11 Years

CBSE
Class 12
English Core

Previous Year-wise Solved Papers

(2013 - 2023) Powered with Concept Notes

DISHA™
Publication Inc

DISHA Publication Inc.

45, 2nd Floor, Maharishi Dayanand Marg,
Corner Market, Malviya Nagar, new Delhi –110017
Tel: 49842349/ 49842350

Typeset By
DISHA DTP Team

Buying books from DISHA

Just Got A Lot More Rewarding!!!

We at DISHA Publication, value your feedback immensely and to show our apperciation of our reviewers, we have launched a review contest.

To participate in this reward scheme, just follow these quick and simple steps:
- Write a review of the product you purchase on Amazon/Flipkart.
- Take a screenshot/photo of your review.
- Mail it to *disha-rewards@aiets.co.in*, along with all your details.

Each month, selected reviewers will win exciting gifts from
DISHA Publication. Note that the rewards for each month
will be declared in the first week of next month on our website.

https://bit.ly/review-reward-disha.

**Write To
Us At**

feedback_disha@aiets.co.in

CONTENTS

Bhagvad Gita

The Story Way

for Students & Parents

- 21 Lessons of Gita explained with Stories & Anecdotes
- Specially written for students & parents

70+ 5 star ratings

by Avinash Agarwal

Author of

- How to raise a Topper
- Topper s' Study Hacks
- The Secret code of UPSC Toppers

CBSE Board Solved Paper

Time Allowed : 3 Hours   *Maximum Marks : 80*

Read the following instructions very carefully and strictly follow them.

(i)   This question paper has 13 questions. All questions are compulsory.

(ii)   This question paper contains **THREE** Sections – Section A : **READING SKILLS** Section B : **CREATIVE WRITING SKILLS** and Section C : **LITERATURE.**

(iii)   Attempt all questions based on specific instructions for each part. Write the correct question number and part thereof in your answer sheet.

(iv)   Separate instructions are given with each question/part, wherever necessary. Read these instructions very carefully and follow them strictly.

(v)   Adhere to the prescribed word limit while answering the questions.

SECTION - A : Reading

1.   Read the passage given below:

(1)   As a form of expression, graffiti is famously characterized by the outlaw values; the creation and display of graffiti countered societal rules and was considered by some as vandalism. Not only was it symbolic of rebel values but was also linked to destruction of property. These links between graffiti culture and rebellion were age-old and some say, were popularized by hip-hop culture.

(2)   Imagine waking up one morning, to see you walls smeared with black paint - names, symbols, messages. the most interesting bit is that these wall artists were never caught red-handed. It was all done stealthily. It was almost as though people were marking their territory using painted symbols and slogans. The change was creeping in. Mobile numbers and captivating phrases gradually became markcting tools for free advertising. Catchy phrases tickled the curiosity and calls were made to those numbers.

(3)   Over a period of time, there was a shift in perception. Blank walls beckoned invitingly and artists saw whitewashed walls as an opportunity to display their work in free and open settings. The city became one large canvas; the illegal 'gang activity' became an art form on display in walking galleries. Graffiti was gradually being replaced and the stigma of illegality was being dropped. There was a move to embrace rather than condemn.

(4)   The colours, shapes, and subjects became cultural themes. What was once rebellious expression is artistic talent at its vibrant best, rich in images of plants, animals and unspoiled landscapes. The painted walls encouraged by residents and governments have created their own ecosystem - a reconciliation of nature with man-made forces.

(5)   The monotony and uniformity of urban life is today infused with human vitality and beauty. Cities speak proudly about the painted walls and clamour to be the first to preserve culture and history through these. Graphic displays of social awareness issues effectively and economically reach out to the common man. Silent art speaks volumes. Be it hygiene, conservation, education, or right and duties - the message is conveyed in an animated, colourful manner without being an imposition.

Based on your understanding of the passage, answer the questions given below: **10 × 1 = 10**

(i) Complete the sentence by choosing an appropriate option.

Graffiti in the earlier years was

(a) Considered a valuable legacy.

(b) done by prominent artists.

(c) an expression of rebellion.

(d) supported by society.

(ii) Comment on the writer's statement, 'It was all done stealthily'.

(iii) List two reasons why graffiti was not popular among people.

(iv) Select the word from para 2 of the passage that conveys the opposite of 'boring'.

(v) The writer would agree with all of the following EXCEPT:

(a) Graffiti art was paid activity.

(b) Wall art was an age-old tradition.

(c) Graffiti became popular as a marketing tool.

(d) People were curious by what scribbled on walls.

(vi) Which word from the following most nearly means 'reconciliation' with reference to the given context? (para 4)

(vii) Why does the writer say that the stigma of 'illegality' was dropped?

(viii) Complete the following sentence with references to the passage: The city became one large canvas because ______.

(ix) The passage states a shift in attitude. Identify the best option that indicates this shift.

(a) rejection to dismissal

(b) confusion to clarity

(c) imposition to acceptance

(d) dislike to acceptance

(x) List two ways in which wall art in beneficial to society.

2. Read the passage given below:

(1) Educational technology is the combined use of computer hardware, software, educational theory, and practice to facilitate learning. When referred to with its abbreviation EdTech, it points to the industry of companies that create educational technology. With education growing online, India's EdTech market size is expected to grow 3.7 times in the next five years.

(2) Education in both rural and urban India is expected to be supported by technology in the near future.

(3) As per a 2019-2020 report, only 23.3 percent of schools had an internet connection, Moreover, 61 percent of schools in the country didn't even have computers.

(4) With the internet rate estimated to reach above 55 percent by the end of 2025 in India, digitisation of education will impact the country's development and become one of the topmost priorities for the government.

(5) Budget 2021-22 allocated ₹93,224.31 crore to the Ministry of Education. It was an increases of over ₹8,100 crore from the revised estimates for the current fiscal year and the Department of Higher Education was allocated ₹38,350.65 crore.

(6) The role of technology in education is more critical now than ever in addressing educational disparity. It has already made learning affordable and accessible. In particular, the use of technology in education in rural India is one of the biggest boons of recent times.

(7) With help from apps and software, teachers can enhance their teaching ability and provide information about the most recent developments. Students can enjoy an interactive learning experience. Teachers can employ animation, PowerPoint slides and graphs to catch the interest of their pupils. Gasification lends interest in the subject.

(8) The only education system is a sector in which growth and development will work for the betterment of many sectors which include educating learners and increasing job opportunities for educators and technical tams.

Use of Technology in Education

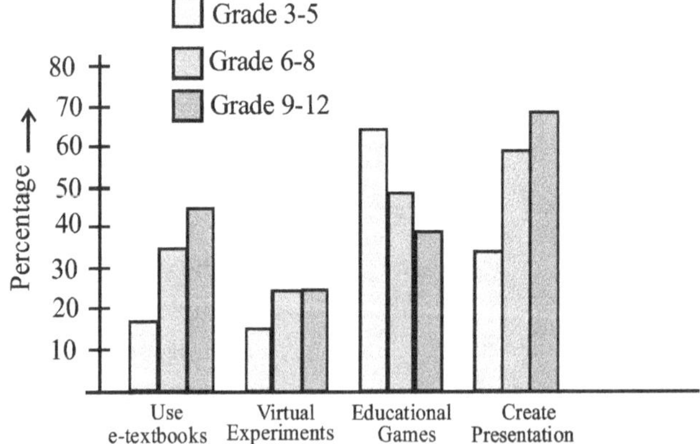

Table I.
REASONS FOR BOOM IN EDTECH
1 Lower cost involved in the dissemination of online education
2 Convenient, flexible and affordable
3 Initiatives by the Government which include programmes like SWAYAM and DIKSHA
4 Increasing number of education-based startups
5 Increment in the interent user base
6 Increasing penetration of mobile devices
7 Inflow of investments and acquisitions in this sector
8 It overcomes the geographical barriers

Based on your understanding of the passage, answer the questions given below:　　　　　　**10 × 1 = 10**

(i) Does the following statement agree with the information given in para 1?

Education technology is the practice of introducing information and communication technology tools into the classroom.

Select from the following:

True - If the statement agrees with the information

False - If the statement contradicts the information

Not Given - If there is no information on this

(ii) What are the two essentials for digitisation of education?

(iii) Select the option which displays that use of technology in education in rural India is one of the biggest boons of recent times.

  (a) Frees up the teacher to the able to concentrate on farming.

  (b) Teachers can enhance their teaching ability and provide more value to the students.

  (c) It understands what is needed and technology is subsequently developed effectively.

  (d) Simplifies assignment management with user-friendly methods.

(iv) Complete the sentence based on the following statement:

The role of EdTech is more critical now ______.

(v) The word 'critical' in para 6 most nearly means

  (a) difficult

  (b) crucial

  (c) complementary

  (d) causative

(vi) Complete the given sentence by selecting the most appropriate option:

Technology in education for the betterment of many sectors such as ______.

  (a) farmers, educators and businessmen

  (b) educating learners, job opportunities for educators and technical teams

  (c) doctors, engineers and technocrats

  (d) banking, construction workers and software technicians

(vii) Digital education will become a top priority for the government because ______.

(viii) Complete the given sentence by selecting the most appropriate option:

The concluding sentence of the passage makes a clear case that ______.

  (a) the growth of educational technology and online education will take some time

  (b) nobody imagined a growth as exponential as in the last two years

  (c) development of EdTech will work for the betterment of many other sectors as well

  (d) the private sector has to play a decisive role

(ix) Based on the graph, state the items which have the highest percentage of technology used by students of grades 9-12 and by students of grades 3-5.

OR

For the Visually Impaired Candidates only in lieu of Q.No. 2 (ix):

(ix) Complete the sentence approximately in two-three words.

With the help of technology, students enjoy ______.

(x) Based on the reading of the passage, state a point to challenge the given statement:

India's EdTEch market size is expected to double in the next five years.

(20 marks)

3.　Attempt any one from (A) and (B) given below:

(A) The Literary Society of your school is setting up a Writer's Guild to encourage and develop the habit of creative writing. Draft a notice in 50 words for the school notice-board, inviting students from classes VI-X to join the Writer's Guild. You are Ragini/Rakesh, President of the Society. Mention relevant details of day, date, time and venue.

OR

(B) The Traffic Police of your district has agreed to hold one-day programme on road safety in your school. Draft a notice in about 50 words to be put up on the school notice-board, informing students of classes 8-12 to assemble at the appointed place. You are Shaili. Sunnet, Sports Incharge. Mention day, date, time and venue.

4. Attempt any one from (A) and (B) given below:

(A) The outgoing batch of Class XII is going on a picnic to the Garden of Five Senses. Send an informal invitation letter in 50 words to your classmates. You are Rita/Ram, the Head Girl/Head Boy of Lotus Public School. Mention day, date, time and venue.

OR

(B) You were invited by your friend Shahid to the marriage of his sister, but due to some unavoidable circumstances, you cannot leave station. Write an informal letter of reply in 50 words expressing your inability to attend the function. You are Hamid/Henna of Aliganj, Nashik. Mention day, date, time and venue.

5. Attempt any one from (A) and (B) given below:

(A) Kavita/Karan Agarwal sees the following advertisement in the local newspaper:

BRIGHT FUTURE COACHING CENTER

Requires Part-time tutors for all subjects for classes 6-12

The applicant must have an excellent and equipped to take online classes.

Good interpersonal skills

Experience - Minimum 2 years

Apply within 10 days to the Director, Bright Future Coaching Center, Meerut

Kavita/Karan decides to apply for the job. Write a letter of application in 120-150 words with detailed biodata in response to the above advertisement.

OR

(B) You have observed that differently abled persons do not get adequate opportunities and facilities from people or the authorities with regard to their participation in the workforce. As a responsible citizen, write a letter to the editor of 'The Times of India' in 120-150 words explaining the measures that should be initiated to provide necessary assistance to make their life meaningful and productive. You are Usha/Umesh

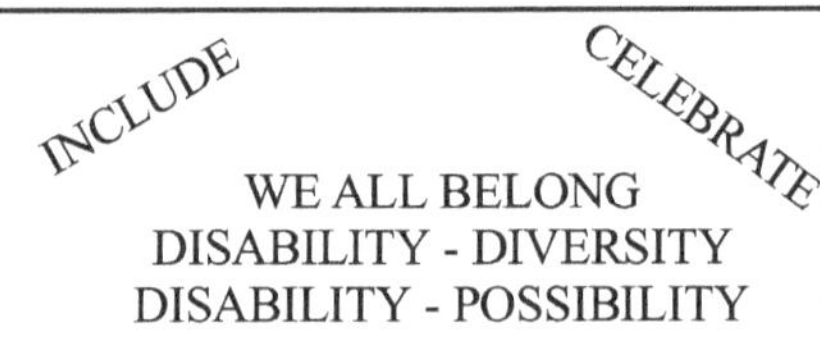

6. Attempt any one from (A) and (B) given below:

STREET THEATER

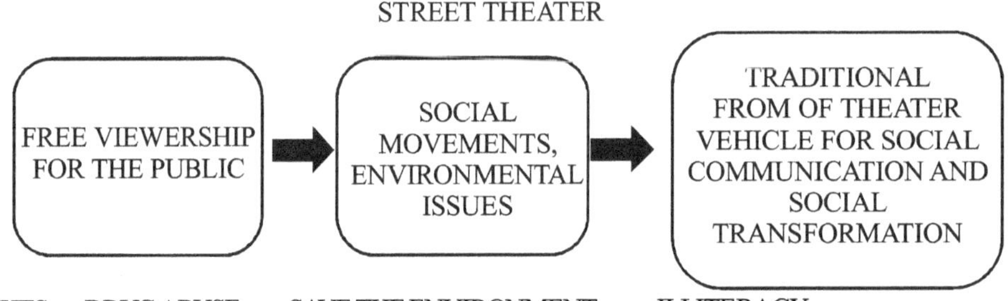

CHILD RIGHTS......DRUG ABUSE....... SAVE THE ENVIRONMENT ....ILLITERACY

OR

(B) The newspapers today have full page advertisements promoting senior citizen living. Write an article in 120-150 words expressing your views on the resonance for this increase and benefits of shifting into these residential complexes. You are Renu/Rajan, a resident of Sachar, a senior living paradise.

Benefits:
• affordable
• community living, companionship
• activities for seniors
• safety
• assisted care
• 24-hour ambulance to nearest hspital
• regular healt check ups

SECTION - C : (Literature)

(40 marks)

7. Attempt any one of the extracts (A) and (B) given below:

(A) Read the following extract and answer the questions that follow: 6 × 1 = 6

Now we will count to twelve
and we will all keep still.
For once on the face of the Earth
let's not speak in any language,
let's stop for one second,
and not move our arms so much.
It would be an exotic moment
without rush, without engines,
we would all be together
in a sudden strangeness.   (Keeping Quiet)

(i) Significance of countering up to twelve is
   (a) it is time to start the race.
   (b) it is symbolic of life.
   (c) it is a measure of time.
   (d) that time does not wait for anyone.

(ii) The word _______ in the extract means unusual and exciting.

(iii) Excessive activity would create an atmosphere of
   (a) productivity
   (b) mechanisation
   (c) confusion
   (d) competition

(iv) The poet would want to create all of the following EXCEPT
   (a) a peaceful environment
   (b) a harmonious world.
   (c) an atmosphere for introduction.
   (d) a world full of hustle and bustle.

(v) Complete the following analogy correctly:
   face of the Earth : _______ : : sudden strangeness : alliteration

(vi) On the basis of the extract, study the two statements, I and II given below:
   I.   People must keep silent at twelve everyday.
   II. Introspection will lead to peaceful coexistence.
   Choose the most appropriate option:
   (a) I is false, but II is true
   (b) Both I and II are false
   (c) Both I and II are true
   (d) I is true, but II is false

OR

(B) Read the following extract and answer the questions that follow: 6 × 1 = 6

Driving from my parent's
home to Cochin last-Friday
morning, I saw my mother,
beside me,
doze, open mouthed, her face ashen like that
of a corpse, and realised with pain
that she was as old as she
looked but soon
Put that though away, and
looked out at Young
Trees sprinting, the merry children spilling
out of their homes ....

(i) The poet's mother looks
   I. exhausted
   II. healthy
   III. rejuvenated
   IV. pale
   V. relaxed
   Choose the most appropriate option:
   (a) Only V   (b) healthy
   (c) I, II and IV   (d) I and IV

(ii) The poet looks out of the car because _______.

(iii) Choose the option that displays the same poetic device as 'her face ashen like that of a corpse'.

    (a) stars winked in the midnight sky

    (b) a bitter sweet experience

    (c) as cold as ice

    (d) grey geese in the green field

(iv) The phrase 'she realized with pain' indicates the poet's

    (a) anxiety of missing the flight.

    (b) fear of losing her mother.

    (c) fear of illness.

    (d) anxiety of taking her mother on the flight.

(v) On the basis of the extract, study the two statements, I and II given below:

    I. The poet was in a hurry to reach the airport.

    II. The poet did not want to think about her mother growing old and infirm.

Choose the most appropriate option:

    (a) I is correct, but II is incorrect

    (b) Both I and II are correct

    (c) Both I and II are incorrect

    (d) II is correct, but I is incorrect

(vi) What does the phrase 'sprinting trees' symbolize?

    (a) youthfulness and forgetfulness

    (b) vitality and youthfulness

    (c) energy and casualness

    (d) pallor and exuberance

8. Attempt any one of the two extracts (A) and (B) given below: 4 × 1 = 4

(A) read the following extract and answer the questions that follow:

"You are to come to the replace," the man said. "The old General is in pain again."

"Oh," Hana breathed, "Is that all?"

"All?" the messenger exclaimed. "Is it not enought?"

"Indeed it is," she replied, "I am very sorry."

When Sadao came to say goodbye, she was in the kitchen, but doing nothing. The children were asleep and she sat merely resting for a moment, more exhausted from her fright then from work. (The Enemy)

(i) Seeing the messenger, Hana was apprehensive of ______.

(ii) The summons for Dr. Sadao were because

    (a) the servants had reported.

    (b) there was medical emergency.

    (c) the General wanted to express his admiration.

    (d) the prisoner of war had escaped.

(iii) Which of the following summarizes Hana's reason for resting momentarily?

    (a) Her physical exhaustion

    (b) Her fear

    (c) Her infirmity

    (d) Her sadness

(iv) Complete the analogy correctly with a word from the extract.

    asleep : awake : : rejuvenated : ______.

(B) Read the following extract and answer the questions that follow: 4 × 1 = 4

Mr. Lamb : Look, boy, look .... what do you see?

Derry: Just..... grass and stuff. Weeds

Mr. Lamb : Some call them weeds. If you like, then .... a weed garden, that. There's fruit and there are flowers, and trees and herbs. All sports. But over there ... weeds. I grow weeds there. Why is one green, growing plant called a weed and another 'flower'? Where's the difference? It's all life ... growing. Same as you and me.

Derry: We're not the same.

(i) In the above extract, what best summarizes Mr. Lamb's attidue towards growing weeds?

    (a) a celebration of life

    (b) an manifestation of his loneliness

    (c) a manifestation of his loneliness

    (d) an example of his gardening skills

(ii) Which of the following best describes Derry's tone when he says "We're not the same"?

    (a) bitter   (b) confused

    (c) defiant   (d) snobbish

(iii) Mr. Lamb brings out the contrast between flowers and weeds in order to:

    (a) explain weeds are important in a garden.

    (b) demonstrate that weeds have medicinal values.

    (c) emphasize the specific purpose of each.

    (d) illustrate that there should be no distinction.

(iv) What word from the above extract most nearly means the opposite of 'difference'?

9. Attempt any one of the two extracts (A) and (B) given below: **6 × 1 = 6**

(A) Read the following extract and answer the questions that follow:

Rudyard Kipling expressed an even more condemnatory attitude towards the interviewer. His wife, Caroline, writes in her diary for 14 October, 1892 that their day was 'wrecked by two reporters from Boston'. She reports her husband as saying to the reporters, "Why do I refuse to be interviewed? Because it is immoral! It is a crime, just as much of a crime as an offence against my person, as an assault, and just as much merits punishment. It is cowardly and vile. No respectable man would ask it, much less give it." Yet Kipling had himself perpetrated such an 'assault' on Mark Twain only a few years before. H.G. Wells in an interview in 1894 referred to the 'interviewing ordeal', but was a fairly frequent interviewee and forty years later found himself interviewing Joseph Stalin. (The Interview)

(i) Kipling viewed interviews with

   (a) compassion   (b) condemnation

   (c) reconciliation   (d) gratitude

(ii) Kipling assaulted __________ with an interview.

   (a) H.G. Wells   (b) Joseph Stalin

   (c) T.S. Eliot   (d) Mark Twain

(iii) Complete the analogy with a word from the extract:

   attack : assault : : committed : ______

(iv) The word 'wrecked' in the extract most nearly means

   (a) ravaged   (b) annihilated

   (c) killed   (d) ruined

(v) Rubyard Kipling uses the phrase 'it is crime' between he feels it is

   (a) illegal

   (b) an offence against his person

   (c) an act of espionage

   (d) a waste of time

(vi) Kipling violated his own observation on interviewing by ______.

OR

(B) Read the following extract and answer the questions that follow: **6 × 1 = 6**

Then the poet spoke, He couldn't have addressed a more dazed and silent audience - no one knew what he was talking about and his accent defeated any attempt to understand what he was saying. The whole thing lasted about an hour; then the poet left and we all dispersed in utter bafflement - what are we doing? What is an English poet doing in a film studio which makes Tamil films for the simplest sort of people? People whose lives least afforded them the possibility of cultivating a taste for English poetry? The poet looked poetry baffled too, for he too must have felt the sheer incongruity of his talk about the thrills and travails of an English poet. His visit remained an unexplained mystery.

(i) Choose the appropriate option with reference to the extract. "The audience were dazed' because

   (a) they were not accustomed to listening to poetry.

   (b) they had never before seen an Englishman.

   (c) they failed to comprehend what the poet was speaking

   (d) they were already bored.

(ii) Complete the sentence with reference to the extract:

   The English poet was ______ when he was addressing the dazed audience.

(iii) Where did the talk take place? Choose the correct option.

   (a) The Main Mall

   (b) Story Writing Department

   (c) Film studio

   (d) Subbu's office

(iv) The English poet's visit is an 'unexplained mystery' because ______.

(v) Complete the analogy with a word from the extract:

   noisy : silent : : assembled : ______

(vi) Explain the following phrase with reference to the extract :

   The poet felt 'the sheer incongruity of his talk'.

10. Answer any five of the following in about 40-50 words each: **5 × 2 = 10**

   (a) Why did Gandhi agree to a settlement of twenty-five percent refund to the peasants? (Indigo)

   (b) What made the ironmaster invite the peddler to his house?

   (c) What was the expectation of the people who had set up the roadside stand?

   (d) Why did Aunt Jennifer create tigers so different from her own character?

   (e) Why can the bangle-makers not organise themselves into a cooperative? (Lost Spring)

   (f) Why did Douglas decide to go to the YMCA pool to learn swimming?   (Deep Water)

11. Answer any two of the following in about 40-50 words each: **2×2 = 4**

   (a) What warning did Judewin give to Zitkala-Sa?

   (b) What were the apprehensions of Derry's mother about his visit Mr. Lamb?

   (c) What dilemma did Dr. Sadao face about the wounded American soldier?

12. Answer any one of the following in about 120-150 words: **5**

   (a) Fantasising and unrealistic dreams sometimes lead to disappointment and disillusionment. Discuss with reference to the story 'Going Places'.

OR

   (b) Firozabad presents a strange paradox - the beauty of the glass bangles and the misery of the people who make bangles. Discuss.

13. Answer any one of the following in about 120-150 words: **5**

   (a) Describe briefly the Third Level. How did it differ from the Second Level?

OR

   (b) What was the Maharaja's mission? How did he resolve to overcome the obstacles in the fulfillment of his mission? (The Tiger King)

SECTION - A

1. (i) (c) an expression of rebellion (1 × 10 = 10 Marks)

(ii) It was done in a hideous manner

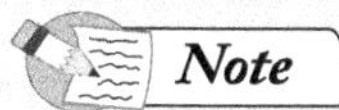

Note

Stealthily - Something that is secret in action.

(iii) symbol of rebellion & destruction of property

(iv) captivating

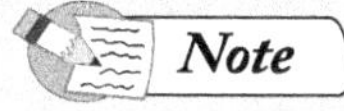

Note

Opposite word for boring is charming or captivating.

(v) (a) Graffiti was a paid activity

(vi) (a) ceasefire

(vii) People started appreciating graffiti as an art form

(viii) artists could display their art for free and in open settings

(ix) (b) confusion to clarity

(x) preserve history & culture; display social awareness issues

(1 × 10 = 10 Marks)

2. (i) True, this statement agrees with the in formation.

(ii) internet connection & computers

(iii) (b) Teachers can enhance their teaching ability and provide more value to the students

(iv) as its market size is expected to grow 3-7 times in next 5 years

(v) (b) crucial

(vi) (b) educating learners, job opportunities for educators and technical terms

(vii) it will impact country's development

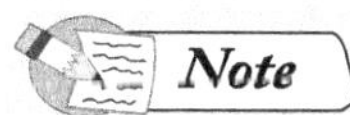

Note

Digital education induces growth and development in many sectors by educating learners.

(viii)(c) development of Edtech will work for the betterment of many other sectors as well

(ix) Grades 3-5 – Educational Games

Grades 9-12 – Create presentations

(x) expected to rise 3-7 times

3. (A) Value Points

ABC LITERACY SOCIETY
NOTICE

24th April, 2023

This is to inform all the students from classes 6th - 10th that the literary society of our school is setting up a writer's guild to encourage the habit of creative writing on 27th April, 2023, at auditorium from 11 am to 2 pm. For further details contact the undersigned.

Ragini

President

Literary society

OR

PQS PUBLIC SCHOOL
NOTICE

24th Feb, 2023

ONE DAY ROAD SAFETY PROGRAMME

The students of classes VIII - XII are hereby informed that the traffic police (East) district has agreed to hold one day programme on Road safety on 28th Feb, 2023 Tuesday from 11 am to 12 pm, in basket ball ground. DCP (Traffic) will be the chief guest for more information, contact the undersigned.

Suneet

Sports Incharge

4. (A) Lotus Public School **(5 Marks)**

Saket, New Delhi

24 Feb. '23

Dear batchmates

Outgoing batch of class XII is organising picnic to the Garden of Five Senses – 5/3/23 – charges ₹ 1,500/- inclusive of transportation & food & beverages. Interested students may give names to respective class monitors – limited seats – A/C buses – will leave school 9:00 A.M. – join for unlimited fun yours sincerely.

Rita

(HEAD GIRL)

OR

4. **(B)** 17/9 Gulabganj

Aliganju, Nasik

24.02.23

Dear Shahid

Many thanks for inviting me to the marriage of your sister, Sameena on 11 March 2023 at Grand Bauquets, Najafgarh, Delhi at 8:00 P.M. with deep regret, I express my inability to attend the same due to unavoidable circumstances.

Best wishes to the bride and groom!

Yours truly

Hamid

5. **(A)** 5-46/9 Ram Nagar   **(5 Marks)**

Meerut-41

24 February, 2023

The Director

Bright Future Coaching Centre

193 Ravi Kunj

Meerut

Sub : Application for the post of part-time tutors

Sir,

With reference to your advertisement published in local newspaper dated 24th March, 23, inviting application for the post of Part time tutors for all subjects for classes 6th to 12th. I wish to be considered for the same.

I am a determined educator having experience of 4 years well versed in taking online classes.

I shall be glad to be favoured with an interview with you at your convenience.

Yours sincerely

Kavita Aggarwal

Encl. - Bio data

BIO-DATA

Name – Kavita Aggarwal

Father's name – Om Pal Aggarwal

Mother's name – Rajni Aggarwal

D.O.B. – 11.03.1994

Address – S-46/9, Ram Nagar, Meerut-41

Phone no. 99123456xx

Educational Qualifications

YEAR	COURSE	BOARD/UNIVERSITY	
2017	M.Sc.	Delhi University	96.4
2015	B.Sc.	Delhi University	89.7
2012	XII	C.B.S.E	97.7
2010	X	C.B.S.E	93.9

Professional Qualifications

(a) B.Ed – Rohtak University (2021) 82.3%

(b) 6 months' Diploma MS-Office

Hobbies – Painting, Theatre

Achievements – Best Athlete - District level (2014)

– Best Debator – Zonal level (2013)

– Top All-Rounder at College (2016)

References –   (A) Anil Tha

Professor, Hindi

Amity University

9999886xxx

(B) Dr. Anjana Das (M.S)

Max Hospital, Saket

98182345xx

24.02.2023

Kavita Aggarwal   Meerut

OR

5. **(B)** A-106 Priya Vihar

Delhi - 93

24 Feb. 2023

The Editor

The Times of India

B.S.Z. Marg

Delhi

Sub.- Lack of opportunities for the disabled

Sir

Columns of esteemed newspaper - draw attention towards inadequate opportunities for the differently abled in India

Inclusivity in workforce – need of the hour – disability not a block, but a possibility – part of diversity – govt. & private sector must ensure robust participation of the disabled in jobs – provide ample opportunities corrective measures must be ensured – awaken the authorities from deep slumber

Yours truly

Usha

(5 Marks)

6.   **(A)**   **3-DAY STREET THEATRE FESTIVAL**

By- Salman, HT correspondent

24 Feb. 2023, Monday

Three-day Street Theatre Festival – at Central Lawrns – organised by student members – 5 NGOs – Amit Das, renowned theatre personality inaugurated event – performances put up on Child Rights, Drug Abuse, Junk Food etc. free viewership for public – wonderful performances – followed by open house session – experiences shared – food stalls & book stalls – event culminated with soulful rendition of the National Anthem

OR

(B)   **Senior Citizens' Community**

By: Renu

Steady increase in senior citizens' community – active members – generally whose children are staying away – wish to live a meaningful life – with like – minded same age group – sachar, a senior living paradise provides affordable stay – safety, assisted care, regular health checkups are some of the highlights – wonderful way of living in companionship during the twilight years great way of living a cheerful & meaningful life

7.   **(A)**   **(1 × 6 = 6 Marks)**

     (i)   (c)   its a measure of time

     (ii)   exotic

     (iii)   (b)   mechanisation

     (iv)   (d)   a world full of hustle & bustle

     (v)   personification

     (vi)   (a)   I is false but II is true

OR

(B)   (i)   (d)   I & IV

     (ii)   she wants to escape from the harsh reality of life- ageing mother

     (iii)   (c)   as cold as ice

     (iv)   (b)   fear of losing her mother

     (v)   (d)   II is correct but I is incorrect

     (vi)   (b)   vitality & youthfulness

8.   **(A)**   **(1 × 4 = 4 Marks)**

     (i)   Dr. Sadao being arrested on charges of treasor

     (ii)   (b) there was a medical emergency

     (iii)   (a) her physical exhaustion

     (iv)   exhausted

OR

8.   **(B)**

     (i)   (a)   a celebration of life

     (ii)   (a)   bitter

     (iii)   (c)   emphasize specific purpose of each

     (iv)   same

9.   **(A)**   **(1 × 6 = 6 Marks)**

     (i)   (b)   condemnation

     (ii)   (d)   Mark Twain

     (iii)   ferpetrated

     (iv)   (d)   ruined

     (v)   (b)   an offence against his person

     (vi)   by interviewing

OR

9.   **(B)**

     (i)   (c)   they failed to comprehend what the poet was speaking

     (ii)   equally baffled

     (iii)   Gemini Studios - film studio

(iv) none of them could comprehend the reason of the English poet's visit

(v) dispersed

(vi) poet felt 'out of place' or 'misfit' in that studio

(5 × 2 = 10 Marks)

10. (a) Gandhiji agreed on the settlement of 25% refund to peasants as money was not important for him. The British landlords parting away with then prestige had a bigger impact.

(b) The Ironmaster mistook the peddler to be his old acquaintance – his comrade, friend from the days of army.

(c) People who had set up roadside stand expect to feel the city money in their hands and also pray silently that any passers by would stop by and purchase something from them.

(d) Aunt Jennifer's creation is different from her own character as she is submissive whereas her tigers are majestic and move freely.

(e) The banglemakers are stuck in the vicious circle of poverty-middlemen, sahukars and policemen. They don't have strength and will to speak against them.

(f) Doughlas wanted to shed inhibitions of fearing water. Moreover, the YMCA pool had gradual slope and an instructor as well.

(2 × 2 = 4 Marks)

11. (a) In order to maintain uniformity amongst students, Zitkala-Sa was warned by Judewin that her long heave hair would be chopped off and made to wear tight clothes.

(b) Derry's mother was apprehensive about Mr. Lamb as she had heard a lot about him. Hence, she instructed Derry not to go there.

(c) Dr. Sadao's dilemma was whether to save Tom the U.S. Prisoner of war as a humanitarian gesture or to throw him back into the sea as he was an enemy.

(5 Marks)

12. (a) Sophie fantacized about her idol, Danny Casey - an Irish footballer wherein she move an imaginary conversation with him. In that fantasy, Danny promised to meet her, making Sophie wait endlessly. The disillusioned Sophie was totally dejected when he didn't 'turnup'.

OR

(b) The city of Firozabad showcases a strange paradox as the timeless beauty of glass bangles completely overshadows the misery of the people who make them. These people add colour and happiness to the lives of others while their own lives are totally dark and bleak.

(5 Marks)

13. (a) The suburban trains used to leave from the second level of the Grand Central station, whereas the third level had smaller rooms, fewer ticket windows and train gates. The information booth was wooden and old-looking. In addition to this, it had gaslights, brass spittoons and Currier & Ives locomotive engine on the track.

OR

(b) The Maharaja's mission was to kill hundred tigers as the state astrologer had prophecized his death at the hands of a tiger. He resolved to overcome the obstacles by marrying a girl from a kingdom that boasted of a huge tiger population. He also provided unduc benefits to the villagers and even bribed the British officer's wife.

CBSE Board Solved Paper

Time Allowed : 3 Hours   *Maximum Marks : 80*

Read the following instructions very carefully and strictly follow them.

(i)   This question paper has 13 questions. All questions are compulsory.

(ii) This question paper contains **THREE** Sections – Section A : **READING SKILLS** Section B : **CREATIVE WRITING SKILLS** and Section C : **LITERATURE.**

(iii) Attempt all questions based on specific instructions for each part. Write the correct question number and part thereof in your answer sheet.

(iv) Separate instructions are given with each question/part, wherever necessary. Read these instructions very carefully and follow them strictly.

(v)   Adhere to the prescribed word limit while answering the questions.

SECTION - A : Reading

1.   Read the passage given below: **20 Marks**

(1) I know many friends of mine who drink coffee regularly but do not know that coffee exists in different forms other than instant coffee. There are many who swear by Flora cafe classic or Coco gold, which they consider premium coffee. I may sound offensive but instant coffee is not the only way; in fact it's a very bad way of making coffee! Instant coffee cannot match up to brewed coffee's flavour nor does it have Arabica beans. It uses Robusta beans that are lower in flavour. Don't know the difference ? ! Read on...

(2) That plant might be a genius! It created a chemical that would keep pests away. Fortunately for us and unfortunately for the plant - that plan did not work the way it was intended to. The chemical might have averted a few pest attacks, but attracted a far greater threat - human beings. The plant I am talking about is coffee and the chemical is caffeine.

(3) To begin from the beginning - coffee is from a more mature part of the tree - the seed - unlike other stimulants. The ripe berry is picked and de-pulped leaving us with a seed called 'green bean' or 'green coffee'. Green bean is uncharacteristically bland with a taste nowhere close to that of coffee, but it is valued for its higher antioxidant levels.

(4) It's an interesting phenomenon to see how this bland green bean turns to a flavourful coffee bean. Coffee bean is a seed and like any other seed is rich in proteins fats and all necessary ingredients for giving birth to a new plant. When exposed to heat, the fats and carbohydrates in the bean turn into essential oils, which give the characteristic taste and aroma to the coffee bean. The degree of roasting depends on the need or purpose of use.

(5) These beans are ground so that the surface area of the bean is increased, which makes extraction easier. The bean can be ground or crushed but making the particles uniform will ensure equal extraction or else the smaller particle will get over extracted and the larger one under extracted. Hence, the burr grinder is used to ensure that the coffee bean gets ground in a uniform way in which all particles are of similar sizes.

(6) Does under extraction give a lighter coffee and over extraction a stronger one? No. For a lighter or stronger coffee less or more coffee powder has to be used. Why? Under extraction will not get all the flavours of the coffee as the water runs too quickly. It will not get what you want - it will taste sour. Over - extraction will bring out all unnecessary flavours rendering the taste bitter.

On the basis of your understanding of the above passage, answer the questions given below:

10 × 1 = 10

(i) Complete the sentence by choosing an appropriate option The author complained that his friends ________ .
   (a) consumed only Flora classics.
   (b) were not aware of different forms of coffee.
   (c) were severely addicted to drinking coffee.
   (d) considered Coco gold as premium coffee.

(ii) Comment on the writer's reference to the unique feature of coffee plant. (paragraph 2)

(iii) List the reason why the author refers to humans as 'great threat to coffee' plants.

(iv) Select an option that conveys the same meaning as 'energiser' from words used in. (paragraph 3)
   (a) bland   (b) mature
   (c) antioxidant (d) stimulants

(v) Complete the given sentence with an appropriate inference with respect to the following:
Fats and carbohydrates turn into essential oils leading to ______ .

(vi) Comment on the writer's reference to the interesting phenomenon in paragraph 4.

(vii) Over extraction does not give a stronger coffee. Based on your understanding of paragraph 6, list one method to get stronger coffee.

(viii) The writer would not agree with the given statements based on paragraph five EXCEPT
   (a) The burr grinder grinds coffee beans uniformly.
   (b) Less surface area makes extraction easier.
   (c) Grinding gives stronger aroma.
   (d) Good coffee is a mix of smaller and bigger particles.

(ix) Why is it fair to say that the right degree of extraction of coffee is important?

(x) Select the most suitable title of the above passage.
   (a) The Art of Coffee Making
   (b) Benefits of Consuming Coffee
   (c) Green Coffee - The perfect antioxidant
   (d) The Coffee Addict

2. Read the passage given below:

(1) News - If you can't remember the last time, you saw a teenager reading a book, newspaper or magazine, you're not alone. In recent years, less than 20 percent of teens report reading a book, magazine or newspaper daily for pleasure. More than 80 percent say they use social media every day, according to research published by the World Psychological Association.

(2) "Compared with previous generations, teens in the 2010s spent more time online and less time with traditional media, such as books, magazines and television," said lead author of the book yGen and professor of psychology at ABC University. "Time on digital media has displaced time once spent enjoying a book or watching TV."

(3) Swaner and her colleagues analysed data concluded from an ongoing study of a nationally representative sample of approximately 50,000 eighth, tenth and twelfth grade students annually. They looked at survey results from 1976 to 2016, representing more than 1 million teenagers. While the study started with only twelfth - graders in the 1970s, eighth and tenth - graders were added in 1991.

(4) Use of digital media increased substantially from 2006 to 2016. Among twelfth-graders, internet use during leisure time doubled from one to two hours per day during that period. It also increased 75 percent for tenth-graders and 68 percent for eighth-graders.

(5) "In the mid- 2010s, the average twelfth-grader reported spending approximately two hours a day texting, just over two hours a day on the internet - which included gaming - and just under two hours a day on social media," said Swaner. That's a total of about six hours per day on just three digital media activities during their leisure time."

(6) In comparison, tenth-graders reported a total of five hours per day and eighth-graders reported four hours per day on those three digital activities. Consequently the spent time in the digital world is seriously degrading the time they spend on more traditional media such as print book and newspapers.

(7) The decline in reading print media was especially steep. In the early 1990s, 33 percent of tenth-graders said they read a newspaper almost every day. By 2016, that number was only 2 percent. In the late 1970s, 60 percent of twelfth-graders said they read a book or a magazine almost every day; by 2016, only

16 percent did. Twelfth-graders also reported reading fewer books each year in 2016 compared to how much they read in 1976 and approximately one-third did not read a book (including e-books) for pleasure in the year prior to the 2016 survey.

(8) There's no lack of intelligence among young people. However due to over dependence on digital media they find it difficult to focus for long periods of time and to read long-form text. Subsequently they find it challenging to understand complex issues and develop critical thinking skills.

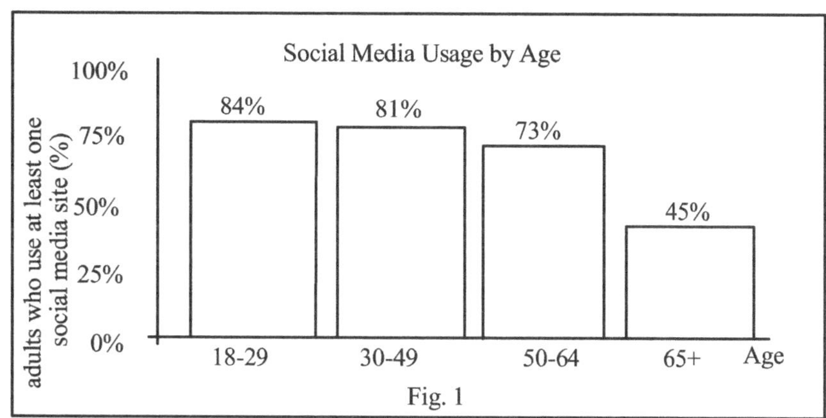

Fig. 1

On the basis of your understanding of the passage, answer the questions given below: **10 × 1 = 10**

(i) Does the following statement agree with the information given in paragraph 1 ?

The writer believes that very few teens indulge in reading as a pleasurable activity.

Select from the following:

True : if the statement agrees with the information.

False: if the statement contradicts the information.

Not given : if there is no information on this.

(ii) Select the option that displays the most likely reason for this research.

In order to find out.......

(a) reading choices of teenagers.

(b) digital competency of teenagers.

(c) speed of reading text.

(d) the decline of time spent on traditional media.

(iii) Complete the statement based on the following statement:

Traditional media has been replaced by digital media. We can say this because ________.

(iv) Do you think that the researchers of study added tenth and eighth graders to the survey deliberately? Support your answer with reference to the text.

(v) Complete the given sentence by selecting the most appropriate option:

The concluding sentence of the text makes a clear case for ________ by listing it as a core competency for analysis and application.

(a) following social media

(b) reading long texts

(c) building focus and concentration

(d) developing constructive habits

(vi) Complete the given sentence by selecting the most appropriate option:

The digital activities that the twelfth-graders indulge in are ________.

(a) texting, gaming, television

(b) texting, gaming, social media

(c) newspaper, books, magazine

(d) television, books, gaming

(vii) Complete the sentence appropriately with one/two words:

Teens today hardly read print media for ________.

(viii) Based on the reading of the text, state a point to challenge the given statement:

"Time on digital media has displaced time once spent enjoying a book or watching T.V."

(ix) What does the author mean by degrading the time in para 6?

(a) spending less time

(b) waste of time

(c) consuming more time

(d) saving time

(x) As per Fig.1, the percentage of people above 50 yrs is ________ the percentage of teenagers using social media.

(a) greater than (b) less than

(c) equal to (d) negligible to

FOR VISUALLY IMPAIRED CANDIDATES.

In lieu of Q. 2 (x)

(x) The decline in reading print media was especially steep. What does 'steep' mean in the above sentence?

   (a) slow   (b) sharp

   (c) steady   (d) gradual

SECTION - B : (Writing & Skills)

20 Marks

3. Attempt any ONE of the following in about 50 words.

   (a) You are Vijay/Veena. Head Boy/Girl of Minerva Public School, Bhopal. Your school is planning to organise a Career Counselling Workshop for the students of classes 9-12. Draft a notice in about 50 words informing students about the workshop mentioning day, date, time and venue. **5**

OR

3. (b) Your school is planning to organise a Water Conservation Awareness Programme for the students. As school captain of SLV Public School, Lucknow, draft a notice in about 50 words informing the students about the programme mentioning day, date, time and venue. You are Sanjay/Sanjana. **5**

4. Attempt any ONE from (a) and (b) given below:

   (a) You have bought a new house in Meerut. Write an informal letter of invitation inviting your friends and relatives to the house warming ceremony. Mention day, date, time and venue. As Rajesh Sharma, draft an invitation in about 50 words. **5**

OR

4. (b) You are Manoj/Meena. You have received an invitation from your friend Vijay to a party to celebrate his admission in a prestigious Management Institute. Write an informal letter in about 50 words accepting the invitation. Mention day, date, time and venue. **5**

5. Attempt any ONE from (a) and (b) given below:

   (a) You have recently come across an advertisement for the post of software engineer in S.K. Global Solutions. Write an application with bio-data in about 120-150 words to The Manager, S.K. Global Solutions, J.P. Nagar, Bangalore. You are Ranjan/Ritu of Indra Nagar, Bangalore. **5**

SK GLOBAL SOLUTIONS
Required Software Engineer
Job Responsibilities:
• Write well-designed software
• Develop layouts
• Execute software development cycle
Preferred Skills & Qualifications:
• B.Tech. - Computer Science
• Experience - 3-5 years.

OR

5. (b) You are Sujoy/Sujata of Nehru Colony, Indore. You recently visited Shimla with your family. You were perturbed to see the tourists throwing empty water bottles and cans all over the place. Write a letter to the editor of national daily in about 120-150 words expressing your concern and offering suggestions to improve the situation. Use the given cues along with your own ideas to compose this letter. **5**

Eco Friendly Travel

create less waste

dispose garbage properly

40% pollution increase during tourist season

do sustainable travel

waste and pollution have far reaching impact on wildlife, environment, visitors & communities

create-clean and healthy vacation destination

Ecological Conservation - A need of the hour.

6. Attempt any ONE from (a) and (b) given below:

(a) You are Rahul/Rekha. There are frequent power cuts in your locality. You strongly feel that it is time to shift to solar power. Write an article in about 120-150 words on the topic 'Solar Power. An Apt Global Solution for Energy Crisis'. Support your ideas with the cues given below. **5**

• renewable energy
• reduce energy bill
• completely clean - no air or water pollution, no greenhouse gas effects, carbon free: no emissions
• low maintenance cost

OR

6. (b) Your school recently conducted an inter-school Heritage Quize Contest. As a student reporter, write a report of the event in about 120-150 words to be published in your school magazine. You are Amit/Archana. Mention day, date, time and venue. **5**

Know Your Heritage
An Inter-School Quiz Contest

- History
- Mythology
- Culture
- Monuments
- Handicraft
- Attractive prizes for audience question
- Friday 14th March, St. Marks School

SECTION - C : (Literature)

40 Marks

7. Read the following extract and answer the questions that follow. Attempt any ONE: **6 × 1 = 6**

(a)   A thing of beauty is a joy forever
Its loveliness increases, it will never
pass into nothingness : but will keep
A bower quiet for us, and a sleep
Full of sweet dreams, and health and quiet
and breathing.
Therefore, on every morrow are we wreathing
A flowery band to bind us to the earth:
Spite of despondence, of the inhuman dearth
Of noble natures, of the gloomy days
Of all the unhealthy and o'er darkened ways
Made for our searching.

(i)   Keats defines beauty as
  (a)   transient   (b)   eternal
  (c)   illusionary   (d)   short lived

(ii)   'will keep a bower quiet for us' means all of the following EXCEPT
  (a)   create a peaceful, shady place
  (b)   provide a shelter
  (c)   will decrease noise pollution
  (d)   nature's canopy

(iii)   On the basis of the extract, choose the correct option with reference to the two statements given below:
  1.   Beautiful things uplift the soul.
  2.   Beauty is overhanging.
  (a)   1 can be inferred from the extract but 2 cannot.
  (b)   2 can be inferred from the extract but 1 cannot.
  (c)   both 1 and 2 can be inferred from the extract.
  (d)   both 1 and 2 cannot be inferred from the extract.

(iv)   The things that cause unhappiness are
  (1)   lack of noble nature
  (2)   old tunes

(3)   dull days
(4)   calm mind
(5)   a flowery hand
(6)   strong relationships
Choose the most appropriate option:
  (a)   (1) and (2)   (b)   (1) and (3)
  (c)   (4) and (5)   (d)   (3) and (6)

(v)   Complete the analogy. Do not repeat from used example:
flowery band : metaphor ::   : alliteration

(vi)   According to the poet 'every morrow' we are ________.

OR

7.   (b)   Aunt Jennifer's tigers prance across a screen,
                                6 × 1 = 6
Bright topaz denizens of a world of green,
They do not fear the men beneath the tree;
They pace in sleek chivalric certainty.
Aunt Jennifer's fingers fluttering through her wool
Find even the ivory needle hard to pull.
The massive weight of uncle's wedding band
Sits heavily upon Aunt Jennifer's hand.

(i)   Denizens of the world of green refer to ________.
  (a)   huntsmen   (b)   Aunt Jennifer
  (c)   uncle   (d)   tigers

(ii)   Choose the option that displays the same poetic device as used in the second line of the extract.
  (a)   heart of stone   (b)   trees sprouting
  (c)   silver spoon   (d)   white murder

(iii)   The men setting beneath the tree are ________.

(iv)   What quality of uncle can be inferred through these lines?
  (a)   compassionate nature
  (b)   courageous
  (c)   confident
  (d)   dominating

(v)   The tigers in the extract are symbolic of
  (a)   creativity and courage
  (b)   confidence and gentleness
  (c)   cruelty and fear
  (d)   aggression and starving

(vi)   Aunt Jennifer's tigers prance across
  (1)   the screen
  (2)   the fields
  (3)   the embroidered tunic
  (4)   the cage
Which of the following is the most appropriate choice?
  (a)   (1) and (2)   (b)   (2) and (4)
  (c)   (1), (2) and (3)   (d)   (1) and (3)

8. Read the following extract and answer the questions that follow. Attempt any ONE: **4 × 1 = 4**

   (a) To make sure, I walked over the newsboy and glanced at the stack of papers at his feet. It was The World and The World hasn't been published for years. The lead story said something about President Cleveland. I've found that front page since, in the Public library files and it was printed June 11, 1894.

        I turned toward the ticket windows knowing that here - on the third level at Grand Central - I could buy tickets that would take Louisa and me anywhere in the United States we wanted to go. In the year 1894. And I wanted two tickets to Galesburg, Illinois.

(i) The newspaper that covered the lead story about President Cleveland was

   (a) The Pioneer   (b) The New York Times

   (c) The World   (d) The Times

(ii) The narrator wanted to buy tickets to __________ .

(iii) Which of the following in the extract most nearly means the opposite of 'stare' ?

   (a) glance   (b) peek

   (c) ignore   (d) examine

(iv) Charley wanted two tickets because he wanted to go with

   (a) Sam   (b) Cleveland

   (c) Louisa   (d) the Psychiatrist

OR

8. (b) When I was studying in the third class, I hadn't yet heard people speak openly of untouchability. But I had already seen, felt, experienced and been humiliated by what it is.

        I was walking home from school one day, an old bag hanging from my shoulder. It was actually possible to walk the distance in ten minutes. But usually it would take me from half an hour to an hour to dawdle along watching all the fun and games that were going on all the entertaining novelties and oddities in the streets, the shops and the bazaar.   **4 × 1 = 4**

(i) The narrator was humiliated because _________.

(ii) The narrator 'dawdled along' as she _________.

   (a) enjoyed looking at the various sights

   (b) was getting late for school

   (c) she didn't like going home

   (d) she enjoyed haggling and shopping

(iii) On the basis of the extract, choose the correct option with reference to the two statements given below:

   (I) The distance from school to home was very short.

   (II) She was feeling upset and so dawdling her way home.

   (a) (I) can be inferred from the extract but (II) cannot.

   (b) (II) can be inferred from the extract but (I) cannot.

   (c) Both (I) and (II) cannot be inferred from the extract.

   (d) Both (I) and (II) can be inferred from the extract.

(iv) The word 'novelties' in the passage most nearly means

   (a) colourful trinkets

   (b) wooden toys.

   (c) unique and interesting items

   (d) expensive souvenirs

9. Read the following extract and answer the questions that follow. Attempt any ONE.   **6 × 1 = 6**

   (a) "I sometimes find a rupee, even a ten rupee note", Saheb says, his eyes lighting up when you can find a silver coin in a heap of garbage, you don't stop scrounging, for there is hope of finding more. It seems that for children, garbage has a meaning different from what it means to their parents. For the children it is wrapped in wonder for the elders it is a means of survival.

        One winter morning I see Saheb standing by the fenced gate of the neighbourhood club, watching two young men dressed in white, playing tennis. "I like the game", he hums, content to watch it standing behind the fence. "I go inside when no one is around" he admits. "The gate keeper lets me use the swing."

(i) Saheb found a rupee

   (a) on the street

   (b) in the garbage dump

   (c) in Firozabad

   (d) on the tennis court

(ii) Which emotion of Saheb is revealed in the phrase 'his eyes lighting up' ?

   (a) anxiety   (b) envy

   (c) happiness   (d) greed

(iii) For the elders garbage is _________ and for children it is _________.

(iv) On the basis of the extract, choose the correct option with reference to I and II given below:

   I.   Saheb watches the game from outside.

   II. Saheb had lost the previous match.

   (a) I is true but II is not

   (b) II is true but I is not

   (c) Both I and II are true

   (d) Both I and II are untrue.

(v) 'Scrounging' in the passage most nearly means.

   (a) digging   (b) searching

   (c) flinging   (d) burying

(vi) 'There is hope for finding more'. Explain with reference to the above extract.

OR

9. (b) "Or an actress, Now there's real money in that. Yes, and I could may be have the boutique on the side. Actresses don't work full time, do they ? Anyway, that or a fashion designer. You know-something a bit sophisticated". And she turned in through the open street door leaving Jansie standing in the rain. "If I ever come into money I'll buy a boutique". "Huh, if you ever come into money ... if you ever come into money you'll buy us a blessed decent house to live in thank you very much."

Sophie's father was scooping shepherd's pie into his mouth as hard as he could go, his plump face still grimy and sweat - marked from the day. "She thinks money grows on trees, don't she Dad? Said little Derek hanging on the back of his father's chair.

$6 \times 1 = 6$

Their mother sighed.

(i) Sophie wants to become an actress to

(a) become famous   (b) to earn money

(c) to support her father   (d) to compete with Jansie

(ii) Jansie wanted Sophie to spend her money on

(a) her marriage

(b) her career

(c) to open a boutique

(d) buying a house

(iii) Sophie is daydreaming about__________.

(iv) The phrase 'money grows on trees' indicates that Sophie __________.

(v) Sophie's mother's sigh is one of

(a) regret   (b) delight

(c) relief   (d) helplessness

(vi) From the extract Jansie comes across as a __________ person.

(a) practical   (b) dominating

(c) immature   (d) starstruck

10. Answer any FIVE out of six questions given below in about 40-50 words. $5 \times 2 = 10$

(a) What does Gandhi refer to as 'conflict of duties'?

(b) What does the expression 'polished traffic' refer to? What does it reveal about city people?

(c) Why did the iron master compare Edla to a person?

(d) What is the significance of the word 'but' in but all I said was see you soon. Amma? (My Mother at Sixty-Six)

(e) What handicap did Doughlas suffer from? How did he overcome that?

(f) What according to Pablo Neruda in the poem 'Keeping Quiet' is the lesson that we should learn from mother earth?

11. Answer any TWO out of three questions given below in about 40-50 words: $2 \times 2 = 4$

(a) Why was Dr. Sadao not sent abroad with the troops?

(b) What was the hidden agenda behind the Tiger King's marriage with the princess in the neighbouring state?

(c) What are the significant features of 'Students on Ice Programme'?

12. Answer any ONE in about 120-150 words:

(a) The last lesson reflects the flaws in human character that led to the sad plight of people in Alsace. Substantiate your answer with evidences from the text.   **5**

OR

(b) A Roadside Stand is a social satire depieting the two contrasting worlds existing in society. Justify this statement with reference to the poem.   **5**

13. Answer any ONE in about 120-150 words:

(a) Mr. Lamb stands as a symbol of optimism and hope. Support your answer with examples from the text.   **5**

OR

(b) Dr. Sadao emerges as a saviour of humanity. Substantiate your answer with evidence from the text.   **5**

SECTION - A

(1 × 10 = 10 Marks)

1. (i) (b) were not aware of different forms of coffee.

(ii) The writer refers to the unique feature of coffee plant as it created a chemical called caffeine that kept pests away.

(iii) The author refers to humans as a 'great threat to coffee' plants because caffeine was intended to keep pests away, but instead, it attracted humans who consume coffee as a stimulant.

(iv) (d) stimulants.

(v) Fats and carbohydrates turn into essential oils leading to the characteristic taste and aroma of the coffee bean.

(vi) The writer's reference to the interesting phenomenon in paragraph 4 is that the bland green coffee bean turns into a flavourful coffee bean when exposed to heat.

(vii) To get stronger coffee, more coffee powder has to be used.

(viii) The writer would not agree with the statement that grinding gives stronger aroma based on paragraph five.

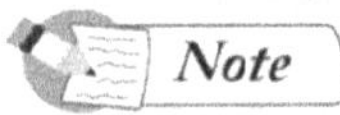 **Note**

Grinding gives a characteristic taste and aroma to the coffee bean, but it's the oils that give the aroma, not the grinding.

(ix) It is fair to say that the right degree of extraction of coffee is important because if the extraction is underdone, the flavour and aroma will be incomplete, and if it is overdone, the taste will be bitter and unpleasant.

(x) (a) The Art of Coffee Making.

2. (i) True **(1 × 10 = 10 Marks)**

(ii) (d) the decline of time spent on traditional media.

(iii) Research published by the World Psychological Association found that less than 20% of teens report reading a book, magazine, or newspaper daily for pleasure, while over 80% say they use social media every day.

(iv) Yes, the researchers of the study added tenth and eighth graders to the survey deliberately. As mentioned in paragraph 3, the ongoing study started with only twelfth-graders in the 1970s, and eighteenth tenth-graders were added in 1991.

(v) (c) building focus and concentration.

(vi) (b) texting, gaming, social media.

(vii) Pleasure.

(viii) The given statement assumes that time spent on digital media cannot be enjoyed, which may not be true for everyone.

 **Note**

Additionally, it suggests that time spent on traditional media is inherently more enjoyable than time spent on digital media, which is a subjective assertion.

(ix) (a) spending less time.

(x) (b) less than.

SECTION - B

3. (a) **(5 Marks)**

Minerva Public School, Bhopal
Notice

March 5, 2023

Attention all students

The school is delighted to announce a career counselling workshop for students on March 15, 2023, from 10:00 am to 1:00 pm in the school auditorium. The workshop aims to provide insights and guidance to help you choose the Right Career Path. This workshop will be conducted by School. Interested students can register their names with the undersigned on or before March 10, 2023.

Vijay/Veena
Head Boy/Girl

OR

3. (b)

S.L.V Public School, Lucknow
Notice
WATER CONSERVATION AWARNESS

February 26, 2023

We are pleased to announce that S.L.V Lucknow is organising a Water Conservation Awareness Program for the students. The program aims to create Awareness about the Importance of water Conservation and Sustainable use of Water Resource. The Program will begin from 10th March 2023 and will be held every Wednesday and Friday from 3 PM to 5 PM. The venue for the Program will be in the School. All interested students are requested to register their names with the sports department by 8th March 2023.

Sanjay/Sanjana
School Captain, SLV Public School Lucknow

4.   (a)   **(5 Marks)**
H-21
Rithala
Delhi
24 Feb' 23
Dear [Name of Friend/Relative],
I hope this letter finds you in good health and in high spirits. I am writing to inform you that I have recently bought a new house in Meerut, and I would be delighted if you could join me at the housewarming ceremony. The ceremony will be held on Sunday, 6th March 2023, from 11:00 AM to 2:00 PM at my new residence: [A-42 Bawana Nagar, Meerut]. I am looking forward to having you over and sharing this special occasion with you. Please do let me know if you are able to attend.
Warm regards, Rajesh Sharma.

OR

4.   (b)
B-23
Rohini
Delhi
24 Feb'23
Dear Vijay,
Thank you so much for inviting me to your party to celebrate your admission in the prestigious Management Institute. I am really happy for you, and I would love to be a part of your celebrations. The day, date, time and venue you have mentioned in the invitation suit me perfectly. So, I will be there at your party on Saturday, 4th March 2023, at 7:00 PM, at your residence: [A-42 Bawana Nagar, Meerut]. I am really looking forward to meeting you and celebrating your success. Thank you once again for inviting me.

5.   (a)   **(5 Marks)**
The Manager
S.K Global Solutions
J.P Nagar
Bangalore
Subject: Application for the post of Software Engineer.
Respected Sir/Madam
I am writing to apply for the post of Software Engineer in your esteemed organization. I came across your advertisement in the local newspaper, and I feel that my qualifications and experience make me a suitable candidate for this position. I am a B.Tech. Graduate in Computer Science from Bangalore University and have 3 years of experience in software development. I have attached my resume, which highlights my educational qualifications, work experience, and skills. I am confident that my skills and experience align with the job responsibilities and preferred qualifications mentioned in the advertisement. I would be grateful for the opportunity to further discuss my qualifications with you in person. Thank you for considering my application.
Yours Sincerely,
Ranjan/Reetu

BIO DATA

Name- Rajan/Reetu
Date of Birth- 15 September,1970
Address- 3/5 Model Town, Kurukshetra
Educational Qualifications

Exam	Board	University/name	Percentage
X	CBSE	XYZ Public school	97%
XII	CBSE	XYZ Public School	95%
B.Tech	Bangalore University	Bangalore University	80%

Languages; Java, python and C++
Working Experience;
(a)   Software Engineer at Infosys from 1991 to 1994.
(b)   Senior Staff Engineer at Microsoft from 1994 to 2000.
(c)   Lead Engineer at Microsoft from 2000 to 2008.
(d)   Director, Engineering at Facebook from 2008 to now.
Extra – curricular Activities;
(a)   Awarded prizes in Declamation Consents.
(b)   Awarded Best Actor Award in Dramatics.
References:
1.   A.K. Poddar Professor, Head of Dept. Bangalore University, Delhi
2.   Ram Prakash Professor and Dean Bangalore University, Delhi

OR

5.   (b)
C-25
Nehru Colony Indore
24 Feb'23
The Editor
The Times of India
NRK Business Park Indore
Subject: Concerns over increasing pollution and waste during tourist season Respected
Sir/Madam
I am writing this letter to express my concern over the increasing pollution and waste during the tourist season, which I recently observed during my visit to Shimla with my family. It was disheartening to see tourists throwing empty bottles and cans all over the place, spoiling the natural beauty of the place.
As we know, tourism has become an important source of income for many places, but it also has a negative impact on the environment. Waste and pollution have far-reaching impacts on wildlife, the environment, visitors, and communities.
The ecological conservation of the place is a need of the hour. I suggest some measures to create a clean and healthy vacation destination. Firstly, we should encourage eco-friendly travel by promoting public transport, cycling, and walking. Secondly, we should create less waste by carrying our own reusable water bottles and avoiding single-use plastics. Lastly, we should dispose of garbage properly by using designated bins.

I believe that sustainable travel is the key to preserving the beauty of tourist destinations. We must ensure that tourism does not come at the cost of environmental degradation. I urge the concerned authorities to take immediate action towards ecological conservation and create a safe and healthy environment for tourists and locals.

Yours truly,

Sujoy/Sujata

6. **(a)** **(5 Marks)**

Solar Power: An Apt Global Solution

By Rahul/Rekha

In recent times, the demand for energy has been on a constant rise. However, our conventional sources of energy are depleting at an alarming rate. The need of the hour is to switch to renewable energy sources, and solar power is the perfect solution. It is the most abundant and readily available source of energy on earth. Solar power has numerous benefits. Firstly, it helps to reduce energy bills significantly. Once the initial installation cost is covered, solar energy is virtually free. Secondly, solar energy is completely clean and has no adverse impact on water pollution, air pollution or greenhouse gas effects. It is carbon-free and emits no harmful gases. Hence, it is environmentally friendly and sustainable. Furthermore, solar energy requires low maintenance cost. It only needs to be cleaned periodically to remove dust and dirt. It is a one-time investment that has long-term benefits. Solar panels have a lifespan of 20-30 years, and they can be used to generate electricity for a long period.

To conclude, solar power is an apt global solution for the energy crisis. It is renewable, environmentally friendly, and cost-effective. Governments and individuals must take necessary steps towards shifting to solar power to ensure a sustainable and greener future. It is high time we realise the importance of renewable energy sources and take action towards creating a brighter and cleaner future.

(b)

Know your Heritage

By Amit/Archana

St. Marks School hosted an exciting Inter- School Quiz Contest called 'Know Your Heritage' on Friday, 14th March. The contest was focused on topics related to history, mythology, culture, monuments, and handicrafts. Students from various schools in the city attended the event.

The quiz contest consisted of multiple rounds of challenging questions. Each round tested the participant's knowledge and awareness of Indian heritage. The questions were based on various aspects of Indian culture and tradition, which made the event informative and engaging. Apart from the quiz, there was an audience question round, where the audience could win attractive prizes. The quiz was conducted in a fun, and interactive manner, which kept the participants and the audience engaged throughout the event.

The students' enthusiasm and eagerness to participate made the event a great success.

The winners were awarded exciting prizes, and all the participants were appreciated for participants and the audience engaged throughout the event.

The students' enthusiasm and eagerness to participate made the event a great success. The winners were awarded exciting prizes, and all the participants were appreciated for their efforts. In conclusion, 'Know Your Heritage' was a successful and informative event that educated the participants and audience about the rich heritage of India. The quiz contest served as a platform for students to showcase their knowledge and love for their culture and tradition. The event was a great opportunity for students to learn and have fun at the same time.

7. **(a)** **(i)** eternal. **(6 × 1 = 6 Marks)**

(ii) will decrease noise pollution. This is incorrect, as the phrase means that beauty creates a peaceful, shady place or provides a shelter or nature's canopy. It does not necessarily refer to a decrease in noise pollution.

(iii) 1 can be inferred from the extract but 2 cannot is correct.

The extract suggests that beautiful things are a source of joy that lasts forever, but there is no indication that beauty is ever-changing.

(iv) (1) and (3) are the correct options.

The extract mentions "despondence" and "gloomy days" as causes of unhappiness, which corresponds to option (3), and "inhuman dearth of noble natures" corresponds to option (1).

(v) Flower band: metaphor: : silly sally : alliteration

(vi) According to the poet, "every morrow" we are "wreathing a flowery band to bind us to the earth" despite the negative aspects of life mentioned earlier in the extract.

OR

7. **(b)** **(i)** tigers.

(ii) Metaphor is a figure of speech in which a word or phrase is applied to an object or action to which it is not literally applicable.

(iii) The men setting beneath the tree are the human beings who are the hunters but tigers do not afraid of them as they are full of strength and power.

(iv) Based on the lines provided, it can be inferred that Uncle is a dominating person. The line "The massive weight of uncle's wedding band/Sits heavily upon/Aunt Jennifer's hand" suggests that Aunt Jennifer feels oppressed or burdened by her marriage to Uncle.

(v) The tigers in the extract are symbolic of confidence and gentle. They are described as "prancing" with "sleek chivalric certainty" and not fearing the men beneath the tree, which suggests a sense of fearlessness and self-assuredness.

(vi) Aunt Jennifer's tigers prance across the screen. The first line of the extract states "Aunt Jennifer's tigers prance across a screen," which suggests that the tigers are being displayed on a screen, likely in the context of a work of art or a decorative piece. Therefore, the most appropriate choice is (a) (1) and (2)

(4 × 1 = 4 Marks)

8. (a) (i) The newspaper that covered the lead story about President Cleveland was The World.

(ii) The narrator wanted to buy tickets to Galesburg, Illinois.

(iii) The word that most nearly means the opposite of 'stare' in the extract is ignore.

(iv) Charley wanted two tickets because he wanted to go with Louisa.

OR

8. (b) (i) The narrator was humiliated because of untouchability that she had experienced and felt, even though she had not yet heard people speak openly about it.

(ii) The narrator 'dawdled along' as she enjoyed looking at the various sights, fun and games that were going on in the streets, the shops and the bazaar.

(iii) On the basis of the extract, option (a) is correct: (I) can be inferred from the extract but (II) cannot. The passage does not provide any indication that the narrator was feeling upset.

(iv) The word 'novelties' in the passage most nearly means unique and interesting items.

(6 × 1 = 6 Marks)

9. (a) (i) Saheb found a rupee in the garbage dump.

(ii) The emotion of Saheb revealed in the phrase 'his eyes lighting up' is happiness.

(iii) For the elder's garbage is a means of survival and for children, it is wrapped in wonder.

(iv) On the basis of the extract, the correct option is (a) I is true but II is not. Saheb watches the game from outside, but there is no indication that he had lost the previous match.

(v) 'Searching.

(vi) The statement "when you can find a silver coin in a heap of garbage, you don't stop scrounging, for there is hope of finding more" suggests that finding a valuable item in the garbage gives a sense of hope to the children that there might be more treasures to be found. This encourages them to continue searching through the garbage.

OR

9. (b) (i) to earn money.

(ii) Jansie wanted Sophie to spend her money on opening a boutique.

(iii) Sophie is daydreaming about becoming an actress or a fashion designer and having a boutique on the side.

(iv) The phrase 'money grows on trees' indicates that Sophie has unrealistic expectations about money and its availability.

(v) regret.

(vi) practical

(5 × 2 = 6 Marks)

10. (a) Gandhi referred to 'conflict of duties' as a situation where an individual has to choose between two or more equally important moral obligations or duties, and fulfilling one duty would mean neglecting the other. First, he did not want to set a bad example as a law breaker. Second, he wanted to render the humanitarian and national service for which he had come.

(b) The expression 'polished traffic' in the poem 'My Mother at Sixty-Six' by Kamala Das refers to the smooth and efficient flow of traffic in the city. It reveals the busy and practical nature of city people who are used to such a fast-paced lifestyle.

(c) The iron master compared Edla to a parson because of her compassionate and kind nature towards her father's workers. She showed concern and empathy towards them just as a parson would show towards his congregation.

(d) In the sentence "but all I said was see you soon, Amma," the word 'but' is used to contrast the speaker's casual remark with the heavy emotional weight of the situation. It highlights the speaker's attempt to be nonchalant in order to hide their true feelings.

(e) Fear of water was a handicap Douglas developed during his childhood. It stayed with him as he grew older. It ruined his pursuits of pleasure such as canoeing, boating, swimming and fishing. He used every method he knew to overcome this fear. Finally, he determined to get an instructor and learn swimming.

(f) According to Pablo Neruda in the poem 'Keeping Quiet,' the lesson that we should learn from mother earth is to take a moment to stop and listen to the world around us. By keeping quiet and being still, we can connect with nature and find peace within ourselves.

(2 × 2 = 4 Marks)

11. (a) Derry's thinking towards people and life completely changed and he became self-confident when he met with lamb. Mr. Lamb successfully infused in him Courage and self-determination. He advised him to ignore the comments made by people on his physical impairment and enjoy beauty of life and nature That was why Derry went back to Mr. Lamb's garden in spite of his mother's refusal. Now, Derry had understood the importance and true meaning of life And understanding himself better than before.

(b) The astrologers predicted that the newly-born prince will grow up to become the hero of the heroes, brave of the bravest and a great warrior. He also predicted that the baby was born in the hour of the bull. The bull and the tiger were enemies. Therefore, he would die because of the tiger.

(c) The astrologers predicted that the newly-born prince will grow up to become the hero of the heroes, brave of the bravest and a great warrior. He also predicted that the baby was born in the hour of the bull. The bull and the tiger were enemies. Therefore, he would die because of the tiger.

(5 × 1 = 5 Marks)

12. (a) The last lesson reflects the flaws in human character that led to the sad plight of People in Alsace. This is evident in the text when M. Hamel talks about how the People of Alsace had a habit of putting off learning until tomorrow. He says, "Every day we have said to ourselves, 'Bah! I've plenty of time. I'll learn it tomorrow.' And now you see where we've come out. Ah, that's the great trouble with Alsace; she puts off learning till tomorrow." This reflects the lack of foresight and the tendency to procrastinate, which led to the people of Alsace not being able to speak or write their Language. This is further evident when M. Hamel talks about how the parents of the Children in his class were not anxious enough to have them learn and how he had often sent them to water his flowers instead of learning their lessons. This reflects the lack of emphasis on education and the tendency to prioritize other activities over r learning, which is why the people of Alsace missed their opportunity to speak or write their language.

OR

(b) In the poem "A Roadside Stand" by Robert Frost, the author portrays a sharp contrast between two worlds that exist in society. On one hand, there is the world of the wealthy, represented by the cars that pass by the roadside stand, who are seemingly indifferent to the struggles of the people who run the stand. On the other hand, there is the world of the poor, represented by the people who run the roadside stand, who are struggling to make ends meet and are at the mercy of those who pass by. The author uses satire to highlight the injustice and inequality that exists in society.

The wealthy drivers in their cars are portrayed as selfish and unconcerned about the plight of the poor, as they drive by without stopping to offer any help or support. The people who run the roadside stand are depicted as helpless victims of a system that favors the rich and powerful. Furthermore, the author also criticizes the government for its lack of action in addressing the issues of poverty and inequality. The line "no matter if we have no money, not enough to keep open more than one eye at a time highlights the government's failure to provide basic necessities to its citizens.

In conclusion, "A Roadside Stand" is a social satire that highlights the contrast between the wealthy and the poor, and criticizes the government's inaction in addressing the issues of poverty and inequality. The poem serves as a reminder of the need for empathy, compassion, and action in creating a more just and equitable society.

13. (a) In the story "On the Face of It" Mr. Lamb is presented as a symbol of optimism and hope. He is a kind and compassionate man who offers comfort and understanding to the protagonist, Derry, in his time of need.

Firstly, Mr. Lamb's positive attitude and kindness inspire Derry to overcome his feelings of despair and self-pity. Despite his own physical disabilities, Mr. Lamb remains optimistic and hopeful, and encourages Derry to do the same. He teaches Derry that even though life may be difficult, there is always something to be grateful for, and that one should never give up hope.

Secondly, Mr. Lamb's character embodies the idea that one's physical appearance does not define who they are as a person. Despite his disfigured face and missing eye, Mr. Lamb is a kind, intelligent, and caring individual who sees the best in others. He teaches Derry that true beauty comes from within, and that one should never judge others based on their appearance.

Lastly, Mr. Lamb's character represents the idea that there is always a way out of difficult situations. He encourages Derry to face his fears and to overcome his physical limitations. He teaches Derry that with determination and a positive attitude, one can achieve anything they set in their mind.

OR

(b) In the story "The Enemy" Dr. Sadao emerges as a saviour of humanity, displaying compassion and humanity despite the prejudice and hatred surrounding him. Here are some examples from the text to support this claim:

Firstly, Dr. Sadao demonstrates his humanity and compassion when he saves the life of an enemy soldier, a wounded American soldier he finds on the beach near his house. He risks his own life and reputation by taking the soldier into his home and nursing him back to health, despite the fact that the soldier is a member of the enemy army. His actions show that he values human life above political and national affiliations, and that he is willing to do what is right, regardless of the consequences.

Secondly, Dr. Sadao's decision to help the American soldier is driven by his commitment to the Hippocratic Oath, which requires him to treat all patients, regardless of their background or nationality. His actions demonstrate that he is a true professional who upholds the highest ethical standards of his profession.

Thirdly, Dr. Sadao's actions inspire his wife, Hana, to share in his compassion and humanity. Despite her initial shock and fear, Hana learns to see the wounded soldier as a human being, rather than an enemy, and she assists her husband in nursing him back to health. Her transformation shows that Dr. Sadao's actions have a ripple effect, inspiring others to act with compassion and humanity.

All India *2022*
CBSE Board Solved Paper Term-II

Time Allowed : 2 Hours   *Maximum Marks : 40*

Read the following instructions very carefully and strictly follow them.
(i)   This question paper contains **THREE** sections – READING, WRITING and LITERATURE
(ii)   Attempt questions based on specific instructions for each part.

SECTION A: Reading

(14 Marks)

1.   Read the passage given below :   **(1 × 8 = 8 Marks)**

1.   Very often, we do not take the first step towards a good cause because we say to ourselves, "The task is so big. What can I do alone ?" So nothing gets done. There is much talk about environmental protection, air pollution and saving our forests. Do we really care? If we do, here are a few things we can do to make our surroundings more pleasant.

2.   It is good to adopt a two–uses - attitude ! By putting an article to a second use, we are giving it a longer lease of life and using up less raw material from nature. One of the, worst things we do is the abuse of paper. The clean sides of envelopes can be used to write small notes, lists and reminders around the house. The more paper we use, the more trees will have to be cut down. For the same reason, we should avoid the use of paper napkins or paper plates. Cloth napkins are just as good, for they can be washed and used over and over again.

3.   Another area which needs the most urgent attention is effective garbage disposal. People who are conscious about it follow rules and laws strictly. As a result, their neighbourhoods are clean and beautiful. Similarly, each one of us can contribute to a cleaner environment. All kitchen waste should be collected separately. Those of you who have green fingers can turn this into valuable manure. Dig a pit and put the kitchen waste into it. When the pit is a little over half full, cover it up with mud. Let nature do the rest. Within three or six months, we will have a good garden manure. It can also be done as a community project by digging a large pit in the colony. Do take help of all the members, for nothing succeeds like co–operation.

4.   A lot of people don't care about the environment because they don't understand the adverse effect that society has on it. It is important to convince people to care about the environment. The first step would be to convince people to change by providing simple alternative solutions and ways of doing things. The internet is a powerful tool and a group on social media of like–minded people can be formed. People can share environmental stories and issues, as well as pool in solutions and alternatives to educate one another. With the current state that our planet is in, it is imperative that people actively care about the environment and most importantly to act now.

Based on your understanding of the passage, answer **ANY EIGHT** questions from the nine given below :

(i)   Why don't we take the first step towards a good cause ?   **(1 Mark)**

(ii) What is a two – uses attitude?   **(1 Mark)**

(iii) What can we do to avoid the abuse of paper ? (any two points)   **(1 Mark)**

(iv) What is the result of an effective way of garbage disposal ?   **(1 Mark)**

(v) What procedure can one adopt for kitchen waste?   **(1 Mark)**

(vi) How can making of garden manure be done as community project ?   **(1 Mark)**

(vii) How long does it take to make good garden manure ?   **(1 Mark)**

(viii) Select a suitable word from the passage which means – being concerned or interested. (Para 3)   **(1 Mark)**

(xi) Pick out the word from the passage which means – completely necessary? (Para 4)   **(1 Mark)**

2. Read the passage below :

1. Our history makes it evident that the Indians Plastics Industry made a vigorous beginning in 1957 but it took more than 30 years for it to pervade Indian lifestyles. In 1979, 'the market for plastics' was just being seeded by the state-owned Indian Petro-Chemicals and it was only in 1994 that plastic soft drink bottles became a visible source of annoyance.
2. In the same year, people in other cities were concerned about the state of public sanitation and also urged regulatory bodies to ban the production, distribution and use of plastic bags. However the challenge was greater than it apeared at first.
3. The massive generation of plastic waste in India is due to rapid urbanisation, spread of retail chains, plastic packaging from grocery to food and vegetable products, to consumer items and cosmetics. The projected high growth rates of GDP and continuing rapid urbanisation suggest that India's trajectory of plastic consuption and plastic waste is likely to increase.

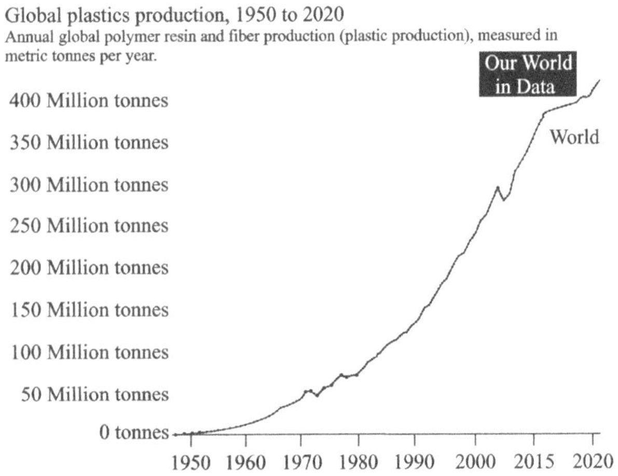
Global plastics production, 1950 to 2020
Annual global polymer resin and fiber production (plastic production), measured in metric tonnes per year.
Our World in Data
400 Million tonnes
350 Million tonnes
300 Million tonnes
250 Million tonnes
200 Million tonnes
150 Million tonnes
100 Million tonnes
50 Million tonnes
0 tonnes
World
1950 1960 1970 1980 1990 2000 2015 2020

4. According to the United Nations Environment Programme (UNEP) report of 2018, India stands few other countries like France, Mongolia and several African countries that have initiated total or partial national - level bans on plastics in their jurisdictions. On World Environment Day in 2018, India vowed to phase out single-use plastics by 2022, which gave a much needed impetus to bring this change.
5. In this context, thereafter ten state(Andhra Pradesh, Chhattisgarh, Gujrat, Himachal Pradesh, Karnataka, Madhya Pradesh, Meghalaya, Odisha, Rajasthan and Tamil Nadu) are currently sending their collected waste to cement plants for co-processing, twelve other states/UTs are using plastic waste for polymer bitumen road construction and still four other states are using the plastic waste for waste-to-energy plants and oil production. A world of greater possibilities has now opened up to initiate appropriate and concrete actions to build up the necessary institutions and systems before oceans turn, irreversibly into a thin soup of plastic.
6. However there is no one single masterstroke to counter the challenges witnessed by the staggering plastic waste management in the country. The time is now to formulate robust and inclusive National Action Plans and while doing so, the country will establish greater transparency to combat the plastic jeopardy in a more sustainable and holistic way.

Based on your understanding of the passage answer **ANY SIX** out of the seven questions given below :

i. What does the writer mean by 'visible source of annoyance' ? **(1 Mark)**

ii. Why did people demand a ban on plastics ? **(1 Mark)**

iii. What created a demand for plastics in India ? **(1 Mark)**

iv. With reference to the graph write one conclusion that can be drawn about the production of plastics in 2019 (aproximately). **(1 Mark)**

FOR THE VISUALLY IMPAIRED CANDIDATES (in lieu of Q . No . iv)

What accelerated the plastic waste in India ?

v. What does the upward trend of the graph indicate? **(1 Mark)**

FOR THE VISUALLY IMPAIRED CANDIDATES (in lieu of Q . No. v)

How are certain states in India recycling plastic waste, productively ?

vi. What does the line, oceans turning 'irreversibly into a thin soup of plastic', suggest ? **(1 Mark)**

vii. What step must be taken to combat the challenges of plastic waste management ? What will be its impact ? **(1 Mark)**

SECTION B: (Writing)

(8 Marks)

3. Mr. and Mrs. Agarwal of pushp Farms, Kolkata, are hosting a party on the occasion of the twenty - first birthday of their daughter, Vinita. Write a letter of invitation to Sonakshi, their niece, giving details of the date, time and venue in about 50 words.   **(3 Marks)**

4. Attempt **ANY ONE** from A and B given below :

(5 Marks)

4A. You are Chitra/Chetan Deshpande, residing at Akash Nagar, Agra. You come across the following classified advertisement in the newspaper. Write a letter, in about 120-150 words, applying for the position of a computer teacher at Sunrise Global School, Agra.

SITUATION VACANT

WANTED a qualified computer teacher for Sunrise Global School, Agra Applicant must be post graduate in Computer Science with minimum 3 years of work experience. Mention additional skills and interests. Apply with full particulars within a week to the principal, Sunrise Global School, Agra.

4B. You are Sunil/ Megha, School Leader of Sudheer Public School, Chennai On the completion of 25 years of meritorious service to the cause of education, your school celebrated its Silver Jubilee with great pomp and show. the celebrations lasted three days and in the true tadition of the school, each day was devoted to a noble cause of service. Special attention was paid to Children With Special Needs, Old Age Homes Orphanages, Students shared experiences of voluntary service and the Theatre Club put up short skits highlighting social concerns. Write a report in 120 - 150 words abourt the event to be published in your school magazine.

SECTION C: (Literature)

(18 Marks)

5. Attempt **ANY FIVE** of the six questions given below within 40 words each   **(2 × 5 = 10 Marks)**

   i   The iron master accuses the peddler of not being quite honest. What does the peddler say to justify the situation ?   **(2 Marks)**

   ii. Gandhi effectively managed to redress the problems of the indigo sharecroppers with the Lieutenant Governor. What did he achieve ?   **(2 Marks)**

   iii. Explain the irony at the end of the poem, ' Aunt Jennifers Tigers'.   **(2 Marks)**

   iv. After mother Skunk and Roger Skunk return home, she hugs him before he sleeps. What does this show about mother Skunk ?   **(2 Marks)**

   v.   How did Mr. Lamb's conversation and company change Derry's desire to isolate himself from the world ?   **(2 Marks)**

   vi. How did Evans manage to smear himself with blood ? What effect did it have on the officers ? **(2 Marks)**

6. Answer **ANY TWO** Of the following in about 120-150 words each :   **(4 × 2 = 8 Marks)**

   i.   In Edla's dealing with the peddler, she was compassionate and generous. discuss with reference to the story 'The Ratrap'.   **(4 Marks)**

   ii. Gandhi not only alleviated economic conditions of the Champaran people but also their social and cultural background. Justify.   **(4 Marks)**

   iii. Justify the title of the lesson 'On The Face Of It'.

(4 Marks)

Solutions

SECTION - A

1. (i) 'We don't take the first step towards a good cause because we think work to be big and can't be completed alone. So, we end up doing nothing.' **(1 Mark)**

(ii) 'It is good to adopt a two-uses-attitude! By putting an article to second use, we are giving it a longer lease of life and using up less raw-material from nature.' **(1 Mark)**

(iii) 'The clean sides of envelope can be used to write small notes, lists and reminders around the houses. Instead of using paper napkins, one can use cloth napkins.' **(1 Mark)**

(iv) People who are conscious about it follow rules and laws strictly. The neighbourhoods are clean and beautiful. **(1 Mark)**

(v) 'All kitchen waste can be collected separately. Those who have green fingers can turn this into valuable manure. Dig a pit and put the kitchen waste into it.' **(1 Mark)**

(vi) Digging a large pit in the colony and putting the kitchen waste into it can turn kitchen waste into a good manure. Help of all the members of the group will make the work easier by co-operation. **(1 Mark)**

(vii) Within three or six months, one will have good garden manure. **(1 Mark)**

(viii) Conscious **(1 Mark)**

(ix) Imperative **(1 Mark)**

2. (i) In 1992 plastic soft drink bottles were so much prevalent in the society that it became annoying seeing them. **(1 Mark)**

(ii) People were concerned about the state of public sanitation and urged regulatory bodies to ban the production. **(1 Mark)**

(iii) 'Rapid urbanisation, spread of retail chains, plastic packaging from grocery to food.' **(1 Mark)**

(iv) Plastic production in 2019 is more than previous years but less than 2020. **(1 Mark)**

(v) Plastic production has been growing with every passing years. **(1 Mark)**

(vi) Since we dump our plastic waste in oceans, so there is not much time left when the whole sea turns into a thin plastic later. **(1 Mark)**

(vii) There can be no single masterstroke to combat the challenge of plastic waste management. There should be robust and inclusive Notional Action Plans to establish greater transparency.

For Visually Impaired

(iv) The projected high growth of GDP and continuous rapid urbanisation accelerated plastic waste in India

(v) Ten states are sending either collected waste to cement plants and twelve other are sending for polymer, bitumen road construction and oil production.

SECTION - B

3. Pushp Farms, **(3 Marks)**
Kolkata
Date: 20th June 2022
Dear Sonakshi,

I hope you are in good shape and taking good care of your mother and father.

Vinita is turning 21 this Friday. So, we have decided to hold a party on the 26th June 2022. The party will start at 6 pm at Celebration Banquet Hall.

Waiting for your presence with your parents,

Mr. and Mrs. Agarwal

Note: Be crisp and precise. Since we have limited words, we cannot exceed the word limit by 10 words. Marks will be deducted if word limit forfeited.

4. **4A.** **(5 Marks)**

Akash Nagar,

Agra

The principal,

Sunrise Global School,

Agra

Date: 20th June 2022

Sub.: Application for the post of computer teacher.

Dear Mam/Sir,

It is with reference to your advertisement for a computer teacher in the newspaper. I am Chetan Deshpande. I wish to apply for the post of computer teacher in your school.

I received a gold medal for securing the first position in graduation and completed post graduation with first division in Computer Science, both from Agra University. I have a teaching experience for more than 5 years and still teaching at Sarvpriya School in Agra. Here, I have been working for 2 years.

But now I wish to switch from Sarvpriya School to your school because it is very far from my home. Therefore, to lessen my commutation time and better opportunity, I want to join Sunrise Global School.

I promise to work hard and stand up to your expectations. I have excellent communication skills with utmost sincerity and dedication to teaching. I have also won many medals in athletics at the school level.

Here, I enclose my bio data.

Expecting a positive reply,

Warm Regards,

Chetan Deshpande,

Enclosure: A bio data

Bio Data

Name :	Chetan Deshpande
Address :	Akash Nagar, Agra
Father's Name :	Harsh Deshpande
Date of Birth :	25th Nov. 1995
Marital Status :	Unmarried
Phone No. :	982823xxxx
E-mail address :	smartsagar25@gmail.com

Qualification	School	Subjects	Passing year	Percentage
Secondary	Kendriya Vidyalaya	English, Hindi, Maths, Science, Social Science	2010	95%
Senior Secondary	Kendriya Vidyalaya	Physics, Cemistry, Maths, Computer Science, English	2012	97%
Graduation	Agra University	Computer Science	2012-15	90%
Post-Graduation	Agra University	Computer Science	2015-17	85%

Name of School	Working tenure	Classes
Wisdom Public School	Jan, 2017- April, 2020	Secondary Classes
Sarvpriya School	April,2020 - Present	Senior Secondary

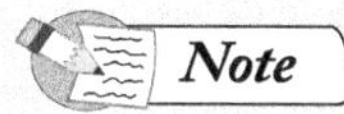

Note

Since it is a form of formal letter, one has to stay professional and to the point. One should be able to provide a valid argument for getting selected. Bio data should contain all necessary information. Wrong format may end up in deduction of one mark.

4B. Silver Jubilee of Services for Educational cause

(5 Marks)

By Sunil
Sudheer Public School

On 10th June 2022, the school completed 25 years of meritorious service to the cause of education. On the occasion of Silver Jubliee, we held a three-day event.
The first day is devoted to the educational development of Children with Special Needs. 4th class students of Special Needs school were invited to the school. Here, they spent a day with the students of our school. They matched toe with toe with the Dance club and participated in various other activities. Rohan wanted an inclusive policy where we could include such students in our school.

On the second day, elderly people from Shivam NGO were invited to the school. They gave their words of wisdom to the students of our school. Students of the theatre group performed an overwhelming skit for them. Students learned moral lessons through their life experiences. Ritika felt blessed to be a part of the lecture.

On the third and final day, children from Nidhi Orphanage were invited to spend a day with our school students. They interacted with our school students in a homely environment. Later, they participated in various sports activities and attended career guidance and orientation. Samridhi, part of the volunteering group, said she realized the importance of sharing love and caring for each other. Like this, we concluded the event and bade farewell to all our chief guests from various Diasporas.

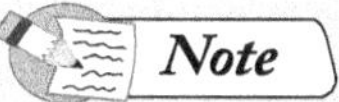

Note

Report writing should be in passive form. One should keep hold of the tense used. Title should be short, concise and to the point. The concluding paragraph should be progressive in nature.

SECTION - C

5. (i) The ironmaster, in 'The Rattrap' by Selma Lagerlof, accused the peddler of not being honest when he was inquired about his identity. Peddler, in return, reiterated his rattrap theory. All the comforts and pleasures of society are nothing but a rattrap, and one day everyone gets trapped in one or the other such rattraps. **(2 Marks)**

(ii) Gandhi had 'four protracted interviews' with the Governor who then appointed an official commission. This commission consisted of landlords, government officials, and Gandhi as the representative of the peasants. After many rounds of discussion, a 50% refund of the money extorted deceitfully and illegally was decided. But the planters demanded a 25% return to which Gandhi immediately agreed. Gandhi meant that the amount is not important but by giving money, the planters bowed down to the peasants and had given their honour too. **(2 Marks)**

(iii) Aunt Jennifer's Tigers written by Adrienne Rich highlights an ironic aspect of society. When Aunt Jennifer will die, her fingers will still be holding those 'ringed ordeals'. She still would be loyal to her rituals and religion. But the tigers which she stitched on the cloth will go on 'prancing, proud and unafraid.' Unlike the artist, her art is fearsome, amber-eyed, sinewy strength and independent.

(2 Marks)

(iv) This attribute of mother Skunk portrays her care and love for her child Roger Skunk. She explained to her that their natural smell is the most beautiful gift of God for them. They should not change themselves as per society. Instead, they should stay the same and society will accept them in the coming time.

(2 Marks)

(v) Mr. Lamb told Derry about a story of a man who had locked himself up in a room. He was afraid of everything. 'A bus might run him over, or a man might breathe deadly germs, or lightning might strike or kick him to death or he might love a girl and the girl would leave him and he might slip on a banana skin and heads off.' **(2 Marks)**

(vi) It was the invigilator who got that blood for Evans. It was brought in the rubber-ring that McLeery carried with him in his briefcase. It was pig's blood which was mixed with human blood to stop clotting. This blood was smeared on his face by Evans. General didn't believe in its possibility. Other officers were left stunned after knowing the details of the situation. **(2 Marks)**

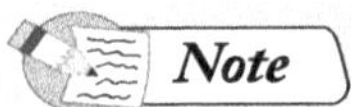 *Note*

These answers give us full opportunity to write at our will. But we need to be concise and divide our time accordingly. Incorporate name of the text and author in every answer. This gives a positive response in the minds of the checker.

6. (i) 'The Rattrap' is a story written by Selma Lagerlof. Edla was the ironmaster's daughter who stayed with him. She portrayed the character of a compassionate, brave, and intellectual girl. She noticed that the peddler was afraid of going to the house of the ironmaster's home and relieved his suspicions by giving him free will to leave. When Mr. Ironmaster was infuriated by the deceit of the peddler, she was thinking from the peddler's point of view. It portrays her level of understanding and maturity toward the situation. Unlike her father considered the peddler a thief, she gave him the status of a human. She even asked to share the Christmas meal with the vagabond as promised. It showed her courage and intelligence to fulfill her father's promises even in opposing situations. All these efforts turned into a character change for the peddler. He thanked her for her 'nobility' and consideration. Instead of stealing silver spoons, he packed thirty kroner which he stole from the old man. The vagabond elevated his stature from a rat to 'Captain von Stahle.' **(4 Marks)**

(ii) Gandhi not only planned and perforated economic development but social as well as cultural up-gradation. For educating society, Mahadev Desai and Narhari Parikh were appointed. Many other teachers from Bombay, Poona, and other places also reached Champaran. Devad with Kasturbai taught the ashram rules on personal cleanliness and community sanitation. Gandhi called for a doctor for six months of service. Only three medicines were available- castor oil for a coated tongue, quinine with castor oil for malaria fever, and ointment with castor oil for skin eruptions. Even after staying far away from Champaran, he stayed in touch by mail. He wrote to the residents that it was time to dig new pits otherwise the old ones would begin stinking. He read through the financial statements of the state at regular intervals. Through all those processes Gandhi not only freed them but made them self-reliant to take informed decisions judiciously.

(4 Marks)

(iii) 'On the face of it' is written by Susan Hill. As the title suggests, Derry faced discrimination for his burned face. People's comments like 'ugliest thing', 'poor boy' had infuriated him and brought his self-esteem down. But Mr. Lamb's insightful understanding of life gave a new meaning to life. Mr. Lamb guided Derry by giving the instance of weeds. Weeds are also like any other 'green growing plant'. They also have similar attributes to any other flower. 'It's all life.' Mr. Lamb revoked the story of beauty and the beast. Moreover, he asked Derry to explain its relevance to the present context. Derry accurately pointed out that it's a matter of inner beauty. Mr. Lamb gave Derry an example of the man who lived in fear of rejection and death. He closed himself inside a room. But eventually, a painting fell on him and he died. Through man's example, Mr. Lamb wanted Derry to stay fearless. Death is inevitable. One should remain ready for all sorts of situations. Derry understood that what he thinks, feels, sees, and hears is more important than his burned face. He was ready to accept his reality and focus on more productive factors. Hence, one should look beyond personal shortcomings and focus on available resources. **(4 Marks)**

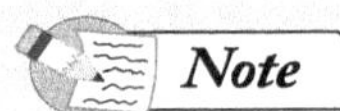 *Note*

These are full length answers. One should at least give 4 points in each answer. Here word limit can be exceeded. But time should be used judiciously. Begin with name of the text and its author. With every point, give some explanation of the story.

All India *2022*
CBSE Board Solved Paper Term-I

Time Allowed : 90 Minutes   *Maximum Marks : 40*

Read the following instructions very carefully and strictly follow them.

(i) This question paper contains **60** questions out of which 50 questions are to be attempted. All questions carry equal marks.

(ii) This question paper consists of three Sections – Section A, Section B and Section C.

(iii) **Section – A – Reading** – contains **18** questions. Attempt any **14** questions from **Q.** No. **1** to **18**.

(iv) **Section – B – Writing Skills** – contains **12** questions. Attempt any **10** questions from **Q.** No. **19** to **30**.

(v) **Section – C – Literature** – contains **30** questions. Attempt any **26** questions from **Q.** No. **31** to **60**.

(vi) First **14** questions in Section A, **10** questions in Section B and **26** questions in Section C will be evaluated.

(vii) There is only one correct option for every multiple choice question (MCQ). Marks will not be awarded for answering more than one option.

(viii) There is no negative marking.

SECTION A: Reading

I. Read the passage given below :

1. What's the one thing that you associate with your college days ? For me, it was consuming copious amounts of chai. A cup of tea was a panacea to all troubles and the companion to all joys. In this exclusive interview, we caught up with 66-year-old Deepak Garg, owner of Ganga Dhaba, a spot that every officer from National Academy of Administration has visited multiple times.

2. Deepak begins, "My family has been here for almost 90 years. It was my grandfather who first started working here as the supplier to the hotel that existed then. "In 1964, when Deepak was all of eight, he lost his father and the responsibility of raising four children, fell on his mother.

3. "Our growing up years were a huge struggle. My mother used to teach home science at a local balwadi school, and which was also where my siblings and I studied," he says . In 1978, Deepak says that he started a food joint that he named Om Chinese restaurant. "In those days, there was a huge liking for Chinese food and hence the name and the choice of cuisine," he says.

4. For almost 17 years, things continued and then Deepak got a Public Call Office (PCO) installed for the Officer Trainees. The business did so well that soon he had installed more than ten telephones, with separate cabins, to allow them some privacy while they made and received their calls.

5. "The OTs who would talk on the PCO from here would always refer to the place as 'Ganga Dhaba'. It was because this place is so close to the Ganga hostel inside the academy, that slowly the name changed and it became Ganga Dhaba, "Since it was the OTs that gave us our identity, we decided to change the name and call it Ganga Dhaba," he says.

6. There have been instances when Deepak and his family members have learnt dishes from the OTs. He says, "So many dishes on our menu today are because some officer came in and decided to teach us how to make them."

7. We have seen two generations of officers, served the parents, who now as the parents come back to drop their children at the academy and tell us to take care of them. What more can we ask for ? While the money we make is not great, the respect and the love we have accumulated over the years is what keeps us going," says Deepak, proudly. (400 words)

Based on your understanding of the passage, answer **any eight** out of the ten questions by choosing the correct options :

1. What, according to the author, gave him solace during his bad times in his college days ?

  (a) Friends   (b) Family

  (c) Tea   (d) Telephone

2. Read the following statements :

(i) Mr. Deepak named his food joint Om Chinese.

(ii) Chinese food was then popular among people.

(a) (ii) is the cause for (i).

(b) (i) is the cause for (ii).

(c) (i) is true and (ii) is false.

(d) (i) is false and (ii) is true.

3. 'Soon he had installed ten telephones.'

In the light of the above statement select the option that lists the right inference.

(a) He was kind enough to do social service for the OTs.

(b) He was successful and flourishing in his business.

(c) He expanded his canteen to accommodate more people.

(d) He switched his business from canteen to telephone booths.

4. The gesture of changing the name of the food joint to 'Ganga Dhaba' speaks of Deepak's

(a) wavering mind

(b) tendency to change with times

(c) respect and tribute to OTs

(d) dogmatic approach

5. 'his family members learnt dishes from OTs."

Choose the option that lists the inference with reference to the above statement.

(a) OTs were equally good connoisseurs of food.

(b) his family was mediocre in cooking.

(c) his family had close association and good rapport with OTs.

(d) his family wanted to learn more recipes to expand their business.

6. As per paragraph 7, select the option that sums up the personality of Deepak Garg.

(a) He is a struggler, lacks business acumen to make his business profitable.

(b) He is a very social and friendly person and enjoys good relationship with OTs.

(c) A responsible son who shared the burden of his family.

(d) A person who upholds dignity and esteem in life, not materialistic.

7. "......OTs that gave us our identity." He means to say

(a) His canteen was in the vicinity of OT's hostel.

(b) The canteen was named after the OTs hostel.

(c) It was OTs who helped his family to learn new recipes.

(d) It was OTs who patronized his canteen business.

8. Choose the option that aptly defines Deepak Garg's life story "from struggling childhood days to becoming a successful businessman".

(a) Where there is a will, there is a way.

(b) Make Ray while the Sun shines.

(c) A good fire make a good cook.

(d) Despair gives courage to a coward.

9. '...... many dishes on our menu today are because some officer came in and decided to teach us.'

Choose the option that rightly reflects the tone of the speaker.

(a) Ignorance   (b) Humility

(c) Pride   (d) Regret

10. "...... tell us to take care of them."

Choose the option that lists the appropriate reason behind the statement.

(a) Parents make a request as they stay away from their children.

(b) Deepak Garg can take care as he stays close to the hostel.

(c) Parents trust and respect Deepak Garg's hospitality.

(d) Parents pay Deepak Garg for the facilities he offers.

II. Read the passage given below :

1. Air pollution is a major threat to human health. The United Nations Environment Programme has estimated that, globally, 1.1 billion people breathe in unhealthy air. The World Health Organization (WHO) has estimated that urban air pollution is responsible for approximately 800,000 deaths and 4.6 million people lose their lives every year around the globe.

2. Traffic and transportation problems, inadequate drainage facilities, lack of open spaces, carbon emission, and the accumulation of waste aggravate the problem. Air pollution is associated with increased risk of acute respiratory infections (ARI), the principal cause of infant and child mortality in developing countries.

3. Urban air quality in most mega cities has been found to be critical and Kolkata is no exception to this. An analysis of ambient air quality in Kolkata was done by applying the Exceedance Factor (EF) method, where the presence of listed pollutants' (RPM, SPM, NO_2, and SO_2) annual average concentration are classified into four different categories; namely critical high, moderate, and low pollution. Out of a total of 17 ambient air quality monitoring stations operating in Kolkata, five fall under the critical category, and the remaining 12 locations fall under the high category of NO_2 concentration, while for RPM, four record critical, and 13 come under the high pollution category. The causes of high concentration of pollutants in the form of NO_2 and RPM have been identified in earlier studies as vehicular emission (51.4%), followed by industrial sources (24.5%) and dust particles (21.1%).

4. Later, a health assessment was undertaken with a structured questionnaire at some nearby dispensaries which fall under areas with different ambient air pollution levels. Three dispensaries have been surveyed with 100 participants. It shows that respondents with respiratory diseases (85.1%) have outnumbered waterborne diseases (14.9%) and include acute respiratory infections (ARI) (60%), chronic obstructive pulmonary diseases (COPD) (7.8%), upper track respiratory infection (UTRI) (1.2%), influenza (12.7%), and acid-fast bacillus (AFB) (3.4%).

Pollution in India

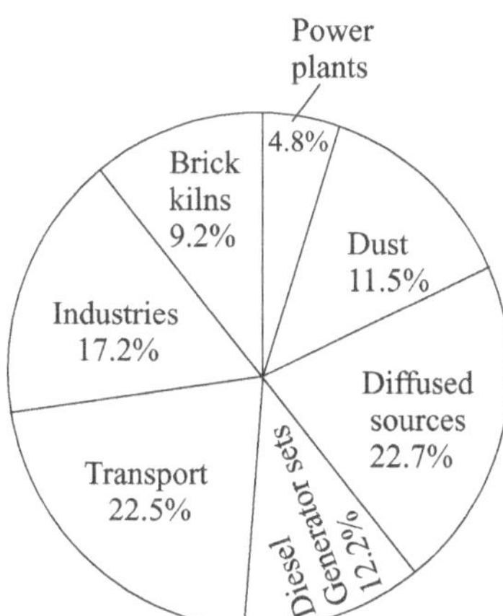

Fig. 1

5. To live a healthy life and have better well-being, practising pollution-averting activities in one's day-to-day activites is needed. These pollution-averting practices can only be possible when awareness among the masses is generated that the air, they breathe outdoors, is not found to be safe.

Based on your understanding of the passage, answer any six out of the eight questions by choosing the correct options:

11. Select the option that highlights the main idea of the passage.
    (a) To educate people about the threat of air pollution.
    (b) To warn people of the threat of air pollution and educate them about the safety measures.
    (c) To discuss the status of pollution in Kolkata and share the details of the study.
    (d) To educate people on Exceedance Factor method and share the results of the study.

12. Select the option that displays the correct 'cause and effect' relationship.

	Cause	Effect
(a)	Traffic and transportation problem	4.6 million deaths
(b)	Lack of open spaces	Mega cities
(c)	Air pollution	Respiratory diseases
(d)	Air quality monitoring stations	Emission of NO_2

13. Read the following statements:
    (i) Air pollution kills 4.6 million people every year in India.
    (ii) Air pollution is causing health hazards to more people than water pollution.
    (a) (i) is true and (ii) is false.
    (b) (i) is false and (ii) is true.
    (c) (i) is true and is responsible for (ii).
    (d) Both (i) and (ii) are false.

14. The author's opinion on the development of Mega cities is
    (a) Cities face transportation problem due to heavy traffic
    (b) Urbanization leads to deterioration of air quality.
    (c) Mega cities are the right spots to study air pollution.
    (d) Cities face the problem of congestion.

15. Select the option that lists the author's recommendation to the people.
    i. He wants people to be aware that air pollution is a major threat.
    ii. He urges people not to live in mega cities.
    iii. He advises people to follow pollution averting activities seriously.
    iv. He wants people to reduce vehicular emissions.
    (a) i & ii   (b) ii & iii   (c) i & iii   (d) iii & iv

16. Select the option that displays the true statement as per fig. 1.
    (a) Dust and power plants are the causes for maximum pollution.
    (b) Pollution caused by transport is much more than the pollution caused by industries.
    (c) The use of diesel generator is responsible for more than 50% of air pollution.
    (d) Dust stands fourth in the list that causes air pollution.

For the visually impaired candiates

16. As per paragraph 3, select the option that holds true.
    (a) Only urban air pollution is responsible for deteriorating human health condition.
    (b) The higher intensity of pollutants in the form of NO_2 and RPM is mainly due to vehicular emissions.
    (c) Dust particles in air are the major contributors of pollution.
    (d) Traffic and transport plays a negligible role in increasing pollution.

17. Read the following statement :
    (i) Air quality in Kolkata is less than critical.
    (ii) 12 locations were selected for measuring ambient air quality.
    (iii) Most of the mega cities are suffering from the problem of poor air quality.
    (a) (i) is true and (ii) and (iii) are false.
    (b) (i) and (ii) are true and (iii) is false.

(c) (i) and (iii) are true and (ii) is false.

(d) (i) and (ii) are false and (iii) is true.

18. "accumulation of waste aggrrvates the problem."

Select the option that best describes the 'problem' with reference to the above statement.

(a) Increase in pollution leads to huge accumulation of waste.

(b) Lack of space for waste disposal.

(c) More developments lead to more waste.

(d) Lack of sustainable and effective waste management.

SECTION B: (Writing & Skills)

III. Answer any four out of the five questions given below with reference to the context.

19. Mrs. Sujata wants to rent out the first floor of her house. She decides to draft an advertisement to be published in a national daily.

Choose the correct option under which heading she can publish her advertisement.

(a) For Sale

(b) Accommodation Wanted

(c) Situation Vacant

(d) To let

20. Select the option that lists the important information that Sujata needs to include in her advertisement.

i. Size of the house

ii. People in the neighbourhood

iii. Location

iv. Amenities and facilities

v. Distance from Metro Rail Station

vi. Contact address

(a) i, iii, v & vi   (b) i, iii, iv & vi

(c) ii, iii, v & vi   (d) i, ii, iv & v

Vineeta is the Head girl of Gandhi Memorial School, Nagpur. She is asked to draft a notice informing students of class XII about a workshop on stress management.

21. Select the option that best justifies the title for the notice.

(a) Workshop for class XII students

(b) How to manage stress

(c) Stress management workshop for class XII students

(d) Attention ! class XII students

22. Select the appropriate option that lists important details that Vineeta should include in her notice.

(a) Time to reach the venue, dress code for students, date, name of the resource person

(b) Date, venue, time, name of the resource person

(c) Date, duration, reason to attend, name of the resource person

(d) Date, venue, time, dress code for students

23. Help Vineeta by choosing the right option to complete the statement in her notice.

The workshop will be _______ and will teach some _______ to effectively manage stress.

(a) conducted, time   (b) effective, tips

(c) interesting, students (d) beneficial techniques

IV. Answer any six of the seven questions given below with reference to the context.

Rashmi is President of her school Library Club. She decides to write an article on the need to develop the habit of reading as she strongly feels it is fading among the present day students.

24. Select the option that lists an appropriate title for Rashmi's article.

(a) Develop reading habit to be successful.

(b) Why is reading important?

(c) Reading skill – A requisite to be a good communicator

(d) Reading is the best exercise for mind

25. Help Rashmi complete her ideas in the following sentence by choosing the right option.

Every book opens up new _______ of thoughts for the reader. Reading books is one of the _______ habits that helps one improve his or her focus.

(a) ideas, common

(b) dimensions, constructive

(c) doors, interesting

(d) views, best

26. What major reason can Rashmi state in her article for deteriorating reading habits among students?

(a) Academic pressure   (b) Sports

(c) Digital technology   (d) Friends

27. Select the option that lists suitable steps to be taken to improve reading habits among children.

i. Gift them books

ii. Take them on trips to a library

iii. Encourage them to read text books.

iv. Create a reading space for children.

v. Take children on field trips.

(a) i, ii & iv   (b) i, iii & v

(c) ii, iii & iv   (d) i, iv & v

28. Select the option that best describes the importance of reading habit:

(a) A book is a gift you can open again and again – Garrison Keillor

(b) Reading is a conversation. All books talk, but a good book listens as well – Mark Haddon

(c) The greatest gift is a passion for reading – Elizabeth Hardwick

(d) Books are a uniquely portable magic – Stephen King

29. Read the following statements :

   (i) An article is a written piece of communication published for a large/targeted audience.

   (ii) An article is an interactive communication with a selected audience.

   (a) (i) is false and (ii) is true.

   (b) (i) is true and (ii) is false.

   (c) Both (i) and (ii) are true.

   (d) Both (i) and (ii) are false.

30. The title of an article must not be

   (a) clear and attractive   (b) eye-catching

   (c) interesting   (d) lengthy

SECTION C: (Literature)

This section has sub-sections V, VI , VII, VIII & IX. There are a total of 30 questions in the section. Attempt any 26 questions from section V-IX.

V. **Read the extract given below to attempt the questions that follow:**

Mukesh insists on being his own master. "I will be a motor mechanic", he announces.

'Do you know anything about cars ?' I ask.

"I will learn to drive a car." he answers, looking straight into my eyes. His dream looms like a mirage amidst the dust of streets that fill his town Firozabad, famous for its bangles. Every other family in Firozabad is engaged in making bangles. It is the centre of India'a glass blowing industry where families have spent generations working around furnaces, welding glass, making bangles for all the women in the land it seems.

Mukesh's family is among them. None of them know that it is illegal for children like him to work in the glass furnaces with high temperatures, ...

31. What does the author try to convey by the expression 'being his own master' ?

   (a) Mukesh is disobedient to the elders.

   (b) Mukesh is adamant in his behavior.

   (c) Mukesh takes his own decisions.

   (d) Mukesh does not listen to others.

32. Through the expression "... looking straight into my eyes" the narrator is trying to convey.

   (a) Mukesh displayed no fear in his eyes.

   (b) Mukesh was not feeling shy while speaking to the narrator.

   (c) Mukesh was conversing in a very friendly manner with the narrator.

   (d) Mukesh displayed his courage and determination in expressing his opinion.

33. 'His dream looms like a mirage.' This indicates

   (a) Mukesh has no clear vision of his dream.

   (b) His dream is distorted and misleading.

   (c) His dream is illusive and elusive.

   (d) Mukesh's dream is different from others.

34. "None of them know that it is illegal for children to work in glass furnaces." Select the inference in reference to the above statement.

   (a) The children are innocent and do not realise the hardships of life.

   (b) Their illiteracy and ignorance are exploited by the unsurpulous businessmen.

   (c) They have no one to support them legally to get out of the situation.

   (d) The children are ready to work in glass furnaces due to their poverty.

35. Select the option that lists the facts about Firozabad.

   i.   Almost all the families are engaged in bangle making.

   ii. The children work as motor-mechanics.

   iii. The children work in a hazardous situation.

   iv. Firozabad is the centre for car making.

   (a) i & ii   (b) ii & iii   (c) i & iii   (d) iii & iv

VI. **Read the extract given below and answer the questions that follow:**

I went to the pool when no one else was there. The place was quiet. The water was still, and the tiled bottom was as white and clean as a bathtub. I was timid about going in alone, so I sat on the side of the pool to wait for others.

I had not been there long when in came a big bruiser of a boy, probably eighteen years old. He had thick hair on his chest. He was a beautiful physical specimen with legs and arms that showed rippling muscles. He yelled.

"Hi Skinny ! 'How'd you like to be ducked ?

36. What impression do you form about the narrator ?

   (a) He is a beginner in swimming lessons.

   (b) He has made friends during his swimming lessons.

   (c) The big boy was well built and handsome.

   (d) The narrator lacks courage and confidence to enter the pool alone.

37. The description of the big boy by the narrator is one of

   (a) Complaint   (b) Admiration

   (c) Criticism   (d) Poise

38. Select the option that lists the probable reason for the big boy's behavior towards the narrator.

   (a) his intention to frighten the narrator.

   (b) his desire to give him a surprise.

   (c) The place was quiet and odd.

   (d) The narrator was skinny and alone.

39. The figure of speech in the expression 'as white and clean as a bath tub' is _______ .

   (a) Metaphor   (b) Alliteration

   (c) Simile   (d) Irony

40. The writing style of the narrator indicates that the passage can be classified under a/an _______

   (a) Interview   (b) Autobiography

   (c) Fiction   (d) Short story

VII. Read the extract given below and answer the questions that follow:

What I want should not be

confused

with total inactivity

Life is what it is about;

I want no truck with death.

If we were not so single-minded

about keeping our lives moving -

and for once could do nothing

Perhaps a huge silence

might interrupt this sadness

of never understanding ourselves

and of threatening ourselves with

death.

41. The poet's intention is the first line is to

   (a) give warning to the readers

   (b) give right direction to the readers

   (c) give choice to the readers

   (c) give a clarification to the readers

42. Select the option that best explains the stand of the poet in the expression : "I want no truck with death".

   (a) He advises people to escape death.

   (b) He asserts that death is inevitable.

   (c) He assures that he does not advocate death.

   (d) He expresses his desire not to die.

43. Select the option that aptly describes the tone of the poet in the expression :

"If we were not so single minded'.

   (a) regretful   (b) critical

   (c) encouraging   (d) friendly

44. According to the poet who is to blame for the condition of threatening ourselves with death ?

   (a) Stressful life   (b) Keeping quiet

   (c) Lack of understanding   (d) State of confusion

45. The tone of the poet in the expression

"perhaps a huge silence

might interrupt this sadness" is

   (a) unsure yet optimistic

   (b) sure and confident

   (c) poetic & melodramatic

   (d) hopeful but not confident

VIII. Read the extract given below and answer the questions that follow :

"You are well", Sadao agreed. He lowered his voice. "You are so well that I think if I put my boat on the shore tonight, with food and extra clothing in it, you might be able to row to that little island not far from the coast. It is so near the coast that it has not been worth fortifying. Nobody lives on it because in storm it is submerged. But this is not the season of storm. You could live there until you saw a Korean fishing boat pass by. They pass quite near the island because the water is many fathoms deep there.'

The young man stared at him, slowly comprehending. 'Do I have to ? he asked.'

"I think so", "Sadao said gently. "you understand – it is not hidden that you are here."

46. The arrangements of food and clothing by Dr. Sadao portrays him as

   (a) a kind and compassionate person

   (b) an experienced sailor

   (c) a good event organizer

   (d) a good advisor

47. 'not been worth fortifying' indicates that it _______ .

   (a) has been left uncared for and neglected.

   (b) can be easily spotted by the Korean boats.

   (c) will be easy for the white man to enter the island.

   (d) is dangerous to stay there alone.

48. The speaker's tone in the expression : "Do I have to ?" is

   (a) pleading   (b) commanding

   (c) irritated   (d) fear and doubt

49. "But this is not the season of storm." Dr. Sadao tries to

   (a) explain the situation

   (b) assure him of safety

   (c) educate him on climate

   (d) display his knowledge

50. "... it is not hidden you are here."

Dr. Sadao's intention is :

   (a) to explain why he cannot stay there anymore.

   (b) to remind him that he has tried to hide his presence.

   (c) to explain that it is necessary and good for both of them.

   (d) to assert that his house is not a hiding place.

IX. Attempt the following :

51. "I had counted on the commotion to get to my desk without being seen." In the light of Franz's statement select the option that rightly brings out his intention.

(a) He tried to avoid his friends.

(b) He tried to cheat his teacher M. Hamel.

(c) He did not want to face the villagers in the class.

(d) He wanted to escape M. Hamel's scolding.

52. The poet Kamala Das brought in the image of 'spilling children' with the intention

(a) of praising children.

(b) of reminiscing her childhood.

(c) of bringing in a contrast to the mood of the poet.

(d) of making her mother happy and cheerful.

53. "The stunted, unlucky heir of twisted bones'.

Select the option that best explains the expression : 'unlucky heir'.

(a) leagcy to inherit the father's possessions.

(b) unlucky to live in a slum.

(c) unfortunate to inherit his father's disease.

(d) unfortunate to study in dim classroom.

54. Select the option that aptly describes Hana as a wife :

(a) Hana is very possessive about her husband.

(b) Hana is a very caring and responsible wife.

(c) Hana is a very dominant wife.

(d) Hana is a very fussy and nagging wife.

55. She did not wish to be left alone with the white man. This thought of Hana reveals the fact that

(a) Hana hates white man

(b) white men are dangerous.

(c) War makes people enemies.

(d) Hana is timid and cautious

56. "And then sheer, stark terror seized me",

Which of the following options has used the same figure of speech as in the underlined phrase above ?

(a) Sea <u>waves roared frighteningly</u> on a stormy night.

(b) Fear <u>is a poison</u>.

(c) He roared <u>like a lion</u> in anger.

(d) I am <u>frightfully sorry</u> for my mistakes.

57. "The young men echo the lament of their elders.' Select the option which indicates Anees Jung's view on young men.

(a) They don't take any initiative.

(b) They are as poor as their elders.

(c) They are as helpless as their elders.

(d) They don't support their elders.

58. 'would put on <u>clean clothes</u>.' What does Pablo Neruda mean by 'clean clothes'?

(a) white dress to reflect peace.

(b) mind without courage and confidence

(c) mind without confusion and fear

(d) mind without hatred and prejudice

59. 'But the jump made no difference.' Select the option that reflects the tone of Douglas.

(a) fear (b) regret

(c) anger (d) grief

60. 'Suppose you were condemned to death and the next day I had to have my operation ?" The tone of the General indicates he is

(a) worried about Dr. Sadao as he is a good scientist.

(b) working against the law and order of the country.

(c) uncertain about his health condition.

(d) selfish and dependent on Dr. Sadao for his treatment.

Solutions

SECTION - A

1. **(c)** 'For me, it was consuming copious amounts of chai. A cup of tea was a panacea to all troubles and the companion to all joys.'

2. **(a)** 'Deepak says that he started a good joint that he named Om Chinese restaurant. "In those days, there was a huge liking for Chinese food and hence the name and the choice of cuisine." He says'

3. **(b)** The business did so well that soon he had installed more than ten telephones, with separate cabins.

4. **(c)** "Since it was the OTs that gave us our identity, we decided to change the names and call it Ganga Dhaba."

5. **(c)** Since his family had a close association and good rapport with OTs, they taught his family members dishes to cook and earn in the coming days.

6. **(d)** Deepak Garg values 'respect and love' he has accumulated over the years and not 'money.'

7. **(d)** It was OTs who patronised his canteen business.

8. **(a)** Deepak Garg and his family were determined and continued doing the hard work.

9. **(b)** He acknowledged the fact that he didn't know everything. Instead, he learned from OTs.

10. **(c)** Parents trust and respect Deepak Garg's hospitality

11. **(a)** The passage is providing facts and figures for showing the threats of pollution. Therefore, they are educating people about the threats of air pollution.

12. **(c)** 'Urban air pollution is responsible for approx. 800,000 deaths and 4.6 million.'

'Lack of open spaces aggravates the problem of air pollution'

'The causes of high concentration of pollutants in the form of NO_2 and RPM have been identified .... as vehicular emission'

13. **(a)** There is no comparison laid between air and water pollution.

14. **(b)** Urbanization leads to deterioration of air quality.

15. **(c)** 'To live a healthy life and have better well-being, practising pollution averting activities in one's day-to-day activities is needed.'

16. **(b)** Pollution caused by transport 22.5%

Pollution caused by Industries 17.2%

For visually impaired candidate

(b) The higher intensity of pollutants in the form of NO_2 and RPM is mainly due to vehicular emissions.

17. **(d)** 'Urban air quality in most mega cities is critical and Kolkata is no exception'

18. **(c)** More developments lead to more waste.

SECTION - B

19. **(d)** For renting of a house, we use 'to let' as the heading of the advertisement.

20. **(b)** The size of the house, location amenities, and facilities and contact address are essential.

21. **(c)** The title of the notice should be self-sufficient to provide the gist of the whole notice. Topic of the workshop with the specified class is apt for the notice.

22. **(b)** The dress code for students is not important in the workshop on stress management. The name of the resource person is important to bring interest and add value to the workshop.

23. **(d)** Beneficial and techniques are correct as per the situation.

24. **(b)** The article is to be written on the need to develop the habit of reading. Hence the importance of reading will include all sorts of benefits and phenomena associated with reading.

25. **(b)** Dimensions, constructive suits best for the blanks.

26. **(c)** Since students are addicted to digital technology and audio-visual aids, they are unable to comprehend long texts and read for hours.

27. **(a)** Gifts are prized possessions. Gifting books will add value to the books. People will also gain knowledge while reading texts. It is a better option than encouraging them to read.

28. **(c)** This quote by Elizabeth Hardwick is direct and to the point for developing reading habits among the students.

29. **(b)** An article is not an interactive communication.

30. **(d)** Long titles will not interest the readers.

SECTION - C

31. Phrase 'being his own master' conveys the meaning to be independent and able to make your own decisions. Mukesh in the story by Anees Jung lives in Firozabad where their chief occupation is bangle-making. There he 'insists' on being a motor mechanic.

32. **(d)** 'looking straight into my eyes' literally means to look at someone directly to convince them that what he/she is saying is true, even though the situation may not be pragmatic. The narrator is trying to convey that even in a grim situation Mukesh is determined and courageous. He aspires to go beyond the boundaries of his surroundings.

33. **(c)** Mirage is an optical phenomenon, especially in the desert, by which the image of some object appears displaced above, below, or to one side of its true position as a result of spatial variations of the refractive index of air. It also means something illusory, without substance or reality. Here, his dream is illusionary and quite difficult.

34. **(b)** The children of Firozabad don't know the legality of their work. Neither do they have education and awareness nor ambitions to think beyond bangle-making.

They have been working in glass furnaces with high temperatures, in dingy cells without air and light and this is illegal as per the Indian Constitution. As bangle-making is the sole occupation of the whole community, people don't have time to think about other aspects of life like health, education, infrastructure, cleanliness, etc.

35. **(c)** As evident from the extract, almost all families were engaged in bangle-making. Children and adults both were working in this hazardous situation.

36. **(d)** The statement, " I was timid about going in alone, so I sat on the side of the pool to wait for others." clearly implores that the narrator lacked the courage and confidence to enter the pool alone. Timid means are afraid of.

37. **(b)** The narrator admired the big boy.

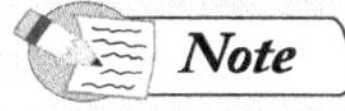

'He was a beautiful physical specimen with legs and arms that showed rippling muscles.' signify the heroic image of the big boy in the narrator's mind. Poise means a calm, confident way of behaving.

38. **(d)** Narrator was sitting alone 'when no one else was there.' He was addressed as 'Skinny' by the big boy. Hence, these two are probable reasons for the big boy's behaviour.

39. **(c)** Simile is a word or phrase that compares something to something else, using the words 'like' or 'as', for example 'face like a mask' or 'white as snow' etc.

40. **(b)** An Autobiography is the story of a person's life written by that person himself/herself. The story is written in the first person. The reader feels the situation through the eyes of the narrator.

41. **(d)** The poet wants to clarify to the readers.

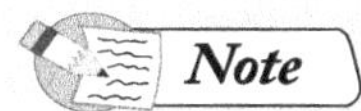

The title of the poem as well as words like 'keep still', 'let's not speak', 'not move' indicate stillness and halt to life but it 'should not be confused' with 'doing nothing'. Poet wants people to go for inner peace and self-realization.

42. **(c)** The poet completely dissociates himself from 'total inactivity' and 'death'. He doesn't want to support or talk good about death.

43. **(b)** The poet is criticizing our single-mindedness. He is nowhere happy with our behaviour. But he also knows that there is still hope.

44. **(c)** 'Perhaps a huge silence

might interrupt this sadness

of never understanding ourselves

and of threatening ourselves with death'

These statements signify that we were ignorant of our death.

45. **(a)** The use of 'might' indicate uncertainty but the poet is optimistic. He ends the poem on a positive and hopeful note.

46. **(a)** Dr. Sadao was a kindhearted and considerate man. Apart from his boat, he is ready to give food and clothing to the young man for his safe journey.

47. **(a)** Since the island gets submerged in the storm no one lives there. And hence it has been left uncared for and neglected.

48. **(d)** The speaker doesn't want to go out of Sadao's home. He is suspicious and fearful that anyone else might shoot him.

49. **(b)** There are many storms on the shore of the island. But that wasn't the season of the storm. Dr. Sadao is assuring him of safety.

50. **(c)** Dr. Sadao is also living in fear of getting caught by the Japanese army. This will bring hard times in both of their lives. Hence it is for the safety of both of them.

51. **(d)** This excerpt is from 'The Last Lesson' by Alphonso Douglas. Franz has always been scolded. Therefore, he wishes to escape his regretful daily routine.

52. **(c)** The poet Kamala Das portrayed the contrasting situations through this incident. Poet was sad because this could be her last journey with her mother. But children were happy outside.

53. **(c)** The student has inherited a disease from his father. Heir means the person with the legal right to receive (inherit) money, property, or a title when the owner dies. Here he has received the disease of twisted bones.

54. **(b)** When Dr. Sadao decided to take the enemy into her house and operate upon him, she fully supported his decision and assisted him in the operation. She hated the enemy soldier but still served him because her husband had sheltered him.

55. **(d)** Hana is timid and cautious. She was apprehensive about the white man.

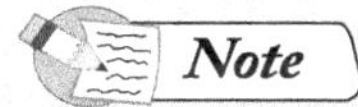

She also got nervous and scared when she saw a messenger at the door in an official uniform. Her hands went weak and she could not draw her breath. She thought that the servants must have told about the American man and the man had come to arrest Dr. Sadao.

56. **(a)** In these two statements personification is used. Personification is the attribution of personal qualities especially the representation of a thing or abstraction as a person or by the human form.

57. **(c)** Echo is a sound that is repeated as it is sent back off a surface such as the wall of a tunnel. Here it signifies economic condition. Since young men don't have enough money, they too are helpless. Note: 'The cry' of not having money is prevalent in every home of Firozabad. They don't even have enough money to feed their bellies. Moreover, 'Little has moved with time'. This situation is passed on to generations to come. 'Years of mind-numbing toil have killed all initiative and the ability to dream.' Hence, they have lost hope of a revival and become ignorant of their grievances.

58. **(d)** People will wear clean clothes and 'walk about with brothers' with 'no hatred and prejudice.'

59. **(a)** Douglas is already drowning in the swimming pool. When he tried to jump and come out of the pool, he couldn't. This brought fear in him.

60. **(d)** General was selfish and depended on Dr. Sadao for his treatment because he was one of the best surgeons in the whole of Japan.

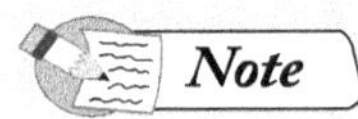

Note

The General had self-embodied himself as a strict communist heroic personality. People knew about the cruel and ruthless beating of her wife by him behind closed doors. This subjugated their desire of questioning, if any.

All India *2020*

CBSE Board Solved Paper

Time Allowed : 3 Hours   *Maximum Marks : 100*

General Instructions:

Read the following instructions very carefully and strictly follow them.

  (i) The quesitons paper comprises three sections - A, B and C.

       Section A - 20 Marks

       Section B - 30 Marks

       Section C - 30 Marks

  (ii) There are **10** questions in the question paper. **All** questions are compulsory.

  (iii) There is no overall choice. However, an internal choice has been provided in one que4stion in Section A, four questions in Section B and three questions in Section C. Make your choice correctly.

  (iv) However, separate instructions are given with each section and question, whereever necessary.

  (v) Do not exceed the prescribed work limit while answering the questions.

SECTION A: Reading

(20 Marks)

1. Read the passage given below :

Donated Organs and their Transportation

1. Once an organ donor's family gives its consent and the organs are matched to a recipient, medical professionals are faced with the onerous challenge of transporting organs while ensuring that the harvested organ reaches its destination in the shortest, possible time. This is done in order to preserve the harvested organs and involves the police and especially the traffic police department.

2. The traditional method of transporting organs by road is referred to as a "green corridor". This process entails police escorting an ambulance, so as to move around traffic – usually a specific traffic lane is chosen and all signals on the route stay green to ensure it to reach its destination in the shortest possible time. A 'green corridor' is a route cleared and cordoned off by the traffic police to ensure the smooth and steady transportation of harvested organs, on most occasions, to those awaiting a life-saving transplant. Organs tend to have a very short preservation time, such as the heart which has to be harvested and transplanted within four hours or the lungs which can be preserved for only six hours once they are harvested.

3. The first green corridor in India was created by Chennai Traffic Police in September 2008 when they accomplished their task of enabling an ambulance to reach its destination within 11 minutes during peak hour traffic. That organ saved a nine-year-old girl whose life depended on the transplant.

4. Similarly, such green corridors have been created by traffic police of various cities such as Pune, Mumbai, Delhi, NCR etc. Personnel are sationed at selected points to divert, control and clear the traffic giving way to the ambulance. Apart from this, a motorcade of police vehicles accompanies the ambulance ensuring that it does not face any problems. Delhi Traffic Police provided a green corridor from IGI Airport to Institute of Liver and Biliary Sciences in Vasant Kunj for transportation of a liver. The distance of 14 kms was covered in 11 minutes.

5. Experts point out the lack of a robust system to transport organs to super-speciality hospitals in least possible time. National Organ & Tissue Transplant Organisation (NOTTO), the country's apex organ donation agency, is now framing a proposal to airlift cadaver organs and will send a report to the Union Health Ministry. "Cadaver organs have a short life and so transplant should be done within a few golden hours," Director (NOTTO) expressed, "Therefore, we are preparing a proposal for airlifting organs at any given moment."

6. Most states do not have enough well-trained experts to retrieve or perform transplant procedures. Also, there is an acute shortage of advanced healthcare facilities to carry out a transplant. So, it is referred to other big centres in metropolitan cities. Organs

retrieved from Aurangabad, Indore, Surat, Pune are sent to Mumbai as these cities do not have super-specialty healthcare centres, informed officials.

7. "In India, about fifty thousand to one lakh patients are suffering from acute heart failure and need heart transplant at any point of time. In a private set-up, a heart transplant costs ₹15-20 lakhs, which is followed up by postoperative medication of about ₹30,000 per month lifelong."

1.1 On the basis of your understanding of the above passage, answer any five of the following questions by choosing the most appropriate options:

(a) The first green corridor in India was created in:
 (i) New Delhi   (ii) Chennai
 (iii) Mumbai   (iv) Pune

(b) The organization which is framing a proposal to airlift cadaver organs is :
 (i) Union Health Ministry
 (ii) Regional Organ and Tissue Transplant Organisation
 (iii) National Organ and Tissue Transplant Organisation
 (iv) State Organ and Tissue Transplant Organisation

(c) The onerous task the author is talking about in Para 1 is :
 (i) finding organ donors.
 (ii) finding doctors capable of performing transplants.
 (iii) to carry the harvested organ in the shortest possible time.
 (iv) to arrange the requisite facilities for the transplant.

(d) Most of the people do not go for the heart transplant as:
 (i) it is very risky.
 (ii) it is very painful.
 (iii) it may cause death of the recepient.
 (iv) the cost is probibitive.

(e) Most states refer organ transplant cases to big hospitals because:
 (i) they don't have well trained experts.
 (ii) the patients don't trust local doctors.
 (iii) the state hospitals are very crowded.
 (iv) they don't have a pool of harvested organs.

(f) Heart retrieved from a body is alive only for ____ hours.
 (i) two   (ii) three
 (iii) four   (iv) five

1.2 Answer the following questions briefly:
(a) What is a 'green corridor'?
(b) Why is smooth transportation of the retrieved organ necessary?
(c) What opinion do you form of Chennai Police with regard to the transportation of the harvested heart?

(d) What does the author mean by a few golden hours?
(e) How much does a heart transplant cost a patient in a private hospital?

1.3 Pick out the words from the passage which mean the same as the following:
(a) save (para 1)
(b) achieved / carried out (para 3)

2. Read the following passage:

1. How does television affect our lives? It can be very helpful to people who carefully choose the shows that they watch. Television can increase our knowledge of the outside world; there are high quality programmes that help us understand many fields of study, science, medicine, the different arts and so on. Morever, television benefits very old people, who can't leave the house, as well as patients in hospitals. It also offers non-native speakers the advantages of daily informal language practice. They can increase their vocabulary and practice listening.

2. On the other hand, there are several serious disadvantages of television, of course, it provides us with a pleasant way to relax and spend our free time, but in some countries people watch television for an average of six hours or more a day. Many children stare at the TV screen for more hours a day than they spend on anything else, including studying and sleeping. It's clear that TV has a powerful influence on their lives and that its influence is often negative.

3. Recent studies show that after only thirty seconds of television viewing, a person's brain 'relaxes' the same way that it does just before the person falls asleep. Another effect of television on the human brain is that it seems to cause poor concentration. Children who view a lot of television can often concentrate on a subject for only fifteen to twenty minutes. They can pay attention only for the amount of time between commercials.

4. Another disadvantage is that television often causes people to become dissatisfied with their own lives. Real life does not seem so exciting to these people. To many people, television becomes more real than reality and their own lives seem boring. Also many people get upset or depressed when they can't solve problems in real life as quickly as television actors seem to.

5. Before a child is fourteen years old, he or she views eleven thousand murders on the TV. He or she begins to believe that there is nothing strange about fights, killing and other kinds of violence. Many studies show that people become more violent after viewing certain programmes. They may even do the things that they see in a violent show.
 (a) On the basis of your reading of the above passage, make notes on it using Headings and Sub-headings. Use recognizable abbreviations

(minimum four) and a format you consider suitable. Supply a suitable title to it.

(b) Make a summary of the above passage in about 80 words.

SECTION B: Advanced Writing Skills

(30 Marks)

3. At Rohini, in Delhi you have a three-bedroom flat with all modern amenities. It is fully air-conditioned and has power backup. For the sale of this flat draft a suitable advertisement in not more than 50 words to be published in a local daily. Give all the necessary details. Your contact number is 9911223344.

OR

You are Secretary, Social Service League of your school. Design a poster to be displayed in your colony and in a local hospital premises inspiring people to make a pledge to donate eyes and other organs of their bodies.

4. You are Tapas/Tapasya of A-150, Mount Road, Chennai. You have seen an advertisement in the newspaper, 'The Chennai Times' for the post of Manager (Accounts) in Sundaram Westside, Chennai. Apply for the post with your complete biodata. (120–150 words)

OR

Write a letter to the Editor, 'The Indian times', Jaipur highlighting the need to tap the sports talent at a young age by sports teachers, coaches etc. so that it does not go unrecognized. Thus we shall have a large pool of young talented sports persons who can be groomed. You are Poorva Paras 78, Inderpuri, Jaipur. (**120-150** words)

5. 'No detention policy for classes sixth to eighth is academically very unsound.' Write a debate in **150-200** words either for or against the motion.

OR

As per last census, the literacy rate in India was around 74%. In our day- to-day life, we find people who cannot even read or write. Looking at the gravity of the situation you decide to deliver a speech in your school morning assembly on the topic, "Each One, Teach One'. Write your speech in **150-200** words. You are Vinitha/Bojo.

6. A programme on 'Swachh Bharat Mission' was organized in your school on Mahatma Gandhi's birthday. Posters were prepared and pasted in the colony near your school. A procession was taken out. School premises and its suroundings were cleaned by the students. Public was advised to make the mission successful. Write a report on the programme in **150-200** words. You are Srinivasan/Latha.

OR

The word 'father' is synonymous with strict discipline etc. but it is not completely true. The father fulfils his responsibilites affectionately for the family. Write an article in 150-200 words on the topic, 'Role of father in the family'. You are Dhruv/Deepa.

SECTION C: Textbooks and Long Reading Text

(30 Marks)

7. Read the extracts given below and answer the questions that follow each of them.

(a) He couldn't have addressed a more dazed and silent audience – no one knew what he was talking about and his accent defeated any attempt to understand what he was saying.

   (i) identify the chapter who is 'he'

   (ii) what was 'he' in real life

   (iii) how did the audience react to his speech

   (iv) why was his speech not a success

(b) Driving from my parent's
home to Cochin last Friday
morning, I saw my mother,
beside me,
doze, open mouthed, her face
ashen like that
Of a corpse and realised with
pain
that she was as old as she
looked ... ...

   (i) Where was the poet driving to? Who was sitting beside her?

   (ii) What did the poet notice about her mother?

   (iii) Which thought made the poet feel painful?

   (iv) Name the figure of speech used in the expression : 'her face ashen like that of a corpse'

8. Answer any **five** of the following questions in **30-40** words each :

(a) What explanation did the children offer the writer for not wearing footwear? Did she agree to it ? (Lost Spring)

(b) How did Douglas' experience at the beach in California affect him? (Deep Water)

(c) Why has Raj Kumar Shukla been described as being resolute? (Indigo)

(d) How will 'Keeping Quiet' protect our environment?

(e) How did Charley 'reach' the third level of the Grand Central Station?

(f) What is common between Derry and Mr. Lamb?

(g) Why was Dr. Sadao not arrested on the charge of harbouring an enemy?

9. Answer the following question in **120-150** words :
Why did the Crofter repose confidence in the peddler? How did the peddler feel after betraying the crofter?

OR

Educating children is the responsibility of society. Justify the statement in view of 'The Last Lesson'.

10. Answer the following question in **120-150** words:
What was the prediction of the astrologers regarding the ultimate fate of the Tiger King? How did it come to be true? Describe with reference to the story.

OR

What are phytoplankton? How are they important to our ecosystem? (Journey to the End of the Earth)

Solutions

SECTION - A

1. 1.1   **(1 × 5 = Marks)**

(a) (ii) Chennai

(b) (iii) National Organ and Tissue Transplant Organisation

(c) (iii) to carry the harvested organs in the shortest possible time.

(d) (iv) the cost is prohibitive

(e) (i) they do not have well trained experts

(f) (iii) four

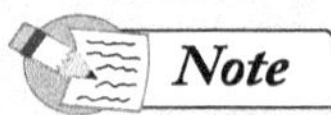

Note

1. *When answering MCQs choose the option which is the closest answer from amongst the options.*

2. *For Factual questions like e.g. "How much does a heart transplant cost……", include only the information given in the passage.*

3. *While answering the 'Why' question like "Why is smooth transportation of the retrieved organ necessary", you may begin your answer with 'Smooth transportation of the retrieved organ is necessary because ………or a similar phrase.*

4. *While answering the vocabulary questions, check the part of speech, the tense of the word etc. Your answer should have the same part of speech, tense etc.*
For e.g. save – preserve (NOT preserves or preserving or preserved)

1.2   **(1 × 5 = 5 Marks)**

(a) The traditional method of transporting organs by road is referred to as a "green corridor". It is a short route which is cleared and cordoned off by the traffic police for the smooth and steady transportation of the harvested organs.

(b) Smooth transportation of the retrieved organ is necessary since the harvested organs have a very short preservation time. Therefore it is necessary to help those awaiting a fresh lease of life.

(c) I have formed an excellent opinion of Chennai Police with regard to the transportation of a harvested heart since they not only performed a noble task of saving a precious life, but that they were able to do so with utmost efficiency and responsibility by reaching the destination within 11 minutes during peak hours of traffic.

(d) The few hours during which the harvested organ is alive and within which time the harvested organ should be transplanted into the recipient is referred to as 'a few golden hours' by the author.

(e) The heart transplant in a private hospital costs about 15-20 lakh per operation excluding the postoperative treatment and medicines which cost about Rs. 30,000 per month throughout one's life.

1.3   **(1 × 2 = 2 Marks)**

(a) save - preserve

(b) achieved/carried out - accomplished

2. (a) Note Making   **(8 Marks)**

Title – Pros and Cons of Watching Television/ Effects of Television on Our Lives

1. Television and its Effects
   1.1 Advantages
      a. Good for those - choose their shows
      b. Increases knowledge
      c. High quality progrms. help
        (i) study
        (ii) medicine
        (iii) science
        (iv) art and craft
      d. Old people, patients etc pass time
      e. Benefits non-native speakers - daily informal lang. practice
      f. Increases vocab.
      g. Can help in practicing listening
   1.2 Disadvantages
      a. children watch tv - < 6 hours
      b. effect on human brain
        (i) poor conc.
      c. Kids - pay attention - a subject for 15-20 min.

2. Effects our daily life
   2.1 Comparing reel life to real life
   2.2 Rise in dissatisfaction
   2.3 depression - not able to solve issues like actors
   2.4 Violence acceptable
      a. A child of 14 years – views 11000 murders on TV
      b. Emulates the show

Key to Abbreviation

Abbreviation	Word
progrms.	programs
etc	etcetra
lang.	language
vocab.	vocabulary
tv	television
<	more than
conc.	concentration
mint.	minutes
	leads to

(b) **Summary:** Television affects life in many ways. If watched with discretion, it increases knowledge through programmes based on study and medicine. It helps in enhancing language skills through daily informal practice and enriches vocabulary. The patients and extremely old people have access to entertainment at home. However, the disadvantages of television comes through mostly in children. Watching TV for more than 6 hours leads to poor concentration and increases violence among all age groups. The adults too are affected adversely since they cannot differentiate between real and reel life and find their life boring.

SECTION - B

3. (4 Marks)

ADVERTISEMENT

FLAT ON SALE

A 3 BHK, 1950 sq.ft. newly constructed, centrally AC flat on sale. Fully equipped with all modern amenities, attached bathrooms, 24 × 7 power backup, ground floor, front lawn, parking space for two vehicles, East facing in Sector 27, Rohini, New Delhi. Owner migrating to Canada. Expected Price-1.8 crores – negotiable. Contact Vinod/Vinneta on 9911223344.

OR

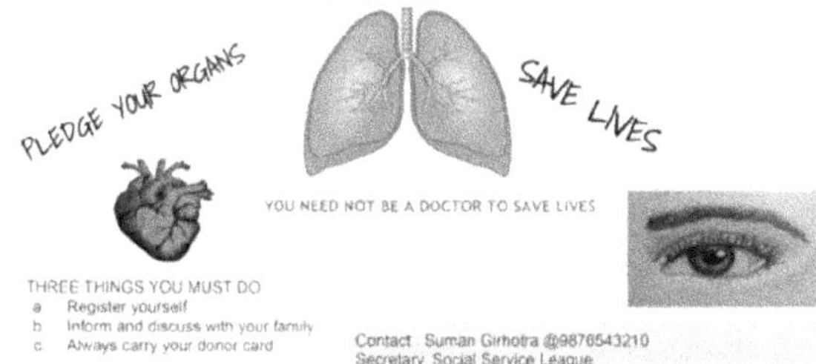

4. Letter (6 Marks)

A-150
Mount Road
Chennai

27 February 20XX

Head HR
Sundaram westside
Chennai

  Sub: Application for the post of Manager (Accounts)

Respected Sir/ Madam,

This is with reference to the advertisement in 'The Chennai Times' dated 26 February, 20XX for the post of Accounts Manager in Sundaram Westside, Chennai. I wish to put forth my application for the same. I have a bachelor's degree in business administration from Narsee Monjee Institute of Management Studies, Mumbai and have previously worked with Pantaloons, Navi Mumbai. I have strong inter-personal skills too.

I would request you to consider my application for the post.

Looking forward to a positive response.

Yours Truly
Tapas/Tapasya
Encl: Bio-data

BIO-DATA

Name:	Ms Tapas/ Tapasya Sinha
Father's Name:	Mr Akash Sinha
Gender:	Male/Female
Marital Status:	Unmarried
Address:	A-150 , Mount Road, Chennai
Email:	xxxx.sinha@gmail.com
Date of Birth:	05.07.20XX
Academic Qualifications:	Bachelor's Degree in Business Administration
Work Experience:	Worked at Pantaloon, Navi Mumbai
Languages Known:	Hindi, English, Marathi &Tamil
Hobbies:	Gardening, Listening to Music & travelling

OR

78,
Inderpuri
Jaipur

23 March, 20XX

The Editor
The Indian Times
Jaipur

 Sub: Highlighting the need to tap young sporting talent

Respected Sir/ Madam,

The performance of Indian sportspersons has raised the red flag regarding the future of Sports in a country like India. Not only has it amply reflected the casual attitude of all towards Sports but also raised questions on the multitude of resources which are being used for the promotion of Sports.

While we wish to rub shoulders with the great sporting nations of the world one day, the fact is that we continue to neglect our largely untapped pool of talent at the grassroot level. This has resulted in dismal and largely forgettable performance by Indians in the international arena. School curriculum too is stringent with little space for sports, lack of praise for the players at school level and more emphasis on academics. We need to follow countries like China who tend to tap into the talents of young sportspersons early at the school, district and state level. Initiatives like 'Khelo India School Games' should also be encouraged. Athletes should get a stipend in order to encourage people to take up sports and better infrastructure at the grassroot level {Like in cricket} would help in betterment of the level of sports in the country.

I hope this letter inspires the concerned authorities to take up the matter in all earnest.

Yours Truly
Puurva/Paras

5. Debate & Speech (10 Marks)

FOR THE MOTION

Respected Chairperson, Members of the Jury, my worthy opponents and dear audience! Today, I, XXX, stand before you to present my views for the motion on the topic 'No detention policy for classes 6-8 is academically very unsound'. The policy at hand here is a classic example of shortsightedness on the part of the policymakers, with the practice of non-detention obliterating the very reason, the students study for- to pass.

The policy rather than helping the students has led to the propagation of a callous attitude, leading to not imbibing what's taught in the class and ultimately resulting in difficulties later in their academic years.

While non-detention was initially touted to reduce the dropout rate, it is pertinent to note that rather than arresting the trend, it has only delayed it leaving the students to feel the heat later in Std IX, not only in terms of the examination but understanding the concepts too in std IX. Since some students do not ready their lessons seriously, disrupting classes and inhibiting the learning of the other students, problems of discipline arises. To conclude I would like to lay emphasize on the fact that it would be a great disservice to the students to promote them even though they are unable to grasp concepts at a lower level.

Against the motion

Respected Chairperson, Members of the Jury, my worthy opponents and dear audience! Today, I, XXX, stand before you to present my views against the motion on the topic 'No detention policy for classes 6-8 is academically very unsound'. Let me begin by thanking the educationists who thought of such a revolutionary idea. By implementing this, the cartographers of the education policy have not only eased the burden of the students but also combatted the problem of increasing school drop-outs.

By not detaining students uptill class VIII the policy makers have ensured that the financial resources spent on the student have not been wasted and as a result the students have not turned into delinquents. This policy also has eased the burden on the students and as a result helped them to excel in sports and other extra-cocurricular activities, focus on their interests and hobbies and showcase their skills. In other words it has been able to bring about the holistic development of the child.

I would like to conclude by stressing upon the fact that this policy enables the teacher to go for a continuous evaluation of the child's skills rather than a single, year end examination and hence helps in imbibing the very essence of learning.

Thank you.

OR

Speech

A very cheerful morning to one and all present here! I, Vinitha/Bejo, am standing in front of you to present a speech on the topic 'Each one teach one'. As per last consensus, the literacy rate in India was around 74%. However, it is hardly a cause for celebration since we find people who cannot even read or write in our daily lives. Even though India is a free democratic country since the last seven decades, we are yet to do justice to the principles which are the lifeline to our constitution. Despite having government and private schools, the government schools have not been able to get the requisite number of children despite running a multitude of programs aimed at attracting the children to school. Out of the few who attend, a large number drop out soon after. Having parents with little schooling themselves, difficult living conditions, widespread poverty and an urgent need to feed the mouth rather than the brain- it is not surprising that there are few takers. Therefore, what one needs to do is to take the school to the homes of the children and you can play a major role here.

I implore you to join the "Each One Teach One" initiative in large numbers wherein you become the teacher, guide and mentor for one student. You would be responsible for your own student. These activities can be taken up in the evenings and continued during vacations. Let us also create awareness regarding the importance of literacy through rallies, street plays and media coverage. This will motivate the Parents to send their children to the school. To conclude I ask you to contribute in the whole process of nation building. Are we all willing to be the change makers in times to come?

Thank You

6. **Report and Article**   **(10 Marks)**

Report

Tribute to the Father of Nation
Through Swachh Bharat Mission

By *Srinivasan/ Latha*

Hyderabad, October 3: All the students, staff and Management of XYZ Public School came together to provide impetus to the dream of our Prime Minister for a cleaner India and what better day to do the same but the birthday of the Father of Nation.

It all started at 5:00 am in the morning with the 'Prabhat Pheri' of the locality by the school choir and selected students of std XII. It was indeed heartwarming to see the residents of the area come out of their houses and join the group in large numbers. This support could be attributed to the awareness campaign which was undertaken a day in advance through beautiful posters prepared by the Picasso Club of the school and pasted at vantage points in the colonies near the school. After the pheri, cleanliness drives were run cleaning the school premises, its surroundings, the colonies and the market areas by the students amply supported by the local populace. The bystanders were also advised to follow suit and make the mission successful. Overall, it was a highly successful initiative by the school well supported by the residents.

OR

Article

Role of the Father in the Family

By *Dhruv/Deepa*

Fathers throughout ages have been viewed as secondary caregivers and strict disciplinarians in almost all cultures. In addition to this the expectations out of both parents along with their roles and responsibilities were clearly set.

While mothers' primary duties were children and household chores, fathers were to be the breadwinner. However, this perception is slowly changing. Today the roles have expanded beyond yesterday's expectations with either both parents working or quite a few fathers becoming primary caregivers, while mothers go to work. All said and done, fathers today, are more present in their children's lives. The father of the new millennium does not always earn. He is also happy being the stay home Dad. This trend is beneficial for the overall growth of the child since fathers, like mothers are pillars in the development of a child's emotional well being.

To conclude , the stereotypes about the role of the fathers is slowly changing and people are realizing more than ever before that being a good Parent has nothing to do with gender, it's all about time and effort.

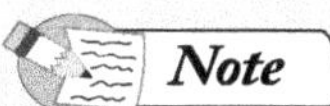 *Note*

1. *The passage is on the effects of television on people of all age groups. So the title must be related to the main idea and should have the key words 'Effects', 'Advantages,' 'Television' etc*
2. *It should always contain phrases. Avoid using complete sentences. For e.g.*
   1. *Television and its Effects*
      1.1 *Advantages*
       a. *Good for those - choose their shows*
       b. *Increases knowledge*
       c. *High quality progrms. help*
          (i) *study*
          (ii) *medicine*
          (iii) *science*
          (iv) *art and craft*
   AND NOT The effects of Television is that it is good ....
3. *Include a minimum of 4-6 distinctly different recognizable short forms i.e. abbreviations of the words in the notes as done in the solution.*

SECTION - C

7. (a)   **(4 Marks)**
  (i) The name of the chapter is "Poets and Pancakes". He is Stephen Spender – the poet who had visited Gemini Studio.
  (ii) He was an English poet and an editor of an English magazine in real life.
  (iii) The audience was extremely quiet and dazed while the speaker addressed his audience. In other words, the audience was non-responsive to his speech.
  (iv) His speech was not a success since no one knew what he was speaking about. Furthermore, his accent was too alien and any attempt to understand what he was saying was defeated by his accent.

(b)   **(4 Marks)**
  (i) The poet was driving to the Cochin airport. Her mother was sitting beside her.
  (ii) The poet noticed that her mother's face was ashen while she dozed off at her side. She realised that her mother was getting old with time.
  (iii) The thought that her mother was getting old and would eventually die was painful to the poet. The age old fear of the impending separation from her mother was painful for her.
  (iv) The figure of speech used in the expression : 'her face ashen like that of a corpse' is a simile.

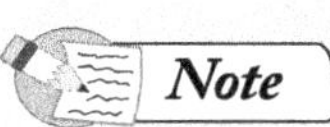 *Note*

1. *Be precise and to the point.*
2. *Since there is no internal choice in this question, try answering all the questions.*
3. *For questions like "Identify the chapter" write the full name of the chapter with the correct spellings.*
4. *Use the language as used in the question. For e.g. "Why was his speech not a success"? Your answer should start with – His speech was not a success because ....*

8.   **(2 × 5 = 10 Marks)**
  (i) The explanation that the children offer to the writer for not wearing footwear was that their mother did not bring them down from the shelf. No. She did not agree to it.
  (ii) Douglas's experience at the beach at California affected him adversely. He developed a deep aversion to water so much so that he kept himself away not only from swimming but also all water related activities.
  (iii) Raj Kumar Shukla had requested Gandhiji to visit Champaran. Since Gandhi was committed to Cawnpore and other places, he told Shukla that he would come later. However, Shukla accompanied him everywhere and did not leave his side even at the Ashram. Gandhi finally asked him to meet at Calcutta and take him from there. Shukla was present on the appointed date and time. It is for these reasons that he has been described as being 'resolute'.
  (iv) Keeping Quiet will protect our environment since it will allow men some time for introspection. It will stop the fishermen from harming the whales and the men gathering salt will look at his hurt hands. In other words, it will stop men from the indiscriminate exploitation of nature for his vested interest and environment will be protected.
  (v) Charley reached the third level of the Grand Central Station accidently. He had worked late at the office and was in a hurry to get uptown to his apartment. Therefore, he decided to take the subway from the Grand Central since it was faster than the bus. He went to the Grand Central and was lost. That is how he reached the third kevel which he initially thought to be the second level.
  (vi) The common thing between Derry and Mr Lamb was that both suffered from physical impairment. Derry's half face was burnt with acid and Mr Lamb had an artificial leg.
  (vii) Dr Sadao was not arrested on the charge of harbouring an enemy because of the General. The General suffered from a fatal condition and none except Sadao was skilful enough to save the General's life. Therefore the General kept him safe.

Note

1. *Choose your questions with care since there is internal choice in this question.*
2. *Each 2-mark question must have at least two value points.*
3. *So, for example – for the question "What explanation did the children offer the writer for not wearing footwear? Did she agree to it?" Answer both parts separately and be to the point.*
4. *For questions requiring specific answer for e.g. " How will 'keeping quiet' protect the environment?" Pick out only those examples which related to the environment.*

9.   **(6 Marks)**

The crofter reposed confidence in the peddler since he was a lonely man who craved for human companionship. He was without any wife or child and therefore happy to get someone to talk to throughout the night in his loneliness. Therefore he not only welcomed the peddler but provided him food and shelter too. He was equally generous with his confidences and shared with the peddler that earlier he was a crofter at Ramsjo Ironworks and now it was his cow that sustained him. It was only last month that he had received thirty kronor in payment from the creamery. Since the peddler looked unconvinced, he even took out the notes to show him and then put it back at the same place.

The peddler felt quite pleased with his smartness after betraying the crofter. He knew that he had to avoid the public highway and turn off the road into the woods to avoid being caught. However, once he got lost in the forest, he realised with a shock that he himself had got waylaid into the rat trap and regretted his action.

OR

It is indeed true that educating children is the responsibility of the whole society in close coordination with the school and its teachers. The story 'The Last Lesson' in addition to being a story about how language is inextricably linked to one's sense of identity and how one feels threatened at the core of one's being when forbidden from using their own language is also about how each member of the society is responsible for making them learn the language and thereby imparting education. In their regret for not having utilized their time to learn their own native language and their collective response to the last lesson of M Hamel, the story underlines each one's responsibility. M. Hamel blames himself for giving a holiday when he wanted to go fishing himself and for having got his flowers watered by the students at the cost of their lessons. He also underlines the responsibility of the Parents who were not anxious enough to make their children learn. Rather they preferred to put them to work to have a little money. The villagers too regretted having paid less heed to learning the language themselves and show their regret by sitting quietly at the usually empty last rows of the class. Franz himself wished he had attended the classes more often and paid more attention to the lessons. If all of them would collectively fulfilled their responsibility, they would still have had their language to cling to.

✎ *Note*

1. *Each 6-mark question must have at least four value points*
2. *Answer to the point including your own opinion in places where it is deemed necessary by the question.*
3. *Pick out specific examples from the text to support your answer*
4. *Quote straight from the text wherever required but do so only when you are sure of the words.*
    For e.g. the question "Why did the crofter repose confidence in the peddler? How did the peddler feel after betraying the crofter"? answer both parts separately.

Pick the value points from those given below:
FIRST PART
    a.   Crofter - a lonely man

    b.   Craved for human companionship
    c.   Without any wife or child
    d.   Happy to get someone to talk to throughout the night
    e.   Welcomed the peddler
    f.   Provided him food and shelter
    g.   Equally generous with his confidences
    h.   Shared with the peddler - earlier - a crofter cow sustained him
    i.   Thirty kronor in payment from the creamery
    j.   Peddler looked unconvinced
    k.   Show him and then put it back at the same place
FEELING OF PEDDLER
    a.   Quite pleased with his smartness initially
    b.   Goes in the woods to avoid being caught
    c.   Gets lost in the forest
    d.   Realises he himself is into the rat trap
    e.   Regretted his action.

10.   **(6 Marks)**

The prediction of the astrologer regarding the ultimate fate of the Tiger King was that his death would be brought about by a tiger. When this prediction was done at the time of the birth of the Tiger King, the infant gave a deep growl and said "Let tigers beware"! The events thereafter proved detrimental to the tiger population. The Tiger King vowed to kill hundred tigers for which he indulged in massive hunting. His marriage too was not guided by the virtue and the goodness of the princess but the criterion of a kingdom with more tiger population since he wanted to fulfil his vow. Each action of the Tiger King is guided by the predication right from taking the risk of losing his kingdom to the bribes and the taxes. However ironically even after fulfilling his vow of killing hundred tigers it is a tiger, albeit a toy, which becomes the cause of his death. While playing with the toy tiger, a birthday present for his son, he gets hurt by the sliver of wood from the toy tiger and dies later. So, at the end of the story the prediction of the astrologer comes true.

OR

Phytoplankton are microscopic grasses of the sea that nourish and sustain the entire Southern Ocean's food chain. These single-celled plants use the sun's energy to assimilate carbon and synthesise organic compounds through photosynthesis.

They are extremely important to our ecosystem since as said earlier it is phytoplankton which nourish and sustain the entire Southern Ocean's food chain. Any further depletion in the ozone layer will affect the activities of the phytoplankton. This in turn will affect the lives of all the marine animals and birds of the region and ultimately the global carbon cycle. The entire food chain will collapse. Therefore they are the life line to our ecosystem.

✎ *Note*

1. *Each 6-mark question must have at least four value points*
2. *Answer to the point including your own opinion in places where it is deemed necessary by the question.*
3. *Pick out specific examples from the text to support your answer*
4. *Quote straight from the text wherever required but do so only when you are sure of the words.*
5. *Only write whatever is required. Do not try to stretch the answer even if it is less than the required words. For some questions like "What are phytoplankton? How are they important to our eco system", you can only write whatever is required.*

Delhi *2020*

CBSE Board Solved Paper

Time Allowed : 3 Hours   *Maximum Marks : 80*

General Instructions:

Read the following instructions very carefully and strictly follow them.

(i) The question paper comprises **three** sections: A, B and C.

     Section A - 20 Marks

     Section B - 30 Marks

     Section C - 30 Marks

(ii) There are **10** questions in the question paper. **All** questions are compulsory.

(iii) There is no overall choice. However, an internal choice has been provided in one questions in Section A, four questions in Section B and three questions in Section C. Make your choices correctly.

(iv) However, separate instructions are given with each section and question, wherever necessary.

(v) Do not exceed the presecrbied word limit while answering the questions.

SECTION A: Reading

(20 Marks)

1. Read the passage given below :

Donated Organs and their Transportation

1. Once an organ donor's family gives its consent and the organs are matched to a recipient, medical professionals are faced with the onerous challenge of transporting organs while ensuring that the harvested organ reaches its destination in the shortest possible time. This is done in order to preserve the harvested organs and involves the police and especially the traffic police department.

2. The traditional method of transporting organs by road is referred to as a "green corridor". This process entails police escorting an ambulance, so as to move around traffic - usually a specific traffic lane is chosen and all signals on the route stay green to ensure it to reach its destination in the shortest possible time. A 'green corridor' is a route cleared and cordoned off by the traffic police to ensure the smooth and steady transportation of harvested organs, on most occasions, to those awaiting a life-saving transplant. Organs tend to have a very short preservation time, such as the heart which has to be harvested and transplanted within four hours or the lungs which can be preserved for only six hours once they are harvested.

3. The first green corridor in India was created by Chennai Traffic Police in September 2008 when they (accomplished) their task of enabling an ambulance to reach its destination within 11 minutes during peak hour traffic. That organ saved a nine-year-old girl whose life depended on the transplant.

4. Similarly, such green corridors have been created by traffic police of various cities such as Pune, Mumbai, Delhi NCR etc. Personnel are stationed at selected points to divert, control and clear the traffic giving way to the ambulance. Apart from this, a motorcade of police vehicles accompanies the ambulance ensuring that it does not face any problems. Delhi Traffic Police provided a green corridor from IGI Airport to Institute of Liver and Biliary Sciences in Vasant Kunj for transportation of a liver. The distance of 14 kms was covered in 11 minutes.

5. Experts point out the lack of a robust system to transport organs to super-speciality hospitals in least possible time. National Organ & Tissue Transplant Organisation (NOTTO), the country's apex organ donation agency, is now framing a proposal to airlift cadaver organs and will send a report to the Union Health Ministry. "Cadaver organs have a short life and so transplant should be done within a few golden hours." Director (NOTTO) expressed, 'Therefore, we are preparing a proposal for airlifting organs at any given moment."

6. Most states do not have enough well-trained experts to retrieve or perform transplant procedures. Also, there is an acute shortage of advanced healthcare facilities to carry out a transplant. So, it is referred to other big centres in metropolitan cities. Organs retrieved from Aurangabad, Indore, Surat, Pune are sent to Mumbai as these cities do not have super-speciality healthcare centres, informed officials.

7. "In India, about fifty thousand to one lakh patients are suffering from acute heart failure and need heart transplant at any point of time. In a private set-up, a heart transplant costs ~ 15-20 lakhs, which is followed up by postoperative medication of about ₹30,000 per month lifelong."

1.1 On the basis of your understanding of the above passage, answer any five of the following questions by choosing the most appropriate options :

(a) The first green corridor in India was created in :
   (i) New Delhi   (ii) Chennai
   (iii) Mumbai   (iv) Pune

(b) The organization which is framing a proposal to airlift cadaver organs is :
   (i) Union Health Ministry
   (ii) Regional Organ and Tissue Transplant Organisation
   (iii) National Organ and Tissue Transplant Organisation
   (iv) State Organ and Tissue Transplant Organisation

(c) The onerous task the author is talking about in para 1 is :
   (i) finding organ donors.
   (ii) finding doctors capable of performing transplants.
   (iii) to carry the harvested organ in the shortest possible time.
   (iv) to arrange the requisite facilities for the transplant.

(d) Most of the people do not go for the heart transplant as :
   (i) it is very risky.
   (ii) it is very painful.
   (iii) it may cause death of the recipient.
   (iv) the cost is prohibitive.

(e) Most states refer organ transplant cases to big hospitals because
   (i) they don't have well-trained experts.
   (ii) the patients don't trust local doctors.
   (iii) the state hospitals are very crowded.
   (iv) they don't have a pool of harvested organs.

(f) Heart retrieved from a body is alive only for ______ hours.
   (i) two   (ii) three
   (iii) four   (iv) five

1.2 Answer the following questions briefly :
(a) What is a 'green corridor'?
(b) Why is smooth transportation of the retrieved organ necessary?
(c) What opinion do you form of Chennai Police with regard to the transportation of a harvested heart ?
(d) What does the author mean by 'a few golden hours'?
(e) How much does a heart transplant cost a patient in a private hospital?

1.3 Pick out the words from the passage which mean the same as the following :
(a) save (para 1)
(b) achieved / carried out (para 3)

2. Read the following passage :

1. How does television affect our lives? It can be very helpful to people who carefully choose the shows that they watch. Television can increase our knowledge of the outside world; there are high-quality programmes that help us understand many fields of study, science, medicine, the different arts and so on. Moreover, television benefits very old people, who can't leave the house, as well as patients in hospitals. It also offers non-native speakers the advantages of daily informal language practice. They can increase their vocabulary and practise listening.

2. On the other hand, there are several serious disadvantages, of television. Of course, it provides us with a pleasant way to relax and spend our free time, but in some countries people watch television for an average of six hours or more a day. Many children stare at the TV screen for more hours a day than they spend on anything else, including studying and sleeping. Its clear that TV has a powerful influence on their lives and that its influence is often negative.

3. Recent studies show that after only thirty seconds of television viewing, a person's brain 'relaxes' the same way that it does just before the person falls asleep. Another effect of television on the human brain is that it seems to cause poor concentration. Children who view a lot of television can often concentrate on a subject for only fifteen to twenty minutes. They can pay attention only for the amount of time between commercials.

4. Another disadvantage is that television often causes people to become dissatisfied with their own lives. Real life does not seem so exciting to these people. To many people, television becomes more real than reality and their own lives seem boring. Also many people get upset or depressed when they can't solve problems in real life as quickly as television actors seem to.

5. Before a child is fourteen years old, he or she views eleven thousand murders on the TV. He or she begins to believe that there is nothing strange about fights, killings and other kinds of violence. Many studies show that people become more violent after viewing certain programmes. They may even do the things that they see in a violent show.

(a) On the basis of your reading of the above passage, make notes on it using Headings and Subheadings. Use recognizable abbreviations (minimum four) and a format you consider suitable. Supply a suitable title to it.

(b) Make a summary of the above passage in about **80** words.

(30 Marks)

3. You are Dhruv/Nidhi, Student Editor of your school magazine, 'The Buds'. Write a notice in not more than 50 words to be placed on your school notice board, inviting short stories, articles, poems etc from students of all classes for the school magazine. Give all the necessary details.

OR

You are Vinod / Vineeta, General Manager, Global Solutions, Meerut. You want to rent a bungalow to be used as a guest house. It should have all the modern amenities. Draft a suitable advertisement in not more than 50 words to be published in a local newspaper.

4. A book fair was organized in your city, Bhopal. Thousands of people including a large number of students visited the fair. It aroused a great interest in reading and buying books. You want that such book fairs are held in other cities of the state also to promote the habit of reading. Write a letter in 120-150 words to the editor of a local newspaper giving your views. You are Navtej / Navita, F-112 Malviya Nagar, Bhopal.

OR

You carried a hit and run accident victim to a local hospital. You were shocked to see that in its casualty ward the conditions were chaotic. The patient was attended to after a lot of precious time was lost. You are Deepak / Deepa, A-114 Roop Nagar, Delhi. Write a letter of complaint in 120-150 words to the Chief Medical Officer of the hospital.

5. Every year there are floods or droughts in the country. Victims suffer a lot. The government does a lot to help the people, but it is not enough. Society also must do its bit. Write a speech in 150-200 words to be delivered in the school morning assembly describing how the students can also help by collecting clothes, money and medicines from their neighbourhoods. You are Arun / Aruna.

OR

'Rain harvesting is the only solution to water crisis in the present times.' Write a debate either for or against the motion in 150-200 words. You are Sujatha / Ajith.

6. Raising prices of essential commodities make life difficult for the common man. You are Nalini / Ranbir. Write an article in 150-200 words describing the causes, possible solutions and how students can help their parents to cope with the problem.

OR

On your way to school, right in front of the school gate, you saw a verbal dispute leading to a physical fight between an auto rickshaw driver and his passenger. A teacher of your school intervened, found out the cause of the quarrel and amicably resolved the issue (problem). Write a report on the incident in 150-200 words. You are Balbir / Bimla.

(30 Marks)

7. Read the extracts given below and briefly answer the questions that follow each.

(a) But just as he laid his head on the ground, he heard a sound – a hard regular thumping. There was no doubt as to what that was. He raised himself. "Those are the hammer strokes from an iron mill", he thought.
   (i) Who is he?
   (ii) Where was 'he' at that moment?
   (iii) Why did he lay his head on the ground?
   (iv) Did he feel comfortable on hearing the thumping sound? Why?

(b) And such too is the grandeur of the dooms
   We have imagined for the mighty dead;
   All lovely tales that we have heard or read;
   An endless fountain of immortal drink,
   Pouring unto us from the heaven's brink.
   (i) Which two things of beauty are mentioned in these lines?
   (ii) Why are the lovely tales' called an endless fountain?
   (iii) Where is this fountain situated?
   (iv) Explain : 'grandeur of the dooms'.

8. Answer any five of the following questions in 30-40 words each :
(a) How was Saheb's life at the tea-stall?
(b) What are some of the positive views on interviews?
(c) Why is Jansie so critical of Sophie?
(d) How do we know that children at the elementary school are coming from a slum?
(e) Why does Mr. Lamb leave the gate of his house always open?
(f) How did Zitkala – Sa feel when her hair was shingled?
(g) When did the Tiger King' decide to get married?

9. Answer the following question in 120-150 words :
How did the swimming instructor build a swimmer out of Douglas?

OR

How did the court scene at Motihari change the course of India's struggle for freedom?

10. Answer the following question in 120-150 words :
Describe briefly the scene at the third level of Grand Central as seen (or seemed to be seen) by Charley.

OR

How did Dr. Sadao resolve the conflict in his mind between his loyalty to his country and his duty as a doctor?

Solutions

1.   **(1 × 5 = 5 Marks)**

1.1

   (a) (ii) Chennai

   (b) (iii) National Organ and Tissue Transplant Organisation

   (c) (iii) to carry the harvested organs in the shortest possible time.

   (d) (iv) the cost is prohibitive

   (e) (i) they do not have well trained experts

   (f) (iii) four

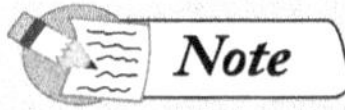

Note

1. *When answering MCQs choose the option which is the closest answer from amongst the options.*
2. *For Factual questions like e.g. "How much does a heart transplant cost……", include only the information given in the passage.*
3. *While answering the 'Why' question like "Why is smooth transportation of the retrieved organ necessary", you may begin your answer with 'Smooth transportation of the retrieved organ is necessary because ………or a similar phrase.*
4. *While answering the vocabulary questions, check the part of speech, the tense of the word etc. Your answer should have the same part of speech, tense etc.*

For e.g. save – preserve (NOT preserves or preserving or preserved)

1.2   **(1 × 5 = 5 Marks)**

   (a) The traditional method of transporting organs by road is referred to as a "green corridor".

   (b) Smooth transportation of the retrieved organ is necessary to help those who are awaiting a life-saving transplant of an organ since the organs tend to have a very short preservation time.

   (c) I have formed an excellent opinion of Chennai Police with regard to the transportation of a harvested heart since they not only performed a noble task of saving a precious life, but that they were able to do so with utmost efficiency by reaching the destination within 11 minutes during peak hours of traffic.

   (d) The author underlines the importance of time by using the term 'a few golden hours'. Since cadaver organs have a short span of life, thus the transplant should be done within a few hours only and those few hours are 'golden'.

   (e) The heart transplant in a private hospital costs about 15-20 lakh per operation excluding the postoperative treatment and medicines which cost about ₹ 30,000 per month throughout one's life.

1.3   **(1 × 2 = 2 Marks)**

   (a) save - preserve

   (b) achieved/carried out - accomplished

2. **(a) Note Making**   **(8 Marks)**

Title – Pros and Cons of Watching Television/ Effects of Television on Our Lives

1. Television and its Effects

   1.1 Advantages

     (a) Good for those - choose their shows

     (b) Increases knowledge

     (c) High quality progrms. help - study, medicine, science, art and craft

     (d) Old people, patients etc pass time

     (e) Benefits non-native speakers - daily informal lang. practice

     (f) Increases vocab.

     (g) Can help in practicing listening

   1.2 Disadvantages

     (a) children watch TV - < 6 hours

     (b) Causes poor concen.

     (c) Kids - pay attention - a subject for 15-20 min.

2. How it affects our daily life

   2.1 Comparing reel life to real life

   2.2 Rise in dissatisfaction

   2.3 depression - not able to solve issues like actors

   2.4 Violence acceptable

     (a) A child of 14 years – views 11000 murders on TV

     (b) Emulates the show

Key To Abbreviation

Abbreviation	Word
progrms.	programs
etc	etcetera
lang.	language
vocab.	vocabulary
tv	television
<	more than
concen.	concentration
mint.	minutes
	leads to

(b) **Summary:** Television affects life in many ways. If watched with discretion, it increases knowledge through programmes based on study and medicine. It helps in enhancing language skills through daily informal practice and enriches vocabulary. The patients and extremely old people have access to entertainment at home. However, the disadvantages of television is seen mostly in children. Watching TV for more than 6 hours leads to poor concentration and increases violence among all age groups. The adults too are affected adversely since they cannot differentiate between real and reel life and find their life boring.

Note

1. *The passage is on the effects of television on people of all age groups. So the title must be related to the main idea and should have the key words 'Effects', 'Advantages,' 'Television' etc.*

2. *It should always contain phrases. Avoid using complete sentences. E.g.*

   1. *Television and its Effects*

      1.1 Advantages

         (a) *Good for those - choose their shows*

         (b) *Increases knowledge*

         (c) *High quality progrms. help - study , medicine, science, art and craft*

         (d) *Old people, patients etc. pass time*

   AND NOT The effects of Television is that it is good ....

3. *Include a minimum of 4-6 distinctly different recognizable short forms i.e. abbreviations of the words in the notes as done in the solution.*

SECTION - B

3.   **(4 Marks)**

NOTICE
SPRINGDALES SCHOOL, UTTAM NAGAR
February 27, 2020
INVITING ARTICLES FOR 'THE BUDS'
All the students are hereby informed that original articles, short stories, poems etc are being invited for the thirteenth edition of our school magazine "The Buds". The interested students can submit it latest by March 15 , 2020 to the undersigned in Room No. 201.
It is reiterated that all the submitted material must be original in nature.
Dhruv/ Nidhi
(Student Editor)
The Buds

OR

NOTICE
WANTED A BUNGALOW ON RENT
Wanted a newly constructed independent bungalow to serve as a guest house for a leading IT company, minimum 7 rooms, attached bathrooms including space to create work stations, preferably ground floor, a front lawn, adequate parking space, uninterrupted power supply in City Light Road, Meerut. Rent no bar. Contact Vinod/Vinneta, G M, Global Solutions on 45645678.

4. Letter   **(6 Marks)**

F-112

Malviya Nagar

Bhopal

                                                              27 February, 20XX

The Editor

Daily Mirror

Bahadur Shah Zafar Marg

Bhopal

    Sub: Appreciation for the Book Fair organized

Sir/Madam,

Through the columns of your esteemed newspaper, I would like to express my happiness and appreciation for the recently organized week- long Bhopal Book Fair by The Readers Hub at the Ranga Rao Stadium.

It was a heart-warming sight to see thousands of people visit the fair on the first day itself. The fair which began on 17th of February had publishers from both India and abroad as participants. The books displayed were not only academic but also non-academic with subjects ranging from adventure, sports, science-fiction, self-help, cookery etc. It was a pleasant sight too to see schools taking an initiative and arrange browsing sessions for the children. The sale of books touched a record high on the first day itself. This is a testimony to the fact that books have not lost their relevance in the world of Internet.

I would like to draw the attention of all citizens towards such initiatives and I hope this initiative by the Readers Hub is taken to the other parts of the state too.

Yours sincerely

Navtej/ Navita

OR

A- 114

Roop Nagar

Delhi

27 February, 20XX

The Chief Medical Officer

The Millennium Hospital

Lodhi Road

New Delhi

Sub: Chaotic condition in the Casualty Department of the Hospital

Respected Sir/Madam

This is to bring to your notice the chaotic situation which is prevalent in the casualty department of your hospital resulting in precious time being lost in tending to cases requiring immediate medical attention.

It was only yesterday that I had the ill fortune of coming to the casualty department with the victim of a hit and run case. Given the fact that the hospital has created a name for itself in a short duration of time and its proximity to the accident site, I took the profusely bleeding man to your hospital. However far from attending to the critical patient, nobody was even willing to listen. It was only after an angry display of my frustration at the callous attitude at the reception, was I given a hearing. While the victim bled and finally lost consciousness, I was subjected to a lot of paperwork. It was three hours after our arrival that the actual treatment of the victim started. I was even told by a visitor that I should consider myself lucky that the victim was attended to in three hours!

I would like to take this opportunity to request you to take some corrective measures like setting up of a special team to look into the critical victims, mock drills of such situations and CCTV recording to be played in front of the staff so that they are able to understand the frustration of the victims. A hospital like yours deserves a good reputation and I'm sure you will be able to save many more lives if things were improved at the department.

Thanking you in anticipation

Yours truly

Deepak/Deepa

5. **Speech and Debate** (10 Marks)

Good Morning Everyone!

Respected Principal Mam, dear teachers and my dear friends. I am Arun/ Aruna of class XII A and I stand before you to make you aware of the current situation prevalent in our country and implore you to contribute your bit as a conscious member of the society in this hour of need.

India is a land where the vicissitudes of weather are known to everyone. Due to different climatic and rainfall patterns in different regions of India, it wouldn't be wrong to say that, while some parts are suffering from devastating floods, another part of India is facing a drought like condition at the same time.

Every year there is a great national loss both in terms of human and financial resources even though the Government and the NGOs come to the forefront and help people. However, isn't it time we questioned our own lack of involvement and motivated ourselves to volunteer for such a worthy cause? We the students can also do our bit by visiting the neighborhood and requesting people to contribute clothes, food and medicines for distribution. We can even start from our own homes and serve as an example. Dear Friends! I think it is high time that we the student community came together to put a smile on the faces of the victims.

Debate

Rain Harvesting is the only solution to water crisis in the present times.

A very Good Morning! Respected Chairperson, Members of the Jury, my worthy opponents and dear audience! Today I, Sujatha/ Ajith, stand before you to put forth my views for the motion on the topic "Rain Harvesting is the only solution to water crisis in the present times".

It is said that India is facing the worst water crisis in its history with at least 21 cities of India poised to run out of groundwater. To add to the woes, much of the Indian population is still dependent on groundwater. According to a report by WaterAid around 80% of India's surface water is polluted and approximately 200,000 people are dying each year due to inadequate access to safe water. It is pertinent to mention here that water conservation and water management is slowly proving to be a survival issue not only in India but the world over. The causes for the same can be attributed to unprecedented development, population explosion, accelerating water shortage, global warming and the ever-increasing demand for the natural water resources.

In such a scenario it is advisable that we look at alternatives to saving the already depleting water. Therefore, Rainwater harvesting becomes a viable option. If adequate efforts are made, approximately 620 gallons of water can be saved in every 1000 sq feet of roof space every time it rains. This water can easily be used in flushing of toilets, laundry, watering of plants etc leading to reduction of pressure on the already scarce groundwater. Awareness campaigns along with incentives for the families who switch to this could give a fillip to the idea.

To conclude , Rain water harvesting is the only solution to water crisis in the present times.

Rain Harvesting is the only solution to water crisis in the present times.

A very Good Morning! Respected Chairperson, Members of the Jury, my worthy opponents and dear audience! Today I, Sujatha/ Ajith, stand before you to put forth my views against the motion on the topic "Rain Harvesting is the only solution to water crisis in the present times".

I am indeed perturbed when I look at the topic of discussion today. By saying that rainwater harvesting is the only solution to water crisis in the present times we are looking only at one side of the coin completely ignoring the disadvantages of such an approach. In a country where the rainfall is highly unpredictable, to depend on the vicissitudes of the weather God to fulfil your needs is highly utopian.

In addition to this, the high cost of installation is detrimental to the desire of installing and using it. The systems also require regular maintenance as it is prone to rodents, algae growth, mosquitoes etc. The collection and storage systems may also prove to be restrictive in nature. E.g., in case of heavy downpour, it might not be feasible to hold and conserve all the rainwater. Therefore, in my opinion we need a two-pronged approach- avoiding the wastage of water and looking for alternatives like river water harvesting too. This in fact will take care of the yearly floods as well.

Therefore, to conclude rain harvesting is not the only solution to water crisis in the present times.

6. **Article & Report** **(10 Marks)**

Rising Prices : The causes and the solutions

By *Nalini/ Ranbir*

The rising prices of the essential commodities is a cause of concern for all. In the last five years, the prices of eight essential commodities have gone up by nearly 72% with condiments, milk products and essentials like fruit, vegetables and coffee witnessing an increase between 158.0 % to 73.6. Surprisingly the per capita income of an average Indian in a metro has gone up only by 38%.

The causes of the rising prices can be many but the major cause is the sharp divide between the demand and supply of a particular item either due to unfavourable weather conditions or politically maneuvered. Apart from increasing population which itself is a major cause of

rising demand, changing food habits are also a catalyst. E.g., the growing demand for pizzas has made cheese and butter coveted items.

In addition to the Government role in curbing the prices through subsidies and support price, the children can also play a major role to help their parents cope with this problem. The monthly budgets can be made with the help of the children so that they can fulfil their desire in moderation. Home initiatives like kitchen garden and cook at home options can also be helpful.

To conclude, the family needs to work as a unit so that the solutions can be reached.

Report

A Fracas on the Road: How Impatient are we as a Generation

By *Balbir/ Bimla*

New Delhi, February 27: Yet another case of an auto rickshaw driver entering a dispute with his passenger has come to light. However, this time the general public did not turn a blind eye to the incident and helped to resolve the issue.

It all happened in the early hours of the morning in front of Arya Vidya Mandir. The passenger, a parent, left the driver standing in front of the school and went inside to deposit his son's lunch box. Even though the Parent had promised to return soon, the driver was left standing for an hour with the meter running.

When the Parent returned, the driver demanded for the full payment and wanted to be relieved. However, the Parent was not willing to relent. What initially started as a verbal altercation between the driver and the passenger slowly turned ugly with physical blows being exchanged between the two. However, before the situation turned out of hand, Mr. Abhinav Mathur, PGT English of Arya Vidya Mandir intervened and amicably resolved the matter. It was due to his intervention that the matter was not reported to the police and the poor driver got his due.

One really wishes that there were more Good Samaritans like him.

7. (a) **(4 Marks)**

   (i) 'He' is the rat trap seller.

   (ii) He was in the woods at that moment, having lost his way while trying to escape with the thirty kronors.

(iii) He laid his head on the ground since he was completely exhausted having circled the woods multiple times trying to find his way out. Laying the head on the ground was a sign of exhaustion and giving up completely.

(iv) Yes. He felt comfortable on hearing the thumping sound. He could make out that there was an iron mill somewhere nearby and that meant since he could get some rest and finally a way out of the forest.

(b)   **(4 Marks)**

(i) The two things of beauty which are mentioned in the extract are the 'grandeur of the dooms' and the lovely tales of the mighty princes who are dead now.

(ii) The 'lovely tales' are called an endless fountain since the lovely tales keep motivating and inspiring us endlessly. The way a fountain is a perennial source of sustenance, similarly these tales are a source of sustained motivation for all the human beings.

(iii) This fountain is situated at the brink of heaven.

(iv) The poet wants to underline the fact that even though kingdoms and their rulers have perished with time , there is a grandeur associated with it and human beings can draw inspiration from it . The grandeur of these tales continue guiding us and enhancing the quality of life that one leads.

Note

1.   Be precise and to the point.

2.   Since there is no internal choice in this question, try answering all the questions.

3.   Use the language as used in the question. E.g., "Where was 'he' at the moment" ? Your answer should start with - He was in the woods at that moment, having lost his way……

4.   For question where explanation of the phrase from a poem is required , try to bring it within the context of the poem while explaining the phrase. E.g., Explain: 'grandeur of the dooms', you should not try explaining it independently.

8.   **(2 × 5 = 10 Marks)**

(a) Saheb's life at the tea stall was not what he wanted to make of it. He was no longer his own master. The steel canister seemed to be heavier than the plastic bag that he would carry so lightly on his back. This was because he had lost his independence since now he was working for his master.

(b) Some of the positive views on interviews are that it is a source of truth in its highest form. It helps us to know that part of the person which till date would be unknown. It is also an art in practice. The most vivid impressions of the contemporaries are through the interviews as per Denis Brian.

(c) Jansie is critical of Sophie because she realizes that Sophie's ambitions for herself are impractical and pure fantasies because she neither has the skills nor the means to achieve those dreams. Since she is a friend of Sophie, Jansie wants Sophie to have dreams that are practical and achievable.

(d) There are various pointers in the poem to suggest the fact that the children at the elementary school are coming from a slum. Firstly, the children' faces which is like rootless weed, lacking the healthy colour. The 'stunted' malnourished boy, the tall girl with her head weighed down – all point towards a life which is full of worries, disease and poverty.

(e) Mr Lamb leaves the gate of his house always open to welcome anyone who wants to visit him. He never closes the gate of his garden which also has an apple orchard.

(f) Zitkala-Sa felt miserable and humiliated when her hair was shingled. She cried for her mother and then lost all spirit. She felt as if she was one of the many little animals, driven by a herder.

(g) Since the time the 'Tiger King' had occupied the throne, he was busy killing tigers. Within a period of ten years, he had killed seventy tigers, but the result was that the tiger population in his kingdom became extinct. It was then that he decided to get married to the girl in the royal family of a state with the largest population.

Note

1.   Choose your questions with care since there is internal choice in this question.

2.   Each 2-mark question must have at least two value points.

3.   So, for example – for the question "Why is Jansie so critical of Sophie", include any two value points from those given below.

   (a)   Knows Sophie's ambitions for herself - impractical and pure fantasy

   (b)   Sophie neither has the skills nor the means

   (c)   Impossible to achieve the dreams

   (d)   Since she is a friend – she wants Sophie's welfare

   (e)   Sophie should have dreams - that are practical and achievable

9.   **(6 Marks)**

Douglas had an aversion for water since his childhood due to his experiences on the beach at California followed by an equally harrowing experience at the YMCA pool. The result was a deep fear of water which stopped him from enjoying any water related activity. So finally, he employed an instructor who made him practice 5 days a week - an hour each day. He used a pulley with one end of the rope in his hand and the other tied to Douglas' waist to help him swim back and forth in the water with the entire control resting with the instructor. After three months, Douglas was taught how to breathe while swimming and this made him loose his fear of water slowly. Finally, he was taught how to kick the water with his legs at the side of the pool. Thus, piece by piece the instructor built a swimmer out of Douglas.

OR

The court scene at Motihari changed the course of India's struggle for freedom by reigniting self-belief in the Indians. Not only did it bring the peasants and the lawyers together but also exemplified the powerlessness of the British in the wake of combined demonstration by the masses. The morning when the hearing was to take place, the whole town of Motihari was black with peasants. The spontaneous demonstration of the peasants, in thousands, around the courthouse was the beginning of their liberation from the fear of the British. Since the officials felt powerless in regulating the crowd without Gandhi's support, Gandhiji helped them out, giving concrete proof that their power, till date, dreaded and unquestioned, could now be challenged by the Indians. The Government, baffled, requested for postponement of the trial to which Gandhiji read out a statement pleading guilty and asked for the due penalty. The magistrate deferring the judgement to after the two-hour recess, asked Gandhiji to furnish bail. Upon denial by Gandhiji, finally the judge said he would not deliver the judgement for several days and allowed Gandhiji to remain at liberty.

The entire episode reflected the powerlessness of the Britishers and consolidated Gandhiji's role as the leader of the masses. This proved to be a milestone in India's struggle for Independence.

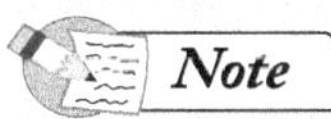 *Note*

1. *Each 6-mark question must have at least four value points*

2. *Answer to the point including your own opinion in places where it is deemed necessary by the question.*

3. *Pick out specific examples from the text to support your answer*

4. *Quote straight from the text wherever required but do so only when you are sure of the words.*

   E.g., the question "How did the swimming instructor build a swimmer out of Douglas" start from the childhood experiences and build your answer.

10.   **(6 Marks)**

Charley arrives or seems to arrive at the third level accidently. He notices that the room was smaller, there were fewer ticket windows and train gates, and the information booth in the centre was of wood and old looking. The man in the booth wore sleeve protectors and a green eye shade. There were open flame gas-lights, brass spittoons and newspapers like "The World" which hadn't been published since a long time. Even the people around wore old fashioned clothes with beards, sideburns and moustaches. When he went to the ticket counter to buy two tickets to Galesburg, Illinois, the clerk calculated the fare but became angry when Charley offered him the money. He shouted that Charley was trying to 'skin' him by offering something which wasn't money. Only after Charley glances into the cash drawer that he realizes the veracity of the clerk's comment. The whole drawer was full of old-style bills!

OR

Dr Sadao faced the conflict between his loyalty to his country and his duty as a doctor. In other words, it was a dilemma of whether to use his surgical skills to save the life of the wounded person or hand over an escaped American prisoner of war to the Japanese General. However, he was able to resolve his conflict by striking a wonderful balance between the two duties without compromising on either. A strong believer of professional loyalty and human kindness he was aware of his primary duty as a doctor which implied making the ailing, injured and sick people fully whole irrespective of his own notions about Americans. Therefore, notwithstanding the risk inherent in treating an enemy, and ignoring the fact that he did not like Americans, the surgeon in him instinctively inspires him to take the person home, operate upon him and provide post-operative treatment. He rises above narrow national prejudices and extends help and services to an enemy. In course of time his faithful servants and even his wife either desert him or fail to see his viewpoint. Despite all these encumbrances on his way, he single-mindedly focusses on his primary duty.

However, Dr Sadao does not fail as a patriot too while he is fulfilling his responsibility as a doctor. He saved the life of the General by operating on him, informed him about the injured man whom he has treated since he is an escaped prisoner of war. He also accepts the General's decision to send the assassins without any reluctance. He even keeps the door open for the assassins to enter thereby keeping his integrity as a Japanese citizen, intact.

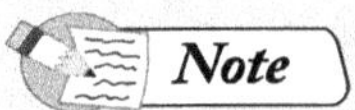

Note

1. *Each 6-mark question must have at least four value points*

2. *Answer to the point including your own opinion in places where it is deemed necessary by the question.*

3. *Pick out specific examples from the text to support your answer*

4. *Quote straight from the text wherever required but do so only when you are sure of the words.*

    E.g., the question "How did Dr. Sadao resolve the conflict in his mind………….","" divide your answer into: 1. The conflict and 2.The solution to the conflict. Use the value points from those given below :

THE CONFLICT

   (a) Between loyalty to his country and his duty as a doctor

   (b) Dilemma whether to use his surgical skills to save the life of the wounded person

   (c) Or hand over an escaped American prisoner to the General

   (d) Strikes a wonderful balance between the two duties without compromising on either

RESOLUTION TO THE CONFLICT : AS A DOCTOR

   (a) Primary duty as a doctor-making the ailing, injured and sick people fully whole

   (b) Did not care his own notions about Americans

   (c) Did not like Americans-still did his duty

   (d) Takes the person home, operates, provides post-operative treatment

   (e) Able to rise above narrow national prejudices, extends help and services to an enemy

CBSE Board Solved Paper

Time Allowed : 3 Hours   *Maximum Marks : 100*

General Instructions:

(i) This paper is divided into three sections : A, B and C. All the sections are compulsory.

(ii) Separate instructions are given with each section and question, wherever necessary. Read these instructions very carefully and follow them faithfully.

(iii) Do not exceed the prescribed word limit while answering the questions.

SECTION A: Reading

(30 Marks)

1. Read the passage given below carefully and answer the questions that follow :

    1. "But have you been to Nimtita? Have you been to the palace there?" asked the old man in the tea-shop, with the thatched roof. We were in the village of Lalgola, one hundred and fifty miles from Kolkata, and we had just seen our thirteenth nobleman's palace and found it unsuitable.

    2. "Nimtita? Where is that?" we asked without much interest. We had never heard of the place. "It is sixty miles to the North of here. You drive up the highway. Then you come to a river which you have to cross. A ferry will take your car across. Then up the highway again for twenty miles. A sign tells you where to branch off... It's on the river Padma, on the eastern bank. It's the palace of the Choudharys. I've been listening to your talk, and I feel you ought to see this one before you give up."

    3. We were not very hopeful. We had had enough trouble taking free advice from people who had no idea of our needs. Anyway, the question was : do we or do we not undertake this last trip? If we did not like the palace, it might mean either giving up making this film altogether, or seriously changing its nature. We tossed a coin to decide whether to go or not. The coin said, 'Go!', and we set out on our sixty-mile journey.

    4. It was when I was in bed with my right leg in plaster that I had decided the film on Tarasankar Banerji's famous short story, 'The Music Room' (Jalsaghar). A nasty fall on the stone steps at Banaras had brought about a serious knee injury. I lay in bed and read all the Bengali books I could lay my hands on. Just then, the film distributors were not too keen to take my film for distribution, and may be this was one of the things that made me choose 'The Music Room'.

    5. Here was a dramatic story which could naturally bring in music and dancing, and distributors loved music and dancing. But here, too, was a story full of feelings. So it would be satisfying for me as an artist. I would cast Chabi Biswas, our greatest actor, in the leading role of the zamindar — the zamindar whose love of the big musical entertainments brings about his ruin. But the most important thing was to find a palace. As we had a low budget, there was no question of having studio-built sets. I knew that, if we had the money, my art director could easily build a set which looked like our old palace with the right style. But we just didn't have the money for it.

    6. Nimtita turned out to be everything that the old man had claimed — and more. No one could have described in words the feeling of utter sadness that surrounded the palace. The river Padma had changed its course over the years, so that now there were endless stretches of sand where once had been villages. The palace itself — Greek pillars and all — was a perfect realization of my dream image. It stood looking out over the stretches of sand with a sad dignity. It had somehow escaped being totally destroyed when the river changed its course. The river had reached within ten yards of the front of the palace — having swallowed the garden — and then stopped. Ganendra Narayan Choudhary, who is seventy and owns a British title and the palace, told us how it happened : "We were having breakfast one morning when we heard a low rumble. We went out to the verandah and saw a big chunk of our estate — almost a square mile of it — going under water, disappearing forever. It all happened in a few seconds. Padma's appetite is legendary."

7. "But aren't you afraid that the river might encroach further?"

8. "Oh, yes, the rains bring with them the usual fears."

9. On returning from our first trip to Nimtita, I telephoned the author, Mr. Banerji. He had been just as anxious about the location as we were.

10. "We've found our palace at last, Mr. Banerji," I said.

11. "Have you? And where is it?"

12. "At a little known place called Nimtita."

13. "Nimtita? There was a note of recognition in his voice." You don't mean the palace of the Choudharys, do you?"

14. "That's the one."

15. "But that's extraordinary ! I have't been to Nimtita myself, but I have read about the Choudharys in a history of Bengal zamindars, and it was the music-loving Upendra Narayan Choudhary who served as the model for my rajah."

1.1. On the basis of your understanding of the above passage, answer each of the questions given below by choosing the most appropriate option.

(a) The writer of the passage is a ________ by profession.
   (i) painter   (ii) filmmaker
   (iii) photographer   (iv) journalist

(b) What helped the author and his friends to decide whether or not to go to Nimtita?
   (i) the suggestion made by the old man at the tea-shop
   (ii) their own intuitive feeling
   (iii) description of the palace in a travel book
   (iv) tossing of a coin

(c) Why was the idea of building a set for shooting given up?
   (i) Shooting at a set would not give a real life effect.
   (ii) They didn't have money for a set.
   (iii) Building a set is very time consuming.
   (iv) Shooting at the actual palace would be more authentic.

(d) Who is the central character in the story, 'The Music Room'?
   (i) A local raja   (ii) A zamindar
   (iii) A British official   (iv) An artist

(e) What did the author like most about the palace?
   (i) facilities for the visitors
   (ii) wood carvings at the ceiling
   (iii) its huge central hall
   (iv) its Greeks pillars

1.2. Answer the following questions briefly :

(a) What suggestion did the old man at the tea-shop make to the author and his friends?

(b) Why did the author not like the idea of taking free advice?

(c) How did the author sustain a serious injury?

(d) What brought about the ruin of the zamindar in the story, 'The Music Room'?

(e) Who was Ganendra Narayan Choudhary?

(f) How did Mr. Banerji react to the information about the palace?

1.3. Answer any three of the following questions in 25 – 30 words each :

(a) Why did the author choose the story, 'The Music Room' for his film?

(b) How do you know that reaching Nimtita was not easy?

(c) What havoc did the river Padma cause when it changed its course?

(d) How had the palace escaped being totally destroyed?

1.4. Find words/phrases from the passage which are similar in meaning to each of the following :

(a) main (para 5)   (b) nobility (para 6)

(c) concerned (para 9)

2. Read the passage given below carefully and answer the questions that follow :

1. Physical education which is commonly part of the curriculum at school level includes training in the development and care of the human body and maintaining physical fitness. Physical education is also about sharpening overall cognitive abilities and motor skills via athletics, exercise and various other physical activities like martial arts and dance.

2. Physical education promotes the importance of inclusion of a regular fitness activity in the routine. This helps the students to maintain their fitness, develop their muscular strength, increase their stamina and thus stretch their physical abilities to an optimum level. Physical fitness helps them to inculcate the importance of maintaining a healthy body, which in turn keeps them happy and energized.

3. Participating in sports, be it team sports or dual and individual sports, leads to a major boost in self-confidence. The ability to go on the field and perform instills a sense of self-confidence, which is very important for the development of a person's character. Every victory achieved on the field, helps to boost a person's self-confidence. Moreover, the ability to accept defeat on the field and yet believe in your capabilities brings a sense of positive attitude as well.

4. Physical education classes are about participating in the physical fitness and recreation activities, but they are also about learning the overall aspects of physical health. For example, in today's world the problems of obesity, or anaemia and bulimia are common amongst teenagers. Physical education provides an excellent opportunity for teachers to promote the benefits of healthy and nutritious food and warn against the ill effects of junk food.

Promoting sound eating practices and guidelines for nutrition are some of the very valuable lessons that can be taught through physical education classes at school level.

5. Participation in team sports and even dual sports helps to imbibe a sense of team spirit amongst the students. While participating in team sports, the children have to function as an entire team, and hence they learn how to organize themselves and function together. This process of team building hones a person's overall communication skills and the ability to get along with different people.

6. Participation in sports and physical education activities helps to sharpen the reflexes of the students. It also brings order and discipline to the body movements and helps in development of a sound body posture. The hand-eye coordination improves as well.

7. Physical education classes also include lessons about the importance of personal hygiene and importance of cleanliness. Thus, these classes help the students to know the important hygiene practices that must be practised in order to maintain health and wellness throughout life.

8. Physical education classes help to enhance the overall cognitive abilities of the students, since they get a knowledge of the different kinds of sports and physical activities that they participate in. For example, a person who is participating in a specific type of martial arts class, will also gain knowledge of the origins of the martial arts, and the other practices and historical significance associated with it.

2.1. On the basis of your understanding of the above passage, make notes on it using headings and subheadings. Use recognizable abbreviations (wherever necessary – minimum four) and a format you consider suitable. Also supply an appropriate title to it.

2.2. Write a summary of the above passage in about 100 words.

SECTION B: Advanced Writing Skills

(30 Marks)

3. Mr. Virendra Sehwag, who was to deliver a talk to help the cricket players to do well in the game is not able to come on the given day. Write a notice in about 50 words informing the students about the new date on which he is coming. You are Gopal/Garima, Secretary Sports Club, Uday School, Green Park, Kanpur.

OR

Your old friend, Suresh Upreti has invited you to join him on his 10th marriage anniversary. Unfortunately, you are not able to attend the function. Write a message in about 50 words expressing your inability to be present on the occasion. You are Gitika/Ganesh, 10, Pandit Nagar, Nashik.

4. You are Rodrigues/Maria, Principal of Sea View Senior Secondary School, Vasco da Gama. Your school needs to formulate and submit an evacuation plan by the end of the month. You are clueless about how this is to be done. You write a letter in 120–150 words to the State Disaster Management Authority, Goa asking them for advice and help on how to formulate a disaster evacuation drill for 1500 students.

OR

The Gandhi Foundation is recruiting graduates for an intensive leadership-training programme during the summer, in villages across India. You are Anjana/Benji from 21, Ratnapur Village, Bilaspur. You are very excited to see the advertisement and decide to apply for the same. Draft a letter in 120–150 words applying for the advertised programme. Include a biodata showing how suitable you are for the training.

5. Air pollution in our cities is increasing alarmingly. According to environmentalists, vehicles are one of the major contributors to air pollution. They recommend use of public transport by private vehicle owners. People in general are willing to switch over from private to public transport if there is a good system in place. Write an article in 150 – 200 words on the topic, 'Importance of an efficient public transport system'. You are Raghu/Ragini.

OR

It is true that water will become a scarce commodity in the near future. We are notorious for wasting water. We waste water during weddings. We waste water at our homes and also at our schools. Write a speech in 150–200 words on the topic, 'Water is precious; use it wisely' to be delivered in the school morning assembly. You are Govind/Govindi.

6. The eminent psychologist, Dr. Madhumita was invited by your school authorities to speak to the students on the topic, 'How to maintain robust mental health'. She delivered a lively speech without using any medical technical terms. After the lecture the students asked many questions especially about how to cope with stress during examinations. Dr. Madhumita addressed their concerns very patiently and gave them some very useful tips. Write a report in 150 – 200 words for your school magazine describing the session with the psychologist. You are Noor/Hilal Head-girl/Head-boy, National School, Sonepat.

OR

The Nilgiris Senior Secondary School is holding an interschool debate on the topic, 'School bullies are a menace; they should be expelled'. You will be participating from your school in the debate. Write your debate in 150– 200 words choosing a stand for or against the motion.

SECTION C: Textbooks and Long Reading Text

(40 Marks)

7. Read the extract given below and answer the questions that follow :

On their slag heap, these children Wear skins peeped through by bones and spectacles of steel With mended glass, like bottle bits on stones. All of their time and space are foggy slum. So blot their maps with slums as big as doom.

(a) Name the poem and the poet.

(b) Which image is used to describe the poverty of these children?

(c) What sort of life do these children lead?

(d) Identify and name the figure of speech used in line 3.

OR

but soon

put that thought away, and

looked out at young,

trees sprinting, the merry children spilling

out of their homes.

(a) Name the poem and the poet.

(b) What thought did the poet put away?

(c) Why are the young trees described as sprinting?

(d) How do you know that the joyful scene did not help her drive away 'that thought' from her mind?

8. Answer any four of the following questions in 30–40 words each :

(a) How do symbols in the poem, 'Aunt Jennifer's Tigers' help us understand her plight?

(b) What is your impression of Sophie's brother Geoff?

(c) What frantic efforts did Zitkala-Sa make to save her hair from being cut?

(d) How did the Tiger King's marriage bring him closer to his target?

(e) Why were the old men of the village sitting in the classroom on the last day of the lesson?

(f) What precautions did the authorities take for the smooth conduct of the O-level examination?

9. Answer any one of the following questions in 120–150 words :

(a) Childhood fears are deeply entrenched in our mind. Determination, hard work and right training are needed to get rid of them. Comment on the statement in the light of Douglas' efforts to overcome his fear of water.

(b) When and why did the author say that civil disobedience had triumphed for the first time in modern India?

(c) How does the story, 'The Rattrap' show the redemptive power of love and compassion?

10. Answer any one of the following questions in 120–150 words :

(a) "Things that matter. Things nobody else has ever said. Things I want to think about." What are the 'things' that Derry is referring to? How did Derry's chance meeting with Mr. Lamb prove meaningful for him?

(b) 'The Enemy' portrays the victory of humanity in a moment of crisis. Illustrate this fact through the actions taken by Dr. Sadao for the enemy soldier.

(c) How does the story, 'Should Wizard Hit Mommy' bear testimony to the fact that the frustrations faced by adults and their personal experiences often intrude upon their interaction with their children? Elaborate.

11. Answer any one of the following questions in 120–150 words :

(a) Why did Teddy Henfrey feel insulted after his encounter with the strange man at the 'Coach and Horses'? What did he do to relieve himself from his nasty mood on his way back from the inn?

(b) Griffin calls Dr. Kemp a traitor as he cheated Griffin and let out all his secrets. Do you agree with this depiction of Kemp? Give reasons.

(c) How do the misfortunes of Silas at Raveloe transform him in the eyes of the community?

(d) Describe Nancy's personality and approach to life in 'Silas Marner'.

12. Answer any one of the following questions in 120–150 words :

(a) 'A most remarkable story,' commented Mr. Bunting. Which story was he referring to? Why was it so remarkable?

(b) Griffin allows the destructive desires to dominate his life. Substantiate the statement with reference to 'The Invisible Man'.

(c) What is the most important internal conflict presented at the beginning of the story, 'Silas Marner'?

(d) Narrate the unfortunate incident of the theft of Silas' gold.

Solutions

1.   1.1.   **(1 × 5 = 5 Marks)**

(a) (ii) filmmaker

Refer to paragraph 3, line 4: '…it might mean either giving up making this film altogether…'

(b) (iv) tossing of a coin

Refer to last sentence of paragraph 3.

(c) (ii) They didn't have money for a set.

Refer to paragraph 5, particularly the last sentence.

(d) (ii) A zamindar

Refer to lines 4-5, paragraph5: '…in the leading role of the zamindar…'

(e) (iv) its Greek pillars

Refer to lines 5-6, paragraph 6: 'The palace itself— Greek pillars and all—was a perfect realization of my dream image.'

1.2.   **(1 × 6 = 6 Marks)**

(a) The old man at the tea-shop suggested that the author and his friends go to the palace of the Chaudharys at Nimtita before giving up their search for a suitable location to shoot.

(b) The author did not like the idea of taking free advice because he and his unit had already faced a lot of trouble by listening to free advice from people who had no idea of their specific needs.

(c) A nasty fall on the stone steps at Banaras had caused the author a serious knee injury.

(d) In the story, ' The Music Room', the zamindar's love of the big musical entertainments had brought about his ruin.

(e) Ganendra Narayan Chaudhary was the seventy year old British title holder who owned the Chaudharys palace at Nimtita.

(f) Mr. Banerji exclaimed that it was extraordinary for the author to have decided to shoot 'The Music Room' at the Chaudharys palace at Nimtita because it was the music loving zamindar Upendra Narayan Chaudhary of the same palace on whom he had modelled the zamindar/ rajah of the story.

1.3.   **(3 × 2 = 6 Marks)**

(a) The distributors were not too keen to take the author's films for distribution at that time. 'The Music Room' was a dramatic story which would naturally bring in music and dance which was loved by the film distributors. Therefore, the author chose it for his film.

(b) The journey to Nimtita was not straight or easy. It constituted driving up the highway; then crossing a river with a ferry carrying the car across; and then again driving twenty miles up the highway before branching off to the eastern bank of river Padma where the palace was situated.

(c) When river Padma changed its course, it submerged many villages and destroyed much of the Chaudharys palace, reaching as far as within ten yards of its front, having swallowed the garden.

(d) The palace escaped being totally destroyed as the river Padma stopped ten yards away from the front of the Chaudharys palace after swallowing its garden.

1.4.   **(1 × 3 = 3 Marks)**

(a) leading   (b) nobility   (c) anxious

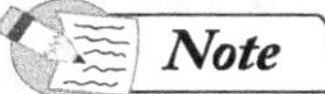 **Note**

1. *When answering MCQs (Question No.1.1)choose the option which is the closest answer from amongst the options.*

2. *For Factual questions like e.g. "What suggestion did the old man at the tea-shop make to the author and his friends", include only the information given in the passage.*

3. *While answering the 'Why ' question like "Why did the author not like the idea of taking free advice?", you may begin your answer with 'the author not like the idea of taking free advice because' ………or a similar phrase.*

2.   2.1.   **(5 Marks)**

(a) Notes

Title: Utility of Physical Education

1. ensures overall devpt.
   - 1.1 helps maintain fitness
   - 1.2 promotes cogn ability
   - 1.3 dev. motor skills
   - 1.4 promotes hygiene
   - 1.5 includes var. acts
     - 1.5.1. ath.
     - 1.5.2. exercise
     - 1.5.3. martial arts
     - 1.5.4. dance
2. promotes fitness regimen
   - 2.1. develops musc. strength
   - 2.2. inc. stamina
   - 2.3. keeps happy & enrgd
3. raises self-confidence
   - 3.1. dev. character
   - 3.2. instils positive att.
4. promotes health awareness
   - 4.1. promotes healthy food
   - 4.2. warns against junk food
   - 4.3. promotes sound eating practices
5. promotes sportsmanship
   - 5.1. builds team spirit
   - 5.2. teaches team work

5.3. dev. social & comm.. skills

6. dev. mind & body

    6.1. sharpens reflexes

    6.2. disc. body movts.

    6.3. dev. good posture

    6.4. improves hand-eye coord.

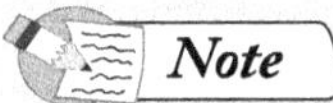 *Note*

1. *The passage is on Physical education and its importance in the life of a student including the ways in which a student can benefit from it. So the title must be related to the main idea and should have the key words viz.' Importance', 'Physical Education,' 'utility' etc*

2. *It should always contain phrases. Avoid using complete sentences. For e.g.*

    1. ensures overall devpt.

      1.1 helps maintain fitness

      1.2 promotes cogn ability

      1.3 dev. motor skills

      1.4 promotes hygiene

      1.5 includes var. acts

        1.5.1. ath.

        1.5.2. exercise

    AND NOT The utility of Physical Education in a student's life is that it ensures overall etc........

3. *Include a minimum of 4-6 distinctly different recognizable short forms i.e. abbreviations of the words in the notes as done in the solution.*

Key to abbreviations			
1.	devpt.–development	8.	enrg^d–energised
2.	cog^n–cognitive	9.	dev.–develops
3.	var.–various	10.	att.–attitude
4.	act^s–activities	11.	comm.–communication
5.	ath.–athletics	12.	disc.–disciplines
6.	musc.–muscular	13.	movts.–movements
7.	inc.–increase	14.	coord.–coordination

2.2 Summary   (5 Marks)

Physical education ensures overall development of an individual. It helps maintain physical fitness; and develops cognitive abilities and motor skills through various activities like exercise, athletics, martial arts and dance. It increases stamina and muscular strength and keeps one happy and energised. Physical education promotes hygiene and fitness regimen. It raises self-confidence and instils a positive attitude. It promotes health awareness and healthy eating. It promotes sportsmanship and team work which in turn develop the individual's social and communication skills. Physical activities sharpen reflexes, discipline body movements, improve hand-eye coordination and develop a good posture.

3.   **(4 Marks)**

NOTICE
UDAY SCHOOL, GREEN PARK, KANPUR

March 2, 2019

VIRENDRA SEHWAG TALK POSTPONED

Students are informed that the talk by renowned cricketer Virendra Sehwag which was scheduled to be delivered on March 5, 2019 has been postponed to **March 10, 2019**.

              Venue: Main auditorium

              Time: 10 am

Gopal/Garima

Secretary, Sports Club

OR

Reply to decline invitation

Gitika/Ganesh expresses his/her thanks to Suresh for the kind invitation to attend his 10th wedding anniversary celebration, but regrets to inform that he/she will be unable to attend the function due to some prior commitment. He/she sends heartfelt wishes to the blessed couple for many more years of blissful marriage.

10, Pandit Nagar, Nashik

4.   **(6 Marks)**

Sea View Senior Secondary School,

Vasco da Gama, Goa

March 2, 2019

The State Disaster Management Authority,

Goa

Sub: Seeking advice on how to formulate a disaster evacuation drill

Sir,

The school has been directed to formulate and submit an evacuation plan to be carried out in the school in the event of a disaster, by the end of this month.

Unfortunately, we have no clue about how this is to be done. We would require professional advice from experts in this domain to train us.

Therefore, we solicit your advice and help in this regard.

Kindly oblige.

Thanking you

Yours faithfully

Rodrigues/Maria

Principal

OR

21, Ratnapur Village

Bilaspur

March 2, 2019

The Gandhi Foundation,

New Delhi

Sub: Application for Leadership-Training Programme

Sir/Ma'am,

With reference to the advertisement in leading national dailies dated 30th March, 2019, I would like to apply for the leadership-training program which is going to be organised during summers. I fulfil the qualifications required for the programme. I am enclosing my CV and attested copies of my testimonials.

Anticipating a positive response from your organisation.

Yours faithfully

Anjana

Enclosures: 1. CV

              2. Educational Certificates

CV

Name:	Anjana Sharma
Father's Name:	Mr. Rajiv Sharma
Address:	21, Ratnapur Village, Bilaspur
Contact:	0322-6411321, 98713XXXXX
Email:	Anjana71@gmail.com
Date of Birth:	21st July, 1998
Religion:	Hinduism
Marital Status:	Unmarried

Educational Qualification:

Exam	College/Board/University	Year	Percentage
Class X	CBSE	2013	95%
Class XII	CBSE	2015	92%
B.Com (Honours)	Maharishi University of Management, Bilaspur	2018	87%

Extracurricular Activities:

         Sports Captain in School President of Debate Society in College

Strengths: Excellent Communication Skills

              Team Player

              Time Management

5.   **(10 Marks)**

Importance of an Efficient Public Transport

By *Raghu/Ragini*

It is seen that with increase in population, the number of vehicles has also increased; resulting in rise in air pollution. The effects of vehicular pollution on health are dangerous, and hence, to reduce its harmful effects on society, environmentalists recommend the use of public transport.

The use of public transport not only helps in keeping traffic congestion lower, but also reduces air pollution from idling vehicles caught in traffic snarls. Taking public transportation is a good option during high traffic days. It keeps commuters more active and develops community feeling among them. Public transport saves stress of driving and cuts travelling cost. It reduces pollution as buses run on cleaner fuel, such as CNG; and the Metro, on electricity. The Metro even saves time, compared to road travel. However, people will not switch to public transport unless there is a good system available. Governments often fail to ensure the required frequency and snag free service, which ultimately makes people switch back to private vehicles. Therefore, the need of the hour is to have an efficient public transport system with focus on reducing personal vehicular use. Optimization through carpooling and vehicle sharing will also help.

OR

A very good morning to the excellencies, respected teachers and my dear colleagues.

I, Govind/Govindi of Class XI-A, stand before you to speak on the topic, 'Water is precious; use it wisely'. We all know that water is vital for the continuation of life on earth. We need it essentially for drinking as human body is around 65% water by weight. It is required for many a human activity such as cooking, washing, cultivating crops. Water falling from an elevation generates hydroelectric power. However due to surging population growth, climate change, and reckless, wasteful use, a global water crisis is impending in the near future. People tend to use water carelessly while bathing, gardening, washing fruits, vegetables or clothes. A lot of water is wasted during family functions, particularly weddings! Global reports have given a grim assessment of the planet's freshwater supply. Lack of access to water spells poverty and deprivation and breeds the potential for unrest and conflict. Hence, as responsible global citizens, we need to use water judiciously; and, conserve and save every bit of it. We must adopt concrete measures for preventing wastage of water and preserving it for our future generations.

6.   **Report**   **(10 Marks)**

An Interactive Session By Dr. Madhumita

By *Noor/Hilal, Head Girl/Head Boy*

As a part of its literacy program, National School, Sonepat organized an event to promote mental health awareness among its students on 2nd of March, 2019, in the Central Auditorium of the school. The Chief Guest was an eminent psychologist, Dr. Madhumita Iyer, who also runs an N.G.O for the mentally challenged.

The event began with the Principal, Mrs. Sangeeta Rajput's speech on 'Mental Health and its side effects on Youth', followed by an inspiring short film. The highlight of the event was the motivating speech by Dr. Madhumita Iyer on 'How to Maintain Robust Mental Health'. She delivered a lively speech discussing the whole range of issues students generally struggle with, without using complex medical terms. It was followed by an interactive session in which students asked her many questions, especially about how to cope with stress during exams. Dr. Madhumita addressed their concerns very patiently and gave them some very useful tips. Students appeared visibly happy with their numerous queries being answered to their satisfaction.

The event ended with high tea and snacks followed by a vote of thanks by our Director, Mr. Rampal.

OR

Debate

For The Motion

Honourable Chairperson, respected judges and my worthy opponents!

I stand here to present my arguments in favour of the motion, 'School bullies are a menace; they should be expelled'.

Of the various societal issues prevailing, school bullying constitutes one that hasn't been paid much attention to in all these years. Some children, individually or in a group, bully others who are weak, meek or different, in a show of strength, smartness or superiority. The trend is only worsening with time. It is definitely a hidden threat that not only mars the victim child's confidence but also causes deferred disturbances appearing in future life. Victims of bullying are likely to suffer a variety of psychological disorders, including depression, anxiety or attempt to suicide. Bullying has become a menace and must be addressed immediately. It is necessary to expel such children, as they are a threat to both the victim and the school. Thus, it is important for caregivers, guardians, parents, authorities, counsellors and psychologists to notice signs of bullying and act promptly. It's high time we took a strict action and stopped this crime permanently.

Thank You!

Against The Motion

Honourable Chairperson, respected judges and my worthy opponents!

I stand here to argue against the motion, 'School bullies are a menace; they should be expelled'.

There's no denying the fact that school bullying continues to be a widespread and pernicious problem. However, the area of concern is how the problem is addressed. It is often considered a 'hate crime' with a zero tolerance policy with bullies being subjected to suspension, expulsion, detention, enforced isolation, and so on. Punishing bullies may seem like the obvious, natural response to the problem, but it does not truly address it. Researchers are of the view that punishing kids who bully not only fails to address the source of the problem, but actually makes things worse. It only encourages the bully to retain the image and be more aggressive and hurtful. Moreover, such studies also suggest that students who bully may have behavioural or emotional problems

themselves that require intervention in order to address the root cause of bullying.

Therefore, if schools focus on effective early intervention and counselling for bullies instead of punishing them, it is likely they would see a decrease in bullying and suspensions and expulsions. In addition, it could prevent some tragic consequences of bullying.

SECTION - C

7.   **(1 × 4 = 4 Marks)**

(a) The poem is 'An Elementary School Classroom In A Slum' and the poet is Stephen Spender.

(b) 'Their slag heap' is used to describe the poverty of the children. Here 'their slag heap' refers to the hunger-stricken wasted bodies of the children. The poet is comparing the extremely starved and malnourished bodies to the large pile of industrial waste.

(c) The children lead miserable and pathetic lives. Their life is full of misery, hopelessness and suffering.

(d) The comparison, 'like bottle bits of stones' is a simile; 'bottle bits' is alliteration with '*b*' sound repeated.

OR

(a) The poem is 'My Mother At Sixty Six' and the poet is Kamala Das.

(b) The poet put the thought of losing her mother, away. The thought of separation from her mother was very unpleasant. She felt uneasy and disturbed, so she decided to ignore the thought.

(c) The young trees are a contrast to the poet's old mother who is old, weak and pale. The trees are sprinting as they symbolise youth and are full of life.

(d) The joyful scene did not help her drive away the thought of losing her mother because in contrast to the merry children who were full of energy and life, her mother was weak, dull and lifeless at the age of sixty-six. The enthusiasm and vitality of the young children led to the painful realisation that her mother may breathe her last any day in the near future.

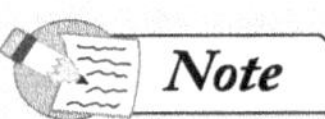

Note

1. *Be precise and to the point.*

2. *Since there is an internal choice in this question, try picking up the extract which you are familiar with.*

3. *Try answering all the questions of the extract that you have picked up.*

4. *For questions like "Name the poem and the poet" write the full name of the poem and the poet with the correct spellings.*

5. *For questions like "Which image is used to describe the poverty of these children," pick out the exact phrase from the poem 'slag heap' and then describe it.*

6. *Use the language as used in the question. For e.g. "How do you know that the joyful scene did not help her drive away "that thought" from her mind? "Your answer should start with – The joyful scene did not help her...................*

8. 　　　　　　　　　　　　　　　　**(3 × 4 = 12 Marks)**

(a) A number of symbols have been used by the poet in the poem 'Aunt Jennifer's Tigers' which depict her plight. Aunt Jennifer herself represents women wedged under the tyrannical hand of a patriarchal society. Aunt Jennifer's tigers are used as a symbol of the fear and terror perpetrated on women by the male world. The wedding band is symbolic of male authority and power.

(b) Geoff is Sophie's elder brother, the oldest child in the family. He is an apprentice mechanic who had to travel each day to the far side of the city for his work. He is a self-involved individual who did not speak much but listened to his sister's wild stories. Though he is fascinated by Danny Casey, he cautions Sophie to stop day-dreaming about him.

(c) As soon as Zitkala came to know about the decision of cutting her long hair, she decided to fight. She crept up the stairs into a large empty room and then crawled under a bed. She did not come out even when she heard Judewin calling her name. But they found her and dragged her out. She cried, shook her head all the while but could not avoid her hair from being shingled.

(d) In order to defeat the astrologer's prophecy, the Maharaja had to kill a hundred tigers. He had already killed all seventy tigers in his kingdom. For this reason, he wished to marry a girl in the royal family of a state with a rich tiger population, where he could kill the rest of the thirty tigers. He actually reached the tally of 99 after marriage.

(e) Several of the elderly people from the village were sitting on the back benches during M. Hamel's last lesson. The villagers had come there to attend his last lesson as it was their way of paying respect to the master, who had given forty years of faithful service to the school.

(f) Many precautions were taken by the Governor for the smooth conduct of the O-level examination. The examination was arranged in the prison's cell itself which was secured by two heavy doors. Jackson conducted a thorough search leaving no chance for Evans to run away. Evan's cell was carefully examined and all potential weapons were removed. A transceiver was implanted in his cell so that the Governor could listen to the proceedings therein. Stephens was positioned at the door of the cell throughout the exam. In addition, the whole prison was on high alert.

Note

1. *Choose your questions with care since there is internal choice in this question.*

2. *Each 3-mark question must have at least two-three value points.*

3. *For questions like "What is your impression of Sophie's brother Geoff" you must give your own impression. Your answer can be creative as long as it is supported by substantial evidence.*

4. *For questions requiring specific answers like "What precautions did the authorities take for the smooth conduct of the O-level examination" pick out the most relevant examples from the text. Be specific and clear.*

9. 　　　　　　　　　　　　　　　　**(6 Marks)**

(a) Douglas' first two experiences with water instilled a fear of being drowned in him. The first occurred at the age of three or four years, when a sea wave washed him ashore. The next happened at the age of ten or eleven, when he was thrown into the deep end of the YMCA pool. This frightful experience left a permanent impression on Douglas' mind. The fear gripped him and he was unable to enjoy any of the sports activities. To overcome his fear of water, he hired an instructor to learn swimming. The instructor gave him hundreds of exercises and taught him how to exhale and inhale in water. The practice went on for three months and Douglas was able to counter his fear. To gain confidence, he went to Lake Wentworth and dived off a dock at Triggs Island. His determination and hard work with right amount of training had succeeded in banishing his fear of water.

(b) When Gandhiji visited Champaran to look into the problems of the poor peasants, he was served an official notice to quit Champaran. Gandhi signed the receipt and remarked that he would disobey the order. This was the beginning of civil disobedience. As a result, Gandhi received a summons to appear in court the next day. The peasants thronged the courtroom. They wanted to help the 'Mahatma' who was in trouble with the authorities for trying to help them. The officials were powerless. Gandhi helped them regulate the crowd. This baffled the officials.

The magistrate postponed announcing the sentence by two hours and asked Gandhi to furnish bail. Gandhi declined. The judge released him without bail. The judge said he would not deliver the judgment for several days. Later, the case was dropped by the Lt. Governor himself. It was then that the author said that civil disobedience had triumphed for the first time in modern India.

(c) The peddler had been living a miserable life of poverty, despair and frustration. His only aim was to accomplish things in life through any means. His view towards the society was in fact shaped by the indifferent attitude of the society towards him. He viewed the whole world as a rattrap and felt that the riches and luxuries were only baits to entice people into a vicious cycle of struggles, from which there was no escape. It was only when he met the ironmaster's daughter, Edla that his outlook towards the life changed. Edla's warmth, kindness, compassion and genuineness touched him. He left a rattrap as a Christmas gift for Edla and enclosed a letter thanking her for her kindness. He also confessed to stealing money from the crofter and left the money to be restored to the owner. Thus, through the character of the peddler, the story 'Rattrap' shows the redemptive power of love and compassion. The peddler redeemed himself from his dishonest ways and emerged as a transformed person.

10. **(6 Marks)**

(a) Though Derry's association with Mr. Lamb is brief, the boy benefits greatly from the old man's company. Derry had lost all zest for life due to his burnt face. After meeting Mr. Lamb, he is filled with new enthusiasm for life. He undergoes a major transformation and develops into a confident youth from the meek boy that he earlier was. Mr. Lamb's words have a profound effect on him and inspire him to see the brighter side of life. He categorically tells his mother that he wants to go back to Mr. Lamb and talk about '"things that matter. Things nobody else has ever said. Things he wants to think about." Here 'things' are Derry's perturbed thoughts which he has never discussed with anyone. It is only after meeting Mr. Lamb that Derry is full of hope and positivity and wants to live his life to the fullest.

(b) 'The Enemy', by Pearl S. Buck portrays the victory of humanity in a moment of crises through the character of a Japanese surgeon, Dr Sadao. Dr Sadao was a skilled surgeon trained in America and a famous scientist. He was devoted to his work and to the cause of the needy. When he saw the American soldier in a wounded condition, he was torn between his duty towards the country and compassion towards mankind. But his humanitarian virtues to save a man's life as a doctor superseded and he operated the man and saved his life. It was the victory of humanity in a moment of crisis. He also arranged for a boat and helped Tom to escape. This act of Dr Sadao was an act of humanism and compassion. His spirit of humanity surpassed everything else and he saved the life of a man rising above any prejudice.

(c) The story, 'Should Wizard Hit Mommy' bears testimony to the fact that frustrations faced by adults and their personal experiences often intrude upon their interaction with their children. It was customary for Jack to weave a story of Roger every Saturday night to make his daughter Jo fall asleep. But the story of Roger Skunk threw up something unusual. Jo questioned his ideas for the first time. Jack was not very comfortable with having his word or authority questioned. He had the typical parental attitude and opinion that parents knew what was best for their children. He did not like women to take anything for granted, to the extent that he did not go to help his pregnant wife paint the woodwork. He stuck to his ending of the story with Roger Skunk getting his foul smell back, and refused Jo's demand of changing the end.

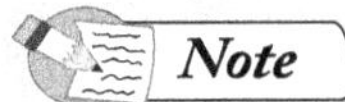

Note

1. *Each 6-mark question must have at least four value points*

2. *This question has internal choice. Therefore, choose with care.*

3. *Answer to the point including your own opinion in places where it is deemed necessary by the question.*

4. *Pick out specific examples from the text to support your answer*

5. *Quote straight from the text wherever required but do so only when you are sure of the words.*

6. *For e.g. for question like "'The Enemy' portrays the victory of humanity in a moment of crisis. Illustrate this fact through the actions taken by Dr. Sadao for the enemy soldier"- you can build your answer on the following value points.*

    (a) *Portrays the victory of humanity in a moment of crisis- character of a Japanese surgeon, Dr Sadao*

    (b) *Skilled surgeon trained in America - devoted to his work and to the cause of the needy*

    (c) *Saw American soldier in a wounded condition*

    (d) *Was torn between duty towards country and compassion towards mankind*

    (e) *Humanitarian virtues superseded*

    (f) *Operated the man -saved his life*

    (g) *Victory of humanity in a moment of crisis*

    (h) *Arranged for a boat -helped Tom escape*

    (i) *Act of Dr Sadao-act of humanism and compassion- rose above all prejudice.*

11. **(6 Marks)**

(a) Teddy Henfrey, the clock-repairer, was an inquisitive inhabitant of Iping who had an unpleasant meeting with the strange man. Mrs. Hall called him to mend the clock in Griffin's room. The first time Teddy encountered the bandaged head, he was taken aback. When he was left alone in his company, he worked as slowly as possible in the hope of getting some details about the stranger. But the stranger caught him wasting time and rebuked him. He was snubbed by the former to do the mending fast. He felt insulted because Griffin did not entertain him or treat him well.

After quickly fixing the clock, he went out quite annoyed and suspecting that the strange man was definitely wanted by the police. On his way home, he met Mr. Hall and set him against Griffin by talking ill about him. Describing him as an incongruent and suspicious character, he relieved himself of the hurt by spreading rumours against the strange man.

(b) Since Dr. Kemp and Griffin were known to each other since college days, Griffin thought Kemp would be supportive and understanding. He extracted a promise from Kemp not to reveal his presence to anyone. He told his story and revealed all his sinister plans as well. All these revelations alerted Kemp though he gave an assurance to Griffin that he would not break his confidence. Griffin hoped that he would get all the support from him, and would work along with him. However, Kemp informed Col. Adye and his betrayal was revealed. Kemp planned to hand him over to the police, as he felt Griffin could prove extremely dangerous to people. Therefore, Kemp became a traitor in Griffin's eyes by letting out all his secrets.

(c) With the loss of his gold, Silas had undergone a big change, both in his own character and also in the way he was perceived and viewed by others in Raveloe. When his money was stolen, the villagers felt sorry for him. What changed his life was the child he believed was sent from above. Eppie brought him much more joy and happiness than he ever received from the gold. It was due to Eppie that his faith in human relationships got restored. He finally experienced reciprocated love and companionship from the villagers. So far, he had been considered strange and mysterious but with Eppie in his life, he got accepted by the people of Raveloe. They now understood him clearly and became sympathetic towards Silas.

(d) Nancy Lammeter, the elder of the two daughters of Mr. Lammeter, comes from a family that is wealthy by Raveloe standards. She follows her father's teaching to live virtuously and is proud of her roots. She is a young charming girl who lives completely up to the standards expected of a lady. Her hands are described as coarse as they show the traces of butter-making, cheese-crushing, and other work typically performed by rural women. Though she adheres to her moral code of ethics and disapproves Godfrey's weakness of character, she is exhilarated by Godfrey's attention, in part because of the status he embodies. She is a typical country girl because of her peculiar belief in omens. It is through the course of the novel that she matures from a young girl to a competent housewife. Thus it can be said that Nancy is a pretty and caring young lady who lives her life according to her own code of behaviour and belief.

12. **(6 Marks)**

(a) After Mr. Cuss's encounter with the stranger, he was in a state of panic and shock. So he rushed hurriedly to Mr. Bunting and narrated him the whole incident. But Mr. Bunting did not believe the story of the doctor. Instead, he reacted by saying, "It's a most remarkable story." Mr. Bunting's reaction was justified because he had never heard about such an incident as had happened with Dr. Cuss. He couldn't believe that there could be such a man who had invisible limbs. He guessed that perhaps mirrors were used to trick Mr. Cuss or it was some sort of hallucination produced by a good magician. Hence, he termed Dr. Cuss's encounter with Griffin as 'a most remarkable story'.

(b) It can be said that Griffin allowed destructive desires to dominate his life which turned him into a criminal. He was a self-centered man who had no conscience. He appeared to be at war with the entire mankind. When he was short of money to continue his experiments, he robbed his own father, who committed suicide because the money was not his. He burnt down the house at Great Portland Street when the landlord and his sons found about his experiments. He looted a small costume shop, and left after striking the old owner on his head. His plan to spread a reign of terror among people using his powers of invisibility scared Dr. Kemp. Griffin even tried to kill him for betraying him to the police. Griffin is portrayed as a negative character with destructive and harmful instincts. He becomes unbearable to the society and finally meets his end.

(c) The most important internal conflict presented at the beginning of the story, 'Silas Marner' is his conflict with God. Though an honest and faithful member of a religious sect In Lantern Yard, he was excommunicated from his community for a theft he had not committed. His best friend William's plot to implicate him in the case of theft in the church destroyed his faith in mankind completely and made him leave Lantern Yard for good. The two-fold condemnation by the treachery of his best friend and by the community of God left him desolate. He renounced his religion and faith in God for the injustice done to him and came to adopt the life of a recluse in Raveloe.

(d) On his way back after causing the death of Wildfire, Godfrey's horse, Dunstan remembered the miser Silas's money and decided to stop at his cottage to discuss borrowing some of it for paying off Godfrey's debt. He wanted to borrow a lantern and discuss the money matter with Silas. On finding that Silas was not in the cottage, he walked in and seated himself in front of the fire. Dunstan wondered whether the old man was dead. If so, no one would need his money. He started looking for his money and discovered the two leather bags containing Silas's gold coins in a hiding place under some bricks below the loom. He replaced the bricks and quickly made off with the gold treasure, stepping out into the darkness of the night.

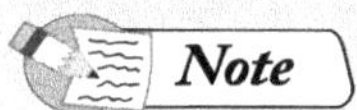 **Note**

1.   Each 6-mark question must have at least four value points.

2.   This question again has internal choice. Therefore, choose with care.

3.   Answer to the point including your own opinion in places where it is deemed necessary by the question.

4.   Pick out specific examples from the text to support your answer.

5.   Quote straight from the text wherever required but do so only when you are sure of the words.

6.   Only write whatever is required. Do not try to stretch the answer even if it is less than the required words.

7.   In questions requiring answer to be written in two parts, remember to show the transition in your answer through a change in paragraph as done in the solutions. For e.g. in question like "Why did Teddy Henfrey feel insulted after his encounter with the strange man at the 'Coach and Horses'? What did he do to relieve himself from his nasty mood on his way back from the inn?"- you can build your answer on the following value points.

Part I of the question

1.   Teddy Henfrey, the clock-repairer- inquisitive inhabitant of Iping

2.   Had an unpleasant meeting with the strange man

3.   Mrs. Hall called - mend the clock in Griffin's room

4.   The first time taken aback - encountered the bandaged head

5.   Left alone in his company, worked as slowly as possible- hopeful of getting some details about the stranger

6.   Caughtwasting time- rebuked

7.   Snubbed- asked to do the mending fast

8.   Felt insulted because Griffin did not entertain him or treat him well

Part II of the question

1.   After fixing the clock- went- annoyed - suspected the strange man was wanted by the police

2.   Met Mr. Hall on his way back - and set him against Griffin by talking ill about him

3.   Described him as an incongruent andsuspicious character

4.   Relieved himself of the hurt by spreading rumours against the strange man

Delhi *2019*

CBSE Board Solved Paper

Time Allowed : 3 Hours   *Maximum Marks : 100*

General Instructions:
  (i) This paper is divided into three Sections : A, B and C. All the sections are compulsory.
  (ii) Separate instructions are given with each section and question, wherever necessary. Read these instructions very carefully and follow them faithfully.
  (iii) Do not exceed the prescribed word limit while answering the questions

SECTION A: Reading

(30 Marks)

1. Read the passage given below :

1. All of Earth's oceans share one thing in common: plastic pollution. Discarded plastic bags, cups, and bottles make their way into the sea. Today, it seems that no part of the ocean is safe from plastic trash. In recent years, oceanographers have searched in vain for a pristine marine environment. They have found plastic everywhere they have looked. "It is a common global problem, we can't point to a single habitat or location with no plastic."

2. Plastic harms wildlife and introduces dangerous chemicals into marine ecosystems — communities of organisms interacting with their surroundings. Once plastic enters the environment, it lasts a long time. Scientists are working to prevent plastic pollution from entering the sea.

3. When people litter, or when trash is not properly disposed of, things like plastic bags, bottles, straws, foam beverage cups get carried to the sea by winds and waterways. About 80 percent of ocean plastic originates on land. The rest comes from marine industries such as shipping and fishing.

4. In 2015, engineer Jenna Jambeck at the University of Georgia and other researchers calculated that at least 8 million tons of plastic trash is swept into the ocean from coasts every year. That's the equivalent of a full garbage truck of plastic being dumped into the sea every minute. If current trends in plastic production and disposal continue, that figure will double by 2025. A report published by the World Economic Forum last year predicts that by 2050, ocean plastic will outweigh all the fish in the sea.

5. In today's world, plastic is everywhere. It's found in shoes, clothing, household items, electronics, and more. There are different types of plastics, but one thing they all have in common is that they're made of polymers – large molecules made up of repeating units. Their chemical structure gives them a lot of advantages : they're cheap and easy to manufacture, lightweight, water-resistant, durable, and can be moulded into nearly any shape.

6. Unfortunately, some of the properties that make plastics great for consumer goods also make them a problem pollutant. Plastic's durability comes in part from the fact that unlike paper or wood, it doesn't biodegrade, or break down naturally. Instead it just fragments, or breaks into tiny pieces over time. These tiny pieces, known as microplastic, can potentially stick around for hundreds or perhaps even thousands of years.

7. Another problem with plastics is the other chemicals they contain, like dyes and flame retardants. When plastic isn't disposed of properly, these additives end up in the environment. Plastic also tends to absorb harmful chemicals from its surroundings. "It's like a sponge for persistent organic pollutants." These long-lasting, toxic substances include pesticides and industrial chemicals. If plastic absorbs the chemicals, and marine organisms eat the plastic, they may be exposed to higher concentrations of these contaminants.

8. One of the biggest impacts of plastic pollution is its effect on sea life. Seals, sea turtles, and even whales can become entangled in plastic netting. They can starve to death if the plastic restricts their ability to move or eat. Or the plastic can cut into the animals' skin, causing wounds that develop severe infections.

9. Sea turtles eat plastic bags and soda-can rings, which resemble jellyfish, their favourite food. Seabirds eat bottle caps or chunks of foam cups. Plastic pieces may make an animal feel full, so it doesn't eat enough real food to get the nutrients it needs. Plastic can also block an animal's digestive system, making it unable to eat.

10. Plastic and its associated pollutants can even make it into our own food supply. Scientists recently examined fish and shell-fish bought at markets in California and Indonesia. They found plastic in the guts of more than a quarter of samples purchased at both locations. In organisms that people eat whole, such as sardines and oysters, that means we're eating plastic too. In larger fish, chemicals from plastic may seep into their muscles and other tissues that people consume.

11. One way to keep the ocean cleaner and healthier is through cleanup efforts. A lot of plastic waste caught in ocean currents eventually washes up on beaches. Removing it can prevent it from blowing out to sea again. Beach clean-up is ocean clean-up.

12. Cleanup efforts can't reach every corner of the ocean or track down every bit of microplastic. That means it's critical to cut down on the amount of plastic that reaches the sea in the first place. Scientists are working toward new materials that are safer for the environment. For example, Jambeck and her colleagues are currently testing a new polymer that breaks down more easily in seawater.

13. "Individual actions make a big difference," says Jambeck. Disposing of plastic properly for recycling or trash collection is a key step. "And simple things like reusable water bottles, mugs, and bags really cut down on waste," she says. Skipping straws or using paper ones helps too. Ocean pollution can seem overwhelming, but it's something everyone can help address. This is a problem we can really do something about.

1.1 On the basis of your understanding of the above passage, answer each of the questions given below by choosing the most appropriate option :

  (i) Percentage of ocean plastic that originates from land is:
    (a) 20% (b) 50% (c) 80% (d) 25%

  (ii) In which year did Jenna Jambeck and other researchers calculate that at least 8 million tons of plastic trash is swept into ocean every year?
    (a) 2018 (b) 2015 (c) 2005 (d) 2010

  (iii) Plastic is not biodegradable because it is made up of:
    (a) low atomic particles
    (b) tiny particles
    (c) strong big particles
    (d) large molecule polymers

  (iv) Sea turtles eat :
    (a) plastic bottles
    (b) plastic bags and soda-can rings
    (c) bottle caps
    (d) chunks of foam cups

  (v) Scientists bought fish and shell-fish for examination at markets in :
    (a) China and Russia
    (b) Pakistan and Afghanistan
    (c) California and Indonesia
    (d) Australia and Brazil

1.2 Answer the following questions briefly :
  (i) Which articles made of plastic generally cause pollution in the sea?
  (ii) How does plastic in oceans harm marine ecosystems?
  (iii) How is microplastic formed?
  (iv) Why is plastic compared to a sponge?
  (v) What is the biggest impact of plastic pollution on sea life?
  (vi) How are scientists trying to reduce the plastic pollutants?

1.3. Answer any three of the following questions in 25-30 words each :
  (i) How does plastic waste enter the oceans?
  (ii) How is it true to say that plastic is everywhere in today's world?
  (iii) Which property of plastic makes it a problem pollutant?
  (iv) What has scientist Jambeck suggested for having cleaner and healthier oceans?

1.4 Pick out the words/phrases from the passage which are similar in meaning to the following :
  (i) unspoiled (para 1)
  (ii) long lasting (para 5)
  (iii) people working together (para 12)

2. Read the passage given below :

1. Getting enough sleep is as important as taking time out to relax. A good night's sleep is essential for preserving the health of your brain and gives you the best chance to meet the coming day with a razor sharp mind. An average person needs about six to eight hour sleep a night – although it is also true that you need slightly less than this, as you grow older-another advantage of aging stress and sleep deprivation often feed on each other, since stress tends to make it harder for you to fall asleep at night and sleep deprivation in itself causes stress.

2. Eventually, too little sleep can dramatically interfere with the performance of your memory – something you obviously want to prevent. If you are not getting enough sleep, try going to bed 30 to 60 minutes earlier than your normal bed time for a few days. Lie down on the bed and try to relax by dissociating yourself from your daily routine work. This is normally enough to catch up on any sleep deprivation.

3. If, however, you suffer from insomnia you should seek the advice of your doctor. The chances are it is already affecting your ability to remember and recall information – and if you are struggling to improve your memory scores, this could be at the root of your problem. Prolonged periods of insufficient sleep can deplete your immune system, make you more accident prone and even cause depression – this can also reinforce a more negative outlook on life, which can contribute to your stress burden. The good news is that your memory and mood should automatically improve once you improve your sleep patterns. Tackle your sleep issues and everything else should fall into place.

4. Because stress management is so essential to maximize your brain power, if you are not in the habit of setting aside time to relax, make it a priority to do so. Even a minute or two of deep breathing can start to work wonders. Often the best ideas and memories can come to you when you are in a state of relaxation as it is during these moments that your brain stores, processes and plays with the information it has received.

5. Meditation has long been part of religious and spiritual life, specially in Asia. Today, more and more people are adopting it in Western countries also, for its value in developing peace of mind and lowering stress. There is some evidence that regular meditation can have real sleep gain and health benefits particularly in terms of protecting your brain against aging.

2.1. On the basis of your understanding of the above passage, make notes on it using headings and subheadings. Use recognizable abbreviations (wherever necessary – minimum four) and a format you consider suitable. Also supply an appropriate title to it.

2.2 Write a summary of the above passage in about 100 words.

SECTION B: Advanced Writing Skills

(30 Marks)

3. You are Principal of National Public School, Jaipur. You require a TGT (Maths) for your school. Draft a suitable advertisement in not more than 50 words for the 'Situations Vacant' column of 'The National Times' stating essential and desirable qualifications, experience etc of the candidates.

OR

Arts Club of your school is going to organize a drawing and painting competition. Write a notice in not more than 50 words, to be displayed on the school notice board, inviting students to participate in it. Give all the necessary

details. You are Rishabh/Ridhima, Secretary, Arts Club, Sunrise Public School, Gurugram, Haryana.

4. You have realized the necessity of education and financial independence of women for their family, society and in turn for the nation. Write a letter to the Editor, 'The National Times' highlighting your ideas on the importance of education of women leading to a better status for them. You are Tarun/Taruna, B-7/9, Mall Road, Delhi. (100 – 125 words)

OR

You bought a refrigerator two months ago from Mohan Sales, Ashok Vihar, Bangalore. It has developed certain problems regarding its functioning. Cooling has stopped and it is making a lot of noise. Write a letter of complaint to the Manager asking him for immediate repair/replacement of the same. You are Sachin/Shashi, 61 Pratap Enclave, Bangalore. (100 – 125 words)

5. Write a debate in 150 – 200 words either for or against the motion : 'Capital Punishment should be abolished'.

OR

Regular practice of yoga is useful in maintaining good health. It is also important for good concentration and peace of mind. You are Shivam/Shabnam.

Write a speech in 150 – 200 words to be delivered in the morning assembly of your school, highlighting the impact of yoga in our life.

6. Hard work and punctuality are essential for a happy and successful life. They help in meeting the desired targets of our life. You are Kavya/Kanha. Write an article in 150 – 200 words highlighting the importance of hard work and punctuality in a student's life.

OR

In your locality a blood donation camp was organized by an NGO – 'For Your Health'. Many people visited the camp and donated blood. Write a report in 150 – 200 words for a local newspaper covering the arrangements, doctors' team, refreshment served etc.

SECTION C: Textbooks and Long Reading Text

(40 Marks)

7. Read the extract given below and answer the questions that follow :

I looked again at her, wan, pale
as a late winter's moon and felt that old
familiar ache, my childhood's fear,
but all I said was, see you soon, Amma,
all I did was smile and smile and smile …
(i) Name the poet and the poem.
(ii) What was the poet's childhood fear?
(iii) What is the poetic device used in lines
(iv) Explain : 'late winter's moon'.

OR

…… The stunted, unlucky heir

Of twisted bones, reciting a father's gnarled disease,

His lesson, from his desk. At back of the dim class
One unnoted, sweet and young. His eyes live in a dream,
Of squirrel's game, in tree room, other than this.

(i) Who is the unlucky heir?

(ii) What has he inherited?

(iii) Who is sitting at the back of the dim class?

(iv) How is he different from rest of the class?

8. Answer any four of the following questions in 30-40 words each :

(i) Who did M. Hamel blame for the neglect of learning on the part of boys like Franz?

(ii) How did the instructor turn Douglas into a swimmer?

(iii) Why do you think Gandhiji considered the Champaran episode to be a turning point in his life?

(iv) What made the chief astrologer place his finger on his nose?

(v) How did the writer indicate that Dr. Sadao's father was a very traditional and conventional man?

(vi) How does Jo want the story to end? Why?

9. Answer any one of the following in 120-150 words :

(i) "Seemapuri, a place on the periphery of Delhi yet miles away from it, metaphorically." Explain.

(ii) 'The Rattrap' focuses on human loneliness and the need to bond with others. Comment.

(iii) Attempt a character sketch of Sophie as a girl who lives in her dreams.

10. Answer any one of the following in 120 – 150 words :

(i) Derry and Mr. Lamb both are victims of physical impairment, but their attitudes towards life are completely different. Elaborate.

(ii) Write a character sketch of the Governor of Oxford Prison based on the story, 'Evans Tries an O-Level'.

(iii) Why did Bama stroll in the market place instead of hurrying back home? Describe the sights she enjoyed seeing there.

11. Answer any one of the following questions in 120 – 150 words :

(i) Why was Mrs. Hall happy to have a guest at 'Coach and Horses' Inn? How did the stranger behave at the inn?

(ii) Describe Mr. Marvel's meeting with the mariner at Port Stowe. What kind of person was the mariner?

(iii) How did Dunstan Cass meet his end?

(iv) Describe the circumstances under which Silas Marner had to leave Lantern Yard.

12. Answer any one of the following questions in 120 – 150 words :

(i) How does the novel, 'The Invisible Man' highlight the theme of corruption of morals in the absence of social restrictions?

(ii) Compare and contrast Griffin (the invisible man) and Dr. Kemp as scientists and also as members of society.

(iii) George Eliot has portrayed Godfrey as a morally weak character. Comment.

(iv) In 'Silas Marner', describe the role of Dolly Winthrop.

Solutions

1. 1.1 (i) (c) 80% **(1 × 5 = 5 Marks)**
  (ii) (b) 2015
  (iii) (d) large molecule polymers
  (iv) (b) plastic bags and soda-can rings
  (v) (c) California and Indonesia

1.2 **(1 × 6 = 6 Marks)**

(i) Articles like discarded plastic bags, cups, bottles, straws, beverage cups, soda can rings, foam, bottle caps etc cause pollution in the sea.

(ii) Plastic in oceans harm marine ecosystems by introducing dangerous chemicals into the marine ecosystem.

(iii) Microplastic is formed by the natural breaking down of plastic into fragments over the years. Since plastic is not bio-degradable, it just fragments over time forming microplastic.

(iv) Plastic is compared to a sponge because it tends to absorb harmful chemicals from the surroundings. In other words it acts like a sponge to persistent organic pollutants.

(v) The biggest impact of plastic pollution on sea life is its adverse effect. Sea animals like seals, turtles etc get entangled in the plastic netting leading to restriction of movement. This many a times leads to starvation leading to the ultimate death of the concerned animal. Plastic netting also causes wounds leading to severe infections.

(vi) Scientists are trying to reduce the plastic pollutants by trying to cut down on the plastic that reaches the sea in the first place. They are therefore working towards new materials that are safer for the environment and testing a new polymer that breaks down easily in sea water.

1.3 **(2 × 3 = 6 Marks)**

(i) Plastic waste enters the ocean through various means. When people litter, or when trash is not properly disposed of, things like plastic bags, bottles, straws, foam , beverage cups etc get carried to the sea by winds and waterways. A lot of plastic waste also comes from marine industries such as shipping and fishing.

(ii) It is true to say that plastic is everywhere in today's world since there is no single habitat or location without plastic. It is found in shoes, clothing, food, household items, electronics and in many more such items.

(iii) The fact that plastic is durable and non-bio-degradable makes it a problem pollutant. It absorbs harmful chemicals from surroundings and sticks around for hundreds and thousands of years making the problem much worse.

(iv) Scientist Jambeck has placed a lot of emphasis on the "individual actions" making a lot of difference in creating cleaner and healthier oceans. Disposing of plastic properly for recycling or trash collection is a key step. We can take simple steps like using reusable water bottles, mugs and bags, skipping plastic straws and using paper ones etc. This will ultimately cut down on the generation of plastic waste and pave way for cleaner oceans.

Note

1. When answering MCQs (Question No.1.1) choose the option which is the closest answer from amongst the options.

2. For Factual questions like e.g. "Which property of plastic makes it a problem pollutant", include only the information given in the passage.

3. While answering the 'Why question like "Why is plastic compared to sponge", you may begin your answer with 'Plastic is compared to a sponge because ………or a similar phrase.

1.4 (i) unspoiled – pristine **(1 × 3 = 3 Marks)**
  (ii) long lasting – durable
  (iii) people working together- colleagues

2. **(5 Marks)**

2.1 Note Making

Title: Importance of Sleep For Human Well-Being

1. Importnc. of Sleep
  1.1 preserves health
  1.2 sharpens brain & mind
  1.3 six to eight hours sleep – a must
    1.3.1 need less as one grows older

2. Impact of Sleep Deprivan.
  2.1 stress
  2.2 mem'y loss

3. Ways to catch up on sleep deprivan.
  3.1 retiring to bed earlier than usual time
  3.2 lie on bed- disassociate from the day
  3.3 relax → sleep

4. Insomnia

   4.1 affects ability to recall / remember

   4.2 depletes immune sys.

   4.3 makes one accident prone

   4.4 causes depression

   4.5 –ve outlook on life

   4.6 contribute to stress burden

5. Solution to /insomnia

   5.1 consult a doctor

   5.2 Stress Managemt.

       a. through deep breathing

       b. Meditatn.

6. Benefits of Stress Managemt.

   6.1 uplifts mood – sharpens mem'y

   6.2 brain relaxes- stores info.

7. Benefits of Meditatn.

   7.1 dev. peace of mind

   7.2 lowers stress

   7.3 protects brain against aging

Key to Abbreviation

Abbreviation	Word
Importnc.	importance
Deprivan.	deprivation
mem'y	memory
→	leads to
sys.	system
–ve	negative
Managemt.	management
Meditatn.	meditation
info.	information
dev.	developement

(b) Summary: **(5 Marks)**

The importance of adequate sleep for human beings cannot be negated. It not only sharpens our mind but preserves our health too. Even though a person needs approx. 6-8 hours of sleep, the requirement decreases with age. Sleep deprivation can lead to stress and memory loss. Therefore, we must avoid sleep deprivation. If one is suffering from insomnia, one must visit a doctor since insomnia affects our memory, increases stress, makes us accident prone and affects life negatively on the whole. Stress management through deep breathing and meditation also helps. Meditation is also said to protect the brain from aging.

Note

1. The passage is on the importance of sleep and its effects on the general well- being of humans. So the title must be related to the main idea and should have the key words 'Sleep ', 'Importance,' 'well-being' etc

2. It should always contain phrases. Avoid using complete sentences. E.g.
1. Importnc. of Sleep
1.1 preserves health
1.2 sharpens brain & mind
1.3 six to eight hours sleep – a must
*   1.3.1 need less as one grows older*
AND NOT The importance of sleep is that it preserves our health etc……..

3. Include a minimum of 4-6 distinctly different recognizable short forms i.e. abbreviations of the words in the notes as done in the solution.

SECTION - B

3.   **(4 Marks)**

ADVERTISEMENT
MATHEMATICS TEACHER REQUIRED

Required a TGT (Maths) teacher for National Public School, Jaipur. B.Sc. (Maths) degree along with B. Ed. is a must, minimum two years of experience, good computer and communication skills, knowledge of Vedic Maths an added advantage. Salary as per norms.Interested candidates can send their CV's at *national@gmail.com* or contact at 932XXXXX.

OR

NOTICE
SUNRISE PUBLIC SCHOOL, GURUGRAM

16th March 2019

DRAWING AND PAINTING COMPETITION

All the students are hereby informed that the Arts Club of our school is organizing a drawing and painting competition on 20th March 2019 for all the students in the school auditorium from 12 pm to 2 pm. Interested students can come to the venue on that day. No prior registration required. For more information contact the undersigned.

Rishabh/ Ridhima

(Secretary, Arts Club)

4.   **Letter**   **(6 Marks)**

B-7/9

Mall Road

Delhi

                March 16, 2019

The Editor,

The National Times

New Delhi

        Subject: Education of women

Sir/Madam

Through the columns of your esteemed newspaper, I would like to express my views on the importance of education of women leading to a better status for them.

For centuries, women have been viewed as mere caretakers and thus education was not thought important for them. This resulted in them, being pushed and relegated to a dark and abusive environment. Their views were inconsequential, their voices muted, and their financial rights curbed. Even though we claim that today we have been successful in creating a well-balanced society where women are treated at par with men, the ground reality is extremely grim. Women still need to be educated and made financially independent so that they get a better stature and position in the society. It will give them the voice that has hitherto been limited. Even the mind set of the society needs to undergo a transformation so that it is willing to give the space that a woman truly deserves. As is rightly said "Educate a women, and educate the whole family !"

The world is now developing at a fast pace. However, this development is meaningless if the female, half of the society, does not get its due. I hope my words find a place in your newspaper and make the citizens aware of the importance of education of women.

Yours truly

Tarun/Taruna

OR

61 Pratap Enclave

Bangalore

March 16, 2019

The Manager

Mohan Sales

Ashok Vihar

Bangalore

Subject: Complaint regarding Malfunctioning of Refrigerator

Sir/Madam

This is to bring to your notice that I had purchased a Voltas 250 litre double door refrigerator from your showroom on 6th January 2019. It has been just two months, but the appliance has developed certain problems.

The cooling has stopped completely, and it is making a lot of noise. Most of the food and vegetables kept in the refrigerator are getting spoilt. Furthermore, there is some leakage too because of which water comes out after every twenty minutes.

Since the refrigerator is still in the warranty period, I would like you to repair it free of cost as soon as possible.

Yours truly

Sachin/Shashi

5. Debate   **(10 Marks)**

Capital Punishment Should Be Abolished

For the motion: Good morning everyone! Respected Jury members, teachers, students and my worthy opponents. Today, I, Parth/Pritha, stand before you to express my opinion for the motion on the topic 'Capital punishment should be abolished.'

Human life is a precious and irreplaceable commodity and hence no one has the right to deny someone their life. The act of capital punishment being a favoured means of dispensing justice in the medieval times has no place in the modern world.

Not only is it a gross violation of the right to life guaranteed by the constitution of almost every other country of the world, it also highlights the fact that the justice system is more hinged on punishing criminals rather than reforming them. You cannot punish a wrongdoer by doing wrong things against them. Taking revenge is not the same as providing justice.

The law is a set of rules, justice is a matter of moral and ethics and there is nothing more immoral than the act taking away a life. The idea of justice is an abstract concept which has been subject to change over time. As a result, the laws too have changed accordingly and in this modern worldview the act of capital punishment has no place.

Thank you for your patient hearing

Against the motion : Good morning everyone! Respected Jury members, teachers, students and my worthy opponents. Today, I, Parth/ Pritha, stand before you to express my opinion against the motion on the topic 'Capital punishment should be abolished.'

The human society exhibits a symbiotic relation between people. Every person, no matter who they are contribute in their own ways for the overall development for the society. Therefore, people who contribute nothing to this structure and instead work towards destroying it not only should be expelled from this system but also be eliminated due to the threat they pose to the society.

My dear audience - capital punishment is awarded for the gravest and most heinous of crimes and not just any petty crime. People who commit such crimes have almost no redeemable human qualities and keeping them in jails only increases the cost of the manpower and money spent on them. Furthermore capital punishment, if given in the rarest of rare cases will act as a deterrent to others.

A person who has done inhuman things to someone cannot appeal to others to treat them in a humane manner. Ladies and gentleman- I do believe that taking a life is one of the worst things to do. However, any such threats to the society should be eliminated especially if it endangers others.

Thank you for your patient hearing.

OR

Speech:

Importance of Yoga in Our Life

Good morning to one and all present here!

Today I, Shubham/Shivani will deliver a speech to highlight the importance of yoga in our daily lives. Modern life comes with its privileges, but it also comes with its own little issues. Stress and tension are an integral part of our lives today– be it a student or a working person.

One needs to steer clear of these self- limiting issues. Here is where yoga comes into play, being a proven way to reduce stress by enhancing the production of dopamine and cortisol. Practicing yoga also reduces blood pressure hereby curing hypertension.

Yoga is also a form of rehabilitation for people addicted to certain drugs. It improves overall flexibility of the body, energizes and helps reduce weight. For us, students, asanas like Surya namaskar are preferred since it increases blood flow to the brain helping in the brain functioning better. Breathing exercises too help dispel stress and behavioral issues can be curbed. To conclude the ancient practice of yoga has an extremely important role to play in today's fast paced world. It not only is a means of recreation but also stress busting exercise too which promotes general well-being.

Thank You!

6. **Article**   **(10 Marks)**

Hard Work and Punctuality - The Two Pillars of Success

By *Kavya/Kanha*

Hard work and punctuality are important pre-requisites for success in a student's life. A disciplined person understands the value of punctuality. Discipline for some could be an order or a code of behaviour and for others it could be the control that one gains by enforcing a system. Whatever the case might be, we all understand the value of adhering to timelines. Getting up early, reaching school in time, adhering to the set goals of study and sports- all of it shape the personality of a person. If inculcated early in life it leads to cultivation of restraint, good work ethics, self-confidence and an absence of chaos and confusion in life. In addition to this it brings better fruits to the hard work that a person does.

Achievements without hard work are impossible. An idle student can never gain happiness and success in his or her life and will always blame time or other people for their failures. Work is a privilege and a pleasure for those who don't consider work as a burden. Working is a part of living which is considered as worship. Students who work very hard and make the best use of their time can really achieve their dreams which they have envisioned for themselves.

In addition to removing stress and negative attitude, hard work and punctuality makes a person, a role model for others to emulate.

OR

Report:

Blood Donation Camp Organized

By *Raj/Reena*

New Delhi, March 6: A blood donation camp was organized by an NGO- "For Your Health" on Saturday, the 16th of July 2020 in Vikas Nagar in association with the Blood Bank of the town. A large number of people gathered to donate their blood.

The blood donation camp was inaugurated by the local MLA Mr. Akhilesh Singh who donated his blood at around 8:00 in the morning. The camp was very well organized with comfortable seating arrangements for the people in waiting. The recovery room was also spacious and pleasant where the donors were provided not only with some rest after the extraction of blood but also some refreshments. The doctors were efficient and quick to respond to any query or need. Tests were also conducted to ascertain the suitability of the donor to donate blood. Speaking about the arrangements at the venue a donor, Mrs. Shashikala said – "I have donated blood many times, but this is the first time that it's so hassle free. I am impressed."

One only hopes that the NGO continues to take these initiatives in the future too.

SECTION - C

7.   **(1 × 4 = 4 Marks)**

(i) The poet of the above poem is Kamala Das and the name of the poem is My Mother at Sixty-Six.

(ii) The poet's childhood fear was the fear of separation from her mother because of her mother's death.

(iii) The poetic device that is used in lines 1-2 is a "simile". (late winter's moon)

(iv) The phrase 'late winter's moon' is used by the poet to describe the look on her mother's face. The phrase underlines the dull and pale look on her mother's face.

OR

(i) The unlucky heir is the boy with stunted growth who is reciting his lessons from the back of the class.

(ii) He has inherited his father's gnarled disease.

(iii) A sweet young boy with dreamy eyes is sitting at the back of the class.

(iv) He is different from the rest of the class in the sense that he has not lost his capacity to dream and is lost in his thoughts completely untouched by his surroundings.

Note

1. *Be precise and to the point.*

2. *Since there is an internal choice in this question, try picking up the extract which you are familiar with.*

3. *Try answering all the questions of the extract that you have picked up.*

4. *For questions like "Name the poem and the poet" write the full name of the poem and the poet with the correct spellings.*

5. *Use the language as used in the question. For e.g. "How is he different from the rest of the class "? Your answer should start with – He is different from the rest of the class because ………*

8.   **(3 × 4 = 12 Marks)**   **9.**   **(6 Marks)**

(i)   M. Hamel did not put the blame on any one person for the neglect of learning on the part of boys like Franz. He said that parents preferred to send them to work on a farm or at the mills in order to have a little more money. He himself sent them to water his flowers or gave them a holiday when he wanted to go fishing. Therefore it was not only the boys but also their parents and M. Hamel himself who were to be blamed for this neglect of learning.

(ii) The instructor made Douglas practice for five days a week an hour every day. In order to remove his fear of water, the instructor tied a rope attached to a pulley, and made him practice. He also made him practice breathing underwater and kick his legs in water. Piece by piece he built a swimmer out of Douglas.

(iii) Gandhiji considered the Champaran episode to be a turning point in his life since it was for the first time in the history of India that the sharecroppers realised that they too had rights. It was the first success of Civil Disobedience movement in India and marked the beginning of the liberation from fear of the British.

(iv) The chief astrologer placed his finger on his nose in stupefaction. He was shocked beyond belief when the ten day infant tiger king enunciated clearly and raised intelligent questions.

(v)   The writer indicates that Dr. Sadao's father was a very traditional and conventional man since even though Dr Sadao likes Hanna, he does not proceed till the time he gets to know that she is a Japanese too. Even the marriage is solemnized in a traditional manner. For his father education was the chief concern and that is why he sent Dr Sadao to England.

(vi) Jo wants her father to make the wizard hit mommy skunk on her head and change the original smell of Roger to that of roses once again.

She wanted the story to end in this manner since for her Roger Skunk's happiness was more important than an assertion of identity.

1. Choose your questions with care since there is internal choice in this question.

2. Each 3-mark question must have at least two-three value points.

3. So, for example – for the question " How does Jo want the story to end? Why ?" answer both parts separately and be to the point.

4. For questions requiring specific answer for e.g. " How did the instructor turn Douglas into a swimmer?" pick out only those examples which reflect the tricks and efforts of the instructor.

(i)   It is ironic indeed that Seemapuri, a place on the periphery of Delhi is miles away from it metaphorically and stands a sharp contrast to the city. Seemapuri has been the home for the people who came there from Bangladesh in 1971. Having no other skills or adequate education they picked up rag picking as their means of survival and now are living a life of deprivation and perpetual poverty. Living for more than 30 years without an identity or a permit but with ration cards which allows them to buy grains, they move from place to place, living in structures of mud with roofs of tin & tarpaulin or tents which serve as their transit homes. They pitch their tents wherever they can find food. For them garbage is like gold since it brings then food and a roof over their heads, even if it is leaking. Their children also grow up there and become their 'partners in survival'. All this is in sharp contrast to the sheen of Delhi and therefore it is said that Seemapuri although geographically close is poles apart from Delhi.

(ii) The story 'The Rattrap' focusses on human loneliness and the need to bond with others. Each of the four main characters feel lonely or have a negative view of the world. The crofter offers hospitality to the rat trap seller since he has not had company since the time his wife had died. He is so hospitable and full of trust that he shows the three ten kronor notes to the rat trap seller and ends up losing them. The iron master invites the rat trap seller home mistaking him for an old colleague of his. Elda too despite her awareness that something about the tramp is not right invites and insists that he stay since they could do with some Christmas cheer. Each is desirous of some company and it is worth mentioning that it is because of Elda's treatment of the rat trap seller coupled with her sincerity that his heart finally changes.

(iii) Sophie is a typical adolescent for whom dreaming is the most natural thing. She is from a weak socio-economic background and therefore the living conditions of her family aren't very pleasant. In such a scenario, having ambitions to make a better living by becoming a model and opening a boutique is her way of moving up the social ladder. However, she does not have any concrete plan as to how she is going to achieve that and ignoring the ground realities she continues indulging in fantasies. What she needs to understand is that the dreams should be achievable and realistic. She should also have the zeal to work hard for her dreams which this case does not seem possible. For her, the dreams are an escape from reality and there comes a time when dream and reality merge together so much so that she sees things which do not happen at all. Her meeting with Danny Casey is one such case. This kind of dreaming is dangerous and can be fatal. The fact that she involves her brother Derek too in this is all the more damaging.

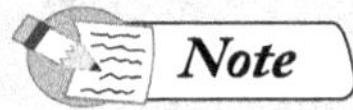

1. *Each 6-mark question must have at least four value points*
2. *This question has internal choice. Therefore choose with care.*
3. *Answer to the point including your own opinion in places where it is deemed necessary by the question.*
4. *Pick out specific examples from the text to support your answer*
5. *Quote straight from the text wherever required but do so only when you are sure of the words.*

10.   **(6 Marks)**

(i) Both Mr. Lamb and Derry suffer from physical impairment, but each has a different response which shapes up their attitude towards life. Mr. Lamb has a tin leg as his real leg had got blown off in the war and Derry had had an accident where more than half his face was burnt by acid. However more than the physical limitation, it is the feeling of alienation from society that bothers Derry. His face is a constant source of pain for him. The lack of friends, remarks of the onlookers on the street, the whispered conversations on the ground floor of his home between his parents and even his mother's kiss on his cheek – all are sources of pain for Derry since all this makes him feel isolated and different from the rest. He therefore shuts himself in and avoids meeting people. There is a lot of negativity in him. However, with Mr. Lamb the case is different. Even though he is mocked at in the streets with children calling him Lamey-Lamb, he does not find it disturbing. Mr. Lamb does not want any sympathy and he derives his happiness from the hum of the bees, his crab apples and his garden. He is more outward looking and positive in nature. To conclude, even though the two are in the same predicament, both have different responses to it.

(ii) The Governor of Oxford Prison in the story 'Evans Tries an O-Level' is a gullible, sensitive, intelligent and understanding person. He agrees to Evans' objections and orders Stephens to stand outside the cell. However, he is also diligent and believes in cross checking everything. He makes his best efforts to cover up for any eventuality in terms of ensuring the security arrangements. He is also smart enough to decode the message in the correction slip and reaches Evans after his escape. However he is gullible enough to be taken for a ride by him the second time too. In the end he turns out to be a 'good-for-a-giggle' governor since Evans is able to dodge him once again and move scot free.

(iii) There were many reasons why Bama strolled in the market place instead of hurrying back home. The distance that could be easily covered in ten minutes would eat up an hour of hers. She would watch all the fun and games going on the road. She enjoyed the novelties like the performing monkey, the snake charmer with the snake, the street lights on the way, the cyclist riding for three days etc. The various food stalls, the street plays, the political meetings, puppet shows, clay beads – all were of interest to her. She could go on and on looking at the beautiful sights at the Maariyaata temple and the Pongal offerings being cooked in front of the temple. These were the colourful sights for which Bama strolled in the market place.

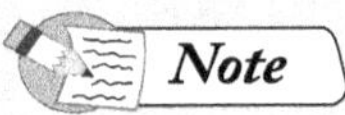

1. *Each 6-mark question must have at least four value points*
2. *This question again has internal choice. Therefore, choose with care.*
3. *Answer to the point including your own opinion in places where it is deemed necessary by the question.*
4. *Pick out specific examples from the text to support your answer*
5. *Quote straight from the text wherever required but do so only when you are sure of the words.*
6. *Only write whatever is required. Do not try to stretch the answer even if it is less than the required words.*

11.   **(6 Marks)**

(i) Mrs. Hall was happy to have a guest at 'Coach and Horses' Inn since it was early February. It was extremely difficult to come across any business in such a cold, biting winter and to find a guest knocking at her door brought in the prospect of earning some money. Therefore she felt overwhelmed at her piece of luck.

The behaviour of the stranger upon arrival however was not very warm. He was in fact very curt and rude. He flung a couple of sovereigns on the table and his demeanour discouraged any conversation. Later he locked himself in the room and said he did not want to be disturbed. His behaviour in fact degenerated as time passed which can be well-exemplified with instances of his behaviour with Teddy, Doctor Cuss etc.

(ii) Marvel meets the Mariner while he is resting on a bench outside a little inn on the outskirts of Port Stowe. Marvel is extremely agitated and his meeting with the mariner isn't pleasant. The mariner reads out the news of the invisible man from the newspaper and says he believes the story. Marvel is on the verge of divulging something about the invisible man but cries out in pain at that juncture. It is obvious that he is intercepted by something. He gets up in a hurry with his face contorted in physical suffering which he attributes to a toothache and leaves, calling the story a 'hoax'. The Mariner is surprised and angry and calls Marvel a 'silly devil'.

The Mariner is elderly and seems to be an observant person. He notices the contrast between Marvel's appearance and the sound of money in his pocket. He also loses his temper and gets angry at Marvel when he leaves without telling him anything about the invisible man.

(iii) Dunstan Cass had blackmailed some money out of Godfrey Cass, his brother, threatening to divulge the secret of his marriage to Molly Farren – a woman who gets into drinking. When Godfrey wants the money back, Dunstan suggests that they sell Wildfire – Godfrey's favourite horse. While taking it to the market, the horse gets killed at a stake. Coming back Dunstan gets caught in the mist and goes to Silas's cottage primarily with an intention of cajoling some money out of him. Finding the cottage empty with a bright fire burning inside, he is tempted to enter it. He goes inside and comes upon the hiding place of the gold. A little bit of an effort and he is able to retrieve the bags from the floor. He has no compunctions about stealing it and runs away with the gold. However, while crossing Stone-pit, he drowns and meets his end. His body is only discovered, wedged between two stones, sixteen years after his death, when Stone-pit went dry from the draining.

(iv) The circumstances under which Silas had to leave Lantern Yard are utterly shameful for him. He was a faithful member of a religious community and well respected in the society. He had a friend William and was also engaged to a young serving woman, Sarah. In other words, he was leading a perfect and a happy life at Lantern Yard. However, he is falsely implicated in stealing from the Church and we later realise that it is his friend, William who is instrumental in his falling from favour. Silas's engagement to Sarah also breaks and a month later William and Sarah get married to each other. All this affects Silas adversely. Completely disillusioned by the way his best friend and fiancée framed and deserted him, Silas leaves Lantern Yard.

12.   **(6 Marks)**

(i) The novel, 'The Invisible Man', highlights the theme of corruption of morals in the absence of social restrictions. Even though a genius, the turn of events in the novel depict Griffins as a scientist gone astray. For him the discovery is not for benefit of the society but self-glorification and self-gratification. From the very beginning Griffin is portrayed as a man with no moral compunctions or societal etiquettes. He is rude, full of avarice, selfish and engulfed in his egoistic pursuits. In order to move further in his experiments, he even robbed his father and caused his death.

In the absence of any social restrictions he degenerates from a man to a maniac. He misuses his powers at every juncture, and this shows his diluted sense of values. He even tries to use Dr. Kemp to unleash a reign of terror. In the end he meets a fitting end.

(ii) Both Griffin and Dr. Kemp are from the University College. While Griffin on one hand is a scientist trying to perfect the art of invisibility not for the benefit of the society but for self-glorification, Dr Kemp is a dignified intellectual and a responsible citizen. Griffin even though a genius, is depicted as a scientist gone astray since after perfecting the trick of invisibility, he becomes a menace to the society. His aggressiveness comes to fore many times in the novel with slamming of doors, furniture flying in the room, threats to Marvel etc. His encounter with Dr. Kemp and the request to join him in unleashing the Reign of Terror shows the remorseless side of his personality. However, Dr. Kemp's refusal to misuse the powers elevates his stature in our eyes. While Griffin has no respect for rules or authority, Dr. Kemp is law abiding and willing to shoulder a responsibility.

(iii) George Eliot has portrayed Godfrey as a morally weak character. He is introduced as an 'open-faced, good-natured young man' but a man of irresolute nature. He is set to inherit all his father's fortunes but he marries Molly Farren, an opium addict, has a child, Eppie, and then deserts Molly. Far from mustering enough courage and confiding in his father, he keeps it a secret since he is attracted to Nancy Lammeter and wants to marry her. He also fears his father disinheriting him and because of this he gives in to younger brother, Dunstan Cass,' blackmailing time and again. When it comes to his wife Nancy, he isn't even able to muster enough of courage to tell her of his secret marriage before his marriage to her. The reaction at Molly's death 'cast only one glance at the dead face on the pillow,' and heaving a sigh of relief shows his moral degradation and selfishness. Even though he is the biological father of Eppie, he does not acknowledge her as his own child. He confesses to his deed only when Dunstan Cass' body is found in Stone Pits virtually at the end of the novel. It is only then that he wants to adopt Eppie. All this amply proves his procrastinating nature and the fact that his is morally a weak character.

(iv) Dolly Winthrop, even though a minor character in the novel 'Silas Mariner' is one of the lovable characters of the novel. She is the wife of the wheelwright, Ben Winthrop and mother of Aaron who later marries Eppie. She is characterized as a "good wholesome woman," "a woman of scrupulous conscience", and someone who takes upon herself to help Silas. She visits Silas along with Aaron and a present of lard cakes and talks to Silas about going to the church. Though initially she does not make any impact on Silas, she is the one who slowly brings him back into the mainstream. She gets Eppie christened and that is the first time that Silas visits the Church. She later raises Eppie along with Silas and in due course of time becomes Eppie's godmother and mother-in-law. She herself believes in customs and traditions and persuades Silas to always trust in God and go to church. She is kind and patient, devoutly religious and open and friendly. Therefore, even though a minor character, Dolly Winthrop has a major role to play.

All India *2018*

CBSE Board Solved Paper

Time Allowed : 3 Hours   *Maximum Marks : 100*

General Instructions:

(i) This paper is divided into three sections : A, B and C. All the sections are compulsory.

(ii) Separate instructions are given with each section and question, wherever necessary. Read these instructions very carefully and follow them faithfully.

(iii) Do not exceed the prescribed word limit while answering the questions.

SECTION A: Reading

(30 Marks)

1. Read the passage given below:

   1. When you grow up in a place where it rains five months a year, wise elders help you to get acquainted with the rain early. They teach you that it is ignorant to think that it is the same rain falling every day. Oh no, the rain is always doing different things at different times. There is rain that is gentle, and there is also rain that falls too hard and damages the crops. Hence, the prayer for the sweet rain that helps the crops to grow.

   2. The monsoon in the Naga hills goes by the native name, khuthotei (which means the rice-growing season). It lasts from May to early or mid-October. The local residents firmly believe that Durga Puja in October announces the end of rain. After that, one might expect a couple of short winter showers, and the spring showers in March and April. Finally, comes the "big rain" in May; proper rainstorms accompanied by heart-stopping lightning and ear-splitting thunder. I have stood out in storms looking at lightning arc across dark skies, a light-and-sound show that can go on for hours.

   3. This is the season when people use the word sezuo or süzu to refer to the week-long rains, when clothes don't dry and smell of mould, when fungus forms on the floor and when you can't see the moon or the stars because of the rainclouds. But you learn not to complain. Rain, after all, is the farmer's friend and brings food to the table. Rituals and festivals centre around the agricultural rhythm of life, which is the occupation of about 70 percent of the population.

   4. The wise learn to understand its ways. I grew up hearing my grandfather say, "It's very windy this year. We'll get good rain." If the windy season was short and weak, he worried there might not be enough rain for the crops. I learned the interconnectedness of the seasons from childhood, and marvelled at how the wind could bring rain. Another evening, many rainy seasons ago, my paternal aunt observed the new moon and worried, "Its legs are in the air, we're in for some heavy rain." She was right. That week, a storm cut off power lines and brought down trees and bamboos.

   5. Eskimos boast of having a hundred names for snow. Norwegians in the north can describe all kinds of snow by an equal amount of names : pudder, powder snow, wet snow, slaps, extra wet snow, tight snowfall, dry snow, and at least 95 more categories of snow. Likewise, in India we have names and names for rain. Some are common, some are passing into history.

   6. The rains are also called after flowering plants and people believe that the blossoming of those plants draws out rain. Once the monsoons set in, field work is carried out in earnest and the work of uprooting and transplanting paddy in flooded terrace fields is done. The months of hard labour are June, July and August. In August, as the phrogü plant begins to bloom, a rain will fall. This August rain, also called phrogü, is a sign that the time for cultivation is over. If any new grain seeds are sown, they may not sprout; even if they do sprout, they are not likely to bear grain. The rain acts as a kind of farmer's almanac.

   7. The urban population of school-goers and office-goers naturally dislikes the monsoon and its accompanying problems of landslides, muddy streets and periodic infections. For non-farmers, the month of September can be depressing, when the rainfall is incessant and the awareness persists that the monsoons will last out till October. One needs

to have the heart of a farmer to remain grateful for the watery days, and be able to observe - from what seems to the inexperienced as a continuous downpour - the many kinds of rain. Some of the commonly known rain-weeks are named after the plants that alternately bloom in August and September. The native belief is that the flowers draw out the rain.

8. Each rain period has a job to fulfil : October rain helps garlic bulbs to form, while kümünyo rain helps the rice bear grain. Without it, the ears of rice cannot form properly. End October is the most beautiful month in the Naga hills, as the fields turn gold and wild sunflowers bloom over the slopes, all heralding the harvest. Prayers go up for protecting the fields from storms, and the rains to retreat because the grain needs to stand in the sun and ripen. The cycle nears completion a few weeks before the harvest, and the rain does retreat so thoroughly from the reaped furrows that the earth quickly turns hard. The months of rain become a distant memory until it starts all over again.

On the basis of your uderstanding of the above passage, complete the statements given below with the help of options that follow:

(a) The rains are called after flowering plants because
   (i) heavy rains kill plants.
   (ii) flowers grow in the rainy season.
   (iii) it is believed that the plants bring the rain.
   (iv) flowers grow all the year round.

(b) The rain is like a calendar for farmers because
   (i) it tells them when to sow and when to harvest.
   (ii) it tells them the birthdays of their children.
   (iii) each month has a time for plantation.
   (iv) different kinds of rain tell different things.

(c) People who live in cities don't like rain because
   (i) it brings mud and sickness with it.
   (ii) they are not bothered about the farmers.
   (iii) they don't like the plants that grow during the rain.
   (iv) going shopping becomes difficult.

(d) People pray asking the rain to retreat because
   (i) the fungus and mould need to dry.
   (ii) children don't get a chance to play.
   (iii) the crops need the sun and heat to ripen.
   (iv) they like to pray.

Answer the following questions briefly:

(e) Why do the elders want you to understand the rains in the Naga hills?

(f) What does Durga Puja mean to the farmers of the Naga hills?

(g) What kind of rain is called sezuo?

(h) What is the occupation of more than half the population of the Naga hills?

(i) How is the heart of the farmer different from that of the city person?

(j) When does rain become a memory in the minds of the people of the Naga hills?

(k) Find words from the passage which mean the same as the following:
   (i) flowering (para 6)
   (ii) nonstop (para 7)

2. Read the passage given below:

1. Every morning Ravi gives his brain an extra boost. We're not talking about drinking strong cups of coffee or playing one of those mind-training video games advertised all over Facebook. "I jump onto my stationary bike and cycle for 45 minutes to work," says Ravi. "When I get to my desk, my brain is at peak activity for a few hours." After his mental focus comes to a halt later in the day, he starts it with another short spell of cycling to be able to run errands.

2. Ride, work, ride, repeat. It's a scientifically proven system that describes some unexpected benefits of cycling. In a recent study in the Journal of Clinical and Diagnostic Research, scientists found that people scored higher on tests of memory, reasoning, and planning after 30 minutes of spinning on a stationary bike than they did before they rode the bike. They also completed the tests faster after pedalling.

3. Exercise is like fertilizer for your brain. All those hours spent on exercising your muscles, create rich capillary beds not only in leg and hip muscles, but also in your brain. More blood vessels in your brain and muscles mean more oxygen and nutrients to help them work. When you pedal, you also force more nerve cells to fire. The result : you double or triple the production of these cells - literally building your brain. You also release neurotransmitters (the messengers between your brain cells) so all those cells, new and old, can communicate with each other for better, faster functioning. That's a pretty profound benefit to cyclists.

4. This kind of growth is especially important with each passing birthday, because as we age, our brains shrink and those connections weaken. Exercise restores and protects the brain cells. Neuroscientists say, "Adults who exercise display sharper memory skills, higher concentration levels, more fluid thinking, and greater problem-solving ability than those who are sedentary."

5. Cycling also elevates your mood, relieves anxiety, increases stress resistance, and even banishes the blues. "Exercise works in the same way as psychotherapy and antidepressants in the treatment of depression, maybe better," says Dr. Manjari. A recent study analyzing 26 years of research finds that even some exercise - as little as 20 to 30 minutes a day - can prevent depression over the long term.

6. Remember: although it's healthy, exercise itself is a stress, especially when you're just getting started

or getting back into riding. When you first begin to exert yourself, your body releases a particular hormone to raise your heart rate, blood pressure, and blood glucose levels, says Meher Ahluwalia, PhD, a professor of integrative physiology. As you get fitter, it takes a longer, harder ride to trigger that same response.

On the basis of your understanding of the passage, complete the statements given below with the help of the options that follow:

(a) Ravi gets his brain to work at peak level by
    (i) drinking three cups of coffee.
    (ii) playing games that need brain activity.
    (iii) cycling on a stationary bike.
    (iv) taking tablets to pump up his brain.

(b) When nerve cells work during exercise then
    (i) the body experiences stress.
    (ii) the brain is strengthened by multiplying them.
    (iii) you start to lose your temper.
    (iv) your stationary cycle starts to beep.

Answer the following questions briefly:

(c) How does exercise help the brain?
(d) Why does Ravi do a circuit of 'ride, work, ride'?
(e) What is the work of neurotransmitters?
(f) What benefits other than greater brain activity does one get from cycling?
(g) Why is exercise so important for adults?
(h) How is exercise itself a stress?
(i) Find words from the passage which mean the same as the following:
    (i) manure (para 3)   (ii) inactive (para 4)

3. Read the passage given below:

Keeping cities clean is essential for keeping their residents healthy. Our health depends not just on personal hygiene and nutrition, but critically also on how clean we keep our cities and their surroundings. The spread of dengue and chikungunya are intimately linked to the deteriorating state of public health conditions in our cities.

The good news is that waste management to keep cities clean is now getting attention through the Swachh Bharat Mission. However, much of the attention begins and stops with the brooms and the dustbins, extending at most to the collection and transportation of the mixed waste to some distant or not so distant place, preferably out of sight.

The challenge of processing and treating the different streams of solid waste, and safe disposal of the residuals in scientific landfills, has received much less attention in municipal solid waste management than is expected from a health point of view.

One of the problems is that instead of focusing on waste management for health, we have got sidetracked into "waste for energy". If only we were to begin by not mixing the biodegradable component of solid waste (close to 60 percent of the total) in our cities with the dry waste, and instead use this stream of waste for composting and producing a gas called methane.

City compost from biodegradable waste provides an alternative to farmyard manure (like cow-dung). It provides an opportunity to simultaneously clean up our cities and help improve agricultural productivity and quality of the soil. Organic manure or compost plays a very important role as a supplement to chemical fertilisers in enriching the nutrient-deficient soils. City compost can be the new player in the field.

Benefits of compost on the farm are well-known. The water holding capacity of the soil which uses compost helps with drought-proofing, and the requirement of less water per crop is a welcome feature for a water-stressed future. By making the soil porous, use of compost also makes roots stronger and resistant to pests and decay. Farmers using compost, therefore, need less quantity of pesticides. There is also evidence to suggest that horticulture crops grown with compost have better flavour, size, colour and shelf-life.

City compost has the additional advantage of being weed-free unlike farmyard manure which brings with it the seeds of undigested grasses and requires a substantial additional labour cost for weeding as the crops grow. City compost is also rich in organic carbon, and our soils are short in this.

Farmers clearly recognize the value of city compost. If city waste was composted before making it available to the farmers for applying to the soil, cities would be cleaned up and the fields around them would be much more productive.

Quite apart from cleaning up the cities of biodegradable waste, this would be a major and sustainable contribution to improving the health of our soil without further damage by excessive chemical inputs. What a marvellous change from waste to health!

The good news is that some states are regularly laying plastic roads. Plastic roads will not only withstand future monsoon damage but will also solve a city's problem of disposing of non-recyclable plastic. It is clear that if the mountains of waste from our cities were to be recycled into road construction material, it would tackle the problem of managing waste while freeing up scarce land.

(a) On the basis of your understanding of the above passage, make notes on it using headings and sub-headings. Use recognisable abbreviations wherever necessary (minimum four) and a format you consider suitable. Also supply an appropriate title to it.

(b) Write a summary of the passage in about 80 words.

SECTION B: Advanced Writing Skills

(30 Marks)

4. You are Faiz/Falak Mazumdar living at 39, Udampur Colony, Shimla. You decide to hold a dinner party to congratulate your grandparents on their golden wedding anniversary. Draft a formal invitation in not more than 50 words to all family members to attend a grand dinner at home.

OR

You are Harish/Harshita of 12, Seva Nagar, Pune. You want to sell your flat as you are shifting to another city for work. Draft a suitable advertisement in not more than 50 words to be published in *The Pune Times* under the classified columns.

5. You are Neeraj/Neeraja Shekhar, Principal, Vasant Public School, Pune. Your school has just started a music department. Write a letter to the Manager of Melody House, Pune, wholesale suppliers of musical instruments, placing an order for musical instruments for the school. Ask for a discount on the catalogue prices. (120 - 150 words)

OR

Bal Vidya Public School, Bhilai, urgently requires a post-graduate teacher to teach political science for which they have placed an advertisement in *The Bhilai Express*. You are Sanjay/Sanjana Sharma from 21, Vasant Marg, Bhilai. Draft a letter including a CV, applying for the advertised post. (120 - 150 words)

6. Recent floods in many metropolitan cities of the country during the monsoon season laid bare the hollowness of the claims of the civic authorities of their preparedness. The poor had to bear the brunt of the problem while no one was ever held accountable. Write an article in 150 - 200 words on the common man's woes during the monsoons and the need for accountability of the officials concerned. You are Sumit/Smita Verma.

OR

You are Ali/Alia, Head girl/Head boy of your school. You are deeply disturbed by the rising cases of aggressive behaviour of students in your school. You decide to speak during the morning assembly about it. Write a speech on 'Indiscipline in Schools'. (150 - 200 words)

7. "Academic excellence is the only requirement for a successful career." Write a debate either for or against the motion. (150 - 200 words)

OR

MMD School, Nashik, recently organised a science symposium on the topic : 'Effect of pollution on quality of life'. You are Amit/Amita Raazdan, editor of the school magazine. Write a report on the event for your school magazine. (150 - 200 words)

SECTION C: Textbooks and Long Reading Text

(40 Marks)

8. Read the extract given below and answer the questions that follow:
... and clear rills
That for themselves a cooling covert make
'Gainst the hot season; the mid forest brake,
Rich with the sprinkling of fair musk-rose blooms;
....
   (a) Identify the poem and the poet.
   (b) What is the role of the clear rills?

   (c) How has the mid forest brake become rich?
   (d) Name the figure of speech in 'cooling covert'.

OR

..... On their slag heap, these children
Wear skins peeped through by bones and spectacles of steel
With mended glass, like bottle bits on stones.
   (a) Name the poem and the poet.
   (b) Explain : 'slag heap'.
   (c) What future awaits these children?
   (d) Name the figure of speech used in the third line.

9. Answer any four of the following questions in 30 - 40 words each:
   (a) What does the poet's smile in the poem, 'My Mother at Sixty-six' show?
   (b) "Listening to them, I see two distinct worlds ... ." In the context of Mukesh, the bangle maker's son, which two worlds is Anees Jung referring to?
   (c) Though the sharecroppers of Champaran received only one-fourth of the compensation, how can the Champaran struggle still be termed a huge success and victory?
   (d) Which article in McLeery's suitcase played perhaps the most significant role in Evans' escape and how?
   (e) Why does Derry's mother not want him to go back to visit Mr. Lamb?
   (f) What considerations influenced the Tiger King to get married?

10. Answer the following question in 120 - 150 words:
In one's approach to life one should be practical and not live in a world of dreams. How is Jansie's attitude different from that of Sophie?

OR

Fear is something that we must learn to overcome if we want to succeed in life. How did Douglas get over his fear of water?

11. Answer the following question in 120 - 150 words:
At the end of the storytelling session, why does Jack consider himself 'caught in an ugly middle position'?

OR

It may take a long time for oppression to be resisted, but the seeds of rebellion are sowed early in life. How did Zitkala-Sa face oppression as a child and how did she overcome it?

12. Answer the following question in 120 - 150 words :
How does the perception and attitude of the villagers of Raveloe towards Silas Marner change from the beginning to the end of the novel?

OR

How do you perceive Dr. Kemp based on his interaction with Griffin? (The Invisible Man)

13. Answer the following question in 120 - 150 words:
How is Godfrey Cass different from his younger brother, Dunstan?

OR

"Misdirected and self-serving ambition essentially remains an exercise in futility." Describe Griffin's character in the light of the above statement.

Solutions

SECTION - A

1.   **(1 × 4 = 4 Marks)**

(a) (iii) it is believed that the plants bring the rain.

(b) (i) it tells them when to sow and when to harvest.

(c) (i) it brings mud and sickness with it.

(d) (iii) the crops need the sun and heat to ripen.

                           (1 × 6 = 6 Marks)

(e) The elders want us to understand the rain because it can do different things at different times. It can be gentle and sweet to help the crops grow, or it can be hard enough to damage the crops. So, it tells us when to sow and when to harvest.

(f) Durga Puja heralds the end of rains.

(g) Sezuo refers to week-long rainstorms accompanied with heart-stopping lightning and ear-splitting thunder, when clothes do not dry and smell of mould, fungus forms on the floor, and you can't see the moon or stars because of the rainclouds.

(h) Agriculture or farming is the occupation of more than half the population of Nagaland.

(i) The heart of the farmer is grateful to the rains for irrigating his crops; the rain is his friend and brings food to his table. On the other hand, the heart of the city person finds rain depressing and dislikes monsoon because of its accompanying problems of landslides, muddy streets and periodic infections.

(j) The rain becomes a memory a few weeks before the harvest, at the end of October.

(k)   **(1 × 2 = 2 Marks)**
    (i) blossoming   (ii) incessant/ continuous

Note

1. *When answering MCQs (Question No.1.1) choose the option which is the closest answer from amongst the options.*
2. *For Factual questions like e.g. "What kind of rain is called sezuo", include only the information given in the passage.*
3. *While answering the 'How' question like "How is the heart of the farmer different from that of the city person", write your answer comparing the two.*
4. *While answering the 'Why' question like "Why does Ravi do a circuit of 'ride, work, ride'", you may begin your answer by explaining the whole reason behind him doing so and then closing the answer by "For this reason, Ravi …….OR you may begin your answer with 'Ravi does a circuit of ………' or a similar phrase.*

2.   **(1 × 2 = 2 Marks)**

(a) (iii) cycling on a stationary bike

(b) (ii) the brain is strengthened by multiplying them.

                          (1 × 6 = 6 Marks)

(c) Exercise acts as a fertilizer for the brain. It creates rich capillary beds which bring in more oxygen and nutrients for it to work; multiplies the nerve cells and releases neurotransmitters which facilitate communication between old nerve cells and new ensuring better, faster functioning.

(d) Cycling for 45 minutes to work gives Ravi's brain an extra boost, peaking his faculties of memory, reasoning and planning at the desk for a few hours. When his mental focus comes to a halt later in the day, he undertakes another short spell at cycling to be able to run errands. For this reason, he takes the circuit of ride, work, ride.

(e) Neurotransmitters are messengers between brain cells. So, they facilitate communication between the cells for better and faster functioning.

(f) Cycling also elevates mood, relieves anxiety, increases stress resistance, banishes the blues, and prevents depression.

(g) Exercise is important for adults because it restores and protects brain cells and thus, checks age-induced deterioration of brain power. Adults who exercise display sharper memory skills, higher levels of concentration, more fluid thinking, and greater problem-solving activity.

(h) Exercise itself is a stress because when one begins to exert oneself, the body releases a particular hormone to raise the heart rate, blood pressure and blood glucose levels.

(i)   **(1 × 2 = 2 Marks)**
(i) fertilizer   (ii) sedentary

3.   **(5 Marks)**

(a) **Note-making**

       MANAGEMENT OF CITY WASTE

1. Cleanliness and health
   1.1. Clean city, healthy resdts
   1.2. Factors of hlth
      1.2.1. Clnlss of city
      1.2.2. Prsnl hygiene and nutrn
   1.3. Lack of clnlss means
      1.3.1. deterng pub. hlth
      1.3.2. chikn.& dengue
2. WM in cities
   2.1. Necessary to keep cities clean
   2.2. Being impltd through SBM
      2.2.1. Only brooms & dustbin
      2.2.2. trnspng mixed waste
3. Challenges of WM
   3.1. Segn of wet waste for composting & CH_4
   3.2. Safe disposal of residuals
   3.3. Prioritising focus
      3.3.1. WM for hlth 1st
      3.3.2. WM for energy(methane)later
4. City compost/org. manure

4.1. Alt. to farm manure

4.2. Serves dual purpose (clean cities, farm benefits)

4.3. Supplements chem. fertilizers

5. Compost benefits for farm

5.1. Holds water

5.1.1. Saves water in water-stressed future

5.1.2. Evades drought

5.2. Makes soil porous & roots resistant to pests & decay

5.2.1. Reduces use of pesticide

5.3. Improves horticulture crops

5.4. Weed-free unlike farm manure

5.4.1. Saves weeding costs

5.5. Rich source of org. Carbon

6. Benefits of plastic roads

6.1. Withstand monsoon damage

6.2. Dispose of plastic waste safely

6.3. Free landfill sites/ scarce land

Note

1. *The passage is on the dirt and slime present in the cities and how proper waste management can help in making the cities clean. So the title must be related to the main idea and should have the key words viz. 'City', 'Waste,' 'Management' etc.*

2. *It should always contain phrases. Avoid using complete sentences. For e.g.*

   1. Cleanliness and health

      1.1. Clean city, healthy resdts

      1.2. Factors of hlth

        1.2.1. Clnlss of city

        1.2.2. Prsnl hygiene and nutrnAND NOT Cleanliness and health are important for every individual . A clean city with healthy residents etc ....

3. *Include a minimum of 4-6 distinctly different recognizable short forms i.e. abbreviations of the words in the notes as done in the solution.*

Key to Abbreviation

Abbreviation	Word
resd^{ts}	residents
hlth.	health
prsnl.	personal
nutr^n	nutrition
deter^{ng}	deteriorating
pub.	public
chikn.	chikangunya
&	and
WM	waste management
impltd	implemented
SBM	Swachha Bharat Mission
transp^{ng}	transporting
seg^n	segregating
CH_4	methane
org.	organic
alt.	alternative
chem.	chemical

(b) **Summary:** (3 Marks)

We must keep our cities clean to ensure public health and to ward off diseases. Waste Management, enforced under Swachha Bharat Mission must focus on waste for health, *i.e.*, on segregating organic waste before processing it for compost and methane. City compost is a weeding-free alternative to farm manure; supplements chemical fertilizers; saves water; enriches soil with organic carbon; reduces pesticide use, and enhances horticulture crops. Plastic roads, safe from monsoon damage, are an effective means of disposing plastic waste and freeing scarce land. (83 words)

SECTION - B

4. (4 Marks)

Falak Majumdar
requests the pleasure of your gracious company at the
GRAND DINNER
to celebrate the joyous occasion of the
GOLDEN WEDDING ANNIVERSARY
of his grandparents
Mrs. Anila Banerjee & Mr. Anirban Badopadhyay
at 8p.m. on Saturday, the 15th of September,
20XX, at his residence.

R.S.V.P.
39, Udampur Colony, Shimla
Ph: XXXXX65431

OR

SALE/PURCHASE

For immediate sale - East facing, freehold, spacious, 3 BHK+ Study, 2 washrooms, 3 balconies, corner flat, 3rd Floor, w/work, new paint, reserved parking, power backup, 24x7 water supply, enclosed society, security, metro stn., school and hospital within 2 km.

Price negotiable. Contact: Harshita at 12, Seva Nagar, Pune; 9999999999

5. (6 Marks)

Vasant Public School
Pune

05 March, 20XX

The Manager,
Melody House
Pune

Subject: Placing an order for certain musical instruments for the school

Dear Sir,

Having decided to start a Music Department in the school from the forthcoming session, I would like to place an order to purchase the following musical instruments from Melody House. With reference to your advertisement claiming you are the leading wholesale suppliers in the city, I expect each instrument supplied to be new, unused and of the best brand.

Kindly send the following items with their price quotations, at the earliest.

Harmonium	-	2
Guitar	-	2
Set of Drums	-	1
Violin	-	2
Tabla	-	2
Cello	-	1

I shall be looking forward to a reasonable discount on the catalogue prices; for, we are likely to place more orders as our music department grows with the passing years.

Thanking you

Yours sincerely,

Neerja Shekhar

Principal

OR

21, Vasant Marg,

Bhilai

05 March, 20XX

The Principal

Bal Vidya Public School

Bhilai

Sub: Application for the position of PGT-Political Science

Dear Sir/Ma'am,

With reference to your advertisement for the requirement of a post-graduate teacher in Political Science, I hereby apply for the same.

I have passed my post-graduation with distinction in Political Science from CV Raman University, Bilaspur.

I have been imparting private tuitions to senior secondary school students for around two years while I was pursuing my B. Ed, and my students have passed with good results. Kindly find attached my CV for the details.

Thanking you

Yours faithfully

Sanjana Sharma

Enclosures: 1. C V

2. Educational Certificates

3. Two passport size photographs

C V

Name: Sanjana Sharma

DOB: Feb 25, 1998

Father's name: Shri. Shyam Sharma

Address: 21, Vasant Marg, Bhilai

Educational qualifications:

Class X   - DPS, Bhilai   89%

Class XII   - DPS, Bhilai   93%   (Pol. Sc.- 99)

B.A. Honours   - CV Raman University   Pol. Sc. -72%

M.A. (Pol. Sc.) - CV Raman University   76%

Professional Qualifications:

B.Ed. (Pol. Sc., History) - CV Raman University   1st Class

Experience: Private tuition to Class XII students for two years.

References: 1. Dr. D.P. Yadav, Principal, DPS, Bhilai.

2. Dr. Adya Gandhi, HOD, Political Science, CV Raman University.

6. Monsoons in India: Rain or ruin?   **(10 Marks)**

By *Sumit Verma*

Monsoons are crucial for India's farming sector. Agriculture is India's mainstay and monsoon its major source of irrigation. So, farmers pray for a good monsoon. The situation is just the opposite in the metropolitan cities that are bursting at their seams under a continual influx of people from rural and suburban areas seeking better earning opportunities. The real estate consumes more and more land to accommodate them, turning metros into dense concrete jungles. Proper drainage is no consideration in this scenario of mindless construction everywhere. So, when monsoon rains lash, they find no outlet and submerge cities. Open manholes suck in people and whole cars too! More people in cities generate more garbage, much of which ends up in rivers, polluting them and raising their beds. So, when monsoon rains arrive, rivers overflow their banks; and, cities already struggling with water logging are caught unawares in the rampaging deluge. Floods indeed have become a routine affair!

Civic authorities routinely parrot their claims that drains have been desilted and everything is under control to take on the monsoon fury. However, it takes just one spell of a heavy downpour to dash all their claims. Commuters struggle through waterlogged roads cursing the authorities. But, the brunt of the civic officials' apathy is borne by the underprivileged section of the society—the homeless, the slum-dwellers, the wanderers. Many homeless die, humble dwellings are swept away in the floods, and inundated roads make sure that no food reaches the starving poor. When the water recedes, mosquitoes breed and diseases consume more poor lives.

The system must fix accountability of lives lost and inconveniences caused on the authorities concerned, so that the monsoon brings rain rather than ruin.

OR

Indiscipline in School

Honourable Madam Principal, respected teachers and my fellow students!

A very good morning to all!

With much distress, I stand before you to speak on the rising incidents of student aggression in our school. Some senior students despite rebukes, impositions, and fines imposed have refused to curb their tendency to enter into brawls over petty issues, play truant, bully others and misbehave with teachers, oblivious to the influence it casts on their juniors, for a few of these issues have been witnessed in junior classes too.

Senior students, you are the beacons to show the right path to the juniors. Show the value education you have received. Follow the ideals of the apostle of peace-Mahatma Gandhi. Ask yourself. Do you feel good after a fight? Does the issue get resolved after an altercation? Doesn't bullying bring out your ugly side? Step into the victim's shoes and discover the emotional trauma your behaviour caused. It is time to act responsibly. Help each other to resolve issues rather than instigate for undesirable behaviour.

Teachers and parents must ensure that their actions do not influence the young the wrong way. They should inspire the young to follow role models. Schools must include Value Education in all classes, including Senior Secondary. The delinquents should be counselled and reformed, not punished. They have lost their way. They only need to be brought back on track.

Together, we all can establish peace and happiness in our lives.

Thank you.

7. **Debate**   **(10 Marks)**

AGAINST THE MOTION

Honourable Chairperson, respected Judges, the esteemed guests, my worthy opponents, and my dear friends!

A very good morning to all!

The motion for the debate is, 'Academic excellence is the only requirement for a successful career' and I stand here to speak **against** the motion.

Academic excellence is the measure of a student's capability to learn what is taught and script it in the answer paper to obtain maximum marks. The education system has been so designed that marks are considered as the determinant of a person's calibre and the ticket to success in one's chosen career. Employers, in general, screen their candidates on the basis of marks obtained in written examination.

However, it has often been seen that the high scorers falter in the dispensation of the work that is expected of them and some average or low scorers exceed expectations. How does one explain this phenomenon?

Well, life is much more than what is learnt in books and reproduced in tests. Academic knowledge aids the understanding of life and helps to live life better. What is learnt in books is of little use, though, unless it is applied to life situations. Life invariably throws contingencies that can be safeguarded with life skills, such as focus, self assurance, communication, interpersonal relations, critical thinking, multitasking, teamwork, leadership, etc. So, one needs to develop an all round personality and be adept in life skills to achieve success.

Times have changed and so has the definition of success. Many new career options have opened that require life skills more than academic excellence. Talent in any domain can be honed to provide recreation; and skills of any kind can be developed to provide life solutions; both, generate income and spell success.

So, academic excellence is not the only requirement for a successful career.

Thank you!

OR

FOR THE MOTION

Honourable Chairperson, respected Judges, the esteemed guests, my worthy opponents, and my dear friends!

A very good morning to all!

The motion for the debate is, 'Academic excellence is the only requirement for a successful career' and I stand here to speak for the motion.

Since the ancient times when language and learning was discovered, man has taken pride in scholarship; has revered men of letters; and, followed the word of the learned. If this is not a measure of success, then what else is?

Students who work hard to obtain maximum marks, develop deep understanding of life through the meticulously prepared curriculum, and strengthen their capabilities to apply their knowledge to life situations. Sincere students go beyond the prescribed texts for the information they are seeking, and develop resourcefulness. Academic excellence opens the doors of higher learning for them. They research for new knowledge and contribute to the advancement of the civilization.

Fierce competition for numbered positions, in the wake of population explosion, makes academic excellence mandatory for aspirants. Civil servants, bank officials, technical experts and other professionals who succeed in competitive examinations designed to test the required competencies, have already been seasoned by their strife as competent individuals who can take decisions in the interest of the nation.

So, academic excellence is indeed the only requirement for a successful career.

Thank you.

OR

Report: Science Symposium on 'Effect of Pollution on Quality of Life' held at MMD School, Nashik

By *Amit Raazdan*

A two-day Science Symposium on the topic, 'Effect of Pollution on Quality of Life' was held in the central auditorium of MMD School Nashik, between 10:30 am to 6:30 pm on the 16th and 17th of December, 20XX. The symposium was chaired by the noted scientist, Dr. Vasudha Narayan.

The following was the agenda of the Symposium:

Day 1

Registration: 10:00-10:30 a.m.

Welcome note: 10:30 a.m. by the Vice-Principal of MMD School, Mr. Hemant Trehan.

Resource person's address:

Morning session (11:00 a.m.-2:00p.m.): Workshop on kinds of pollution

Lunch break: 2:00p.m.-3:00 p.m.

Afternoon session (3:00-6:00p.m.): Causes and Effects of pollution

Day 2

Morning session: Global challenges to pollution

Afternoon session: Intervention strategies: What works for India

High tea: 6:30 p.m.

The resource person for the symposium, Dr. Shishir Dey, Director, Indian Meteorology Department, New Delhi, set the ball rolling with an enlightened talk on the need for humans to mend their ways.

The speakers included research scholars from various universities, science teachers from different schools in the city, and some senior secondary students of science from MMD School.

The keynote address on the first day was delivered by Dr. Rehmat Ali, HOD, Science Department, MMD School; and on the second day, by the Principal MMD School, Dr. Ira Bedi; who also concluded the discussion with her closing remarks. Ankush Rahi, Head Boy, MMD School, delivered the vote of thanks to the esteemed gathering for enlightening the students with their thoughts and opinions. The guests departed after a high tea and informal exchanges with the hosts.

SECTION - C

8. **(1 × 4 = 4 Marks)**

(a) Poem: A Thing of Beauty
Poet: John Keats

(b) The role of the clear rills is to make a cooling covert, *i.e.*, to provide a cool shelter.

(c) The mid-forest brake has become rich because of the blossoming of beautiful musk-roses all over.

(d) 'Cooling covert' creates a beautiful imagery and makes use of alliteration with repeated 'c' sound.

OR

(a) Poem: An Elementary School Classroom in a Slum
Poet: Stephen Spender

(b) 'Slag heap' refers to the mountains of garbage including industrial waste (slag) on which slum children play.

(c) A dismal and miserable future, painted with fog(not bright) awaits these slum kids.

(d) The comparison, 'like bottle bits on stone' is a simile; 'bottle bits' is an alliteration with '*b*' sound repeated.

 *Note*

1. Be precise and to the point.

2. Since there is an internal choice in this question, try picking up the extract which you are familiar with.

3. Try answering all the questions of the extract that you have picked up.

4. For questions like "Identify the poem and the poet" write the full name of the poem and the poet with the correct spellings.

5. For questions like "What is the role of the clear rills ," use the exact phrase from the poem 'cooling covert' and then go on to describe it.

6. Use the language as used in the question. For e.g. " What future awaits these children"? Your answer should either start with – The future that awaits these children is....................OR else you may end the answer with the same phrase.

9. **(3 × 4 = 12 Marks)**

(a) The poet's smile depicts the reassurance that she gives herself as well as her mother in the face of a lurking fear that she may not see her mother alive again, and the guilt of leaving her old mother behind.

(b) The author Anees Jung is talking about Mukesh's poverty-stricken world burdened by the stigma of caste; and, the vicious world of sahukars, policemen, middlemen, law keepers and bureaucrats.

(c) The very fact that the landlords came down to surrender part of their money as well as prestige was in itself a huge victory, the magnitude of the compensation notwithstanding. The agreement broke the deadlock between the peasants and the landlords. The peasants became aware of their rights and learnt to be courageous.

(d) The question paper contained the escape plan which sent the jail authorities in the other direction and facilitated Evans's escape. The semi-inflated rubber tube with pig's blood which Evans used to disguise himself as wounded McLeery could also be taken as the most significant article that helped him escape.

(e) Being new to the area, Derry's mother knew little about Mr. Lamb. Moreover, he lived all alone and had no contact with the outside world. She had seen children tease him and had heard people talk adversely about him. So, she does not want Derry to be in his company.

(f) The astrologers had predicted the Tiger King's death with the hunting of the hundredth tiger. After he had killed all the seventy that were there in his kingdom, he decided to marry a princess from the kingdom with a large population of tigers so that he could reach the count of hundred and prove the astrologers wrong. His vanity, however, proved the prediction right.

Note

1. Choose your questions with care since there is internal choice in this question.

2. Each 3-mark question must have at least two-three value points.

3. For questions like "What does the poet's smile in the poem ' My Mother at Sixty-Six' show " you must write the answer in your own words. Avoid picking up phrases from the poem.

4. For questions requiring specific answers like "Which article in McLeery's suitcase played perhaps the most significant role in Evans' escape and how"- remember to answer both parts of the question separately.

Be very specific and to the point in your answers.

10. **(6 Marks)**

Jansie is a practical girl, aware of her humble moorings and resigned to her situation that she is not one of the fortunate teenagers who can afford to dream, fulfil their aspirations and go places. She has come to terms with the fact that she is destined only to work in the biscuit factory, and it is useless to harbour dreams; for, they will never come true. However, she also believes, that dreams are achievable if one works really hard for it and earns a lot of money.

Sophie, on the other hand, has big dreams and unrealistic, too. She dreams of becoming a manager, actress, fashion designer or boutique owner without being qualified for, and without having to work for, any. She is far removed from reality. The unknown and unexplored fascinates her. She is beguiled by the mystique of her brother's world. She is so engrossed in her dreams that she fantasises about a date with Danny Casey, the football player her brother idolizes, and is left heartbroken.

OR

Douglas developed a terrifying fear of water after a wave knocked him down and suffocated him when he was only three years old. At around eleven, when he joined the YMCA to learn to swim, a bully threw him into the pool one day, and Douglas blacked out struggling hard to escape drowning. This worsened his fears and handicapped him for a long time, until he hired an instructor to learn to swim.

To make Douglas feel safe, the instructor tied a belt around his waist and connected it to a pulley with a rope. Starting like this, Douglas practised swimming in the pool five days a week, an hour per day, for six months; and, finally was able to learn swimming. Though this helped him overcome his fear of water to a good extent, the dread returned when he was all alone in the pool. Determined to get rid of the tiniest vestiges of this terror, he went to Lake Wentworth in New Hampshire, dived off a dock at Triggs Island and swam two miles across the lake. Still not sure, he went to Meade Glacier, dived into Warm Lake and swam across to the other shore and back. Then, he was fully confident that he had left his fears behind, for good.

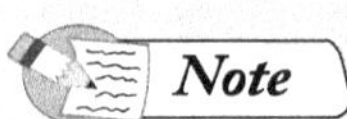

Note

1. *Each 6-mark question must have at least four value points.*

2. *This question has internal choice. Therefore, choose with care.*

3. *Answer to the point including your own opinion in places where it is deemed necessary by the question especially when you are comparing two things.*

4. *Pick out specific examples from the text to support your answer.*

5. *Quote straight from the text wherever required but do so only when you are sure of the words.*

6. *For e.g. for a question like "In one's approach to life one should be practical and not live in a world of dreams. How is Jansie's attitude different from that of Sophie"- you must answer both the parts separately.*

7. *You can build your answer on the following value points.*

JANSIE

1. *Jansie - a practical girl, aware of her humble moorings and resigned to her situation*

2. *Knows is not one of the fortunate teenagers who can afford to dream, fulfil their aspirations and go places.*

3. *Has come to terms with the fact - destined only to work in the biscuit factory- useless to harbour dreams- will never come true.*

4. *Also believes- in the virtue of hard work.*

SOPHIE

1. *Has big dreams.*

2. *Unrealistic.*

3. *Dreams of becoming a manager, actress, fashion designer or boutique own.*

4. *Not qualified for all.*

5. *Far removed from reality- unknown and unexplored fascinates her.*

6. *Beguiled by the mystique of her brother's world.*

7. *Fantasizes about a date with Danny Casey- can prove to be harmful.*

11.   **(6 Marks)**

Jack routinely built a new story out of the basic Roger in trouble seeking the Owl's advice that turned everything right' to make his daughter Jo fall asleep. But this particular Saturday night, she kept interrupting him seeking clarifications in Roger Skunk's story, flagging errors and offering alternatives. Jack was offended by his parental authority as well as authorship being questioned by Jo. He felt possessive about the details of his story and disliked Jo's suggestions. Modifying the storyline to her satisfaction extended it to a fatiguing length. After all his efforts, Jo still wanted him to change the ending of the story. She wanted him to say that the Mommy was stupid in getting Roger Skunk's earlier awful smell back from the endearing rose smell the wizard had given him; and, that the wizard hit Mommy. Jack felt he was caught in an ugly middle position. He felt caged like Clare. He could neither put Jo to sleep nor help his wife clare.

OR

Children living in oppressive societies become aware of the discrimination and injustice meted out to them in every sphere of life and rebel against the authorities in their own way. Informed by her friend Judewin that the authorities were going to shingle their long hair, Zitkala-Sa resolves to rebel rather than submit. Her mother had told her that captured warriors and cowards had their hair shingled; and she was neither. She musters the courage to fight the atrocity to the best of her ability.

She hides herself under a bed in the darkest corner of a hall. When she is detected and dragged out, she kicks and scratches wildly in resistance. She is overpowered and tied to a chair but she keeps screaming and shaking her head vigorously until she loses her braids to the oppressors.

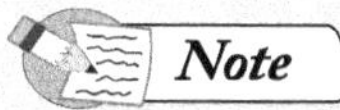

Note

1. *Each 6-mark question must have at least four value points*
2. *This question again has internal choice. Therefore, choose with care.*
3. *Answer to the point including your own opinion in places where it is deemed necessary by the question.*
4. *Pick out specific examples from the text to support your answer*
5. *Quote straight from the text wherever required but do so only when you are sure of the words.*
6. *Only write whatever is required. Do not try to stretch the answer even if it is less than the required words.*
7. *In a question requiring some interpretation For e.g. in question like " It may take a long time for oppression to be resisted, but the seeds of rebellion are sowed early in life. How did Zitkala-Sa face oppression as a child and how did she overcome it" – remember to move from the general to the specific.*
8. *You can build your answer on the following value points.*

GENERAL OBSERVATION

1. *Children living in oppressive societies - aware of the discrimination & injustice.*
2. *Rebel against the authorities in their own way.*

ZITKALA'S REBELLION

1. *Informed byfriend Judewin -shingle their long hair.*
2. *Zitkala-Sa resolves to rebel rather than submit.*
3. *mother had told her - captured warriors and cowards had their hair shingled - she was neither- musters the courage to fight the atrocity.*
4. *Hides herself under a bed in the darkest corner of a hall.*
5. *When detected and dragged out-kicks andscratches wildly in resistance.*
6. *Overpowered and tied to a chair- keeps screaming and shaking her head vigorously until loses braids to the oppressors.*

12.   **(6 Marks)**

Silas Marner is a weaver by profession who leaves Lantern Yard, when his friend William Dane falsely implicates him in a theft of the church gold, to live the life of a recluse in Raveloe. Angry with his fate he relinquishes his religion. The villagers, at first, regard him with awe and suspicion. They fear him for a loner with mystical powers because of his epilepsy and his ability to prepare potions such as the one he cured Sally Oates's dropsy with. So, they create myths about him.

They consider him a miser for he keeps counting his gold coins earned from weaving and fiercely protects them.

However, when Silas finds his gold stolen, and a baby girl at his doorstep, his life turns over a new leaf and soon, the villagers' attitude towards him also undergoes a transformation.

Silas is seen as a doting father and a friendly neighbour. He regains his faith, accepts his destiny and starts attending Church. He decides to leave his past behind and spend the rest of his life in Raveloe. The villagers accept him as one of them. He is no longer an outsider.

OR

The invisible man makes a call on Dr. Kemp, and tells him that he is Giffin, his junior student from University College who had won the medal for chemistry; and, shares his sinister plans with him. Dr. Kemp is aspiring to earn a fellowship with the Royal Society. Their interaction is centred on how Griffin succeeded in achieving invisibility. Dr. Kemp displays his scientist credentials with his queries and skepticism on the subject of invisibility. However, he lacks conviction and doesn't feel the need to tell Griffin that he was not right in doing what he was, nor does he try to dissuade him from carrying out his evil designs. He doesn't realize until much later that Griffin could be rather dangerous. He helps the wounded Griffin; at the same time, realizes he has a responsibility towards the society and informs the police chief to stop Griffin. Thus, he manifests a humane contrast to Griffin's unscrupulous one.

13.   **(6 Marks)**

Godfrey's character is a complete contrast to his younger brother Dunstan's.

Godfrey is a sensible, sober and respectable gentleman, and a deserving successor to his father, Squire Cass. He makes an ideal groom for Nancy Lammeter. However, he displays weakness of character by abandoning his wife Molly. He is unable to make up his mind and lacks the courage to own up his secret marriage to her. He suffers the consequences of his weaknesses.

Dunstan, on the other hand, is a sly and dishonest idler and blackmails his brother with the threat of disclosing his connection to Molly. He is given to reckless ways and squanders his family money. He is constantly in debts and even steals Silas's gold.

OR

Priding himself on being a gold medallist in Chemistry, Griffin misuses his knowledge and expertise to make himself invisible, and carries out 'plans of all the wild and wonderful things' he felt he had now impunity to do.

He nurtures an uninhibited ambition to prove his mettle and enjoy supremacy through invisibility, oblivious to the havoc he wreaks on the lives of others. His was not a pursuit of excellence or a means of sustenance, it was rather, a deranged obsession to satisfy his fancies, amass wealth and comforts of life and eliminate whatever came in his way. He unleashes a reign of terror through this perverted ambition. His arrogance leads him but to his doom.

Griffin misdirected his talent in Science to serve his selfish interests rather than serving humanity. It proved an exercise in futility for it led him only to his doom.

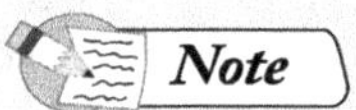

Note

1.   Each 6-mark question must have at least four value points

2.   Both question no. 12 and 13 have internal choice. Therefore, choose with care.

3.   Answer to the point including your own opinion in places where it is deemed necessary by the question.

4.   Pick out specific examples from the text to support your answer.

5.   Quote straight from the text wherever required but do so only when you are sure of the words.

6.   Only write whatever is required. Do not try to stretch the answer even if it is less than the required words.

7.   For question requiring your opinion like " How do you perceive Dr. Kemp based on his interaction with Griffin? (The Invisible Man)- describe the interaction in detail andfeel free to give your own opinion.

8.   You can build your answer on the following value points:

THE INTERACTION

1.   Makes a call on Dr. Kemp-tells him he is Giffin.

2.   Shares his sinister plans.

3.   Dr. Kemp -aspiring to earn a fellowship.

4.   Interaction centred on how Griffin succeeded in achieving invisibility.

5.   Dr. Kemp displaysscientist credentials-queries and skepticism on the subject of invisibility.

HOW I PERCIEVE DR KEMP'S NATURE

1.   Lacks conviction -doesn't feel the need to tell Griffin that he was not right in doing what he was doing.

2.   Doesn't try to dissuade him from carrying out his evil designs.

3.   Realizes much later that Griffin could be rather dangerous.

4.   Helps the wounded Griffin.

5.   Realizes he has a responsibility towards the society and informs the police chief to stop Griffin.

6.   Manifests a humane contrast to Griffin's unscrupulous one.

All India *2017*
CBSE Board Solved Paper

Time Allowed : 3 Hours *Maximum Marks : 100*

General Instructions:

(i) This paper is divided into three sections: A, B and C. All the sections are compulsory.

(ii) Separate instructions are given with each section and question, wherever necessary. Read these instructions very carefully and follow them faithfully.

(iii) Do not exceed the prescribed word limit while answering the questions.

SECTION A: Reading

(30 Marks)

1. Read the passage given below and answer the questions that follow :

   1. We sit in the last row, bumped about but free of stares. The bus rolls out of the dull crossroads of the city, and we are soon in open countryside, with fields of sunflowers as far as the eye can see, their heads all facing us. Where there is no water, the land reverts to desert. While still on level ground, we see in the distance the tall range of the Mount Bogda, abrupt like a shining prism laid horizontally on the desert surface. It is over 5,000 metres high, and the peaks are under permanent snow, in powerful contrast to the flat desert all around. Heaven Lake lies part of the way up this range, about 2,000 metres above sea-level, at the foot of one of the higher snow-peaks.

   2. As the bus climbs, the sky, brilliant before, grows overcast. I have brought nothing warm to wear: it is all down at the hotel in Urumqi. Rain begins to fall. The man behind me is eating overpoweringly smelly goats' cheese. The bus window leaks inhospitably but reveals a beautiful view. We have passed quickly from desert through arable land to pasture, and the ground is now green with grass, the slopes dark with pine. A few cattle drink at a clear stream flowing past moss-covered stones; it is a Constable landscape. The stream changes into a white torrent, and as we climb higher I wish more and more that I had brought with me something warmer than the pair of shorts that have served me so well in the desert. The stream (which, we are told, rises in Heaven Lake) disappears, and we continue our slow ascent. About noon, we arrive at Heaven Lake, and look for a place to stay at the foot, which is the resort area.

   We get a room in a small cottage, and I am happy to note that there are thick quilts on the beds.

   3. Standing outside the cottage we survey our surroundings. Heaven Lake is long, sardine-shaped and fed by snowmelt from a stream at its head. The lake is an intense blue, surrounded on all sides by green mountain walls, dotted with distant sheep. At the head of the lake, beyond the delta of the inflowing stream, is a massive snow-capped peak which dominates the vista; it is part of a series of peaks that culminate, a little out of view, in Mount Bogda itself.

   4. For those who live in the resort, there is a small mess-hall by the shore. We eat here sometimes, and sometimes buy food from the vendors outside, who sell kabab and naan until the last buses leave. The kababs, cooked on skewers over charcoal braziers, are particularly good; highly spiced and well-done. Horse's milk is available too from the local Kazakh herdsmen, but I decline this. I am so affected by the cold that Mr. Cao, the relaxed young man who runs the mess, lends me a spare pair of trousers, several sizes too large but more than comfortable. Once I am warm again, I feel a pre-dinner spurt of energy — dinner will be long in coming — and I ask him whether the lake is good for swimming in.

   5. "Swimming?" Mr. Cao says. "You aren't thinking of swimming, are you?"

   6. "I thought I might," I confess. "What's the water like?"

   7. He doesn't answer me immediately, turning instead to examine some receipts with exaggerated interest. Mr. Cao, with great off-handedness, addresses the air. "People are often drowned here," he says. After a pause, he continues. "When was the last one?" This question is directed at the cook, who is preparing a

tray of mantou (squat, white steamed bread rolls), and who now appears, wiping his doughy hand across his forehead. "Was it the Beijing athlete?" asks Mr. Cao.

On the basis of your understanding of the above passage complete the statements given below with the help of the options that follow :

(a) One benefit of sitting in the last row of the bus was that

(i) the narrator enjoyed the bumps.

(ii) no one stared at him.

(iii) he could see the sunflowers.

(iv) he avoided the dullness of the city.

(b) The narrator was travelling to

(i) Mount Bogda.

(ii) Heaven Lake.

(iii) a 2,000-metre high snow-peak.

(iv) Urumqi.

(c) On reaching the destination the narrator felt relieved because

(i) he had got away from the desert.

(ii) a difficult journey had come to an end.

(iii) he could watch the snow-peak.

(iv) there were thick quilts on the beds.

(d) Mount Bogda is compared to

(i) a horizontal desert surface.

(ii) a shining prism.

(iii) a Constable landscape.

(iv) the overcast sky.

Answer the questions given below briefly :

(e) Which two things in the bus made the narrator feel uncomfortable?

(f) What made the scene look like a Constable landscape?

(g) What did he regret as the bus climbed higher?

(h) Why did the narrator like to buy food from outside?

(i) What is ironic about the pair of trousers lent by Mr. Cao?

(j) Why did Mr. Cao not like the narrator to swim in the lake?

(k) Find words from the passage which mean the same as the following :

(i) sellers (Para 4)

(ii) increased (Para 7)

2. Read the passage given below and answer the questions that follow :

1. Thackeray reached Kittur along with a small British army force and a few of his officers. He thought that the very presence of the British on the outskirts of Kittur would terrorise the rulers and people of Kittur, and that they would lay down their arms. He was quite confident that he would be able to crush the revolt in no time. He ordered that tents be erected on the eastern side for the fighting forces, and a little away on the western slopes tents be put up for the   family members of the officers who had accompanied them. During the afternoon and evening of 20th October, the British soldiers were busy making arrangements for these camps.

2. On the 21st morning, Thackeray sent his political assistants to Kittur fort to obtain a written assurance from all the important officers of Kittur rendering them answerable for the security of the treasury of Kittur. They, accordingly, met Sardar Gurusiddappa and other officers of Kittur and asked them to comply with the orders of Thackeray. They did not know that the people were in a defiant mood. The commanders of Kittur dismissed the agent's orders as no documents could be signed without sanction from Rani Chennamma.

3. Thackeray was enraged and sent for the commander of the Horse Artillery, which was about 100 strong, and ordered him to rush his artillery into the Fort and capture the commanders of the Desai's army. When the Horse Artillery stormed into the fort, Sardar Gurusiddappa, who had kept his men on full alert, promptly commanded his men to repel and chase them away. The Kittur forces made a bold front and overpowered the British soldiers.

4. In the meanwhile, the Desai's guards had shut the gates of the fort and the British Horse Artillery men, being completely overrun and routed, had to get out through the escape window. Rani's soldiers chased them out of the fort, killing a few of them until they retreated to their camps on the outskirts.

5. A few of the British had found refuge in some private residences, while some were hiding in their tents. The Kittur soldiers captured about forty persons and brought them to the palace. These included twelve children and a few women from the British officers' camp. When they were brought in the presence of the Rani, she ordered the soldiers to be imprisoned. For the women and children she had only gentleness, and admonished her soldiers for taking them into custody. At her orders, these women and children were taken inside the palace and given food and shelter. Rani came down from her throne, patted the children lovingly and told them that no harm would come to them.

6. She, then, sent word through a messenger to Thackeray that the British women and children were safe and could be taken back any time. Seeing this noble gesture of the Rani, he was moved. He wanted to meet this gracious lady and talk to her. He even thought of trying to persuade her to enter into an

agreement with the British to stop all hostilities in lieu of an *inam* (prize) of eleven villages. His offer was dismissed with a gesture of contempt. She had no wish to meet Thackeray. That night she called Sardar Gurusiddappa and other leading Sardars, and after discussing all the issues came to the conclusion that there was no point in meeting Thackeray who had come with an army to threaten Kittur into submission to British sovereignty.

On the basis of your understanding of the above passage, complete the statements given below with the help of the options that follow :

(a) Thackeray was a/an

  (i)   British tourist.

  (ii) army officer.

  (iii) advisor to the Rani of Kittur.

  (iv) treasury officer.

(b) British women and children came to Kittur to

  (i)   visit Kittur.

  (ii) enjoy life in tents.

  (iii) stay in the palace.

  (iv) give company to the army officers.

Answer the following questions briefly :

(c) Why did Thackeray come to Kittur?

(d) Why did Kittur officials refuse to give the desired assurance to Thackeray?

(e) What happened to the Horse Artillery?

(f) How do we know that the Rani was a noble soul?

(g) How, in your opinion, would the British women have felt after meeting the Rani?

(h) Why did the Rani refuse to meet Thackeray?

(i) Find words from the passage which mean the same as the following :

(i) aggressive/refusing to obey (Para 2)

(ii) entered forcibly (Para 3)

3. Read the passage given below and answer the questions that follow :

The most alarming of man‖s assaults upon the environment is the contamination of air, earth, rivers and sea with lethal materials. This pollution is for the most part irrevocable; the chain of evil it initiates is for the most part irreversible. In this contamination of the environment, chemicals are the sinister partners of radiation in changing the very nature of the world; radiation released through nuclear explosions into the air, comes to the earth in rain, lodges into the soil, enters the grass or corn, or wheat grown there and reaches the bones of a human being, there to remain until his death. Similarly, chemicals sprayed on crops lie long in soil, entering living organisms, passing from one to another in a chain of poisoning and death. Or they pass by underground streams until they emerge and combine into new forms that kill vegetation, sicken cattle, and harm those who drink from once pure wells.

It took hundreds of millions of years to produce the life that now inhabits the earth and reach a state of adjustment and balance with its surroundings. The environment contains elements that are hostile as well as supporting. Even within the light of the sun, there are short-wave radiations with power to injure. Given time, life has adjusted and a balance reached. For time is the essential ingredient, but in the modern world there is no time.

The rapidity of change and the speed with which new situations are created follow the heedless pace of man rather than the deliberate pace of nature. Radiation is no longer the bombardment of cosmic rays; it is now the unnatural creation of man‖s tampering with the atom. The chemicals to which life is asked to make adjustments are no longer merely calcium and silica and copper and all the rest of the minerals washed out of the rocks and carried in the rivers to the sea; they are the synthetic creations of man‖s inventive mind, brewed in his laboratories, and having no counterparts in nature.

(a) On the basis of your understanding of the above passage, make notes on it using headings and sub-headings. Use recognisable abbreviations (wherever necessary — minimum four) and a format you consider suitable.

(b) Write a summary of the passage in about 80 words.

SECTION B: Advanced Writing Skills

(30 Marks)

4. Your friend, P.V. Sathish, has invited you to attend the wedding of his sister, Jaya. You find that you have an important paper of pre-board examination on the day of the wedding. Thus you cannot attend the event. Write in about 50 words a formal reply to the invitation expressing your regret. You are Puneet/Puneeta Vij, M-114, Fort Road, Chennai.

OR

You are Vikram/Sonia, an electronics engineer who has recently returned from the U.S. and looking for a suitable job in the IT industry. Draft an advertisement in about 50 words for the Situations Wanted column of a national newspaper. Your contact number is 9193010203.

5. Mountview Public School, Kalka is run by an NGO to give quality education to the children of the deprived sections of society. The Principal of the school feels that blackboards in the classrooms need to be replaced. She decides to ask the chairperson of the NGO named ―Education for All‖ for funds. Write her letter in 120 – 150 words. Her name is Shweta Pandit.

OR

National Book Trust organised a week-long book fair at Anna Grounds, Chennai. You visited the fair and bought a few books. You were pleased with the arrangements, enthusiasm of the visitors and the fact that books have not yet lost their relevance in the world of the Internet. Write a letter in 120 – 150 words to the editor of a local newspaper to express your feelings. You are Lalit/Latha, 112, Mount Road, Chennai.

6. Every teenager has a dream to achieve something in life. What they are going to become tomorrow depends on what our youth dream today. Write an article in 150 – 200 words on —What I want to be in lifel. You are Simranjit/Smita.

OR

History Society of Kendriya Vidyalaya, Krishna Nagar sent a group of students to visit a place of historical interest. You, Anant/Anita, were its leader. Write a report in 150 – 200 words for the school newsletter on the tour, describing the place, its history, how you reached there and all that you have learnt.

7. Holi is a festival of colours. It expresses pure and simple joy. Sometimes we start throwing coloured water and that too on strangers. As the Head boy / girl of your school write a speech in 150 – 200 words that you will deliver in the morning assembly of your school, describing why Holi is played and how it should be played.

OR

"It is cruel to put stray dogs to sleep." Write a debate in 150 – 200 words either for or against the motion.

SECTION C: Textbooks and Long Reading Text

(40 Marks)

8. Read the extract given below and answer the questions that follow :
   At back of the dim class
   One unnoted, sweet and young. His eyes live in a dream,
   Of squirrells game, in tree room, other than this.
   (a) Why is the class dim?
   (b) How is the young child different from others?
   (c) What is he doing?
   (d) What is a tree room?

OR

Aunt Jenniferls fingers fluttering through her wool

Find even the ivory needle hard to pull.
The massive weight of Unclels wedding band
Sits heavily upon Aunt Jenniferls hand.
(a) What is Aunt Jennifer doing with her wool?
(b) Why does she find it difficult to pull her ivory needle?
(c) What does —wedding bandl stand for?
(d) Describe the irony in the third line.

9. Answer any four of the following questions in 30 – 40 words each :
   (a) Why were some elderly persons occupying the back benches that day? (The Last Lesson)
   (b) Why did Jansie discourage Sophie from having dreams?
   (c) Having looked at her mother, why does Kamala Das look at the young children?
   (d) How would keeping quiet affect life in and around the sea?
   (e) Why did the Maharaja decide to get married?
   (f) What is mother Skunkls role in the story?

10. Answer the following question in 120 – 150 words :
    "For the children it is wrapped in wonder, for the elders it is a means of survival." What kind of life do the rag-pickers of Seemapuri lead?

OR

The peddler believed that the whole world is a rattrap. How did he himself get caught in the same?

11. Answer the following question in 120 – 150 words :
    In India, the so-called lower castes have been treated cruelly for a long time. Who advised Bama to fight against this prejudice, when and how?

OR

To choose between professional loyalty and patriotism was a dilemma for Dr. Sadao. How did he succeed in betraying neither?

12. Answer the following question in 120 – 150 words :
    Attempt a character sketch of Dr. Kemp as a law-abiding citizen.

OR

Lammeter sisters have money but not class or education. What do you think about them?

13. Attempt the following question in 120 – 150 words :
    Why and how did Griffin burglarise the vicarage?

OR

How did Silasl treatment of Sally Oates affect his life at Raveloe?

Solutions

SECTION - A

1.　(1 × 4 = 4 Marks)

(a) (ii) no one stared at him

(b) (ii) Heaven lake

(c) (iv) there were thick quilts on the beds

(d) (ii) a shining prism

(1 × 6 = 6 Marks)

(e) The two things that made the narrator uncomfortable were the bumpy rides, the leaking windows. Even the man behind him who was eating an overpoweringly smelly goat's cheese was a source of discomfort.

(f) The green ground, the slopes dark with pine, the cattle's drinking from the clear stream made the scene look like a constable landscape.

(g) As the bus climbed higher, the narrator regretted not bringing anything more than a pair of shorts that had served him so well in the desert.

(h) The narrator liked to buy food from outside because he liked the highly spiced kebab and naan and thought of it to be very good.

(i) The ironic part about the trouser which was lent by Mr. Cao was that they were several sizes too large but at the same time were more than comfortable.

(j) Mr. Cao did not want the narrator to swim in the lake because people often drowned in that lake.

(k)　(1 × 2 = 2 Marks)

(i)　sellers- Vendors

(ii)　increased- Exaggerated

Note

When answering MCQs choose the option which is the closest answer from amongst the options.

1. *For Factual questions like e.g. "**What did he regret as the bus climbed higher**," do not include information not given in the passage.*

2. *While answering the 'why' question like "**Why did Mr. Cao not like the narrator to swim in the lake**", you may begin your answer with 'Mr. Cao did not want the narrator to swim in the lake because …… or a similar phrase.*

3. *While answering the vocabulary questions, check the part of speech, the tense of the word etc. Your answer should have the same part of speech, tense etc.*

   For e.g. Sellers – Vendors (NOT Vendor)

   Increased- Exaggerated (NOT Exaggerate or Exaggerating)

2.　(1 × 2 = 2 Marks)

(a) (ii) army officer

(b) (iv) give company to officers

(1 × 6 = 6 Marks)

(c) Thackeray came to Kittur to crush and stop the revolt. He also wanted to terrorize the rulers and the people of Kittur.

(d) The Kittur officials refused to give the desired assurance to Thackeray because they were in a defiant mood and no documents could be signed without sanction from Rani Chennamma.

(e) The Horse Artillery were defeated and completely overrun and routed by Sardar Gurusiddappa and his men, who were on full alert.

(f) Rani was a noble queen because she gave food and shelter to the women and the children who were captured by her men. She also sent a messanger to Thackeray that the women and children were safe and could be taken back anytime.

(g) The British women must have felt safe, relieved, grateful and thankful towards the Rani.

(h) The Rani refused to meet Thackeray because she thought that it was pointless in meeting someone who came to threaten Kittur.

(i)　(1 × 2 = 2 Marks)

(i)　entered forcibly- stormed

(ii)　aggressive/ refusing to obey- defiant

3.　(5 Marks)

(a) **Note-making**

Title- MAN'S ASSAULT ON NATURE

1. Things man contaminates
   1.1　air
   1.2　river
   1.3　earth
   1.4　sea
2. Features of contamination
   2.1　Irreversible
   2.2　Irrevocable
3. Nuclear contamination
   3.1　rad. from nuc. Exp.
   3.2　reaches earth by rain
   3.3　lodges in soil
   3.4　enters human body

4. Chemical contamination
   - 4.1 spd. on crp.
   - 4.2 enter living organisms
   - 4.3 kill vegetation
   - 4.4 kills cattle
5. Role of Man
   - 5.1 tampering atoms
   - 5.2 creating radiation
   - 5.3 synthetic creation thru Man's mind
   - 5.4 brewing in labs

Key to Abbreviations

Abbreviation	Word
nuc.	nuclear
exp.	explosion
crp.	crops
rad.	radiation
spd.	sprayed
thru	through

(b) Summary (3 Marks)

It took us many years and many painful moments to reach to a balanced climate on Earth. However, the ever-growing needs of Man is destroying all. Man has polluted air, river and sea causing a disbalance in Nature. He is doing this through nuclear contamination, which happens due to the radiations from the nuclear warheads and chemical contamination through spraying chemicals on the crops. This goes into the bones of the human beings and acts as slow poison. Man's tampering with atoms and his continuous brewing in laboratories have also contributed towards making the situation worse. (96 words)

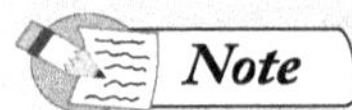

Note

1. *The passage is on how Man is destroying nature. So, the title should have the key words 'Man', 'Nature' and any synonym of the word 'destroy'.*
2. *It should always contain phrases. Avoid using complete sentences. For e.g.*
   Things man contaminates
   - *a. air*
   - *b. river*
   - *c. earth*
   - *d. sea*
   AND NOT Man contaminates air, river, earth and sea.
3. *Include a minimum of 4-6 distinctly different recognizable short forms i.e. abbreviations of the words in the notes as done in the solution.*

4. Reply to invitation (4 Marks)

M-114, Fort Road

Chennai

March 06, 2017

Mr Puneeta thanks Mr Satish for the invitation to the wedding of his sister Jaya, on the 10th of March 2017. However, she expresses her inability to attend the function due to the conduction of the Pre-Board examination of English on that day.

Puneeta

OR

Advertisement

SITUATION WANTED

A dynamic, committed, expert US returned Electronics engineer is looking for an opportunity in a reputed IT company in India. Age: 28 years, M Tech from Massachusetts University, experience of 12 years, Expected salary 95 K per month - negotiable . Contact Sonia- 9193010203

5. Letter (6 Marks)

Mount View Public School

Kalka

March 6, 2017

The Chairperson

NGO 'Education for All'

Kalka

Subject: Requirement of funds for the replacement of blackboards

Respected Sir,

I am to inform you with pleas are that there has been an increase in the number of students since the time the school was started. Lots of students from the nearby slums have enrolled in the school now. As such the total number of sections have also increased. Therefore, we need funds for the improvement in the school academic infrastructure.

There is an immediate requirement for new black boards in the increased sections. Furthermore, in quite a few classrooms the blackboards need replacement because they are either broken or else have become far too shiny making the visibility of the lesson taught on the board a concern. Hence, I would like to request you to release appropriate amount of funds to fulfill the immediate requirement.

Looking forward to your support

Yours sincerely

Shweta Pandit

(Principal)

OR

112
Mount Road
Chennai

23 March, 20XX

The Editor
Daily Herald
Bahadur Shah Jafar Marg
Chennai

Subject: Appreciation for the Book Fair organized by National Book Trust

Sir,

Through the columns of your esteemed newspaper, I would like to express my happiness and appreciation for the recently organized week-long Chennai Book Fair by National Book Trust at the Annamalai Grounds.

The fair which began on 15th of February had publishers from both India and abroad as participants. The books displayed were both academic and non-academic with subjects ranging from adventure, sports, science-fiction, self-help, cookery etc. It was a pleasant sight to see schools taking an initiative to get the children to the Fair and look at the books. The sale of books touched a record high on the first day itself. This was a testimony to the fact that books have not yet lost their relevance in the world of Internet.

I would like to draw the attention of all citizens towards such initiatives and I hope National Book Trust will continue taking these measures in future too.

Yours sincerely
Latha

6. Article   **(10 Marks)**

What I Want to Be in Life

By *Smita*

Every child grows up in an environment which helps him/her shape his/her future. The dreams that one has for oneself is largely dependent on one's own exposure, experiences, the peer group and the guidance of the school and Parents. I grew up in an environment where honesty, integrity, transparency and discipline were the key words. My father, an honest police officer and my mother, a noted academician have been my role models. Whatever I become in life, these values will always be close to my heart.

At this juncture of life, I have many goals and all of these seem equally important to me. What I know for sure is that I will need a lot of hard work and motivation to identify my true potential. Academic regularity and determination to achieve my goal as well as adequate time to pursue my

hobbies, will make me a happier and fulfilled individual. No doubt there will be many obstacles and hiccups on the way but I'm sure I will be able to surmount them all.

At the end of the day, I want to be a happy person who has given back much more to the society than what she has received from it.

OR

Report

The Taj Mahal : A Visitor's Delight

By *Anita*

Agra, December 28: The History Society of Kendriya Vidyalaya, Kishna Nagar organized a trip for the students of Senior Secondary classes to Agra during the Winter vacation as a part of its Heritage Week celebrations. The journey to Agra by train was a delight for all its 40 student and 4 teacher participants. The stay at Agra was at the hotel and the students on reaching Agra hurriedly got ready since they did not want to miss the fun. The top most priority was to visit the Taj Mahal and take maximum benefit out of it.

The Taj Mahal is not only a Mughal architectural wonder but a saga of love. Built in the memory of Mumtaz Mahal, it is a dream in marble on moonlit nights. When we visited the Taj Mahal, we were greeted by our guide who had been hired especially by the school for us. Standing in the gateway we were first able to get a panoramic view of the majestic complex followed by visits to the main chamber. The whole building was decorated with intricate carvings of floral design. As students of the Heritage Club, we were also pained to witness the ill effects of environmental pollution on the structure. However, it is also pertinent to mention here that the efforts of the government to salvage the situation was also visible and praiseworthy.

On the whole it was an educative, exciting and informative trip for all of us.

7. Speech   **(10 Marks)**

Good Morning Madam Principal, respected teachers and my dear friends.

Today I, XXX, the Head Girl of the school, stand before you to apprise you of the importance of the festival of Holi and how it should be played.

I believe there is no need to reiterate that Holi is primarily a festival of colours celebrated by the Hindus in the month of March to celebrate the advent of Spring. The religious connotations link it to Holika Dahan – the sitting of Holika, a lady with powers of remaining unscathed by fire, with Prahlad on her lap on a burning pyre and getting burnt instead. This symbolized the victory of good over the evil.

There are many other mythological stories attached to this festival, Holi. However, without going into the details of these stories, let us come back to the way the festival is celebrated these days.

With passage of time the festival of Holi has also undergone a change. The traditional coloured powders which were made from neem, Kumkum, turmeric, flowers like *tesu* etc have given way to synthetic colours which are infact the irritants to the skin. Therefore, it is my humble request to all gathered here to avoid playing with these synthetic colours especially with people who have sensitive skin. Keeping in view the water scarcity that the Earth faces, it is recommended that all of us switch to dry Holi. Spraying of colours through *pichkari* and water balloons does not suit the students of our school. We must remember that wherever we are, we are also the ambassadors of the school.

Therefore, let us all pledge together to make this Holi a joyful one for all.

Thank you

OR

Debate

Respected Chairperson, Members of the Jury, worthy opponents and my dear audience.

I, XXX, of YYY school stand before you to express my views **against the motion** on the topic "It is cruel to put stray dogs to sleep".

Dogs have been viewed throughout the ages as Man's best friend. We were brought up on stories of how dogs have saved the lives of their masters, we have seen such news clippings on television, we have so many pictures shared on Instagram where dogs of all varieties have come to the rescue of their masters. However while we nod our heads in the affirmative, we tend to ignore the key word in the topic -"**stray**". My dear friends, we are here talking about stray dogs who are without any discipline or control, dogs which exhibit violent behavior, dogs with various diseases, dogs which are infesting the streets huge in number. Haven't we heard stories of dogs mangling new- born babies to pieces? Haven't we seen dogs biting unsuspecting passers by? Dear Friends! Dog bites, if not treated timely and properly can lead to death too. In many cases it is a traffic hazard too. Night times can also lead to a harrowing experience for the two-wheeler riders especially for the pillion rider when the dogs start chasing them barking away to glory.

Keeping all these points in mind I do not think it is cruel to put stray dogs to sleep.

Thank You !

OR

Respected Chairperson, Members of the Jury, worthy opponents and my dear audience. I, XXX, of YYY school stand before you to express my views **for the motion** on the topic "It is cruel to put stray dogs to sleep".

Every living thing has a right to live irrespective of the fact whether they have a home or not. All life is important to support the ecological balance. It is a universal truth that anything that is born will die in the natural course. Then who are we to disturb this flow?

Furthermore, Dogs have been viewed throughout the ages as Man's best friend and a faithful protector. We were brought up on stories of how dogs have saved the lives of their masters. The electronic media is full of news clippings of dogs saving lives of infants too. We have so many pictures shared on Instagram where dogs of all varieties have come to the rescue of their masters. In such a scenario, is it fair to suggest such measures? The Animal Protection Act too prohibits this insane killing.

My worthy opponents might like to stress on the word "stray". However, I would reiterate my initial point that even though we are talking about stray dogs, we are taking about taking away a life and that is something unpardonable.

Thank You!

SECTION - C

8.   **(1 × 4 = 4 Marks)**

(a) The class is dim because it is a classroom in a slum where there is lack of adequate natural light. Further more there is probably no electricity.

(b) The young child is different from others in his ability to dream. He is lost in his own dream world and the surrounding dullness has no negative impact on his ability to dream of a different world.

(c) He is dreaming of a beautiful world where there is the squirrel's game in a tree room.

(d) A tree room is a dwelling place of a squirrel in a tree.

OR

(a) Aunt Jennifer is embroidering tigers on the panel with the wool.

(b) She finds it difficult to pull the ivory needle because her hands are fragile due to the tyrannical married life that she has led.

(c) The wedding band here isn't a sign of mutual trust. Instead it stands for the oppressive control of her husband and this does not allow her to overcome her fears.

(d) The irony of the third line lies in the wedding ring and its weight. A wedding ring is symbol of conjugal happiness. However ironically here, it is a burden and a symbol of oppressive control.

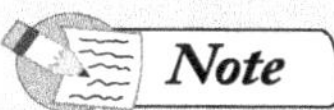 **Note**

1. Be precise and to the point.
2. For e.g. "Why is the class dim" you may begin by ....The class is dim because it is a classroom in a slum where there is lack of adequate natural light and no electricity too.

9.   **(3 × 4 = 12 Marks)**

(a) Some elderly persons were occupying the back benches that day as a mark of respect to the language that was to be banished from the schools of Alsace and Lorraine; and to bid farewell to M. Hamel for his forty years of service . It was to be the last day of a French class and they had gathered there to show their love for their mother tongue.

(b) Jansie discouraged Sophie from having dreams since Sophie's dreams were simply wishful thinking and therefore unrealistic in nature. Jansie knew they were earmarked for the biscuit factory and since she was the more practical of the lot, she wanted Sophie too to become practical.

(c) Kamala Das looks at the young children after looking at her mother to distract herself from the thoughts of her aging mother. Since children are symbolic of youth and energy, it helps her in driving away, momentarily, the pain of the impending separation from her mother.

(d) Keeping quiet would ensure that the fishermen in the seas would not harm the whales, the man gathering salt would look at his hurt hands and introspect. In other words, total inactivity, even though for some time would give everyone some moments to move away from the hurried work that he/she is doing and do some self-analysis.

(e) The Maharaja decided to get married since no tigers were left in the forests of his kingdom and he had killed only seventy tigers till then. In order to reach his aim of killing hundred tigers, he needed to marry a princess from a kingdom with many tigers.

(f) Mother Skunk's role in the story was to make Roger Skunk realize the importance of retaining one's own identity. That is why she hits the wizard on the head since he changes the original smell of Roger Skunk into the rose smell and makes him reverse the magic.

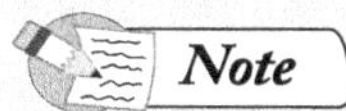 **Note**

Each 3-mark question must have at least two value points.
1. So, for the question "Why were some elderly persons occupying the back benches that day" include any two value points from those given below.
    a.   a mark of respect to the language that was to be banished from the schools of Alsace and Lorraine.
    b.   bid farewell to M.Hamel for his forty years of service.
    c.   It was to be the last day of a French class.
    d.   had gathered there to show their love for the mother tongue.

10.   **(6 Marks)**

The rag pickers of Seemapuri live a life of deprivation and perpetual poverty. A place on the periphery of Delhi, Seemapuri, has been the home for the people who came there from Bangladesh in 1971. Having no other skills or adequate education they picked up rag picking as their means of survival. Living for more than 30 years without an identity or a permit but with ration cards which allows them to buy grains, they move from place to place, living in structures of mud with roofs of tin and tarpaulin or tents which serve as their transit homes. They pitch their tents wherever they can find food. For them garbage is like gold since it brings then food and a roof over their heads, even if it is leaking. Their children also grow up there and become their 'partners in survival'. Rag picking for them is the means of survival. It is also wrapped up in wonder and a source of hope and happiness since they come across a coin or two every now and then in the heap of garbage.

OR

The peddler had a very cynical view of the world which made him consider the whole world as a rat trap and all men and women either trapped by the riches and luxuries of the trap or circling around the bait waiting to be caught. The peddler felt thankful at the beginning of the story that he was, till date, untrapped. However, when he had easy access to the 30 Kronors of the crofter, he stole it. Instead of feeling guilty of having taken advantage of the faith and trust reposed in him, he felt extremely delighted. His primary motive was to keep himself and the stolen thirty kronor safe and therefore he decided to discontinue walking on the public highway and take to the woods. The first few hours in the woods did not pose any difficulty but as time passed, the forest started confusing him. He realized that he was coming back to the same position from where he had originally started. He had not moved an inch further throughout the day. He realized with an alarm that he too had been caught like a rat in the trap. Later he again gets trapped by Elda's sweet words and assurance of a Christmas treat. In spite of his awareness and consciousness, he repeatedly surrenders to worldly temptations. However, at the end of the story he redeems himself.

 *Note*

1. *Each 6-mark question must have at least four value points.*

2. *Answer to the point including your own opinion in places where it is deemed necessary by the question.*

3. *Pick out specific examples from the text to support your answer.*

4. *Quote straight from the text wherever required but do so only when you are sure of the words.*

5. *For e.g.The question "For the children it is wrapped in wonder, for the elders it is a means of survival." What kind of life do the rag-pickers of Seemapuri lead ? You need to use the key words like led a 'life of deprivation and perpetual poverty', - 'Seemapuri - A place on the periphery of Delhi', - the home for the people who came there from Bangladesh in 1971 - no other skills or adequate education - picked up rag picking - means of survival - living for more than 30 years without an identity - ration cards - allows them to buy grains - move from place to place- live in structures of mud with roofs of tin tarpaulin or tents - transit homes - pitch their tents wherever they can find food - garbage is like gold - brings them food and a roof over their heads, even if 'it is leaking'- children grow up there and become 'partners in survival'- Rag picking for them - means of survival - also wrapped up in wonder-source of hope and happiness since they come across a coin or two every now and then in the heap of garbage.*

11.   **(6 Marks)**

As Bama narrates herself, till the time she was studying in the third class, she hadn't heard people speaking openly about untouchability. However, she had already seen, felt, experienced and been humiliated by what it was. Bama's first encounter with untouchability was when she saw a village elder holding a parcel of eatables in a manner which ensured that the parcel stayed away from his body, carrying it to the landlord and giving it to him in a most suppliant manner. She found the sight most amusing but later she gets to know the underlying currents of untouchability behind this action through her elder brother Annan. She finds it totally unacceptable a belief that food of the upper class, if touched by the lower class, was deemed as polluted and unfit for consumption. Her brother Aman gives her some more insights based on what he had faced whenever he came to the village. However, Annan also tells Bama how she can fight against it. Education and being the best in your field are the ways through which one can gain acceptance in a biased society. So, Bama decides to fight against it through education. On the advice of her brother, she studies hard and tops her class and gains acceptance.

OR

To choose between professional loyalty and patriotism was indeed a dilemma for Dr Sadao. However, he succeeded as a doctor and a patriot by striking a wonderful balance between the two and compromising on neither of his duties. As a doctor he is aware of the value of human life and that his primary duty was to make the ailing, injured and sick people fully whole irrespective of one's own prejudices. Therefore, notwithstanding the risk inherent in treating an enemy, and ignoring the fact that he does not like Americans, he takes the person home, operates him and provides post-operative treatment too. In course of time his faithful servants desert him failing to understand the humane side of Dr Sadao. Even his wife to a large extent does not favour his actions because she feels that he is not only risking himself but also putting the life of the family in jeopardy. Despite all these encumbrances on his way, he single-mindedly focusses on his primary duty. However, Dr Sadao does not fail as a patriot too while he is fulfilling his responsibility as a doctor. He informs the General about the injured man whom he has treated since he is an escaped prisoner of war. He also accepts the General's decision to send the assassins without any reluctance. He even keeps the door open for the assassins to enter. It is another matter that the assassins fail to arrive and kill the enemy.

This way he succeeds in betraying neither of his duties.

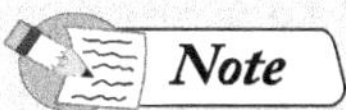
Note

1. *Adhere to the word limit given for the question.*
2. *Quoting from the text always gets more marks but misquotes can backfire. So, be careful.*
3. *The question requires not only your knowledge of the text but also your analysis of the inhuman practice like untouchability. So, include both.*
4. *For the Question "In India, the so-called lower castes have been treated cruelly for a long time. Who advised Bama to fight against this prejudice, when and how, Break the question into parts of WHO, WHEN & HOW and then answer it.*
5. *THE WHO ADVISED part would deal with Bama's own experience - Bama narrates - till the third class - hadn't heard people speaking openly about untouchability- but seen, felt, experienced and been humiliated by what it was - WHEN Bama's first encounter with untouchability - saw a village elder holding a parcel of eatables - carrying it to the landlord - giving it to him in a most suppliant manner- sight most amusing - later gets to know the underlying currents of untouchability- through her elder brother Annan - finds it totally unacceptable - belief that food of the upper class, if touched by the lower class - deemed polluted and unfit for consumption - Aman gives her some more insights - his experience- Annan tells Bama how she can fight against it – HOW - Education and being the best in your field - gain acceptance in a biased society - Bama decides to fight - through education- studies hard and tops her class - gains acceptance.*

12.   **(6 Marks)**

Dr Kemp is a scientist and a fellow student with Griffin at "University College". Griffin accidently reaches Dr Kemp's house when he is shot at. Initially Dr Kemp is surprised at the invisibility of the 'Invisible' Man but later when he understands the identity of the man, he provides shelter, food, rest and clothing to Griffin. He also gives his word that he will protect Griffin. However, as morning approaches and he gets to see the morning newspaper he realizes that Griffin is a threat to mankind due to his maniacal condition. Since Kemp himself is no risk to mankind he refuses to be a part of Griffin's 'Reign of Terror'. Therefore, he denounces Griffin and informs Colonel Adye, the Chief of Burdock Police about Griffin's presence and plans. He also agrees to act as a bait to trap Griffin. In other words, Dr. Kemp puts duty before self and shows himself to be a law- abiding citizen.

OR

The Lammeter sisters were the daughters of Mr Lammeter- a rich person, but they did not have much of education. However, they were virtuous country girls. Nancy Lammeter, had her own individual personality and adhered to her own code of behaviour which encompassed even dressing like her sister Priscilla. She is beautiful and courted by Godfrey Cass whom she later gets married to. She isn't an outdoor person like her sister Priscilla and loves to think inwardly. She is caring and possesses remarkable strength of character coupled with high principles. She refuses to adopt a child after losing her own born as it would be meddling with God's plan. "To adopt a child, because children of your own had been denied you, was to try and choose your lot in spite of Providence" – is what she believes in. However later she agrees to adopt Eppie once she knows the truth about Eppie's parentage.

Priscilla, on the other hand is plain, worldly wise, skilled and self-confident. She is more of an outdoor person and manages the farm and the dairy. Her sole concentration is on getting Nancy married whereas she herself prefers to remain single.

Note

1. *Adhere to the word limit. Answer must reveal your deep knowledge of the text.*
2. *For e.g. the question 'Attempt a character sketch of Dr. Kemp as a law-abiding citizen' use at least 4 value points from those given below:*
    a. *Dr Kemp - a scientist and a fellow student with Griffin at "University College".*
    b. *Griffin accidently reaches Dr Kemp's house.*
    c. *Initially Dr Kemp surprised at the invisibility of the man but later understands the identity- provides shelter, food, rest and clothing to Griffin.*
    d. *Gives his word that he will protect Griffin.*
    e. *See the morning newspaper - realizes Griffin a threat to mankind*
    f. *Refuses to be a part of Griffin's 'Reign of Terror'.*
    g. *Denounces Griffin and informs Colonel Adyeabout Griffin's presence and plans.*
    h. *Also agrees to act as a bait to trap Griffin.*
    i. *Puts duty before self and shows himself to be a law-abiding citizen.*

13.   **(6 Marks)**

The burglary at the Vicarage occurs in the 'small hours of Whit Monday' at around 4 am. It is done by Griffin since all his money was exhausted and he needed cash to continue with his research and make the payment to Mrs Hall. Griffin left the inn and entered the vicarage. Since he was invisible, he was not seen by the vicar and his wife even though they could hear the noise made by the opening and closing of the door. Once they approach the study, they can hear the ruffling sound and see the candle being lighted. A violent sneeze also confirmed the presence of someone. However despite all this, Griffin entered the study room, opened the drawers, searched and stole 'two pounds ten in half sovereigns' which were put in the drawer and left the vicarage without being identified since he was invisible.

OR

Sally Oates was the wife of a cobbler in Raveloe who was suffering from dropsy and heart disease. Silas while taking the shoes to be mended sees Sally Oates and identifies the symptoms as identical to that of his mother's ailment. Silas had inherited some knowledge of herbs from his mother. So, he treated and cured Sally with foxgloves. The news of the miraculous cure of the lady at the hands of an ordinary weaver spread like wild-fire among the villagers. The villagers started flocking to his house with requests for cure to maladies that they were suffering from. However, Silas refused their requests as he wasn't a qualified practitioner and did not believe in falsifying things. Furthermore, he had no need for any extra money. Slowly people became suspicious of him and started gossiping about him. What was thought as an action which could make him closer to the villagers and loved by them, the curing of Sally Oates and the events thereafter make his isolation at Raveloe complete.

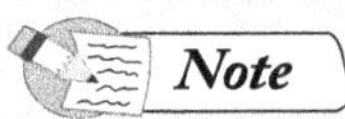

Note

1. *This question tests understanding, appreciation, analysis and interpretation of the incident/character. So, thorough reading of the text is required.*
2. *Adhere to the word limit and answer the question.*
3. *Avoid giving details which you are not sure of.*
4. *For e.g. the question Why and how did Griffin burglarise the vicarage, break the question into Why and How and then answer it.*
5. *why (- all his money was exhausted- needed cash to continue with his research - make the payment to Mrs Hall etc)*
6. *how (Griffin entered the vicarage - Invisible - noise heard but not seen – enters the study - opens drawers- stole 'two pounds ten in half sovereigns'- and left unscathed.*

Delhi *2017*

CBSE Board Solved Paper

Time Allowed : 3 Hours   *Maximum Marks : 100*

General Instructions:

(i) This paper is divided into three sections: A, B and C. All the sections are compulsory.

(ii) Separate instructions are given with each section and question, wherever necessary. Read these instructions very carefully and follow them faithfully.

(iii) Do not exceed the prescribed word limit while answering the questions.

SECTION A: Reading

(30 Marks)

1. Read the passage given below and answer the questions that follow :

1. We sit in the last row, bumped about but free of stares. The bus rolls out of the dull crossroads of the city, and we are soon in open countryside, with fields of sunflowers as far as the eye can see, their heads all facing us. Where there is no water, the land reverts to desert. While still on level ground, we see in the distance the tall range of the Mount Bogda, abrupt like a shining prism laid horizontally on the desert surface. It is over 5,000 metres high, and the peaks are under permanent snow, in powerful contrast to the flat desert all around. Heaven Lake lies part of the way up this range, about 2,000 metres above sea-level, at the foot of one of the higher snow-peaks.

2. As the bus climbs, the sky, brilliant before, grows overcast. I have brought nothing warm to wear: it is all down at the hotel in Urumqi. Rain begins to fall. The man behind me is eating overpoweringly smelly goat's cheese. The bus window leaks inhospitably but reveals a beautiful view. We have passed quickly from desert through arable land to pasture, and the ground is now green with grass, the slopes dark with pine. A few cattle drink at a clear stream flowing past moss-covered stones; it is a Constable landscape. The stream changes into a white torrent, and as we climb higher I wish more and more that I had brought with me something warmer than the pair of shorts that have served me so well in the desert. The stream (which, we are told, rises in Heaven Lake) disappears, and we continue our slow ascent. About noon, we arrive at Heaven Lake, and look for a place to stay at the foot, which is the resort area.

We get a room in a small cottage, and I am happy to note that there are thick quilts on the beds.

3. Standing outside the cottage we survey our surroundings. Heaven Lake is long, sardine-shaped and fed by snowmelt from a stream at its head. The lake is an intense blue, surrounded on all sides by green mountain walls, dotted with distant sheep. At the head of the lake, beyond the delta of the inflowing stream, is a massive snow-capped peak which dominates the vista; it is part of a series of peaks that culminate, a little out of view, in Mount Bogda itself.

4. For those who live in the resort, there is a small mess-hall by the shore. We eat here sometimes, and sometimes buy food from the vendors outside, who sell kabab and naan until the last buses leave. The kababs, cooked on skewers over charcoal braziers, are particularly good; highly spiced and well-done. Horse's milk is available too from the local Kazakh herdsmen, but I decline this. I am so affected by the cold that Mr. Cao, the relaxed young man who runs the mess, lends me a spare pair of trousers, several sizes too large but more than comfortable. Once I am warm again, I feel a pre-dinner spurt of energy — dinner will be long in coming — and I ask him whether the lake is good for swimming in.

5. "Swimming?" Mr. Cao says. "You aren't thinking of swimming, are you?"

6. "I thought I might," I confess. "What's the water like?"

7. He doesn't answer me immediately, turning instead to examine some receipts with exaggerated interest. Mr. Cao, with great off-handedness, addresses the air. "People are often drowned here," he says. After a pause, he continues. "When was the last one?" This

question is directed at the cook, who is preparing a tray of mantou (squat, white steamed bread rolls), and who now appears, wiping his doughy hand across his forehead. "Was it the Beijing athlete?" asks Mr. Cao.

On the basis of your understanding of the above passage complete the statements given below with the help of options that follow :

(a) One benefit of sitting in the last row of the bus was that:

(i) the narrator enjoyed the bumps.

(ii) no one stared at him.

(iii) he could see the sunflowers.

(iv) he avoided the dullness of the city.

(b) The narrator was travelling to :

(i) Mount Bogda.

(ii) Heaven Lake.

(iii) a 2,000-metre high snow-peak.

(iv) Urumqi.

(c) On reaching the destination the narrator felt relieved because :

(i) he had got away from the desert.

(ii) a difficult journey had come to an end.

(iii) he could watch the snow-peak.

(iv) there were thick quilts on the beds.

(d) Mount Bogda is compared to :

(i) a horizontal desert surface.

(ii) a shining prism.

(iii) a Constable landscape.

(iv) the overcast sky.

Answer the following questions briefly :

(e) Which two things in the bus made the narrator feel uncomfortable?

(f) What made the scene look like a Constable landscape?

(g) What did he regret as the bus climbed higher?

(h) Why did the narrator like to buy food from outside?

(i) What is ironic about the pair of trousers lent by Mr. Cao?

(j) Why did Mr. Cao not like the narrator to swim in the lake?

(k) Find words from the passage which mean the same as the following :

(i) sellers (Para 4)

(ii) increased (Para 7)

2. Read the passage given below and answer the questions that follow :

1. Thackeray reached Kittur along with a small British army force and a few of his officers. He thought that the very presence of the British on the outskirts of Kittur would terrorise the rulers and people of Kittur, and that they would lay down their arms. He was quite confident that he would be able to crush the revolt in no time. He ordered that tents be erected on the eastern side for the fighting forces, and a little away on the western slopes tents be put up for the family members of the officers who had accompanied them. During the afternoon and evening of 20th October, the British soldiers were busy making arrangements for these camps.

2. On the 21st morning, Thackeray sent his political assistants to Kittur fort to obtain a written assurance from all the important officers of Kittur rendering them answerable for the security of the treasury of Kittur. They, accordingly, met Sardar Gurusiddappa and other officers of Kittur and asked them to comply with the orders of Thackeray. They did not know that the people were in a defiant mood. The commanders of Kittur dismissed the agent's orders as no documents could be signed without sanction from Rani Chennamma.

3. Thackeray was enraged and sent for the commander of the Horse Artillery, which was about 100 strong, ordered him to rush his artillery into the fort and capture the commanders of the Desai's army. When the Horse Artillery stormed into the fort, Sardar Gurusiddappa, who had kept his men on full alert, promptly commanded his men to repel and chase them away. The Kittur forces made a bold front and overpowered the British soldiers.

4. In the meanwhile, the Desai's guards had shut the gates of the fort and the British Horse Artillery men, being completely overrun and routed, had to get out through the escape window. Rani's soldiers chased them out of the fort, killing a few of them until they retreated to their camps on the outskirts.

5. A few of the British had found refuge in some private residences, while some were hiding in their tents. The Kittur soldiers captured about forty persons and brought them to the palace. These included twelve children and a few women from the British officers' camp. When they were brought in the presence of the Rani, she ordered the soldiers to be imprisoned. For the women and children she had only gentleness, and admonished her soldiers for taking them into custody. At her orders, these women and children were taken inside the palace and given food and shelter. Rani came down from her throne, patted the children lovingly and told them that no harm would come to them.

6. She, then, sent word through a messenger to Thackeray that the British women and children were safe and could be taken back any time. Seeing this noble gesture of the Rani, he was moved. He wanted to meet this gracious lady and talk to her. He even thought of trying to persuade her to enter into an agreement with the British to stop all hostilities in lieu of an *inam* (prize) of eleven villages. His offer was dismissed with a gesture of contempt. She had

no wish to meet Thackeray. That night she called Sardar Gurusiddappa and other leading Sardars, and after discussing all the issues came to the conclusion that there was no point in meeting Thackeray who had come with an army to threaten Kittur into submission to British sovereignty.

On the basis of your understanding of the above passage complete the statements given below with the help of the options that follow

(a) Thackeray was a/an

(i) British tourist.

(ii) army officer.

(iii) advisor to Rani of Kittur.

(iv) treasury officer.

(b) British women and children came to Kittur to

(i) visit Kittur.

(ii) enjoy life in tents.

(iii) stay in the palace.

(iv) give company to thearmy officers.

Answer the following questions briefly :

(c) Why did Thackeray come to Kittur?

(d) Why did Kittur officials refuse to give the desired assurance to Thackeray?

(e) What happened to the Horse Artillery?

(f) How do we know that the Rani was a noble soul?

(g) How, in your opinion, would the British women have felt after meeting the Rani?

(h) Why did the Rani refuse to meet Thackeray?

(i) Find words from the passage which mean the same as the following :

(i) aggressive/refusing to obey (Para 2)

(ii) entered forcibly (Para 3)

3. Read the passage given below and answer the questions that follow :

The most alarming of man's assaults upon the environment is the contamination of air, earth, rivers and sea with lethal materials. This pollution is for the most part irrevocable; the chain of evil it initiates is for the most part irreversible. In this contamination of the environment, chemicals are the sinister partners of radiation in changing the very nature of the world; radiation released through nuclear explosions into the air, comes to the earth in rain, lodges into the soil, enters the grass or corn, or wheat grown there and reaches the bones of a human being, there to remain until his death. Similarly, chemicals sprayed on crops lie long in soil, entering living organisms, passing from one to another in a chain of poisoning and death. Or they pass by underground streams until they emerge and combine into new forms that kill vegetation, sicken cattle, and harm those who drink from once pure wells.

It took hundreds of millions of years to produce the life that now inhabits the earth and reach a state of adjustment and balance with its surroundings. The environment contained elements that were hostile as well as supporting. Even within the light of the sun, there were short wave radiations with power to injure. Given time, life has adjusted and a balance reached. For time is the essential ingredient, but in the modern world there is no time.

The rapidity of change and the speed with which new situations are created follow the heedless pace of man rather than the deliberate pace of nature. Radiation is no longer the bombardment of cosmic rays; it is now the unnatural creation of man's tampering with the atom. The chemicals to which life is asked to make adjustments are no longer merely calcium and silica and copper and all the rest of the minerals washed out of the rocks and carried in the rivers to the sea; they are the synthetic creations of man's inventive mind, brewed in his laboratories, and having no counterparts in nature.

(a) On the basis of your understanding of the above passage, make notes on it using headings and sub-headings. Use recognisable abbreviations (wherever necessary – minimum four) and a format you consider suitable. Also supply a title to it.

(b) Write a summary of the passage in about 80 words.

(30 Marks)

4. You are Vikram/Sonia, an Hon's graduate in history with specialization in Medieval India. You are well acquainted with places of historical interest in Delhi, Agra and Jaipur. You are looking for the job of tourist guide. Write an advertisement in about 50 words for the situations wanted column of a local newspaper. Your contact no. 999751234.

OR

While walking in a park in your neighbourhood you found a small plastic bag containing some documents and some cash. Write a notice in about 50 words to be put on the park notice board asking the owner to identify and collect it from you. You are Amar/Amrita 9399123456.

5. In our society we do not give to our women the respect and status that they deserve. Women are stared at, stalked and even molested. We need to change the male mindset about women. Write a letter in 120-150 words to the editor of a national newspaper giving your views on the problem. You are Omar/Amna, A114 Mall Road, Delhi.

OR

You want to spend a week-long holiday at Shimla in the month of October. You have decided to stay at Hotel Snowview. Write a letter in 120-150 words to the manager to book a room. Mention the dates, facilities in the room, food, sight-seeing facilities etc you will need. You are Amar/Amrita M114, Lake Road, Karnal.

6. Our performance in Rio Olympics has told us that we do not pay enough attention to athletics and outdoor games. It is time we revised our attitude. Sports should be an important part of school's daily routine. Write an article in 150-200 words in 'Importance of Outdoor Games'. You are Sreeja/Thomas.

OR

Cultural Society Sunshine Public School, Nellore organised an adult literacy camp in its neighbourhood. Write a report in 150-200 words on the camp for your school newsletter. You are P.V. Sunitha, Secretary. Use the following clues :

no. of volunteers – hours spent in teaching – location of the class – chairs, blackboards – no. of people attending the camp – benefit.

7. Your PGT English Ms. Geetha is a short story writer also. 'Sky is not Far' is a collection of her latest short stories. This book has won a national award. Write a speech in 150 – 200 words you will deliver in her honour in the morning assembly

OR

'Private cars should be banned in the congested commercial areas of the cities.' Write a debate in 150-200 words either **for** or **against** the motion.

SECTION C: Textbooks and Long Reading Text

(40 Marks)

8. Read the extract given below and answer the questions that follow :

Far far from gusty waves these children's faces.

Like rootless weeds, the hair torn round their pallor;

The tall girl with her weighed-down head.

(a) Who are these children?

(b) Which figure of speech has been used in the first two lines?

(c) Why is the tall girl's head weighed down?

(d) What does the word, 'pallor' mean?

OR

Aunt Jennifer's tigers prance across a screen,

Bright topaz denizens of a world of green.

They do not fear the men beneath the tree;

They pace in sleek chivalric certainty.

(a) Why are the tigers called Aunt Jennifer's tigers?

(b) How are they described here?

(c) How are they different from Aunt Jennifer?

(d) What does the word, 'chivalric' mean?

9. Answer any four of the following questions in 30 – 40 words each

(a) Why did Franz not want to go to school that day?

(b) What was Sophie's ambition in life? How did she hope to achieve that?

(c) What kind of pain does Kamala Das feel in 'My Mother at Sixty-six'?

(d) How can 'mighty dead' be things of beauty?

(e) Why was the Maharaja once in danger of losing his kingdom?

(f) What was the basic plot of each story told by Jack?

10. Answer the following question in 120 – 150 words :

Garbage to them is gold. How do ragpickers of Seemapuri survive?

OR

The peddler thinks that the whole world is a rattrap. This view of life is true only of himself and of no one else in the story. Comment.

11. Answer the following question in 120-150 words :

Untouchability is not only a crime, it is inhuman too. Why and how did Bama decide to fight against it?

OR

Good human values are far above any other value system. How did Dr. Sadao succeed as a doctor as well as a patriot?

12. Answer the following question in 120-150 words

Describe Marvel as an opportunist.

OR

George Eliot has portrayed Godfrey as a morally weak character. Comment.

13. Answer the following question in 120-150 words :

How does Dr. Cuss's encounter with Griffin end in a disaster?

OR

What kind of life did Silas lead at Lantern Yard?

Solutions

SECTION - A

1.   **(1 × 4 = 4 Marks)**

(a) (ii) no one stared at him

(b) (ii) Heaven lake

(c) (iv) there were thick quilts on the beds

(d) (ii) a shining prism

(1 × 6 = 6 Marks)

(e) The two things that made the narrator uncomfortable were the bumpy rides, the leaking windows. Even the man behind him who was eating an overpoweringly smelly goat's cheese was a source of discomfort.

(f) The green ground, the slopes dark with pine, the cattle's drinking from the clear stream made the scene look like a constable landscape.

(g) As the bus climbed higher, the narrator regretted not bringing anything more than a pair of shorts that had served him so well in the desert.

(h) The narrator liked to buy food from outside because he liked the highly spiced kebab and naan and thought of it to be very good.

(i) The ironic part about the trouser which was lent by Mr. Cao was that they were several sizes too large but at the same time were more than comfortable.

(j) Mr. Cao did not want the narrator to swim in the lake because people often drowned in that lake.

(k)   **(1 × 2 = 2 Marks)**

    (i)   sellers- Vendors

    (ii) increased- Exaggerated

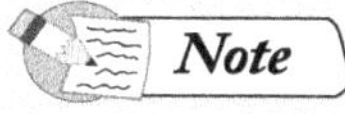 **Note**

When answering MCQs choose the option which is the closest answer from amongst the options.

1. *For Factual questions like e.g. "**What did he regret as the bus climbed higher**," do not include information not given in the passage.*

2. *While answering the 'why' question like "**Why did Mr. Cao not like the narrator to swim in the lake**", you may begin your answer with 'Mr. Cao did not want the narrator to swim in the lake because ………or a similar phrase.*

3. *While answering the vocabulary questions, check the part of speech, the tense of the word etc. Your answer should have the same part of speech, tense etc.*

   For e.g. Sellers – Vendors (NOT Vendor)

   Increased- Exaggerated (NOT Exaggerate or Exaggerating)

2.   **(1 × 2 = 2 Marks)**

(a) (ii) army officer

(b) (iv) give company to officers

(1 × 6 = 6 Marks)

(c) Thackeray came to Kittur to crush and stop the revolt. He also wanted to terrorize the rulers and the people of Kittur.

(d) The Kittur officials refused to give the desired assurance to Thackeray because they were in a defiant mood and no documents could be signed without sanction from Rani Chennamma.

(e) The Horse Artillery were defeated and completely overrun and routed by Sardar Gurusiddappa and his men, who were on full alert.

(f) Rani was a noble queen because she gave food and shelter to the women and the children who were captured by her men. She also sent a messanger to Thackeray that the women and children were safe and could be taken back anytime.

(g) The British women must have felt safe, relieved, grateful and thankful towards the Rani.

(h) The Rani refused to meet Thackeray because she thought that it was pointless in meeting someone who came to threaten Kittur.

(i)   **(1 × 2 = 2 Marks)**

(i) entered forcibly- stormed

(ii) aggressive/ refusing to obey- defiant

3. (a) **Note-making**   **(5 Marks)**

   Title- MAN'S ASSAULT ON NATURE

1. Things man contaminates

   1.1   air

   1.2   river

   1.3   earth

   1.4   sea

2. Features of contamination

   2.1   Irreversible

   2.2   Irrevocable

3. Nuclear contamination

   3.1   rad. from nuc. Exp.

   3.2   reaches earth by rain

   3.3   lodges in soil

   3.4   enters human body

4. Chemical contamination

    4.1   spd. on crp.

    4.2   enter living organisms

    4.3   kill vegetation

    4.4   kills cattle

5. Role of Man

    5.1   tampering atoms

    5.2   creating radiation

    5.3   synthetic creation thru Man's mind

    5.4   brewing in labs

Key to Abbreviations

Abbreviation	Word
nuc.	nuclear
exp.	explosion
crp.	crops
rad.	radiation
spd.	sprayed
thru	through

(b) Summary   **(3 Marks)**

It took us many years and many painful moments to reach to a balanced climate on Earth. However, the ever-growing needs of Man is destroying all. Man has polluted air, river and sea causing a disbalance in Nature. He is doing this through nuclear contamination, which happens due to the radiations from the nuclear warheads and chemical contamination through spraying chemicals on the crops. This goes into the bones of the human beings and acts as slow poison. Man's tampering with atoms and his continuous brewing in laboratories have also contributed towards making the situation worse. (96 words)

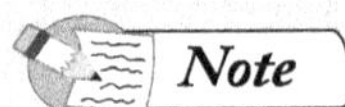 *Note*

1. *The passage is on how Man is destroying nature. So, the title should have the key words 'Man', 'Nature' and any synonym of the word 'destroy'.*
2. *It should always contain phrases. Avoid using complete sentences. For e.g.*
Things man contaminates
    a.   air
    b.   river
    c.   earth
    d.   sea
AND NOT Man contaminates air, river, earth and sea.
3. *Include a minimum of 4-6 distinctly different recognizable short forms i.e. abbreviations of the words in the notes as done in the solution.*

4.   **Advertisement**   **(4 Marks)**

<u>**SITUATION WANTED**</u>

A qualified, experienced History (Hons.) Graduate with specialization in medieval India is seeking employment as a tourist guide: Age:28 years, well-versed with places of historical interest in Agra, Jaipur and Delhi, pleasant personality with good communication and inter-personal skills. Salary negotiable. CONTACT: Sonia @ 9671234712

OR

Feel Good Park, Uttam Nagar
NOTICE
Lost And Found

March 6, 2017

A small blue plastic bag containing some official documents and cash found at Feel Good Park, on the evening of 5th of March, 2017.

Rightful owner can contact the undersigned with proper credentials anytime between 5:00 – 6:00 pm in the park's office to claim the bag.

Amrita

9787896757

5.   **Letter**   **(6 Marks)**

A-114

Mall Road

New Delhi

March 6, 2017

The Editor

The Statesman

New Delhi

Sir,

Subject: <u>Need to change the male mindset</u>

Through the columns of your esteemed newspaper, I would like to draw the attention of all the concerned and well-established members of the society towards the pressing need to change the mindset of the male members of our society so that women are able to enjoy the respect that they deserve.

Even though we claim that we have been successful in creating a well-balanced society where women are treated at par with men, the ground reality is extremely grim. The women are still stared at, stalked and even molested. The crime against women like rape also does not seem to abate despite stringent laws in place. Women are still considered a weaker sex and harassed at every step. We therefore need to work towards changing the mind-set of the people. They need to understand that women are not commodities but an equal and necessary participant in all social, economic and national activity. Without women even Nature stands incomplete.

India is now developing at a fast pace. However, this development is meaningless if the female half of the society does not get its due. The sooner the male members wake up to this challenge and make amends, the better it will be for our society.

Yours truly

Amna

OR

M-114

Lake Road

Karnal

March 6, 2017

The Manager

Hotel Snow view

Shimla

Sir,

Subject: <u>Request for reservation of rooms</u>

This is to request you for the reservation of one room on double occupancy basis from October 12, 2017 to October 19, 2017 since I am visiting Shimla on a holiday.

The room must have a good view, preferably hill facing and well-furnished. I would also like to do some sight seeing for which you can arrange a local guide. Since I would be doing local sight seeing please see to it that the itinerary is such that it allows me to taste some local cuisines as well. Pick and drop facility from and to the nearest railway station would be appreciated.

I look forward to your confirmation at the earliest.

Thanking you

Yours sincerely

Amrita

6. Article   **(10 Marks)**

Importance of Outdoor Sports

By *Sreeja*

The recent performance at Rio Olympics has raised the red flag regarding the future of Sports in a country like India. Not only has it amply reflected the casual attitude of all towards Sports but also raised questions on the multitude of resources which are being used for the promotion of Sports.

Far from producing stellar performers, India is set to pitch forward a generation of couch potatoes who are thriving on the fun provided by the virtual world of outdoor sports. Now a goal is scored with a quick flip of the finger and an ace served without any arch of the body! Even Parents find it difficult to persuade a child to leave the mobile and go to the playground in the evening. School curriculum too is stringent with little space for sports, lack of praise for the players at school level and more emphasis on academics. All this has led to the degeneration of Outdoor sports.

However, we must realize that the aim of education is the development of the overall personality and this is possible only if we give equal importance to both academics and outdoor sports. Outdoor sports make our body agile, tone our muscles and improve our reflex actions. Therefore, the sooner we make efforts to improve the situation, the better.

OR

Report

Adult Literacy Camp Organized

By *P.V. Sunitha, Cultural Secretary*

Nellore, March 6: An Adult Literacy Camp was organized by the Cultural Society of Sunshine Public School on 5th of March 2017 for the residents of the nearby slum areas. The camp was inaugurated by the District Literacy Chairperson Shri Sadashiv Kumar. A total of 450 participants turned up and they were ably looked after by 50 student volunteers. All the participants were divided into groups and were led by a student teacher. Each group had a black board, chalk along with free notebooks and pencils. Classes were conducted for the participants followed by a movie on the importance of personal hygiene and cleanliness in the surroundings. There was a break after the two and half hour class where all the participants were provided with snacks.

At the end of the day the Chief Guest felicitated the student volunteers with certificates and congratulated them for having contributed to this noble event in their own way. The slum dwellers too requested to make this event a monthly affair.

7. Speech   **(10 Marks)**

Good Morning Mam Principal, teachers and students!

I, Anita , a student of class X, feel honoured to have been given the opportunity of speaking about one of our very own teachers Ms Geeta, PGT English who has recently won the National Award for "Sky Is Not Far"- her latest collection of short stories. Mam, you've always been an inspiration for us not only for your teaching style and knowledge but also for the way you have lighted our path and inspired us to perform to the best of our abilities.

Dear students! Each tale in the collection is, as the title suggests, is a journey towards perfection and reaching the sky. These are journeys negotiated by common people who reach uncommon goals. Written in a lucid style, simple language and credible characters, it is a must read for all of us since it makes us aware of Life's struggles and how one can overcome all obstacles with grit and determination.

I would once again like to thank Mam for being in our lives and inspiring us. I hope some of us are able to follow her footsteps and make her proud of us.

Thank You All for your patient hearing!

OR

Debate

Respected Chairperson, Members of the Jury, my worthy opponents and dear audience!

Today, I, XXX, stand before you to present my views **for the motion** on the topic "Private Cars should be banned in the congested commercial areas of the city".

It is common knowledge that cars are the one of the biggest reasons for congestion on the roads. With increase in the paying capacity of the average Indian, the desire to spend on luxuries is increasing. Some ten years back each family had a car and that was considered enough. However now, each member of the family has a personal vehicle resulting in space constraint for the parking of vehicles in the residential areas.

This problem is more acute in the commercial areas of the city where even the pedestrians find it difficult to negotiate their way through the maze of the parked and moving vehicles. Unnecessary honking and waiting for the traffic to clear up adds to noise and air pollution. Gaseous fumes from the vehicles leads to many health problems to the shoppers, sellers and pedestrians too. One dreads to dream of the consequences of this clogging in case of a fire or any other natural or man-made calamity. The situation of the roads is such that it will take hours for the emergency service to arrive at the place of a disaster. Therefore, in my opinion the solution lies in the banning entry of the private vehicles into the congested commercial areas of the city.

Thank You!

OR

Debate

Respected Chairperson, Members of the Jury, my worthy opponents and dear audience!

Today, I, XXX, stand before you to present my views **against the motion** on the topic "Private Cars should be banned in the congested commercial areas of the city".

Let me begin by putting a question to the august gathering – Why do we want to ban the private cars in the congested commercial areas of the city? Is it because we want to control pollution or is it because we want to remove the traffic congestion? I ask this since it is common knowledge that banning private cars in the commercial areas of the city is not a long-term solution for keeping a check on pollution or congestion. Firstly, the pollution that we see engulfing the towns is not because of the private cars. In fact, the commercial vehicles and their poor maintenance and upkeep is the root cause behind this problem. Now moving towards traffic congestion-according to me the solution lies in unearthing the real causes of congestion which is the mismanaged traffic, poor condition of the roads, non – operational traffic lights and many other issues like this. Therefore, rather than banning private cars we should look towards regulating the movement of the traffic with special emphasis on commercial vehicles. We should also try ways by which availability of the public transport is increased so that dependence on personal cars is decreased and there are less vehicles on the roads.

Therefore, in my opinion the solution lies in addressing the problem in a holistic manner.

Thank You !

8.   **(1 × 4 = 4 Marks)**

(a) These children are the students of the elementary classroom who belong to the deprived and poor sections of the society.

(b) There are different figures of speech used in the first two lines. A Simile "like rootless weeds", Alliteration in case of "far from", Repetition in case of "far far" etc.

(c) The tall girl's head is weighed down due to poverty and the responsibilities that lie on her head.

(d) The word "pallor" means the unhealthy and pale appearance. The word describes the pale appearance of the faces of the children.

OR

(a) The tigers are called Aunt Jennifer's tigers because they have been embroidered by her as a representation of her hidden aspirations and desires.

(b) They are described here as elegant, brave, confident and unafraid inhabitants of the jungle who do not 'fear the men beneath the tree'.

(c) These tigers are different from Aunt Jennifer in the sense that the tigers are fearless, confident and chivalric. Aunt Jennifer on the other hand is meek and fearful with fingers 'ringed with ordeals'.

(d) The word 'chivalric' originally means polite and respectful towards women. Here it refers to the confidence of the tigers of their power and certainty.

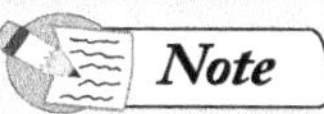 *Note*

1. *Be precise and to the point.*

2. *Pay attention to **the figures of Speech** used in the poems and the **special words** whose meaning can be asked. For e.g "**What does the word, 'pallor' mean**", you must know the meaning of the word as used in the passage.*

9.   **(3 × 4 = 12 Marks)**

(a) Franz did not want to go to school that day because not only was he late for school, but he also hadn't learnt his participles and was in great dread of receiving a scolding from M Hamel. Furthermore, it was a warm and bright day and roaming outside seemed more tempting than school.

(b) Sophie was not happy working in the biscuit factory. Her ambition in life was to rise above her lower middle-class status by becoming a boutique owner or an actress. She wanted to earn money by being a manager and then save enough money to open a boutique herself.

(c) The pain that Kamala Das feels in "My Mother at Sixty-Six" is the pain of eventual separation from her mother on account of her getting old.

(d) The 'mighty dead' can be a thing of beauty through the immortal stories of heroic deeds of the ancestors. The mausoleums and tombs that are erected in the memory of the dead can also be considered being of the same value.

(e) The Maharaja was once in danger of losing his kingdom since he refused to grant permission to the British Officer to hunt tigers in his kingdom. He even refused to allow him to get photographed with a dead tiger and this made the officer angry at the Maharaja.

(f) The basic plot of the story told by Jack was the same except for the change in the kind of animal. A small creature named Roger has a problem. He goes to the wise owl for solution from where he is directed to the wizard who solves the problem after performing a magic spell and asking for a fee which is greater than what the Roger creature has. So, he is directed to a place from where he can get it. The Roger creature then goes home happy where he is in time to hear the train whistle that brought his daddy home from Boston.

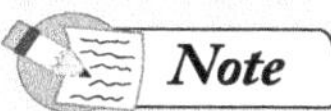 *Note*

You must mention at least two value points while answering these questions.

1. *So, for the question **"Why did Franz not want to go to school that day"** include any two value points from those given below.*

   a.   Franz was late for school.

   b.   He hadn't learnt his participles.

   c.   He was in great dread of receiving a scolding from M Hamel.

   d.   It was a warm and bright day and roaming outside seemed more tempting than school.

10.   **(6 Marks)**

Seemapuri, a place on the periphery of Delhi, has been the home for the people who came there from Bangladesh in 1971 and picked up rag picking as their means of survival. Living for more than 30 years without an identity or a permit but with ration cards which allows them to buy grains, they move from place to place, living in tents which serve as their transit homes. They pitch their tents wherever they can find food. For them garbage is like gold since it brings them food and a roof over their heads, even if it is a leaking roof. Their children also grow up there and become their 'partners in survival'. Rag picking for them is the means of survival. However, for the children the whole art is not only that but more. It is wrapped up in wonder too since they come across a coin or two every now and then.

OR

The peddler has a very cynical view of the world which was probably a result of his own poor and abject living conditions and people's negative treatment of him. He thinks of the whole world as a rat trap and all men and women either trapped by the riches and luxuries of the trap or circling around the bait. The peddler feels thankful at the beginning of the story that he is, yet, un-trapped. However, since he is deprived of food, shelter and money, he gets tempted to steal the 30 Kronors of the crofter. Later the wonderful and unexpected treatment at the hands of Elda changes something at the core of his being and after getting lost in the forest he realizes that he himself is trapped in the rat trap and then makes amends for that. It is of course true that the others like the kind and trusting Crofter, Edla and Ironmaster are not really tempted even though they too lack things in life.

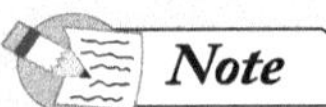

Note

1. *Answer to the point including your own opinion in places where it is deemed necessary by the question.*

1. *Pick out specific examples from the text to support your answer.*

2. *Quote straight from the text wherever required but do so only when you are sure of the words.*

3. *For e.g.The question "Garbage to them is gold. How do ragpickers of Seemapuri survive", you need to use the key words - Seemapuri, a place on the periphery of Delhi-home for those who came there from Bangladesh in 1971 - picked up rag picking - means of survival - living for more than 30 years - no identity - ration cards allows buying grains - move from place to place- living in tents - their transit homes - pitch their tents wherever find food-Garbage is gold - brings them food and a roof over their heads- children too grow up there- become 'partners in survival'- Rag picking - means of survival - for the children the whole art is not only that but more- wrapped up in wonder too - a coin or two every now and then.*

11.   **(6 Marks)**

Bama's first encounter with untouchability was when she saw a village elder holding a parcel of eatables in a manner which ensured that the parcel stayed away from his body and carrying it to the landlord. She found the sight most amusing but later she gets to know about the underlying currents of untouchability behind this action. She finds it totally unacceptable a belief that food of the upper class, if touched by the lower class, was deemed as polluted and unfit for consumption. Her brother Aman gives her some more insights based on what he had faced whenever he came to the village. Education and being the best in your field, according to Aman, are the ways through which one can gain acceptance in a biased society. So, Bama decides to fight against it. On the advice of her brother, she studies hard and tops her class. As a result, many people became her friend.

OR

Dr Sadao succeeded as a doctor as well as a patriot by striking a wonderful balance between the two. As a doctor he was aware of the value of human life and that his primary duty was to make the ailing, injured and sick people fully whole. Therefore, notwithstanding the risk inherent in treating an enemy, he takes the person home, operates him and provides post-operative treatment too. In course of time his faithful servants desert him failing to understand the humane side of Dr Sadao. Even his wife to a large extent does not favour his actions because she feels that he is not only risking himself but also putting the life of the family in jeopardy.

However even while doing his duty as a doctor, Sadao does not fail as a patriot. It is very clear from the lesson that he views all Americans as repulsive and informs the General about the injured man whom he has treated. He also keeps the door open for the assassins to enter. It is another matter that the assassins fail to arrive and kill the enemy.

Note

1. *Adhere to the word limit given for the question.*

2. *Quoting from the text always gets more marks but misquotes can backfire. So, be careful.*

3. The question requires not only your knowledge of the text but also your analysis of the inhuman practice like untouchability. So, include both.

4. For the Question **"Untouchability is not only a crime, it is inhuman too. Why and how did Bama decide** to fight against it", the WHY of the question would require you to relate Bama's first encounter with untouchability. *And the HOW would include Aman's observation that 'Education and being the best in your field were the ways through which one could gain acceptance in a biased society,' which inspires Bama to fight against it.*

12.   **(6 Marks)**

Marvel is an opportunist who benefits due to his association with Griffin. He is introduced in the novel as a tramp, shabby in appearance, who is recruited by Griffin since there are lot of things that Griffin can't perform due to him being invisible. He is also threatened with dire consequences if he does not follow Griffin's command and do as he bids. Marvel agrees to help Griffin since he feels he too can benefit through this association. Later when he suffers physically at the hands of Griffin, he tries to escape and is successful only at the second try. He is also instrumental in getting Griffin shot by a bullet when he takes refuge in the 'Jolly Cricketers'inn. After Griffin's death he is the one who gets to keep the three notebooks along with the money. So, a homeless, jobless, tramp ends up successful keeping everything belonging to Griffin with himself through his shrewdness and keen eye for opportunities. The epilogue shows himstarting a little inn and naming it 'The Invisible Man' through which he becomes quite rich. At times he opens the notebooks to find the secret of invisibility but is not able to understand it.

OR

Godfrey Cass is introduced in the novel as an 'open-faced, good- natured young man' whois set to inherit all his father's fortunes provided he does not go his younger brother's way. He marries Molly Farren, an opium addict and has a child, Eppie, and then leaves her. This is however kept a secret by him since he is attracted to Nancy Lammeter and wants to marry her. Godfrey does not have the courage to reveal this to his father since he fears his father disinheriting him and because of this he gives in to younger brother, Dustan Cass,' blackmailing time and again. He even sells his horse 'Wild Fire' to give Dustan some money. He isn't evenable to muster enough of courage to tell Nancy and his father of his secret marriage before his marriage to Nancy. The reaction at Molly's death'cast only one glance at the dead face on the pillow,' and heaving a sigh of relief shows his moral degradation and selfishness.Even though he is the biological father of Eppie, he only provides for her but does not acknowledge her as his own child. He confesses to his deed only when Dunstan Cass' body is found in Stone Pits virtually at the end of the novel. It is only then that he wants to adopt Eppie. All this amply proves his procrastinating nature and morally weak character.

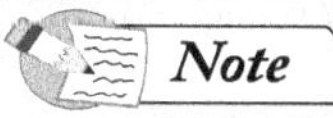 ***Note***

1. *Adhere to the word limit. Answer must reveal your deep knowledge of the text.*

2. *For e.g. the question **'Describe Marvel as an opportunist'** use at least 4 value points from those given below:*

    a. *Marvel an opportunist who benefits due to his association with Griffin.*

    b. *Introduced in the novel as a tramp, shabby in appearance- recruited by Griffin since there are lot of things that Griffin can't perform due to him being invisible- threatened with dire consequences by Griffin's.*

    c. *Feels he too can benefit through this association.*

    d. *Tries to escape and is successful only at the second try.*

    e. *Instrumental in getting Griffin shot.*

    f. *After Griffin's death he is the one who gets to keep the three notebooks along with the money.*

    g. *A homeless, jobless, tramp ends up successful keeping everything belonging to Griffin with himself through his shrewdness and keen eye for opportunities.*

    h. *The epilogue - starting a little inn and naming it 'The Invisible Man' through which he becomes quite rich.*

13.   **(6 Marks)**

Mr Cuss is the general practitioner whose curiosity is ignited by the reports of a stranger with all his face covered with bandages and thousand and one bottles in his room. So, he wants to meet this person and he hits upon the idea of taking the subscription-list for a village nurse as an excuse to meet him. However, this meeting ends in a disaster and Mr Cuss has the most unpleasant and scary experience there. The stranger kept on sniffing and every question of Mr Cuss enraged him. When the prescription caught fire, Griffin wanted to pick up the paper and Mr Cuss was aghast to see an empty sleeve moving. To add to the shock, Griffin nipped Cuss's nose on being questioned further. He could see the entire sleeve but as related by Cuss "there wasn't anything there'. This made Mr Cuss fly away from the inn in terror.

OR

Silas' life at Lantern Yard was diametrically opposed to the kind of life he led at Raveloe. He was a weaver by profession who had inherited from his mother some knowledge of herbs and medicinal plants which could be used to cure certain ailments, but he did not practice it because of two reasons. First, he doubted the lawfulness of such a practice and secondly, he also believed that herbs would not have the required effect without prayers. Since prayers were enough on their own, there was no reason to practice the administration of herbs etc.

At Lantern Yard he was a respected member of the church and known for his honesty, wisdom and exemplary life. He had a close friend William Dane who was a little older than Silas and their friendship was such that the Lantern Yard brethren called them David and Jonathan. Silas also had Sarah, his fiancée, whom he was set to marry in times to come. He led a respected and contented life at Lantern Yard.

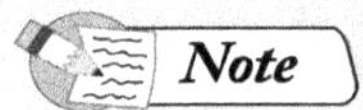

Note

1. *This question tests understanding, appreciation, analysis and interpretation of the incident/character. So, thorough reading of the text is required.*
2. *Adhere to the word limit*
3. *Avoid giving details which you are not sure of.*
4. *For the question –"How does Dr. Cuss's encounter with Griffin end in a disaster", negotiate the question using value points from those given below:*

   a. *Mr Cuss - general practitioner - curiosity ignited by the reports of a stranger with all his face covered with bandages and thousand and one bottles in his room.*

   b. *Wants to meet in person.*

   c. *The idea of taking the subscription-list for a village nurse as an excuse.*

   d. *Meeting ends in a disaster.*

   e. *Most unpleasant and scary experience there.*

   f. *The stranger kept on sniffing and every question of Mr Cuss enraged him.*

   g. *The prescription catches fire- Mr Cuss was aghast to see an empty sleeve moving.*

   h. *Cuss's nose nipped too on being questioned further.*

   i. *Flew away from the inn in terror.*

CBSE Board Solved Paper

Time Allowed : 3 Hours   *Maximum Marks : 100*

General Instructions:

(i) This paper is divided into three sections: A, B and C. All the sections are compulsory.

(ii) Separate instructions are given with each section and question, wherever necessary. Read these instructions very carefully and follow them faithfully.

(iii) Do not exceed the prescribed word limit while answering the questions.

SECTION A: Reading

(30 Marks)

1. Read the passage given below :

1. Maharana Pratap ruled over Mewar only for 25 years. However, he accomplished so much grandeur during his reign that his glory surpassed the boundaries of countries and time turning him into an immortal personality. He along with his kingdom became a synonym for valour, sacrifice and patriotism. Mewar had been a leading Rajput kingdom even before Maharana Pratap occupied the throne. Kings of Mewar, with the cooperation of their nobles and subjects, had established such traditions in the kingdom, as augmented their magnificence despite the hurdles of having a smaller area under their command and less population. There did come a few thorny occasions when the flag of the kingdom seemed sliding down. Their flag once again heaved high in the sky thanks to the gallantry and brilliance of the people of Mewar.

2. The destiny of Mewar was good in the sense that barring a few kings, most of the rulers were competent and patriotic. This glorious tradition of the kingdom almost continued for 1500 years since its establishment, right from the reign of Bappa Rawal. In fact only 60 years before Maharana Pratap, Rana Sanga drove the kingdom to the pinnacle of fame. His reputation went beyond Rajasthan and reached Delhi. Two generations before him, Rana Kumbha had given a new stature to the kingdom through victories and developmental work. During his reign, literature and art also progressed extraordinarily. Rana himself was inclined towards writing and his works are read with reverence even today. The ambience of his kingdom was conducive to the creation of high quality work of art and literature. These accomplishments were the outcome of a longstanding tradition sustained by several generations.

3. The life of the people of Mewar must have been peaceful and prosperous during the long span of time; otherwise such extraordinary accomplishment in these fields would not have been possible. This is reflected in their art and literature as well as their loving nature. They compensate for lack of admirable physique by their firm but pleasant nature. The ambience of Mewar remains lovely thanks to the cheerful and liberal character of its people.

4. One may observe astonishing pieces of workmanship not only in the forts and palaces of Mewar but also in public utility buildings. Ruins of many structures which are still standing tall in their grandeur are testimony to the fact that Mewar was not only the land of the brave but also a seat of art and culture. Amidst aggression and bloodshed, literature and art flourished and creative pursuits of literature and artists did not suffer. Imagine, how glorious the period must have been when the Vijaya Stambha which is the sample of our great ancient architecture even today, was constructed. In the same fort, Kirti Stambha is standing high, reflecting how liberal the then administration was which allowed people from other communities and kingdoms to come and carry out construction work. It is useless to indulge in the debate whether the Vijaya Stambha was constructed first or the Kirti Stambha. The fact is that both the capitals are standing side by side and reveal the proximity between the king and the subjects of Mewar.

5. The cycle of time does not remain the same. Whereas the reign of Rana Sanga was crucial in raising the kingdom to the acme of glory, it also proved to be his nemesis. History took a turn. The fortune of Mewar – the land of the brave, started waning. Rana tried to save the day with his acumen which was running against the stream and the glorious traditions for sometime.

On the basis of your understanding of the above passage answer each of the questions given below with the help of the options that follow :

(a) Maharana Pratap became immortal because :
  (i) he ruled Mewar for 25 years.
  (ii) he added a lot of grandeur to Mewar.
  (iii) of his valour, sacrifice and patriotism.
  (iv) both (ii) and (iii)

(b) Difficulties in the way of Mewar were :
  (i) lack of cooperation of the nobility.
  (ii) ancient traditions of the kingdom.
  (iii) its small area and small population.
  (iv) the poverty of the subjects.

(c) During thorny occasions :
  (i) the flag of Mewar seemed to be lowered.
  (ii) the flag of Mewar was hoisted high.
  (iii) the people of Mewar showed gallantry.
  (iv) most of the rulers heaved a sigh of relief.

(d) Mewar was lucky because :
  (i) all of its rulers were competent.
  (ii) most of its people were competent.
  (iii) most of its rulers were competent.
  (iv) only a few of its people were incompetent.

Answer the following questions briefly :

(e) Who is the earliest King of Mewar mentioned in the passage?

(f) What was Rana Kumbha's contribution to the glory of Mewar?

(g) What does the writer find worth admiration in the people of Mewar?

(h) How could art and literature flourish in Mewar?

(i) How did the rulers show that they cared for their subjects?

(j) What does the erection of Vijaya Stambha and Kirti Stambha in the same fort signify?

(k) Find words from the passage which mean the same as each of the following :
  (i) surprising (para 4)
  (ii) evidence (para 4)

2. Read the passage given below :

1. To ensure its perpetuity, the ground is well held by the panther both in *space* and in *time*. It enjoys a much wider distribution over the globe than its bigger cousins, and procreates sufficiently profusely to ensure its continuity for all time to come.

2. There seems to be no particular breeding season of the panther, although its sawing and caterwauling is more frequently heard during winter and summer. The gestation period is about ninety to hundred days (Whipsnade, ninety-two days). The litter normally consists of four cubs, rarely five. Of these, generally two survive and not more than one reaches maturity. I have never come across more than two cubs at the heels of the mother. Likewise, graziers in the forest have generally found only two cubs hidden away among rocks, hollows of trees, and other impossible places.

3. Panther cubs are generally in evidence in March. They are born blind. This is a provision of Nature against their drifting away from the place of safety in which they are lodged by their mother, and exposing themselves to the danger of their being devoured by hyenas, jackals, and other predators. They generally open their eyes in about three to four weeks.

4. The mother alone rears its cubs in seclusion. It keeps them out of the reach of the impulsive and impatient male. As a matter of fact the mother separates from the male soon after mating and forgets all about their tumultuous union. The story that the male often looks in to find out how the mother is progressing with her cubs has no foundation except in what we wish it should do at least.

5. The mother carries its cubs about by holding them by the scruff of their neck in its mouth. It trains them to stalk, and teaches them how to deliver the bite of death to the prey. The cubs learn to treat all and sundry with suspicion at their mother's heels. Instinctively the cubs seek seclusion, keep to cover and protect their flanks by walking along the edge of the forest.

6. I have never had an opportunity to watch mother panther train its cubs. But in Pilibhit forests, I once saw a tigress giving some lessons to its little ones. I was sitting over its kill at Mala. As the sun set, the tigress materialised in the twilight behind my *machan*. For about an hour, it scanned and surveyed the entire area looking and listening with the gravest concern. It even went to the road where my elephant was awaiting my signal. The *mahout* spotted it from a distance and drove the elephant away.

7. When darkness descended upon the scene and all was well and safe, the tigress called its cubs by emitting a low *haa-oon*. The cubs, two in number and bigger than a full-grown cat, soon responded. They came trotting up to their mother and hurried straight to the kill in indecent haste. The mother spitted at them so furiously that they doubled back to its heels immediately. Thereafter, the mother and its cubs sat under cover about 50 feet (15 m) away from the kill to watch, wait, look, and listen. After about half an hour's patient and fidgetless vigil the mother seemed to say 'paid for'. At this signal, the cubs cautiously advanced, covering their flanks, towards the kill. No longer did they make a beeline for it, as they had done before.

8. The mother sat watching its cubs eat, and mounted guard on them. She did not partake of the meal.

On the basis of your understanding of the passage complete the statements given below with the help of options that follow :

(a) To protect its cubs the mother panther hides them :

(i) among rocks

(ii) in the branches of the trees

(iii) behind the tree trunks

(iv) at its heels

(b) The male panther :

(i) is protective of its cubs

(ii) trains its cubs

(iii) watches the progress of the mother

(iv) is impulsive and impatient

Answer the following questions briefly :

(c) How many cubs does the mother panther rarely deliver?

(d) What may happen if the panther cubs are not born blind?

(e) Why did the mahaut drive his elephant away?

(f) Why did the tigress spit at its cubs?

(g) From the narrator's observation what do we learn about the nature of the tigress?

(h) Why does the panther not face the risk of extinction?

(i) Find words from the passage which mean the same as each of the following :

(i) moving aimlessly (para 3)

(ii) came down / fell (para 7)

3. Read the passage given below :

People tend to amass possessions, sometimes without being aware of doing so. They can have a delightful surprise when they find something useful which they did not know they owned. Those who never have to change house become indiscriminate collectors of what can only be described as clutter. They leave unwanted objects in drawers, cupboards and attics for years in the belief that they may one day need them. Old people also accumulate belongings for two other reasons, lack of physical and mental energy, and sentiment. Things owned for a long time are full of associations with the past, perhaps with the relatives who are dead, and so they gradually acquire a sentimental value.

Some things are collected deliberately in an attempt to avoid wastage. Among these are string and brown paper, kept by thrifty people when a parcel has been opened. Collecting small items can be a mania. A lady cuts out from newspapers sketches of model clothes that she would like to buy if she had money. As she is not rich, the chances are that she will never be able to afford such purchases. It is a harmless habit, but it litters up her desk. Collecting as a serious hobby is quite different and has many advantages. It provides relaxation for leisure hours, as just looking at one's treasure is always a joy. One doesn't have to go out for amusement as the collection is housed at home. Whatever it consists of – stamps,

records, first editions of books, china – there is always something to do in connection with it, from finding the right place for the latest addition to verifying facts in reference books. This hobby educates one not only in the chosen subject, but also in general matters which have some bearing on it.

There are other benefits also. One gets to meet like-minded collectors to get advice, compare notes, exchange articles, to show off one's latest find etc. So one's circle of friends grows. Soon the hobby leads to travelling, perhaps a meeting in another town, possibly a trip abroad in search of a rare specimen, for collectors are not confined to one country. Over the years one may well become an authority on one's hobby and will probably be asked to give informal talks to little gatherings and then, if successful, to larger audiences.

(a) On the basis of your understanding of the above passage make notes on it, using headings and sub-headings. Use recognizable abbreviations (wherever necessary-minimum four) and a format you consider suitable. Also supply an appropriate title to it.

(b) Write a summary of the passage in about 80 words.

(30 Marks)

4. You are Karan Kumar/Karuna Bajaj, a leading lawyer practising in Surat. You want to buy an independent house at City Light Road to be used as office-cumresidence. Draft an advertisement in about 50 words for the classified columns of a local newspaper. You can be contacted at 45645678.

OR

On 30th November your school is going to hold its annual sports day. You want Mr. Dhanraj Pillai, a noted hockey player to give away the prizes to the budding sportspersons of the school. Write a formal invitation in about 50 words requesting him to grace the occasion. You are Karuna/ Karan, Sports Secretary, Sunrise Global School, Agra.

5. Along with air and water pollution, our cities are also under an attack of noise pollution. Marriage processions, DJs during wedding receptions, loud music from neighbourhood flats etc. are all sources of noise which is not good for the old, the ailing and students. Write a letter in 120-150 words to the editor of a local newspaper describing the problem and making a request to the concerned authorities to solve it. You are Karan/Karuna, M 114, Mall Road, Delhi.

OR

In all big cities road rage has become a serious problem. A minor scratch, a little push, or a small brushing past can lead to a scuffle sometimes resulting even in murder. Write a letter in 120-150 words to the Police Commissioner giving your views on the problem and its solutions. You are Karuna/Karan, M 114, Mall Road, Delhi.

6. "Brain drain is not a bane for a developing country like India'. Write a debate in 150-200 words either for or against the motion.

OR

Write a speech in 150-200 words on the topic, 'Discipline shapes the future of a student. It is to be delivered in the morning assembly. You are Karuna/Karan.

7. Education has always been a noble profession. Our ancestors received their learning at gurukuls and ashrams. Even in the near past pathshalas (schools) were associated with places of worship. Today, education is fast becoming commercialised. Parents have to shell out a lot of money on coaching classes, tuition fees etc. Write an article in 150-200 words on 'The State of Education, Today'. You are Karan/Karuna.

OR

According to 2011 census, literacy rate of hundred percent or around has been achieved by only a couple of states in India. Illiteracy is found mostly among the old and the deprived sections of society. What can the youth do to spread literacy in society? Write an article in 150-200 words on 'Role of students in eradicating illiteracy'. You are Karuna/Karan.

SECTION C: Textbooks and Long Reading Text

(40 Marks)

8. Read the extract given below and answer the questions that follow :

Now we will count to twelve
and we will all keep still.
For once on the face of the Earth
let's not speak in any language,
let's stop for one second,
and not move our arms so much.

(a) What is the significance of the number 'twelve'?
(b) Which two activities does the poet want us to stop?
(c) What does the poet mean by 'let's not speak in any language?
(d) Describe the pun on the word, 'arms'.

OR

.... I saw my mother,
beside me,
doze, open mouthed, her face
ashen like that
of a corpse and realised with
pain ....

(a) Who is I?
(b) What did 'I' realise with pain?

(c) Why was the realisation painful?
(d) Identify and name the figure of speech used in these lines.

9. Answer any four of the following questions in 30-40 words each:
(a) What does the reference to chappals in 'Lost Spring' tell us about the economic condition of the rag pickers?
(b) What do we learn about the crofter's nature from the story, 'The Rattrap'?
(c) How is 'Shakespeare wicked and the map a bad example' for the children of the school in a slum?
(d) What picture of male chauvinism (tyranny) do we find in the poem, 'Aunt Jennifer's Tigers'?
(e) How did the Governor, Oxford Prison describe Evans to the Secretary Examination Board?
(f) At the dining table why did Zitkala-Sa begin to cry when others started eating?

10. Answer the following question in 120-150 words:

Every teenager has a hero/heroine to admire. So many times they become role models for them. What is wrong if Sophie fantasises about Danny Casey and is ambitious in life?

OR

Our native language is part of our culture and we are proud of it. How does the presence of village elders in the classroom and M. Hamel's last lesson show their love for French?

11. Answer the following question in 120-150 words:
Both Derry and Lamb are victims of physical impairment, but much more painful for them is the feeling of loneliness. Comment.

OR

How did Jack end the Roger Skunk story? How and why did Jo want to change it?

12. Attempt the following question in 120-150 words:
How did Mrs. Hall show her excitement when Griffin came to stay at Coach and Horses?

OR

How do William Dane's deceit and Sarah's desertion affect Silas?

13. Attempt the following question in 120-150 words:
Marvel is the only character in 'The Invisible Man' who interacts with Griffin and gains something. Comment.

OR

Attempt a character sketch of Eppie.

Solutions

1. (a) (iv) both (i) & (ii)   **(1 × 4 = 4 Marks)**

    (b) (iii) its small area and small population

    (c) (i) the flag of Mewar seemed to be lowered

    (d) (iii) most of its rulers were competent

                 (1 × 6 = 6 Marks)

    (e) Bappa Rawal is the earliest King of Mewar mentioned in the passage.

    (f) Rana Kumbha had given a new stature to the kingdom through victories and developmental work. Literature and Art also flourished during his reign. Rana himself was inclined towards writing and his works are read even today.

    (g) According to the writer, the cheerful nature and liberal character of the people of Mewar is worth admiration.

    (h) Art and Literature could flourish in Mewar due to the peace and prosperity for a long period of time. The rulers of Mewar too were inclined towards Art and Literature.

    (i) The fact that both the Vijaya Stambha and Kirti Stambha stand side by side even today reveal the proximity between the king and the people of Mewar. The rulers also allowed people from other communities to come and do the construction work and that shows the liberal administration on the Kings.

    (j) The erection of Vijaya Stambha and Kirti Stambha in the same fort signifies the proximity between the King and the people of Mewar.

    (k)   **(1 × 2 = 2 Marks)**

       (i) astonishing

       (ii) testimony

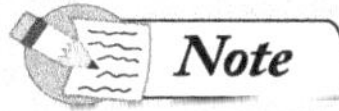

Note

When answering MCQs choose the option which is the closest answer from amongst the options.

1. For Factual questions like e.g. "Who is the earliest King of Mewar mentioned in the passage, "do not include information not given in the passage.

2. While answering the 'How' question like "How could Art and Literature flourish in Mewar", you may begin your answer with 'Art and Literature could flourish in Mewar due to the ……….or a similar phrase.

3. While answering the vocabulary questions, check the part of speech, the tense of the word etc. Your answer should have the same part of speech, tense etc.

4. For e.g. Surprising – Astonishing (NOT astonish or Astonished)

2. (a) option i -among rocks   **(1 × 2 = 2 Marks)**

    (b) option iv - is impulsive and impatient

    (c) The mother panther rarely delivers 5 cubs.

                 (1 × 6 = 6 Marks)

    (d) If the panther cubs are not born blind, they may drift away from their place of safety and might get exposed to the danger of them being devoured by the hyenas, jackals etc.

    (e) The mahaut drove away the elephant so that it would be away from the sight of the panther and not disturb the tigress.

    (f) As soon as the tigress called its cubs, the cubs came hurriedly and hurried straight at the kill. The tigress was furious at their carelessness and she wanted them to be trained to wait and ensure safety first before eating. So, she spat at them and that made them come back to their mother's heels.

    (g) We learn a lot of things about the nature of the tigress from the narrator's observation. We get to know that she is patient, caring and protective. However, she is also strict when she wants to discipline and train the cubs.

    (h) The panther does not face the danger of extinction since it enjoys a much wider distribution across the globe as compared to tigers etc. In addition, it also procreates sufficiently with around 4 to 5 cubs in a litter.

    (i)   **(1 × 2 = 2 Marks)**

       (i) drifting

       (ii) descended

3. (a) **Note Making**   **(5 Marks)**

    Title- Collecting – A Hobby Or An Obsession

    1. Reasons for collection

       1.1 Surprise element

       1.2 No change of house

       1.3 Belief that it might be needed

       1.4 Old people acc.

          1.4.a lack of phy. & mental energy

          1.4.b sentiment

       1.5 Past assn.

       1.6 Deliberate collection

       1.7 A mania

       1.8 Hobby

    2. Advantages

       2.1 Relaxation for leisure

       2.2 No need to go out for amusement

2.3 Meet like- minded collectors for

    2.3.a. get advice

    2.3.b. compare notes

    2.3.c. exchange articles

    2.3.d. to show off one's latest find

2.4 Leads to travelling

2.5 One becomes an authority

2.6 Can give talks to

    2.6.a. small grps

    2.6.b. larger groups as a prof.

Key to Abbreviations

Abbreviation	Word
acc	accumulate
phy	physical
&	And
assn	association
grps	groups
prof.	professional

(b) Summary   **(3 Marks)**

There are various reasons for collecting things. Some do it over the years without even being aware of it. No shifting of house, the belief that something might be needed someday, lack of physical and mental energy, emotional attachment with things of the past are reasons behind collecting things. In addition to it being a mania for some people, collecting has multiple advantages. Spending time creatively, meeting like- minded people, travelling etc leads to one turning into a professional. (79 words)

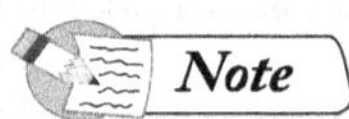

Note

1. *The passage is on the concept of collecting and how it is a hobby as well as an obsession with some people. So, the title shouldhave the key words 'Collect', 'Hobby,' and 'obsession' or any synonym of the words.*

2. *It should always contain phrases. Avoid using complete sentences. E.g.*

    1. *Reasons for collection*

       1.1 Surprise element

       1.2 No change of house

       1.3 Belief that it might be needed

       1.4 Old people acc.

          1.4.a lack of phy. & mental energy

          1.4.b sentiment

    AND NOT The reasons for collecting are many ……..

3. *Include a minimum of 4-6 distinctly different recognizable short forms i.e. abbreviations of the words in the notes as done in the solution.*

4. Advertisement   **(4 Marks)**

<u>**WANTED INDEPENDENT HOUSE**</u>

Wanted an independent house to serve as office-cum-residence for a leading practitioner of law, newly constructed, minimum 6 rooms with attached bathrooms, preferably ground floor with a front lawn and parking space, regular water and power supply in City Light Road, Surat. Price no bar. Contact Karuna Bajaj, 45645678

OR

Formal invitation

Sunrise Global School
Agra

23rd March 20XX

Sh Dharaj Pillai
2/27
Agra

Sir,

Sub: <u>Request to give away the prizes to the budding sportspersons of the school</u>

This is to inform you that our school is organizing its Annual Sports Day on the 7th of April 20XX in Karnail Singh Stadium from 8:00am- 1:00pm. I, on behalf of the staff and students, would like to request you to grace the occasion with your benign presence and give away the prizes to the budding sportspersons of the school. Your presence will be a great motivating factor for them.

Yours faithfully
Karuna

Sports Secretary
Sunrise Global School

5. Letter   **(6 Marks)**

M 114
Mall Road
Delhi

23 March, 20XX

The Editor
The Morning Herald

<u>Sub: Menace of Noise Pollution</u>

Respected Sir

Through the esteemed column of your newspaper, I would like to draw the attention of the concerned authorities towards the increasing menace of noise pollution in our city.

Along with air and water pollution, the city now has to grapple with noise pollution too. Blaring music from the loudspeakers during marriages and birthday parties, continuous honking by the impatient drivers and loud music from the neighboring flats are some of the daily irritants. The problem has become more acute since the time the tiny portable speakers were launched in the market. Now even parks are not spared. This affects people of all age groups – more so- the students whose studies gets affected, the patients and the elderly. It can cause hearing loss, hurt the psychological well -being etc. With the festive and marriage season round the corner, I fear this problem will become more acute.

I therefore request the concerned authorities to solve the problem through better urban planning and some strict legislation so that people of all age groups exist in a peaceful environment.

Yours truly
Karuna

OR

M 114
Mall Road
Delhi

23 March, 20XX

The Police Commissioner
Delhi

<u>Sub: Increase in Incidents of Road Rage</u>

Respected Sir

This is with reference to the increase in the incidents of road rage in Delhi in the last few years. I am a resident of Delhi since the last ten years and I can say with conviction that these incidents have increased in the last couple of years.

Patience and empathy are two virtues that the current generation lacks these days with the result that the show of aggressive and violent behavior has become common by the drivers of the vehicles. People resort to violence sometimes resulting in loss of lives due to their annoyance at petty mistakes. It could be something as simple as a minor scratch, a harmless comment or a glare of the eye. In fact, some routes have become notorious for such behavior due to which people prefer taking alternative routes.

I would request you to take cognizance of the problem and increase the vigilance on the roads using surveillance technology. Some sensitization drives can also be organized by the department.

Thanking you in anticipation

Yours truly

Karuna

6. Debate   **(10 Marks)**

Respected members of the Jury, teachers and my dear friends!

I, XXX, stand before you to present my views on the topic "Brain Drain in not a bane for a developing country like India" and I am speaking **against the motion**. First of all, let us understand the term "brain drain". It refers to a situation where highly qualified and trained people of a country move to another country for work. It is a sad reality of today that the Indian youth are migrating to the other countries due to massive unemployment within the country, lack of lucrative opportunities, low professional standards and work culture etc.

India is a developing country and it needs all the support that it can from its people to become a developed country. In such a scenario when the cream of the country drifts away, there isn't only a loss of talent but also a larger economic loss to one's own country. The expenses incurred on the education and professional training also gets wasted since they do not contribute to the working capital of their own country. Therefore, Brain drain is a bane for a country like India. The sooner the government woke up to this challenge and made stringent laws for compulsory work in one's own country for some years, and take corrective measures to overhaul the professional culture of the country, the scenario will remain dark.

Thank You!

OR

Speech

Good Morning Respected Principal, teachers and my dear friends!

I, Karuna, stand before you today in this bright morning to express my views on the topic "Discipline Shapes the Future of a Student".

Let us first understand what the term discipline is. Discipline is a term whose meaning and values may differ from person to person. For some it could be an order or a code of behavior and for others it could be the control that one gains by enforcing a system. However varied the meanings might be, all will agree that it is one of the important prerequisites for success and essential in all walks of life , more so in a student's life. Getting up early, reaching school in time, adhering to the timelines of study and sports- all of it shape the personality of a person. If inculcated early in life it leads to cultivation of restraint, good work ethics, self-confidence and an absence of chaos and confusion in life. It also promotes a sense of mental well-being since being disciplined removes the stress that comes with lack of proper planning. In addition to this, discipline also inculcates a sense of duty in a person and you slowly become a role model for others to emulate. In other words, discipline becomes the bedrock of character.

Thank You!

OR

Respected members of the Jury, teachers and my dear friends !

I, XXX, stand before you to present my views on the topic "Brain Drain in not a bane for a developing country like India" and I am speaking **for the motion**. First of all, let us understand the term "brain drain". It refers to a situation where the highly qualified and trained people of a country move to another country in search of better opportunities.

It is a reality of the current times that the Indian youth are migrating to the other countries and in my opinion, it is a positive indication. Rather than facing the massive unemployment within the country, the movement abroad gives opportunities to the talented individuals of the country and opens up a vast plethora of possibilities for professional growth. The Indian work force gets recognized abroad and brings prestige to the country. The forex remitted back helps the family and adds on to their economic welfare. Not only does this promote globalization by enhancing the socio- cultural relationship but also brings in a sense of healthy competition among the deserving individuals. Therefore, in my opinion, Brain Drain is not a bane for a developing country like India.

Thank you

7. **Article**   **(10 Marks)**

The State of Education Today

By *Karuna*

Education – the fulcrum of success in a man's life. There was a time when centres of education were considered places of worship and the teachers were held in awe by the students. However, the recent times reflect trends which seem ominous for the education field. Education is becoming increasingly commercialized with each passing day and the burden on the pocket of the Parents is increasing. With the change of family structure from a joint one to nuclear, Parents do not have time for the children since both are earning. It is a sorry sight that greets one on the city streets with children going to tuitions right from the tender age of 3 years to 18 years. The teaching methodologies and the assessment systems are also such that promotes rote learning with little space for design thinking and developing of the creativity and imagination of the students. With the flourishing coaching centres and tutorials, children are being subjected to immense pressure to achieve the required marks and positions in life.

The real purpose of education gets lost in this mindless and unrealistic race to reach the top. Added to this is the paucity of good schools, poor infrastructure and a lack of balance in the student teacher ratio in government schools.

It is time for us to take a stock of the situation and take corrective measures to put things right. Else it will be too late.

OR

Role of Students in Eradicating Illiteracy

By *Karuna*

Even though India is a free democratic country since the last seven decades, we are yet to do justice to the principles which are the lifeline to our constitution. Among many other problems that India faces today is the problem of illiteracy. Even though there are government and private schools, the government schools have not been able to get the requisite number of children despite running a multitude of programs aimed at attracting the children to school. Out of the few who attend, a large number of them drop out soon after. Having parents with little schooling themselves, difficult living conditions, widespread poverty and an urgent need to feed the mouth rather than the brain- the problems are many. What one needs to be done is to take the school to the homes of the children and students can play a major role in the same.

The students can be encouraged to adopt the "Each One Teach One" scheme where they feel responsible for their own students. They can do these activities during their vacations or in the evenings. Even schools where they themselves study can take up these programs. Creating awareness regarding the importance of literacy through rallies, street plays and media coverage can motivate the Parents to send their children to the school. In addition, the student-teacher themselves will benefit since they would be addressing the problem themselves. To conclude, the students can be the change makers in times to come.

SECTION - C

8. **(4 Marks)**

(a) The number "twelve" signifies time. As there are twelve digits in a clock and it encompasses all the 24 hours in it, the poet wants to give us a measure of time till which we need to keep still. Only if we are quiet for a certain period, will we understand the value of stillness.

(b) The two activities that the poet wants us to stop are speaking in any language and moving our arms a lot.

(c) When the poet says "let's not speak in any language" he wants us to bes silent and introspect.

(d) At one level the word "arms" mean the actual physical arms of the human body symbolizing movement. It could also mean the weapons and therefore a plea to practice non-violence.

OR

(a) "I" is the poet Kamla Das.

(b) The "I" realized with pain that her mother was growing old and the it was then that she thought of the impending separation due to death.

(c) The realization was painful since the thought of her mother's eventual death due to old age was difficult for her to accept.

(d) The figure of speech is a simile and it is used in the line "ashen like that of a corpse".

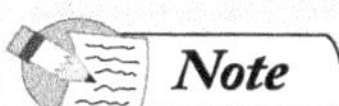 *Note*

1.   Be precise and to the point.

*2.   For e.g. **"Which two activities does the poet want us to stop"** you may begin by ....The two activities that the poet wants us to stop are speaking in any language and moving our arms a lot.*

9. **(3 × 4 = 12 Marks)**

(a) The reference to chappals in "Lost Spring" tells us that the economic condition of the rag pickers is very bad. They are poor and impoverished and do not have enough money to buy chappals.

(b) The crofter in the story "The Rat trap" is very simple and trusting. He is a lonely man who shares vital information about the thirty *kronors* with the peddler very easily not even thinking about the consequences.

(c) The poet calls "Shakespeare wicked and the map a bad example" since both represent a world which is beautiful and has ships and sun and love. This world is in sharp contrast to the world of the slum children which has narrow streets sealed with a lead sky. Therefore, they cannot relate to the examples. In addition to this, aspiring for a world like this might tempt them to steal.

(d) The poem "Aunt Jennifer's Tigers"shows a male chauvinistic society where a married women's life is full of constraint and "ordeals". The uncle's wedding band sits "heavily" upon Aunt Jennifer's hand and the word "heavy" shows the oppressive band of the patriarchal society and how she has been dominated by her husband till date. Even after her death her hands will be "terrified" and ringed with ordeals.

(e) The Governor , Oxford Prison, described Evans as pleasant sort of chap who was one of the stars at Christmas concert. He was good at imitations and a congenital kleptomaniac.

(f) Zitkala -Sa began crying at the dining table when others started to eat because since the timeshe had entered the dining hall, she was committing mistakes not being aware of the systems there. She sat down when others remained standing and then got up while the others started sitting. The matron also caught her eye while she was stealing a glance at the room and this made her feel extremely embarrassed.

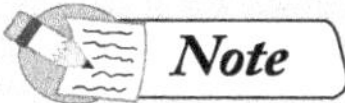 *Note*

Each 3-mark question must have at least two value points.

1.   So, for the question "What do we learn about the crofter's nature from the story 'The Rattrap'", include any two value points from those given below.

   a.   The crofter - very simple and trusting

   b.   Lonely man – not only gives shelter but food too

   c.   Shares vital information about the thirty kronors with the peddler

   d.   Does not even think about the consequence

10. **(6 Marks)**

There is nothing wrong with Sophie fantasizing about Danny Casey and having ambitions in life. In fact, this is the most natural thing for all teenagers to do. The living conditions of her family aren't verypleasant and they are not very well off. In such a scenario, having ambitions to make a better living by becoming a model and opening a boutique is her way to move up the social ladder. However, what she needs to understand is that the dreams should be achievable and realistic. She should also have the zeal to work hard for her dream. As far as fantasizing about Danny Casey is concerned, this too is natural but what she does after that is unpardonable. It is wrong on her part to feed her brother with things that never really happened. The word of caution here is that one must not only dream and live in a make belief world but should follow it up with some concrete plans which can be executed.

OR

Language is a part of one's identity. When a group of people are forbidden from using their own language, one feels threatened at the core of one's being. And it is this threat that unites all people. This is precisely what happens to the entire village of Alsace and Lorraine due to the order from Berlin that French would no longer be taught in the schools there. When Franz arrives in the classroom, he finds the usually empty back row of the class filled with the elderly men of the village who sit quietly at the back of the class paying full attention to the "last" lesson. They look sad as well as sorry for not having gone to school more often and the realization dawns on Franz that this is their way to thank M. Hamel for his forty years of faithful service and at the same time show respect for a country and a language that was theirs no more . M. Hamelspoke about the beauty of French language and appealed to all the people in the class to preserve 'French' since holding on to their language will keep them united. He ends his lesson by writing *"Viva la France"* on the board. Franz too on his part is overwhelmed with emotions and regrets having neglected his native language all these years.

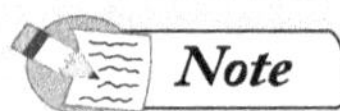

Note

1. *Each 6-mark question must have at least four value points*
2. *Answer to the point including your own opinion in places where it is deemed necessary by the question.*
3. *Pick out specific examples from the text to support your answer*
4. *Quote straight from the text wherever required but do so only when you are sure of the words.*
5. *For e.g. The question **"Our native language is a part of our culture and we are proud of it. How does the presence of the village elders in the classroom and M. Hamel's last lesson show their love for French ,** " you need to use the key words like Language - part of one's identity- when forbidden from using own language, feels threatened - threat unites all people- entire village of Alsace and Lorraine - order from Berlin - French no longer be taught in the schools - When Franz arrives in the classroom he sees elderly men of the village - sitting quietly at the back of the class paying full attention to the "last" lesson- look sad and sorry - their way to thank M. Hamel for his forty years of faithful service - show respect for a country and a language that was theirs no more . M. Hamel - spoke about the beauty of French language-appealed to all the people in the class to preserve 'French'- ends his lesson by writing "Viva la France" on the board.*

11.   **(6 Marks)**

Both Mr. Lamb and Derry suffer from physical disability,but each has a different response to it. Mr. Lamb has a tin leg as his real leg had got blown off in the war and Derry had an accident where more than half his face was burnt by acid. However more than the physical limitation, it is the feeling of alienation from society that bothers Derry. His face is a constant source of pain for

him. The lack of friends , remarks of the onlookers on the street, the whispered conversations on the ground floor of his home between his parents and even his mother's kiss on his cheek – all are sources of pain for Derry since all this makes him feel isolated and different from the rest. However, with Mr. Lamb the case is different. Even though he is mocked at in the streets with children calling him Lamey-Lamb, he does not find it disturbing. Mr. Lamb does not want any sympathy and he derives his happiness from the hum of the bees, his crab apples and his garden. To conclude, even though the two are in the same predicament, both have different responses to it.

OR

Jack ends the Roger Skunk story by making the Mommy Skunk take little skunk to the wizard and making him change the rose smell of Roger Skunk back to its original smell. As per Jack the mother feels that there is nothing wrong in a skunk smelling like a skunk and as a mother, she knew what was right for her baby.

However according to Jo, it was a 'stupid mommy' who would do something like that to her baby and deprive him from the pleasure of being surrounded by friends. Therefore, she wants the ending to be changed the next day. Joe wants the Mommy Skunk to be hit by the wizard and Roger to have the rose smell back. She wants such an ending since the rose smell had earned a lot of friends for Roger and as a child, for Joe, having friends is more important than individuality and a sense of identity.

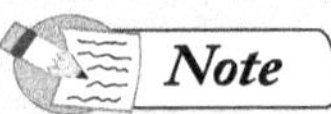

Note

1. *Adhere to the word limit given for the question.*
2. *Quoting from the text always gets more marks but misquotes can backfire. So, be careful.*
3. *The question requires not only your knowledge of the text but also your analysis of the inhuman practice like untouchability. So, include both.*
4. *For the Question "Both Derry and Lamb are victims of physical impairment, but much more painful for them is the feeling of loneliness. Comment, "Break the question into parts of What impairment, Feeling of loneliness and both their response to it.*

   Both Mr. Lamb and Derry suffer from physical disability- each has a different response- Mr. Lamb - tin leg - Derry -an accident - more than half his face burnt by acid- feeling of alienationbothers Derry- face a constant source of pain - lack of friends - remarks of the onlookers -whispered conversations between his parents - mother's kiss on his cheek – all - source of pain for Derry- Mr. Lamb the case is different- children call him Lamey-Lamb- does not find it disturbing- does not want any sympathy - derives his happiness from the hum of the bees-crab apples – garden- even though the two in the same predicament- both have different responses to it.

12. **(6 Marks)**

Mrs Hall was the owner of the inn 'Coach and Horses'. She was a simple, friendly and quite talkative lady who loved to converse with her guests. Since it was winter, Griffin's visit was a god- sent opportunity to make some money since they hardly had any guests in such a harsh and rough weather. Therefore, in her excitement, she ignores the appearance of the guest. Instead, she makes all attempts to make the guest feel at home right from lighting the fire to preparing the meals herselfand offering to take off his coat and hat for drying in the kitchen. Since the maid Millie is sluggish, she carries the plates, cloth and glasses to the parlour on her own. However,Griffin does not give much space to her to strike a conversation. Noticing his covered face, she even asks politely whether he had met with an accident or underwent an operation, but Griffin does not reply. Despite being rebuffed time and again she continues to make herself appear friendly in her excitement.

OR

Silas was a weaver who lived near Raveloe where he had arrived at fifteen years earlier from a city to the North. He was a faithful member of a religious communityand had a friend William. He was also engaged to a young serving woman, Sarah but his engagement did not affect their friendship. In all, he was leading a perfect and a happy life. However, as things turn out, William puts the blame of stealing on Silas and later Sarah too ends her engagement. A month later William and Sarah get married to each other. All this affects Silas adversely. Completely disillusioned by the way his best friend and fiancée framed and deserted him, Silas leaves Lantern Yard. He decides that there isn't any God and becomes a loner. Completely engaged with his loom, day in day out, he starts making more money. For him now, there is only one God – the gold coins that he earns daily.

Note

1. Adhere to the word limit. Answer must reveal your deep knowledge of the text.

2. For e.g. the question 'How do Wiliam Dane's deceit and Sarah's desertion affect Silas' use at least 4 -5 value points from those given below:

   a. Silas- weaver -lived near Raveloe where he had arrived at fifteen years earlier from a city to the North.

   b. Faithful member of a religious community

   c. Had a friend William- also engaged to a young serving woman, Sarah- his engagement did not affect their friendship

   d. In all, was leading a perfect and a happy life

   e. Later William puts the blame of stealing on Silas - Sarah too ends her engagement

   f. William and Sarah get married to each other

   g. Affects Silas adversely- disillusioned by the way his best friend and fiancée framed and deserted him- leaves Lantern Yard

   h. Becomes a loner- completely engaged with his loom- making more money

13. **(6 Marks)**

Marvel was a poor, homeless tramp who did not have any job. He meets Griffin when he was sitting leisurely with his feet in the ditch by the roadside which was one and a half mile away from Iping.Marvel feels his imagination has gone wild when he hears a voice but does not see anyone. Griffin convinces Marvel to be with him and Marvel agrees as he feels he will benefit by the power of Griffin's invisibility. Even though Griffin thought of him as a foolish person , Marvel is far from that. He gives Griffin the slip and takes his notebooks and money to Port Burdock. He gains a lot after Griffin's death too. In the end he starts a little inn and names it 'The Invisible Man' through which he becomes quite rich. At times he opens the notebooks to find the secret of invisibility but is not able to understand it.

OR

Eppie was a child with golden curled hair and the biological daughter of Godfrey Cass & Molly Farren. She is like a daughter to Silas who fills the void left in his heart after the betrayal of William, Sarah and the theft of gold from his house. She is a beautiful, lively and good- natured child who loves Silas unconditionally. Even though she has the choice of a good life because of her rich biological father and his wife Nancy, who want to adopt her, she chooses to be with Silas. She changes him from a recluse to a loving person and heals the hurt of the past. She wants to marry Aaron but only on the condition that all three of them will live together as a family and finally at the end of the novel she walks across the churchyard and down the village to get married with Aaron and Silas by her side as her father.

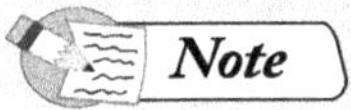

Note

1. *This question tests understanding, appreciation, analysis and interpretation of the incident/character. So, thorough reading of the text is required.*
2. *Adhere to the word limit and answer the question.*
3. *Avoid giving details which you are not sure of.*
4. *For e.g. the question "Attempt a character sketch of Eppie," use at least 4-5 value points from those given below:*
   a. *Eppie- a child with golden curled hair - biological daughter of Godfrey Cass & Molly Farren*
   b. *Like a daughter to Silas - fills the void left in his heart -betrayal of William, Sarah and the theft of gold from his house.*
   c. *Beautiful, lively and good- natured child who loves Silas unconditionally.*
   d. *Even though has the choice of a good life- rich biological father and Nancy who want to adopt her, she chooses to be with Silas.*
   e. *Changes him from a recluse to a loving person - heals the hurt of the past- wants to marry Aaron but condition that all three of them will live together as a family*
   f. *At the end of the novel -walks across the churchyard- down the village - get married - Aaron and Silas by her side as her father.*

Delhi *2016*

CBSE Board Solved Paper

Time Allowed : 3 Hours   *Maximum Marks : 100*

General Instructions:

 (i) Please check that this question paper contains **12** printed pages.

 (ii) Code number given on the right hand side of the question paper should be written on the title page of the answer-book by the candidate.

 (iii) Please check that this question paper contains **13** questions.

 (iv) **Please write down the Serial Number of the question before attempting it.**

 (v) 15 Minute time has been allotted to read this question paper. The question paper will be distributed at 10.15 a.m. From 10.15 a.m. to 10.30 a.m., the students will read the question paper only and will not write any answer on the answer-book during this period.

SECTION A: Reading

(30 Marks)

1. Read the passage given below :

   1. Maharana Pratap ruled over Mewar only for 25 years. However, he accomplished so much grandeur during his reign that his glory surpassed the boundaries of countries and time turning him into an immortal personality. He along with his kingdom became a synonym for valour, sacrifice and patriotism. Mewar had been a leading Rajput kingdom even before Maharana Pratap occupied the throne. Kings of Mewar, with the cooperation of their nobles and subjects, had established such traditions in the kingdom, as augmented their magnificence despite the hurdles of having a smaller area under their command and less population. There did come a few thorny occasions when the flag of the kingdom seemed sliding down. Their flag once again heaved high in the sky thanks to the gallantry and brilliance of the people of Mewar.

   2. The destiny of Mewar was good in the sense that barring a few kings, most of the rulers were competent and patriotic. This glorious tradition of the kingdom almost continued for 1500 years since its establishment, right from the reign of Bappa Rawal. In fact only 60 years before Maharana Pratap, Rana Sanga drove the kingdom to the pinnacle of fame. His reputation went beyond Rajasthan and reached Delhi. Two generations before him, Rana Kumbha had given a new stature to the kingdom through victories and developmental work. During his reign, literature and art also progressed extraordinarily. Rana himself was inclined towards writing and his works are read with reverence even today. The ambience of his kingdom was conducive to the creation of high quality work of art and literature. These accomplishments were the outcome of a longstanding tradition sustained by several generations.

   3. The life of the people of Mewar must have been peaceful and prosperous during the long span of time; otherwise such extraordinary accomplishment in these fields would not have been possible. This is reflected in their art and literature as well as their loving nature. They compensate for lack of admirable physique by their firm but pleasant nature. The ambience of Mewar remains lovely thanks to the cheerful and liberal character of its people.

   4. One may observe astonishing pieces of workmanship not only in the forts and palaces of Mewar but also in public utility buildings. Ruins of many structures which are still standing tall in their grandeur are testimony to the fact that Mewar was not only the land of the brave but also a seat of art and culture. Amidst aggression and bloodshed, literature and art flourished and creative pursuits of literature and artists did not suffer. Imagine, how glorious the period must have been when the Vijaya Stambha which is the sample of our great ancient architecture even today, was constructed. In the same fort, Kirti Stambha is standing high, reflecting how liberal the then administration was which allowed people from other communities and kingdoms to come and carry out construction work. It is useless to indulge in the debate whether the Vijaya Stambha was constructed first or the Kirti Stambha. The fact is that both the capitals are standing side by side and reveal the

proximity between the king and the subjects of Mewar.

5. The cycle of time does not remain the same. Whereas the reign of Rana Sanga was crucial in raising the kingdom to the acme of glory, it also proved to be his nemesis. History took a turn. The fortune of Mewar – the land of the brave, started waning. Rana tried to save the day with his acumen which was running against the stream and the glorious traditions for sometime.

On the basis of your understanding of the above passage answer each of the questions given below with the help of options that follow :

(a) Maharana Pratap became immortal because :
  (i)   he ruled Mewar for 25 years.
  (ii) he added a lot of grandeur to Mewar.
  (iii) of his valour, sacrifice and patriotism.
  (iv) both (ii) and (iii)

(b) Difficulties in the way of Mewar were :
  (i)   lack of cooperation of the nobility.
  (ii) ancient traditions of the kingdom.
  (iii) its small area and small population.
  (iv) the poverty of the subjects.

(c) During thorny occasions :
  (i)   the flag of Mewar seemed to be lowered.
  (ii) the flag of Mewar was hoisted high.
  (iii) the people of Mewar showed gallantry.
  (iv) most of the rulers heaved a sigh of relief.

(d) Mewar was lucky because :
  (i)   all of its rulers were competent.
  (ii) most of its people were competent.
  (iii) most of its rulers were competent.
  (iv) only a few of its people were incompetent.

Answer the following questions briefly :

(e) Who is the earliest king of Mewar mentioned in the passage?

(f) What was Rana Kumbha's contribution to the glory of Mewar?

(g) What does the writer find worth admiration in the people of Mewar?

(h) How could art and literature flourish in Mewar?

(i) How did the rulers show that they cared for their subjects?

(j) What does the erection of Vijaya Stambha and Kirti Stambha in the same fort signify?

(k) Find words from the passage which mean the same as each of the following :
  (i) surprising (para 4)
  (ii) evidence (para 4)

2. Read the passage given below :

1. To ensure its perpetuity, the ground is well held by the panther both in space and in time. It enjoys a much wider distribution over the globe than its bigger cousins, and procreates sufficiently profusely to ensure its continuity for all time to come.

2. There seems to be no particular breeding season of the panther, although its sawing and caterwauling is more frequently heard during winter and summer. The gestation period is about ninety to hundred days (Whipsnade, ninety-two days). The litter normally consists of four cubs, rarely five. Of these, generally two survive and not more than one reaches maturity. I have never come across more than two cubs at the heels of the mother. Likewise, graziers in the forest have generally found only two cubs hidden away among rocks, hollows of trees, and other impossible places.

3. Panther cubs are generally in evidence in March. They are born blind. This is a provision of Nature against their drifting away from the place of safety in which they are lodged by their mother, and exposing themselves to the danger of their being devoured by hyenas, jackals, and other predators. They generally open their eyes in about three to four weeks.

4. The mother alone rears its cubs in seclusion. It keeps them out of the reach of the impulsive and impatient male. As a matter of fact the mother separates from the male soon after mating and forgets all about their tumultuous union. The story that the male often looks in to find out how the mother is progressing with her cubs has no foundation except in what we wish it should do at least.

5. The mother carries its cubs about by holding them by the scruff of their neck in its mouth. It trains them to stalk, and teaches them how to deliver the bite of death to the prey. The cubs learn to treat all and sundry with suspicion at their mother's heels. Instinctively the cubs seek seclusion, keep to cover and protect their flanks by walking along the edge of the forest.

6. I have never had an opportunity to watch mother panther train its cubs. But in Pilibhit forests, I once saw a tigress giving some lessons to its little ones. I was sitting over its kill at Mala. As the sunset, the tigress materialized in the twilight behind my *machan*. For about an hour, it scanned and surveyed the entire area looking and listening with the gravest concern. It even went to the road where my elephant was awaiting my signal. The *mahout* spotted it from a distance and drove the elephant away.

7. When darkness descended upon the scene and all was well and safe, the tigress called its cubs by emitting a low *haa-oon*. The cubs, two in number and bigger than a full-grown cat, soon responded. They came trotting up to their mother and hurried straight to the kill in indecent haste. The mother spitted at them so furiously that they doubled back to its heels immediately. Thereafter, the mother and its cubs sat under cover about 50 feet (15 m) away

from the kill to watch, wait, look, and listen. After about half an hour's patient and fidgetless vigil the mother seemed to say 'paid for'. At this signal, the cubs cautiously advanced, covering their flanks, towards the kill. No longer did they make a beeline for it, as they had done before.

8. The mother sat watching its cubs eat, and mounted guard on them. She did not partake of the meal.

On the basis of your understanding of the above passage complete the statements given below with the help of options that follow :

(a) To protect its cubs the mother panther hides them :

   (i)   among rocks

   (ii) in the branches of the trees

   (iii) behind the tree trunks

   (iv) at its heels

(b) The male panther :

   (i)   is protective of its cubs

   (ii) trains its cubs

   (iii) watches the progress of the mother

   (iv) is impulsive and impatient

Answer the following questions briefly :

(c) How many cubs does the mother panther rarely deliver?

(d) What may happen if the panther cubs are not born blind?

(e) Why did the *mahout* drive his elephant away?

(f) Why did the tigress spit at its cubs?

(g) From the narrator's observation, what do we learn about the nature of the tigress?

(h) Why does the panther not face the risk of extinction?

(i) Find words from the passage which mean the same as each of the following :

(i) moving aimlessly (para 3)

(ii) came down / fell (para 7)

3. Read the passage given below :

People tend to amass possessions, sometimes without being aware of doing so. They can have a delightful surprise when they find something useful which they did not know they owned. Those who never have to change house become indiscriminate collectors of what can only be described as clutter. They leave unwanted objects in drawers, cupboards and attics for years in the belief that they may one day need them. Old people also accumulate belongings for two other reasons, lack of physical and mental energy, and sentiment. Things owned for a long time are full of associations with the past, perhaps with the relatives who are dead, and so they gradually acquire a sentimental value.

Some things are collected deliberately in an attempt to avoid wastage. Among these are string and brown paper, kept by thrifty people when a parcel has been opened.

Collecting small items can be a mania. A lady cuts out from newspapers sketches of model clothes that she would like to buy if she had money. As she is not rich, the chances are that she will never be able to afford such purchases. It is a harmless habit, but it litters up her desk.

Collecting as a serious hobby is quite different and has many advantages. It provides relaxation for leisure hours, as just looking at one's treasure is always a joy. One doesn't have to go out for amusement as the collection is housed at home. Whatever it consists of – stamps, records, first editions of books, china – there is always something to do in connection with it, from finding the right place for the latest addition to verifying facts in reference books. This hobby educates one not only in the chosen subject, but also in general matters which have some bearing on it.

There are other benefits also. One gets to meet like-minded collectors to get advice, compare notes, exchange articles, to show off one's latest find. So one's circle of friends grows. Soon the hobby leads to travelling, perhaps a meeting in another town, possibly a trip abroad in search of a rare specimen, for collectors are not confined to one country. Over the years one may well become an authority on one's hobby and will probably be asked to give informal talks to little gatherings and then, if successful, to larger audiences.

(a) On the basis of your understanding of the above passage make notes on it using headings and sub-headings. Use recognizable abbreviations (wherever necessary-minimum four) and a format you consider suitable. Also supply an appropriate title to it.

(b) Write a summary of the passage in about 80 words.

SECTION B: Advanced Writing Skills

(30 Marks)

4. Principal, Sunrise Global School, Agra requires a receptionist for her school. Draft a suitable advertisement in about **50** words to be published in the classified columns of a national newspaper giving all the necessary details of qualifications and experience required in the receptionist.

OR

Water supply will be suspended for eight hours (10 am to 6 pm) on 6th of March for cleaning of the water tank. Write a notice in about **50** words advising the residents to store water for a day. You are Karan Kumar/Karuna Bajaj, Secretary, Janata Group Housing Society, Palam Vihar, Kurnool.

5. Yesterday you went to Sunrise Hospital, Market Road, New Delhi taking with you the victim of a hit and run accident. There were chaotic conditions in the casualty department. The injured was attended to after a lot of precious time had been lost.

Write a letter of complaint in **120-150** words to the Medical Superintendent. You are Karan/Karuna, M114, Mall Road, Delhi.

OR

Lack of job opportunities in the rural areas is forcing people to migrate to cities. Every big city thus has a number of slums in it. Life in these slums is miserable.

Write a letter in **120-150** words to the editor of a national newspaper on how we can improve the living conditions in these slums. You are Karan/Karuna, M114, Mall Road, Delhi.

6. 'The policy of reservation of seats for admission to the professional courses is good for the deprived sections of society.'

Write a debate in 150-200 words either for or against the motion.

OR

Write a speech in **150-200** words on 'Benefits of early rising' to be delivered by you in the morning assembly of your school. You are Karuna/Karan, Head Girl/Head Boy.

7. India is a land of diversity. One way in which it makes us feel proud of it is the number of festivals we enjoy. Write an article in 150-200 words on 'Festivals of India' . You are Karuna/Karan.

OR

Rising pollution, fast and competitive lifestyle, lack of nutritious food etc. have caused health woes for a large section of our population. Providing health care used to be a charitable and ethical activity. Today it has become commercialized, a money spinning business. Write an article in **150-200** words on 'How to provide proper health care to the common man'. You are Karan/Karuna.

SECTION C: Textbooks and Long Reading Text

(40 Marks)

8. Read the extract given below and answer the questions that follow :

Its loveliness increases, it will never

Pass into nothingness; but will keep

A bower quiet for us, and a sleep

Full of sweet dreams, and health, and quiet breathing.

(a) Whose loveliness will keep on increasing?

(b) Identify the phrase which says that 'it' is immortal.

(c) What is a 'bower'?

(d) Why do we need sweet dreams, health and quiet breathing in our lives?

OR

Old

familiar ache, my childhood's fear,

but all I said was, see you soon,

Amma,

all I did was smile and smile and

smile... ... ...

(a) What does the phrase, 'familiar ache' mean?

(b) What was the poet's childhood fear?

(c) What do the first two lines tell us about the poet's feelings for her mother?

(d) What does the repeated use of the word, 'smile' mean?

9. Answer any four of the following in 30 – 40 words each :

(a) Describe the irony in Saheb's name.

(b) Why was Gandhiji opposed to C.F. Andrews helping him in Champaran?

(c) Aunt Jennifer's efforts to get rid of her fear proved to be futile. Comment.

(d) What does Stephen Spender want to be done for the children of the school in a slum?

(e) When he was only ten days old, a prediction was made about the future of the Tiger King. What was ironic about it?

(f) What was his father's chief concern about Dr. Sadao?

10. Answer the following question in 120 – 150 words :

Our language is part of our culture and we are proud of it. Describe how regretful M. Hamel and the village elders are for having neglected their native language, French. 6

OR

Teachers always advise their students to dream big. Yet, the same teachers in your classrooms find fault with Sophie when she dreams. What is wrong with Sophie's dreams?

11. Answer the following question in 120-150 words :

Derry sneaked into Mr. Lamb's garden and it became a turning point in his life. Comment.

OR

How did Jo want the Roger Skunk story to end? Why?

12. Answer the following question in 120-150 words :

What do we learn about Mrs. Hall and Griffin from their first interaction at Coach and Horses inn?

OR

What kind of life did Silas lead before coming to Raveloe?

13. Answer the following question in 120-150 words :

Everyone who comes into contact with Griffin suffers. Attempt a character sketch of Griffin in the light of this remark.

OR

Attempt a character sketch of Nancy Lammeter.

Solutions

SECTION - A

1. (a) (iv) both (i) & (ii)   **(1 × 4 = 4 Marks)**

(b) (iii) its small area and small population

(c) (i) the flag of Mewar seemed to be lowered

(d) (iii) most of its rulers were competent

(1 × 6 = 6 Marks)

(e) Bappa Rawal is the earliest King of Mewar mentioned in the passage.

(f) Rana Kumbha had given a new stature to the kingdom through victories and developmental work. Literature and Art also flourished during his reign. Rana himself was inclined towards writing and his works are read even today.

(g) According to the writer, the cheerful nature and liberal character of the people of Mewar is worth admiration.

(h) Art and Literature could flourish in Mewar due to the peace and prosperity for a long period of time. The rulers of Mewar too were inclined towards Art and Literature.

(i) The fact that both the Vijaya Stambha and Kirti Stambha stand side by side even today reveal the proximity between the king and the people of Mewar. The rulers also allowed people from other communities to come and do the construction work and that shows the liberal administration on the Kings.

(j) The erection of Vijaya Stambha and Kirti Stambha in the same fort signifies the proximity between the King and the people of Mewar.

(k)   **(1 × 2 = 2 Marks)**

(i) astonishing

(ii) testimony

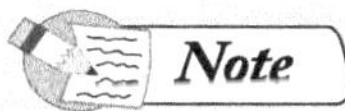

Note

When answering MCQs choose the option which is the closest answer from amongst the options.

1. For Factual questions like e.g. "Who is the earliest King of Mewar mentioned in the passage, "do not include information not given in the passage.

2. While answering the 'How' question like "How could Art and Literature flourish in Mewar", you may begin your answer with 'Art and Literature could flourish in Mewar due to the ………or a similar phrase.

3. While answering the vocabulary questions, check the part of speech, the tense of the word etc. Your answer should have the same part of speech, tense etc.

4. For e.g. Surprising – Astonishing (NOT astonish or Astonished)

2. (a) (i) among rocks   **(1 × 2 = 2 Marks)**

(b) (iv) is impulsive and impatient

(1 × 6 = 6 Marks)

(c) The mother panther rarely delivers 5 cubs.

(d) If the panther cubs are not born blind, they may drift away from their place of safety and might get exposed to the danger of them being devoured by the hyenas, jackals etc.

(e) The mahaut drove away the elephant so that it would be away from the sight of the panther and not disturb the tigress.

(f) As soon as the tigress called its cubs, the cubs came hurriedly and hurried straight at the kill. The tigress was furious at their carelessness and she wanted them to be trained to wait and ensure safety first before eating. So, she spat at them and that made them come back to their mother's heels.

(g) We learn a lot of things about the nature of the tigress from the narrator's observation. We get to know that she is patient, caring and protective. However, she is also strict when she wants to discipline and train the cubs.

(h) The panther does not face the danger of extinction since it enjoys a much wider distribution across the globe as compared to tigers etc. In addition, it also procreates sufficiently with around 4 to 5 cubs in a litter.

(i)   **(1 × 2 = 2 Marks)**

(i) drifting

(ii) descended

3. (a) **Note Making**   **(5 Marks)**

Title- Collecting – A Hobby or An Obsession

1. Reasons for collection

1.1 Surprise element

1.2 No change of house

1.3 Belief that it might be needed

1.4 Old people acc.

1.4.a lack of phy. & mental energy

1.4.b sentiment

1.5 Past assn.

1.6 Deliberate collection

1.7 A mania

1.8 Hobby

2. Advantages

  2.1 Relaxation for leisure

  2.2 No need to go out for amusement

  2.3 Meet like- minded collectors for

    2.3.a. get advice

    2.3.b. compare notes

    2.3.c. exchange articles

    2.3.d. to show off one's latest find

  2.4 Leads to travelling

  2.5 One becomes an authority

  2.6 Can give talks to

    2.6.a. small grps

    2.6.b. larger groups as a prof.

Key to Abbreviations

Abbreviation	Word
acc	accumulate
phy	physical
&	And
assn	association
grps	groups
prof.	professional

(b) Summary   **(3 Marks)**

There are various reasons for collecting things. Some do it over the years without even being aware of it. No shifting of house, the belief that something might be needed someday, lack of physical and mental energy, emotional attachment with things of the past are reasons behind collecting things. In addition to it being a mania for some people, collecting has multiple advantages. Spending time creatively, meeting like- minded people, travelling etc leads to one turning into a professional. (79 words)

SECTION - B

4. Advertisement   **(4 Marks)**

SITUATION VACANT

Wanted a smart, efficient Lady Receptionist for a leading school of Agra. The candidate must be agradute with a pleasing personality, good communication and inter-personal skills and sound knowledge of computers. Salary negotiable. Interested candidates should apply within 10 days with resume and photograph to Principal, Sunrise Global School, Agra or mail the resume at principal.sgc@gmail.com.

OR

NOTICE

JANATA GROUP HOUSING SOCIETY

WATER SUPPLY TO BE SUSPENDED

February 28, 2016

All the members of the Housing Society are hereby informed that water supply would be suspended for 8 hours (10 am to 6 pm) on 6th of March 2016 for the cleaning of the water tanks. All the residents are therefore advised to make adequate arrangements and store water accordingly.

Inconvenience caused is deeply regretted.

Sign

(Karuna Bajaj)

Secretary

Janata Group Housing Society, Palam Vihar

---

5. Letter   **(6 Marks)**

M 114

Mall Road

Delhi

23 March, 20XX

The Medical Superintendent

Sunrise Hospital

Market Road

New Delhi

Sub: Lack of order in the Casualty Department of the Hospital

Respected Sir

This is to bring to your notice the chaotic situation which is prevalent in the casualty department of your hospital resulting in precious time being lost.

It was only yesterday that I had the chance of visiting the casualty department with the victim of a hit and run case. Since the hospital was near the accident site and the hospital has created a name for itself in a short duration of time, I took the profusely bleeding man to your hospital. However far from attending to the critical patient, nobody was even willing to listen. It was only after an angry display of my frustration at the callous attitude at the reception, was I given a hearing. Even after that I was subjected to a lot of paper-work and by then the patient had already lost consciousness. It was three hours after our arrival that the actual treatment of the victim started. I was even told by a visitor that I should consider myself lucky that the victim was attended to in three hours!

I would like to take this opportunity to request you to take some corrective measures like setting up of a special team to look into the critical victims, mock drills of such situations and CCTV recording to be played in front of the staff so that they are able to understand the frustration of the victims. A hospital like yours deserves a good reputation and I'm sure you will be able to save many more lives if things were improved at the department.

Thanking you in anticipation

Yours truly

Karuna

OR

M 114

Mall Road

Delhi

23 March, 20XX

The Editor

Daily Herald

Bahadur Shah Jafar Marg

New Delhi

Sub: Urgent need to improve living conditions in the slums

Respected Sir

Through the column of your esteemed newspaper, I would like to draw the attention of the concerned authorities towards the miserable living conditions in the slums of Delhi.

It is a bitter fact of industrialization and development that while a country on one hand grows by leaps and bounds, a mushrooming of the slums also takes place. It is heartbreaking to look outside the windows of the beautiful high-rise buildings and be greeted by the vast expanse of the slums just adjacent to these buildings. To add to the woe, the people living in these slums do not even have the basic amenities of life. Lack of hygienic conditions, poor drinking water facility, makeshift tenements which are at the mercy of rain and storm, no health care schemes keep the slum dwellers completely at the mercy of God. Even though the Government has floated housing provision schemes, most of the slum dwellers are either unaware of it or get confused because of the processes in the government offices.

I would therefore like to request the government to take some corrective measures as soon as possible to improve the conditions of the slums. Creating work opportunities in the rural areas to stop migration to the cities, improvement in educational opportunities etc would also help. Some NGOs can also be encouraged to adopt the slums. Only when the slum dwellers get their due will the overall condition of the country improve.

Yours truly

Karuna

6. Debate   **(10 Marks)**

Good Morning Everyone!

Today I, XXX, stand before you to put forth my views **for the motion** on the topic "The Policy of Reservation of seats for admission to the professional courses is good for the deprived sections of the society."

It is a well-known fact that caste system in India is deeply entrenched. History stand witness to the caste-based atrocities and discrimination on certain sections of the society. The Government of India in keeping with its philosophy brought in reservation for certain sections of the society so that things could change. Each one of us are only too familiar with the massive protests that shook the country during the Mandal Commission days. These protests amply reflected the fact that the Majority still believes in suppression of the Minority. It was for this reason that despite the nationwide protests, the recommendations of the commission were put into practice. However, till date the inequality in society prevails. The difference between the haves and the have nots still exists.

We must understand that a country can progress in the true sense of the term only if all the sections of society contribute pro-actively. For this to be a reality, the gap needs to be bridged and the marginalized needs to be brought at par with the historically privileged. This can only happen when we provide opportunities to the deprived sections of the society. Therefore in my opinion the policy of reservation of seats for admission to the professional courses is good for the deprived sections of the society.

Thank you

OR

Good Morning Everyone!

Today I, XXX, stand before you to put forth my views **for the motion** on the topic "The Policy of Reservation of seats for admission to the professional courses is good for the deprived sections of the society."

It is a well-known fact that caste system in India is deeply entrenched. History stand witness to the caste-based atrocities and discrimination on certain sections of the society. The Government of India in keeping with its philosophy brought in reservation for certain sections of the society so that things could change. Each one of us are only too familiar with the massive protests that shook the country during the Mandal Commission days. These protests amply reflected the fact that the Majority still believes in suppression of the Minority. It was for this reason that despite the nationwide protests, the recommendations of the commission were put into practice. However, till date the inequality in society prevails. The difference between the haves and the have nots still exists.

We must understand that a country can progress in the true sense of the term only if all the sections of society contribute pro-actively. For this to be a reality, this gap needs to be bridged and the marginalized needs to be brought at par with the historically privileged. This can only happen when we provide opportunities to the deprived sections of the society. Therefore in my opinion the policy of reservation of seats for admission to the professional courses is good for the deprived sections of the society.

Thank You !

OR

BENEFITS OF EARLY RISING

Good Morning Everyone!

I, Karuna, the Head Girl of the school stand before you today in this bright and cheerful morning to share my views on the topic "Benefits of Early Rising".

I start with a quote by Benjamin Franklin - "The early morning has gold in its mouth,". Who knows it better than us students! When we rise early, our stress levels are reduced since we have ample time to attend to our morning chores. There is no morning hour rush to catch the bus with our mothers in tow with our lunch boxes and fathers running behind with something that we had forgotten to pack in the morning. Getting up early takes care of all these morning blues and fills us up with optimism and positivity. Besides allowing you more hours for your work, it also boosts your speed and makes you more adept at taking better decisions, planning and achieving goals. Since we rise up early, we go to bed early too, allowing us those precious 8 hours of sleep. If getting up early is established as a routine in our lives it would translate into better sleep quality as our body's internal clock adapts to our new sleep routine.

It is interesting to relate that as per certain studies in US and UK on University Students, students who were early risers scored significantly higher than the night birds. So, as students we must adhere to this routine of rising early.

Thank you

7. Article   (10 Marks)

Festivals of India

By *Karuna*

The cultural diversity of India is most apparent in the festivals that are celebrated here. The spirit of India is expressed throughout the year in festivals as diverse as the country's landscape and as lively and colourful as its people. The different festivals also emphasize the heterogeneity of our country.

Celebration of all the festivals despite the fact that it might not correlate to one's religion has its own charm. Not only do you get to know about different traditions, folklore and stories, you also understand that beneath all the varied traditions, the cause for celebration remains the same which is the celebration of human life and values. In addition to it breaking the monotony of life it also brings peace and joy to the people. Right from celebration of the new crop to the advent of seasons, the underlying moral of the triumph of the good over evil, celebration of love of familial bonds, gods and goddesses, saints and prophets – all encompass the life of each individual of the country.

Participating in these colorful festivities, you see the vitality of India today as it embraces the traditions of its fascinating past and you understand why India is considered a truly secular country.

OR

How to Provide Proper Health Care to the Common Man

By *Karuna*

With the change in the living standards of the human population and the race to reach the top of the ladder, Man neglected on one of the basic necessities for a happy living – GOOD HEALTH.

Exercise, meditation and visiting the doctor when required aren't the norms today. Added to this is the fast-paced life where you satiate your hunger through "foods on the go" and the pollution that invades your insides while travelling. No wonder providing health care has become a big business in today's world. With the emergence of the privately-owned hospitals with better facility, five star infrastructure, efficient nursing, avant garde technology and easy accessibility, the cost of health care has gone up. The result is that these hospitals have moved out of reach of a common man. So the question is - where does a common man go? Isn't his life precious enough to be saved?

The Government needs to step in here. Strict laws can be made where the common man gets treatment at a subsidized rate in the same hospitals. The condition of the government hospitals also needs to be improved. Better health care facilities at the primary health care centres, provision of free medicines, improvement in the health insurance schemes etc can also be helpful. Moreover awareness drives on hygiene, sanitation and ways to prevent and control disease would nip the problem in the bud.

SECTION - C

8.   **(1 × 4 = 4 Marks)**

(a) The loveliness of a thing of beauty will keep on increasing with passage of time.

(b) The phrase "never pass into nothingness" says that "it" is immortal.

(c) A 'bower' is a pleasant shady place under a tree which gives rest to the human beings.

(d) We need sweet dreams, health and quiet breathing in our lives so that we are clean of all the negative elements that surround our lives, and which may make us feel gloomy. These things will give us the required strength to bear the problems of our lives.

OR

(a) The phrase 'familiar ache' means the painful realization that the poet has that her mother is growing old and the fear of the impending separation due to death. It also means that the pain that she had had in her childhood is revisiting her once again at a much later stage.

(b) The poet's childhood fear was that her mother would grow old and then would die eventually leaving her alone in the world.

(c) The first two lines of the extract tell us that the poet's feelings for her mother are very deep and old. She is pained at seeing her mother grow old because she fears losing her.

(d) The repetition of the word 'smile' only seeks to reiterate that she wants to hide her real feelings from her mother and reassures herself that her mother will be fine.

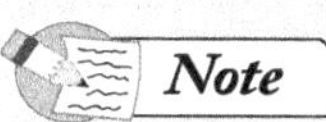 *Note*

1.   Be precise and to the point.

*2.   For e.g. **"Identify the phrase which says that 'it' is immortal'**, pick out the phrase and mention it. You may write your answer as ……..The phrase "never pass into nothingness" says that "it" is immortal*

9.   **(3 × 4 = 12 Marks)**

(a) The irony in Saheb's name lies in its meaning juxtaposed with the work that he does for his living. His full name is Saheb-e-Alam which means the Lord of the Universe. However far from being a lord, he is a refugee from Bangladesh who is a rag picker by profession.

(b) Gandhiji was opposed to CF Andrews since for him the entire struggle was for self-respect and self-reliance. The support of an Englishman would show a weakness of the heart and the seriousness of the cause would be marred.

(c) Even though Aunt Jennifer sews the unafraid tigers and tries to move beyond her fear, she will be unable to do so even after her death. The reference to her 'terrified' hands still 'ringed with ordeals' emphasizes the fact that she has not been able to escape the fear and dominance that she was mastered by in her marriage.

(d) Stephen Spender wants the children to break open from the confines of the classroom and books and learn from nature. Their education should be related to their lives and the rich and the powerful, should get involved in their education.

(e) When the Tiger King was only 10 days old, a prediction that his death would be brought about by a tiger was made. When the king grows up, he ensures that all the tigers are killed and he feels that he has proved the prediction wrong. However, his death is brought about by a wooden tiger toy. This is what is ironical.

(f) The chief concern of Dr Sadao's father was Sadao's education. It was for this that his father had sent him to America at the age of twenty-two.

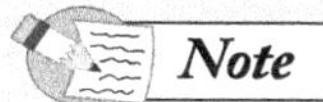 *Note*

1.   Each 3-mark question must have at least two value points.

2.   So, for the question "Why was Gandhiji opposed to C.F. Andrews helping him in Champaran", include any two value points from those given below.

    a.   Opposed to CF Andrews since for Gandhji, the entire struggle was for self- respect and self- reliance

    b.   Support of an Englishman would show a weakness of the heart

    c.   Seriousness of the cause would be marred

    d.   Belief that it could be done alone

10.   **(6 Marks)**

The language of a country is a part of the identity of that nation. When a group of people are forbidden from using their own language, one feels threatened at the core of one's being. It is then that one starts having regrets for the time lost which could have been utilized in learning that language. When an order comes from Berlin forbidding the teaching of French in the schools of Alsace and Lorraine, all are full of regrets at having ignored the language. M. Hamel blames himself for having given a holiday at the cost of a lesson when he wanted to go fishing himself and for having got his flowers watered. The usually empty last rows of the class had elders sitting quietly at back of classroom regretting how they had not paid due attention. Franz himself is on the verge of tears at the last lesson. M Hamel ends the last lesson by appealing to all the people in the class to preserve 'French' since holding on to their language will keep them united and leaves the classroom after writing "*Viva la France*" on the board.

OR

There is nothing wrong with Sophie's dreams and ambitions in life. In fact, this is the most natural thing for all teenagers to do. She is from a weak socio-economic background and therefore the living conditions of her family aren't very pleasant. In such a scenario, having ambitions to make a better living by becoming a model and opening a boutique is her way of moving up the social ladder. However, she does not have any concrete plan as to how she is going to achieve that. What she needs to understand is that the dreams should be achievable and realistic. She should also have the zeal to work hard for her dreams which in her case does not seem possible. For her, the dreams are an escape from reality and there comes a time when dream and reality merge together so much so that she sees things which do not happen at all. This kind of dreaming is dangerous and can be fatal in some cases. The fact that she involves her brother Derek too in this is all the more damaging.

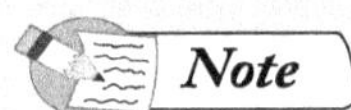 *Note*

1.   *Each 6-mark question must have at least four value points.*
2.   *Answer to the point including your own opinion in places where it is deemed necessary by the question.*
3.   *Pick out specific examples from the text to support your answer.*
4.   *Quote straight from the text wherever required but do so only when you are sure of the words.*

*For e.g., The question **"Our language is part of our culture and we are proud of it. Describe how regretful M. Hamel and the village elders are for having neglected their native language, French,** " you need to use the key words like: language of a country - part of the identity of that nation- forbidden from using their own language - one feels threatened – has regrets for the time lost - could have been utilized in learning that language- order comes from Berlin forbidding the teaching of French - schools of Alsace and Lorraine - all are full of regrets at having ignored the language - M. Hamel - given a holiday at the cost of a lesson- wanted to go fishing himself - got his flowers watered - The usually empty last rows of the class had elders sitting quietly - regretting how they had not paid due attention- Franz - on the verge of tears at the last lesson- M Hamel ends the last lesson - appeals to people in the class to preserve 'French'- holding on to their language - keeps them united - leaves the classroom after writing "Viva la France" on the board.*

11. **(6 Marks)**

Derry, a fourteen year old boy, has half of his face burnt by acid and this face of his is a constant source of pain for him. The lack of friends, remarks of the onlookers on the street, the whispered conversations on the ground floor of his home between his parents and even his mother's kiss on his cheek – all are sources of pain for Derry since all this makes him feel isolated and different from the rest. However, his entry into Mr Lamb's garden and his conversations with him slowly change him. To his surprise Mr Lamb is not scared or repulsed by his scarred face. He comes across as someone who understands Derry and his anguish and doesn't pity him. Mr Lamb's positivity opens up a new world for Derry and he realizes that suffering from a physical problem does not make him different. What makes him different is his way of dealing with the limitation.

It is because of Mr Lamb that Derry is ready to face the world and overcome the obstacles that come his way. A boy who was initially repulsed by human company goes back to Mr Lamb's garden against her mother's advice. He finally finds courage and strength to get what he wants out of life.

OR

Jack ends the Roger Skunk story by making the Mommy Skunk take Roger back to the wizard and making him change the rose smell of Roger back to its original smell. However for Jo, this ending is not acceptable. According to her it was a 'stupid mommy' who would do something like that to her baby and deprive him from the pleasure of being surrounded by friends. Therefore, she wants the ending to be changed the next day. Joe wants Mommy Skunk to be hit by the wizard and Roger to have the rose smell back. She wants such an ending since the rose smell hadearned a lot of friends for Roger and as a child, for Joe, having friends is more important than individuality and a sense of identity. She looks at the story from a child's perspective where acceptance and love from the peer group is more important than uniqueness.

 *Note*

1.   *Adhere to the word limit given for the question.*
2.   *Quoting from the text always gets more marks but mis-quotes can backfire. So, be careful.*
3.   *The question requires not only your knowledge of the text but also your analysis of the inhuman practice like un-touchability. So, include both.*
4.   *For the Question "How did Jo want the Roger Skunk story to end? Why?" break the question into HOW and WHY and use the value points given below.*

Jack ends the story - Mommy Skunk takes Roger back to the wizard - change the rose smell of Roger back to its original smell - Jo - this ending not acceptable - a 'stupid mommy' who would do that to her baby - deprive him from the pleasure of being surrounded by friends - wants the ending to be changed -

Mommy Skunk to be hit by the wizard - Roger to have the rose smell back - wants such an ending since the rose smell had earned a lot of friends for Roger - for Joe, having friends - more important than individuality and a sense of identity - looks at the story from a child's perspective - acceptance and love from the peer group - more important than uniqueness and individuality.

12. **(6 Marks)**

Griffin is a man with unusual appearance who arrives at 'Coaches and Horses' Inn looking for shelter. He doesn't come across as a friendly man. Since he is cold and hungry, he just wants his basic requirements to be fulfilled and be left alone after that. On the contrary Mrs Hall, the owner of the inn was a simple, friendly and talkative lady who loved to strike a friendship with her guests. Since it was winter, Griffin's visit was a god-sent opportunity to make some money since they hardly had any guests in such a harsh and rough weather. So, she tries her best to make Griffin feel at home and even goes to the extent of making the food herself. Mrs Hall's advances however are rebuffed by Griffins. Even though Mrs Hall is unhappy at this treatment, she tolerates Griffin because he has the money to pay and they need guests in this season.

OR

Silas stayed at Lantern Yard before he came to Raveloe. There he was a respected member of the church and known for his honesty, wisdom and exemplary life. He had a close friend William Dane who was a little older than Silas and their friendship was such that the Lantern Yard brethren called them David and Jonathan. Silas also had Sarah, his fiancée, whom he was set to marry in times to come. He had also inherited from his mother some knowledge of herbs and medicinal plants which could be used to cure certain ailments, but he doubted the lawfulness of such a practice. In addition, he also believed that herbs would not have the required effect without prayers and since prayers were sufficient on their own, there was no reason to practice the administration of herbs etc. To conclude, Silas's life at Lantern Yard was diametrically opposed to his life at Raveloe.

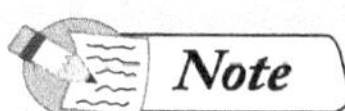 ***Note***

1. *Adhere to the word limit. Answer must reveal your deep knowledge of the text.*
2. *For e.g. the question 'What kind of life did Silas lead before coming to Raveloe' use at least 4 -5 value points from those given below:*
   a. *Stayed at Lantern Yard before Raveloe*
   b. *Was a respected member of the church*
   c. *Known for his honesty, wisdom and exemplary life*

d. *Had a close friend William Dane- little older than Silas - friendship such that the Lantern Yard brethren called them David and Jonathan.*
e. *Sarah, his fiancée, also there whom he was set to marry.*
f. *Inherited from his mother some knowledge of herbs and medicinal plants - doubted the lawfulness of such a practice - also believed that herbs would not have the required effect without prayers - since prayers were sufficient on their own - no reason to practice the administration of herbs etc.*
g. *Silas's life at Lantern Yard was diametrically opposed to his life at Raveloe.*

13. **(6 Marks)**

Griffin is a scientist trying to perfect the art of invisibility. Even though a genius, the turn of events in the novel depict him as a scientist gone astray. The character is enveloped in mystery right from the beginning of the novel with most of his body concealed. His constant rebuffing of Mrs Hall's attempts to be friendly establishes him as a loner and a rude man. After perfecting the trick of invisibility, he becomes a menace to the society. His aggressiveness comes to fore many times in the novel with slamming of doors, furniture flying in the room, threats to Marvel etc. His encounter with Kemp and the request to join him in unleashing the Reign of Terror shows the remorseless side of his personality. Griffin does not even spare his father whose money he steals. The father kills himself because the money belonged to someone else and now with it gone, he would not be able to return it. Griffin has no respect for rules or authority and everyone (except Marvel) who comes in contact with him, suffers.

OR

Nancy Lammeter was the daughter of Mr Lammeter. She has her own individual personality and adheres to her own code of behaviour which encompass even dressing like her sister Priscilla. She is beautiful and courted by Godfrey Cass whom she later gets married to. She isn't an outdoor person like her sister Priscilla and loves to think inwardly. She is caring and possesses remarkable strength of character with high principles. She refuses to adopt a chil dafter losing her own born as it would be meddling with God's plan. "To adopt a child, because children of your own had been denied you, was to try and choose your lot in spite of Providence" – is what she believesin. When she comes to know of Eppie being Godfrey's daughter, she does not chide Godfrey for keeping it a secret even though there is a deep regret in her for husband's action. She in fact surprises Godfrey by saying that she would have adopted Eppie that very time if she had known it. Overall, she is a fine, sensitive woman who empathizes with others.

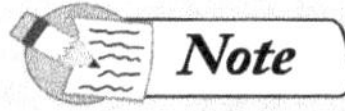 *Note*

1. This question tests understanding, appreciation, analysis and interpretation of the incident/character. So, thorough reading of the text is required.
2. Adhere to the word limit and answer the question.
3. Avoid giving details which you are not sure of.
4. For e.g. the question "Attempt a character sketch of Nancy Lammeter," use at least 4-5 value points from those given below:
    a. Nancy Lammeter- daughter of Mr Lammeter.
    b. Individual personality - adheres to her own code of behavior -encompass even dressing like her sister Priscilla.
    c. Is beautiful and courted by Godfrey Cass - later gets married to him.
    d. Isn't an outdoor person like her sister Priscilla.
    e. Loves to think inwardly - caring - possesses remarkable strength of character with high principles.
    f. Refuses to adopt a child after losing her own born – sees it as meddling with God's plan. "To adopt a child, because children of your own had been denied you, was to try and choose your lot in spite of Providence" – her belief.
    g. Comes to know of Eppie being Godfrey's daughter - does not chide Godfrey for keeping it a secret - deep regret in her for husband's action - surprises Godfrey by saying that she would have adopted Eppie that very time if she had known.
    h. Is a fine, sensitive woman - empathizes with others.

CBSE Board Solved Paper

Time Allowed : 3 Hours   *Maximum Marks : 100*

General Instructions:

(i) This paper is divided into three Sections : A, B and C. All the sections are compulsory.

(ii) Separate instructions are given with each section and question, wherever necessary. Read these instructions very carefully and follow them faithfully.

(iii) Do not exceed the prescribed word limit while answering the questions

SECTION A: Reading

(30 Marks)

1. Read the passage carefully :

   1. For four days, I walked through the narrow lanes of the old city, enjoying the romance of being in a city where history still lives - in its cobblestone streets and in its people riding asses, carrying vine leaves and palm as they once did during the time of Christ.

   2. This is Jerusalem, home to the sacred sites of Christianity, Islam and Judaism. This is the place that houses the church of the Holy Sepulchre, the place where Jesus was finally laid to rest. This is also the site of Christ's crucifixion, burial and resurrection.

   3. Built by the Roman Emperor Constantine at the site of an earlier temple to Aphrodite, it is the most venerated Christian shrine in the world. And justifiably so. Here, within the church, are the last five stations of the cross, the 10th station where Jesus was stripped of his clothes, the 11th where he was nailed to the cross, the 12th where he died on the cross, the 13th where the body was removed from the cross, and the 14th, his tomb.

   4. For all this weighty tradition, the approach and entrance to the church is nondescript. You have to ask for directions. Even to the devout Christian pilgrims walking along the Via Dolorosa - the Way of Sorrows-first nine stations look clueless. Then a courtyard appears, hemmed in by other buildings and a doorway to one side. This leads to a vast area of huge stone architecture.

   5. Immediately inside the entrance is your first stop. It's the stone of anointing this is the place, according to Greek tradition, where Christ was removed from the cross. The Roman Catholics, however, believe it to be the spot where Jesus' body was prepared for burial by Joseph.

6. What happened next? Jesus was buried. He was taken to a place outside the city of Jerusalem where other graves existed and there, he was buried in a cave. However, all that is long gone, destroyed by continued attacks and rebuilding; what remains is the massive– and impressive– Rotunda (a round building with a dome) that Emperor Constantine built. Under this, and right in the centre of the Rotunda is the structure that contains the Holy Sepulchre.

7. "How do you know that this is Jesus' tomb?" I asked one of the pilgrims standing next to me. He was clueless, more interested, like the rest of them, in the novelty of it all and in photographing it, than in its history or tradition.

8. At the start of the first century, the place was a disused quarry outside the city walls. According to the gospels, Jesus' crucifixion occurred 'at a place outside the city walls with graves nearby ....' Archaeologists have discovered tombs from that era, so the site is compatible with the biblical period.

9. The structure at the site is a marble tomb built over the original burial chamber. It has two rooms, and you enter four at a time into the first of these, the Chapel of the Angel. Here the angel is supposed to have sat on a stone to recount Christ's resurrection. A low door made of white marble, partly worn away by pilgrims' hands, leads to a smaller chamber inside. This is the 'room of the tomb', the place where Jesus was buried.

10. We entered in a single file. On my right was a large marble slab that covered the original rock bench on which the body of Jesus was laid. A woman knelt and prayed. Her eyes were wet with tears. She pressed her face against the slab to hide them, but it only made it worse.

On the basis of your understanding of this passage answer the following questions with the help of the given options:

(a) How does Jerusalem still retain the charm of the ancient era?
  (i) There are narrow lanes.
  (ii) Roads are paved with cobblestones.
  (iii) People can be seen riding asses.
  (iv) All of the above

(b) Holy Sepulchre is sacred to
  (i) Christianity
  (ii) Islam
  (iii) Judaism
  (iv) Both (i) and (iii)

(c) Why does one have to constantly ask for directions to the church?
  (i) Its lanes are narrow.
  (ii) Entrance to the church is nondescript.
  (iii) People are not tourist-friendly.
  (iv) Everyone is lost in enjoying the romance of the place.

(d) Where was Jesus buried?
  (i) In a cave
  (ii) At a place outside the city
  (iii) In the Holy Sepulchre
  (iv) Both (i) and (ii)

Answer the following questions briefly :

(e) What is the Greek belief about the 'stone of anointing'?
(f) Why did Emperor Constantine build the Rotunda?
(g) What is the general attitude of the pilgrims?
(h) How is the site compatible with the biblical period?
(i) Why did the pilgrims enter the 'room of the tomb' in a single file?
(j) Why did 'a woman' try to hide her tears?
(k) Find words from the passage which mean the same as:
  (i) A large grave (para 3)
  (ii) Having no interesting features/dull (para 4)

2. Read the passage carefully :

1. We often make all things around us the way we want them. Even during our pilgrimages we have begun to look for whatever makes our heart happy, gives comfort to our body and peace to the mind. It is as if external solutions will fulfil our needs, and we do not want to make any special efforts even in our spiritual search. Our mind is resourceful–it works to find shortcuts in simple and easy ways.

2. Even pilgrimages have been converted into tourism opportunities. Instead, we must awaken our conscience and souls and understand the truth. Let us not tamper with either our own nature or that of the Supreme.

3. All our cleverness is rendered ineffective when nature does a dance of destruction. Its fury can and will wash away all imperfections. Indian culture, based on Vedic treatises, assists in human evolution, but we are now using our entire energy in distorting

these traditions according to our convenience instead of making efforts to make ourselves worthy of them.

4. The irony is that humans are not even aware of the complacent attitude they have allowed themselves to sink to. Nature is everyone's Amma and her fierce blows will sooner or later corner us and force us to understand this truth. Earlier, pilgrimages to places of spiritual significance were rituals that were undertaken when people became free from their worldly duties. Even now some seekers take up this pious religious journey as a path to peace and knowledge. Anyone travelling with this attitude feels and travels with only a few essential items that his body can carry. Pilgrims traditionally travelled light, on foot, eating light, dried chickpeas and fruits, or whatever was available. Pilgrims of olden days did not feel the need to stay in special AC bedrooms or travel by luxury cars or indulge themselves with delicious food and savouries.

5. Pilgrims traditionally moved ahead, creating a feeling of belonging towards all, conveying a message of brotherhood among all they came across whether in small caves, ashrams or local settlements. They received the blessings and congregations of yogis and mahatmas in return while conducting the dharma of their pilgrimage. A pilgrimage is like penance or sadhana to stay near nature and to experience a feeling of oneness with it, to keep the body healthy and fulfilled with the amount of food, while seeking freedom from attachments and yet remaining happy while staying away from relatives and associates.

6. This is how a pilgrimage should be rather than making it like a picnic by taking a large group along and living in comfort, packing in entertainment and tampering with environment. What is worse is giving a boost to the ego of having had a special darshan. Now alms are distributed, charity done while they brag about their spiritual experiences!

7. We must embark on our spiritual journey by first understanding the grace and significance of a pilgrimage and following it up with the prescribed rules and rituals - this is what translates into the ultimate and beautiful medium of spiritual evolution. There is no justification for tampering with nature.

8. A pilgrimage is symbolic of contemplation and meditation and acceptance and is a metaphor for the constant growth or movement and love for nature that we should hold in our hearts.

9. This is the truth!

On the basis of your understanding of the above passage answer the questions that follow with the help of the given options:

(a) How can a pilgrim keep his body healthy?
  (i) By travelling light
  (ii) By eating small amount of food

   (iii) By keeping free from attachments

   (iv) Both (i) and (ii)

(b) How do we satisfy our ego?

   (i) By having a special darshan

   (ii) By distributing alms

   (iii) By treating it like a picnic

   (iv) Both (i) and (ii)

Answer the following as briefly as possible:

(c) What change has taken place in our attitude towards pilgrimages?

(d) What happens when pilgrimages are turned into picnics?

(e) Why are we complacent in our spiritual efforts?

(f) How does nature respond when we try to be clever with it?

(g) In olden days with what attitude did people go on a pilgrimage?

(h) What message does the passage convey to the pilgrims?

(i) Find words from the passage which mean the same as the following:

   (i) made/turned (para 3)

   (ii) very satisfied (para 4)

3. Read the passage given below:

It is surprising that sometimes we don't listen to what people say to us. We hear them, but we don't listen to them. I was curious to know how hearing is different from listening. I had thought both were synonyms, but gradually, I realised there is a big difference between the two words.

Hearing is a physical phenomenon. Whenever somebody speaks, the sound waves generated reach you, and you definitely hear whatever is said to you. However, even if you hear something, it doesn't always mean that you actually understand whatever is being said. Paying attention to whatever you hear means you are really listening. Consciously using your mind to understand whatever is being said is listening.

Diving deeper, I found that listening is not only hearing with attention, but is much more than that. Listening is hearing with full attention, and applying our mind. Most of the time, we listen to someone, but our minds are full of needless chatter and there doesn't seem to be enough space to accommodate what is being spoken.

We come with a lot of prejudices and preconceived notions about the speaker or the subject on which he is talking. We pretend to listen to the speaker, but deep inside, we sit in judgement and are dying to pronounce right or wrong, true or false, yes or no. Sometimes, we even come prepared with a negative mindset of proving the speaker wrong. Even if the speaker says nothing harmful, we are ready to pounce on him with our own version of things.

What we should ideally do is listen first with full awareness. Once we have done that, we can decide whether we want to make a judgement or not. Once we do that, communication will be perfect and our interpersonal relationship will become so much better. Listening well doesn't mean one has to say the right thing at the right moment. In fact, sometimes if words are left unspoken, there is a feeling of tension and negativity. Therefore, it is better to speak out your mind, but do so with awareness after listening to the speaker with full concentration.

Let's look at this in another way. When you really listen, you imbibe not only what is being spoken, but you also understand what is not spoken as well. Most of the time we don't really listen even to people who really matter to us. That's how misunderstandings grow among families, husbands and wives, brothers and sisters.

(a) On the basis of your reading of the above passage make notes on it, using headings and sub-headings. Use recognizable abbreviations (wherever necessary - minimum four) and a format you consider suitable. Also supply an appropriate title to it.

(b) Write a summary of the passage in about 80 words.

SECTION B: Advanced Writing Skills

(30 Marks)

4. Your school, Akash Public School, Agra needs a canteen manager. On behalf of the Principal, write an advertisement in about 50 words to be published in the classified columns of a local daily. Mention the educational and professional qualifications, other qualities required in the manager, who to apply to and the last date for the receipt of applications.

OR

Your club is going to organise an interclass singing competition. Write a notice in about 50 words inviting names of the students who want to participate in it. Give all the necessary details. You are Navtej/Navita, Secretary, Music Club, Akash Public School, Agra.

5. You are Navtej/Navita, Secretary, Environment Club, Akash Public School, Agra, You, along with a group of students, went on a 3-day tour through Corbett National Park. You found how the tourists abuse the available facilities and thus endanger the environment. Write a letter in 120-150 words to the editor of a national daily highlighting the situation. Suggest ways through which the environment of the Park can be saved.

OR

On Teacher's Day, you read in a newspaper that privately owned and managed schools in small towns or even in the suburbs of metropolitan cities exploit their teachers by paying them just a fraction of their authorised salaries. This affects their performance in the classroom and thus the lives of their students. Write a letter in 120 - 150 words to the editor of a national daily raising your voice against such exploitation Suggest ways to solve this problem. You are Navtej/Navita, 112 Taj Road, Agra.

6. The government has banned the use of animals in the laboratories for the purpose of dissection. Write a debate in 150 - 200 words either for or against this decision.

OR

Some people feel that electronic media (TV news) will bring about the end of print media (newspapers). What are your views on the issue? Write a debate in 150 - 200 words either for or against this view.
- use of visuals on TV
- authentic and fast
- not enough news for 24-hour telecast
- may fabricate news
- become repetitive and dull
- even scandals become news
- print media - time tested
- analysed, verified news
- editorial comments
- cater to all interests

7. Ragging has raised its ugly head again. A recent incident at a prestigious school has shown that this evil has not yet come to an end. Write an article in 150 - 200 words on 'Ragging, an Evil'. You are Navtej/Navita.
- a practice from the British era
- original aim, respect for hierarchy
- enforcing traditions, discipline
- Prefect - a teacher substitute
- misuse of authority
- vulgar aspect
- fatalities
- solution

OR

India is a tourist's dream destination. Give your views on the tourism potential of India in an article in 150 - 200 words. You are Navtej/Navita.
- places of worship - religious tourism
- foreigners - places of historical interest
- the rich - hill stations during summers
  - the sun-kissed beaches in winters
  - leisure tourism
- medical tourism
  - world class hospitals

SECTION C: Textbooks and Long Reading Text

(40 Marks)

8. Read the extract given below and answer the questions that follow :

and
looked out at young
trees sprinting, the merry children spilling
out of their homes, but after the airport's
security check, standing a few yards
away, I looked again at her, wan,
pale
as a late winter's moon and felt that

old
familiar ache, ...
(a) How can the trees sprint?
(b) Why did the poet look at her mother again?
(c) What did she observe?
(d) Identify the figure of speech used in these lines.

OR

On their slag heap, these children
Wear skins peeped through by bones and spectacles of steel
With mended glass, like bottle bits on stones.
(a) Who are these children?
(b) What is their slag heap?
(c) Why are their bones peeping through their skins?
(d) What does 'with mended glass' mean?

9. Answer any **four** of the following in 30-40 words each:
(a) What did garbage mean to the children of Seemapuri and to their parents?
(b) How did Rajkumar Shukla establish that he was resolute?
(c) 'Life is what it is all about,....' How is keeping quiet related to life?
(d) Mention any four things of beauty that add joy to our life.
(e) The manner of his (the Tiger King's) death is a matter of extraordinary interest. Comment.
(f) In what condition did Dr. Sadao find the American soldier at the seashore?

10. Answer the following question in 120-150 words:
Even today so many among us believe in superstitions. An astrologer predicted about 'the Tiger King' that he would be killed by a tiger. He 'killed' one hundred tigers yet was himself 'killed' by a tiger. How did the superstitious belief "prevail'?

OR

Dr. Sadao faced a dilemma. Should he use his surgical skills to save the life of a wounded person or hand an escaped American P.O.W. over to the Japanese police? How did he resolve this clash of values?

11. Answer the following question in 120-150 words:
Everybody during the last lesson is filled with regret. Comment. (The Last Lesson)

OR

Sophie lives in a world full of dreams which she does not know she cannot realise. Comment.

12. Answer the following question in 120-150 words:
Describe how Silas Marner is betrayed by his friend, William Dane.

OR

Why and how did Griffin rob the Vicar's house?

13. Answer the following question in 120-150 words:
"Evil begets evil." In the light of this remark, describe the character of Dunstan Cass.

OR

Attempt a character sketch of Mrs. Hall.

Solutions

SECTION - A

1.   **(1 × 4 = 4 Marks)**

(a) (iv) All of the above

(b) (i) Christianity

(c) (ii) Entrance to the church is non-descript

(d) (iv) Both (i) and (ii)

(1 × 6 = 6 Marks)

(e) The Greek belief about the 'stone of anointing' is that this is the place where Christ was removed from the cross.

(f) Emperor Constantine built the Rotunda to protect the Holy Sepulchre.

(g) The Pilgrims were mostly clueless about the traditions and history of the place. They were more interested in photographing it.

(h) The site is compatible with the biblical period as the archaeologists have found tombs from that era which says that Jesus' crucifixion occurred at a place outside the city walls with graves nearby.

(i) The pilgrims entered the 'room of the tomb' in a single file because there was a large marble slab that covered the original rock bench and it made the entrance very narrow.

(j) The woman tried to hide her tears because she didn't want anyone else to see her crying.

(k)   **(1 × 2 = 2 Marks)**

(i) A large grave - Tomb

(ii) Having no interesting features/dull - Non-descript

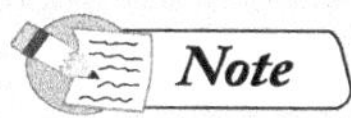 **Note**

Q.1. When answering the MCQs, choose the option which is the closest answer from amongst the options.

Passage 1:

*1. For Factual questions like e.g. **"Why did Emperor Constantine build the Rotunda"**, do not include information not given in the passage.*

*2. While answering the 'Why' question like **"Why did 'a woman' try to hide her tears"**, you may begin your answer with 'The woman tried to hide her tears because ....or a similar phrase.*

Passage 2:

1. When answering MCQs choose the option which is the closest answer from amongst the options.

2. While answering the 'What' question like "What happens when pilgrimages are turned into picnics", you may begin your answer with ...When pilgrimages are turned into picnics, ...or a similar phrase.

3. While answering the vocabulary questions, check the part of speech, the tense of the word etc. Your answer should have the same part of speech, tense etc.

4. For e.g. Made/turned - rendered (NOT render or rendering).

2.   **(2 × 1 = 2 Marks)**

(a) (iv) Both (i) and (ii)

(b) (iv) Both (i) and (ii)

(1 × 6 = 6 Marks)

(c) The change that have taken place in our attitude towards pilgrimages is that we have begun to look for whatever makes our heart happy, gives comfort to our body and peace to the mind.

(d) When pilgrimages are turned into picnics, people take large groups along and live in comfort and tamper with the environment.

(e) We are complacent in our spiritual efforts because we make all the things around us the way we want and more comfortable. We also think that external solutions will fulfil our needs and therefore we do not make any special efforts even in our spiritual search.

(f) When we try to be clever with nature, all our cleverness is rendered ineffective and nature's fury can and will wash away all imperfection.

(g) In the olden days people went into pilgrimage with an attitude of belonging towards all and conveying a message of brotherhood among all.

(h) The message conveyed by the passage is that pilgrimage is symbolic of contemplation, meditation and acceptance.

(1 × 2 = 2 Marks)

(i) (i) Made/turned - rendered

(ii) Very satisfied - complacent

3. (a) Note Making   **(5 Marks)**

Title – The art of listening

1. Hearing

    1.1   phy. phenomenon

    1.2   sound waves reach you

    1.3   hear what said

2. Listening
    2.1   hearing with full conc.
    2.2   applying mind
3. Barriers to listening
    3.1   prejudices / preconceived notion
    3.2   pretend to listen
    3.3   sit in jud.
    3.4   –ive mind-set
4. Importance of listening
    4.1   perfect comm.
    4.2   inter relationship gets better
    4.3   no tension/ negativity
    4.4   reduces misunderstanding

Key to Abbreviation

Abbreviation	Word
phy.	Physical
conc.	Concentration
jud.	Judgement
–ive	Negative
comm.	Communication
inter.	Interpersonal

(b) Summary   **(3 Marks)**

Listening and hearing are a lot different than we originally thought. Hearing refers to the sound waves we hear but do not fully understand and listening means hearing with full concentration. The barrier that comes between us and being good listeners are negative mindset, prejudices, misconceived notions etc. It is important to listen as it can improve communication, remove tension and interpersonal relationship gets better. If we really listen, we not only imbibe what is said but also understand the unspoken. Therefore, we should all try to be good listeners. (90 words)

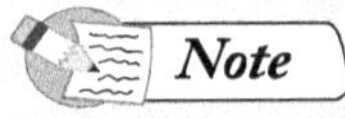

Note

1. *The passage is on the art of listening and the difference between hearing and listening. So, the title should have the key words 'Art', 'Science,' 'listening' or any synonym of the words.*
2. *It should always contain phrases. Avoid using complete sentences. For e.g.*
    1. Hearing
      1.1 phy. phenomenon
      1.2 sound waves reach you
      1.3 hear what said
    AND NOT Hearing is a physical phenomenon when …….
3. *Include a minimum of 4-6 distinctly different recognizable short forms i.e. abbreviations of the words in the notes as done in the solution.*

4.   **Advertisement**   **(4 Marks)**

SITUATION VACANT

Required a Canteen manager for Akash Public School, Agra. Attractive salary, additional benefits. Healthy working environment. Minimum qualification: 12th, 1 year experience in staff management, cleanliness and hygiene. Interested candidates may mail their resumes at principal.akashpublicschool.com or apply on the form available at the school front office on all working days between 8:00- 2:00pm before 30th November 2019.

OR

NOTICE

AKASH PUBLIC SCHOOL, AGRA

10th November 2019

INTERCLASS SINGING COMPETITION

All the students are hereby informed that the Music Club is organizing an Inter-class singing competition on 17th November 2019 for students of classes VIII-XII. Interested students can submit their names to the undersigned by 17th November 2019. The competition will be held in the school auditorium.

Navita

(Secretary, Music Club)

5.   **Letter**   **(6 Marks)**

34 Model Town

Agra

13th November 2019

The Editor

The Times of India

New Delhi

Subject: Dismal state of Corbett National Park

Sir/Madam,

Through the column of your esteemed news paper I would like to draw the attention of the concerned authorities towards the situation prevalent at the Corbett national park.

Every year tourists from all around the World visit this park and they bring many things with them that harms the environment of this park. They litter all over the place thereby making the park filthy. Some trample over the vegetation and even disturb the animals only to see their reactions. Vehicles too are parked at unauthorized places.

This sort of behaviour cannot be tolerated keeping in view the larger interest of the park and the resident animals. Strict penal action must be initiated against the offenders. An increased patrolling by the forest guards can be done to catch the offenders. Some signages instructing tourists can be placed at vantage points. If only we ensure strict adherence to the laid out rules, will the situation improve.

I hope that the concerned authorities will take some action in this matter.

Yours Truly,

Navita

(Secretary, Environment Club, AP S)

OR

112 Taj Road

Agra

13th November 2019

The Editor

The Tribune

New Delhi

Subject: Exploitation of Teachers

Sir/Madam,

Through the columns of your esteemed newspaper, I would like to draw the attention of the concerned authority as well as the general public towards the pathetic condition of a private school teacher.

Teachers are the backbone of the society and they have the great responsibility of shaping the future of the World through their teachings. However, the teachers of privately-owned schools in small towns and the suburbs of the metropolitan cities are being exploited very badly. Despite the fact that they are investing time, even beyond the normal working hours, they are being paid peanuts as compared to their government counterparts. There aren't any perks or allowances or any other form of appreciation for the teachers. This has an adverse effect on the performance of the teachers as they lose interest in their profession. Ultimately it is the student who suffers.

In order to put a stop to this, the government must ensure that schools pay salaries as per government pay scales by monitoring this themselves. All salaries must also be paid through banks. The management too should be more humane towards the teachers.

I hope the concerned authorities take some action in this matter.

Yours Truly

Navita

6. Debate (10 Marks)

Honourable Chairperson, members of the Jury, my worthy opponents and dear audience. I, XXX, stand before you to express my views **for the motion** on the topic," Banning of dissection of animals for research."

Killing innocent animals for research purposes, how inhumane can we be? Agreed that this research will help thousands of humans increase their longevity, but doesn't this propagate unethical values? Dissection of animals is not just wrong but also very inhumane, cruel and dreadful to watch. Not to mention, it also teaches students' animal cruelty. The animals are piled on top of each other, shipped in crowded containers with no regulated temperature, hardly any food or water and brought to the institutions where they would meet death. It also causes death of many animals before they reach the dissection table because of the conditions that they have to live in. Even the drugs used on these animals are not fully safe and often results in their death. How do we justify these deaths? In my opinion the government has done the rightful thing by banning the dissection of animals for research. It can be replaced by using virtual labs and models.

In the end I would like to say that we should stop covering up animal cruelty in the name of scientific research.

Thank You for your patient hearing !

OR

Honorable chairperson, members of the jury, worthy opponents and dear audience.Today I, XXX, stand before you to speak **against the motion** on the topic, "Electronic media will bring an end to the print media."

We all have seen our fathers and grandfathers in the morning, having a cup of tea and reading the newspaper. For people like them it is necessary to have the hard copy of a newspaper rather than reading news on the mobile, tabs or even television for that matter. In fact, their mornings would seem incomplete without the mandatory newspaper in their hands.

Even though electronic media is faster and more of an attention grabber than print media, it is not always to the point and not necessarily with the correct content or information. In contrast to this print media always has analyzed, authentic and verified news. The editorial gives you a better perspective on a given topic in addition to adding to the vocabulary of a person. Furthermore, in our country we do not have internet or 4G network everywhere. So, the people living in these areas can only get to know what's happening around them through the newspaper. Frequent power cuts and affordability also are points of concern in case of electronic media.

In the end I would just like to say that newspaper have been an integral part of our society since a long time and it is going anywhere in the near future.

Thank You for your patient hearing !

7. Article   **(10 Marks)**

Ragging: A Social Evil

By *Navita*

Ragging is a social evil that has been a part of our society since the British rule. It started in English colleges and universities but slowly it spread and corrupted almost the entire Indian educational institutions. The excuse given earlier for ragging was to teach the students respect for the social hierarchy in early career and enforcing traditions and discipline in individuals. However, what started as a disciplining measure, soon became indisciplined itself.

Ragging has let down humanity on innumerable occasions. It is sad to learn that such a malpractice has been going on since decades. The sufferers of this year become the perpetrators of the crime the next year and thus continues the vicious cycle year after year! Ragging of students has led to many serious cases which involved psychological trauma for freshers, physical harm, humiliation and in some cases suicide too. In spite of the strict warning and legislation by the Supreme court, some institutions have failed to abate and control this.

Stringent action against students indulging in ragging should be initiated. Sensitization camps both for freshers and senior students and their Parents needs to be organized. Ragging must be stopped immediately and people ragging others must be punished. In the end I would request all to join hands and stop this dehumanizing activity and create a ragging free world.

OR

India: A Tourist's Delight

By *Navita*

India! The name itself conjures up pictures of unparalleled beauty, with the serene white peaks of the Himalayas to the sun kissed beaches of Goa, with vast expanse of the golden sands of Jaisalmer to the treacherous mangrove forests of the Sunderbans! It is indeed a traveller's delight and has something to offer to suit each taste. India is a land of diversity- diversity of culture, language, food, religion etc. In addition to it has been the birthplace of many religions too. Its places of wordship with Rishikesh,

Kedarnath, Bodhgaya, Shirdi not only appeal to people looking to visit religious places but also people looking for adventure. Attractions like technological parks, science museums, heritage sites, old monuments, war memorials etc abound in almost all the places of tourist interest. Not only this, the Indian handicrafts, jewelry, carpets, leather goods etc have their own place of importance in a tourist's list of souvenirs. Medical tourism is also coming up in a big way with its world class hospitals. Yoga centers, Ayurveda treatment and natural health therapy centers are also figuring in the must visit list of the foreign tourists.

On the whole India has a great potential to become a world player in the tourism industry if only we divert enough resources and attention to this hitherto untapped industry.

8.   **(1 × 4 = 4 Marks)**

(a) The trees themselves are not sprinting. The phrase is used to describe the backward movement of the trees as the car moves forward.

(b) The poet looked at her mother again to see her once again before departing. It is the poet's love for her mother which makes her look at her aging mother once again.

(c) She observed her mother's pale appearance which resembled the late winter moon and realized once again painfully that her mother was aging.

(d) The figure of speech used in these lines is a simile "as a late winter's moon" and personification in "young trees sprinting".

OR

(a) These children are the poor and impoverished children of the slums who are the students of the Elementary school.

(b) Their 'slag heap" is the slum in which they are living like unwanted, waste material.

(c) Their bones are peeping through their skin since they are malnourished.

(d) 'Mended glass' refers to the poor financial condition of the children. They are too poor to even afford proper glasses and manage with broken spectacles.

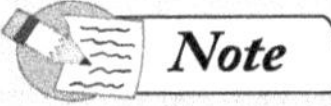

Note

1. *Be precise and to the point.*
2. *Look closely at the figures of speech and the special words.*
3. *For e.g. **"Identify the figure of speech used in these lines"** (My Mother at Sixty Six) you may begin by ………The figure of speech used in these lines is a simile "as a late winter's moon" and personification in "young trees sprinting" (ANY ONE).*

9.   **(3 × 4 = 12 Marks)**

(a) Garbage was a means of survival for the elders of Seemapuri whereas for the children it was wrapped in wonder because they would come across a coin or two in the garbage every now and then.

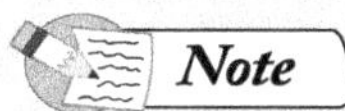

Note

1. *Each 3-mark question must have at least two value points.*
2. *So, for example – for the question "How did Rajkumar Shukla establish that he was resolute", include any two value points from those given below.*
   - *a. Was able to establish that he was resolute - came all the way from Champaran to Lucknow to meet Gandhiji*
   - *b. Waited endlessly to talk to Gandhi*
   - *c. Accompanied him everywhere*
   - *d. Did not leave Gandhi's side for weeks*

(b) Rajkumar Shukla was able to establish that he was resolute because not only did he come all the way from Champaran to Lucknow to speak to Gandhi but also accompanied him everywhere. He did not leave Gandhi's side for weeks.

(c) Keeping quiet is related to life in the sense that people pursue their goals single-mindedly and keep on moving in their lives without pausing for refection. It is therefore important that they keep quiet for sometime and introspect to gain a better perspective on their actions.

(d) The four things of beauty that add joy to our lives are the sun, the moon, the trees both old and young and the daffodils.

(e) The manner of the Tiger king's death is of extraordinary interest since as soon as he was born, the astrologers predicted that the Tiger King would be killed by a tiger. In order to ensure his longevity, the Tiger King vows to kill hundred tigers and he is successful too. However ironically after having killed 100 tigers, his death is brought about by a sliver of wood from a toy tiger.

(f) The American soldier was found motionless on the sca-shore with his face in the sand. He was completely unconscious and had a gun wound on the right side of his lower back which had reopened.

10.   **(6 Marks)**

The story 'The Tiger King' revolves round the predication of the astrologers at the birth of the Tiger King regarding his death and the measures that the Tiger King takes to prove this prediction incorrect. Since the astrologers predict that his death will be brought about by a tiger,

he vows to kill hundred tigers for which he indulges in the hunting of innocent animals. His marriage is also not guided by the virtue and the goodness of the princess but the criterion of a kingdom with more tiger population. Each action of the Tiger King is guided by the predication right from taking the risk of losing his kingdom to the bribes and the taxes. However ironically even after fulfilling his vow of killing hundred tigers it is a tiger, albeit a toy, which becomes the cause of his death. While playing with the toy tiger, a birthday present for his son, he gets hurt by the sliver of wood from the toy tiger and dies later. So, at the end of the story the superstitious belief prevailed.

OR

Yes. Dr Sadao faced the dilemma of whether to use his surgical skills to save the life of the wounded person or hand an escaped American prisoner of war over to the Japanese General. However, he was able to resolve his dilemma by striking a wonderful balance between the two duties without compromising on either. A strong believer of professional loyalty and human kindness he was aware of his primary duty as a doctor which implied making the ailing, injured and sick people fully whole irrespective of his own notions about Americans. Therefore, notwithstanding the risk inherent in treating an enemy, and ignoring the fact that he does not like Americans, the surgeon in him instinctively inspires him to take the person home, operate upon him and provide post-operative treatment too. He rises above narrow national prejudices and extends help and services to an enemy. In course of time his faithful servants and even his wife either desert him or fail to see his viewpoint. Despite all these encumbrances on his way, he single-mindedly focusses on his primary duty.

However, Dr Sadao does not fail as a patriot too while he is fulfilling his responsibility as a doctor. He informs the General about the injured man whom he has treated since he is an escaped prisoner of war. He also accepts the General's decision to send the assassins without any reluctance. He even keeps the door open for the assassins to enter thereby keeping his integrity as a Japanesecitizex intact.

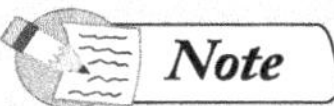

Note

1. *Each 6-mark question must have at least four value points.*
2. *Answer to the point including your own opinion in places where it is deemed necessary by the question.*
3. *Pick out specific examples from the text to support your answer.*

4.   *Quote straight from the text wherever required but do so only when you are sure of the words.*
     For e.g., the question "Dr. Sadao faced a dilemma. Should he use his surgical skills to save the life of a wounded person or hand an escaped American P.O.W. over to the Japanese police? How did he resolve this clash of values,"divide your answer into: 1. The dilemma 2.The solution to the dilemma. Use the value points from those given below:

   a.   *Yes. Dilemma of whether to use his surgical skills to save the life of the wounded person /hand an escaped American prisoner of war over to the Japanese General.*

   b.   *Resolve his dilemma - balance between the two duties without compromising on either- strong believer of professional loyalty and human kindness- aware of his primary duty as a doctor - implied making the ailing, injured and sick people fully whole - irrespective of own notions about Americans - risk inherent in treating an enemy- ignoring the fact that does not like Americans- surgeon in him - inspires to take the person home-operate-provide post-operative treatment - rises above narrow national prejudices -extends help and services to an enemy- faithful servants and even his wife -either desert him -fail to see his viewpoint-he single-mindedly focusses on his primary duty.*

   c.   *Does not fail as a patriot too - informs the General about the injured man-treated -accepts General's decision to send the assassins- no reluctance- keeps the door open for the assassins to enter - keeps his integrity as a Japanese citizen intact.*

11.   **(6 Marks)**

The language of a country is a part of the identity of that nation. When a nation is debarred from using its own language, the identity of its people is threatened. It is then that one starts having regrets for the time lost which could have been utilized. When an order comes from Berlin forbidding the teaching of French in the schools of Alsace and Lorraine, all are full of regrets at having ignored the language. M. Hamel blames himself for having given a holiday at the cost of a lesson when he wanted to go fishing himself and for having got his flowers watered by the students instead of making them attend their lessons. The villagers regretted having paid less heed to learning the language and they reflect their regret by sitting quietly at the usually empty last rows of the class on the day of the last lesson. Franz himself is on the verge of tears at the last lesson and wished he had attended the classes more often and paid more attention to the lessons which he usually found uninteresting. M Hamel ends the last lesson by appealing to all the people in the class to preserve 'French' since holding on to their language will keep them united and leaves the classroom after writing "*Viva la France*" on the board.

OR

Sophie is a young girl from a weak socio-economic background. She is by nature a dreamer and since the living conditions of her family aren't very pleasant, she lives in a make belief world. The limiting scenario at home makes her nurse ambitions to make a better living by becoming a model and opening a boutique. Though she is cut out for the biscuit factory, as Jansie reminds her, she wants to move up the social ladder. However, the only drawback in the world of dreams that she weaves is that it is built on wafer thin ground since she does not have any concrete plan as to how she is going to achieve that. It is not that Sophie does not know that she cannot realize her dreams, for she has Jansie as a friend, who constantly reminds her to keep her feet firmly in the ground. However, for her, the dreams are only an escape from reality and she is happy doing that. There comes a time in the story when her dream world and reality merge together so much that she sees and experiences things and events which do not happen at all and that is where her dreaming becomes dangerous.

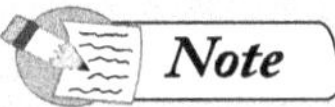

1.   *Adhere to the word limit given for the question.*

2.   *Quoting from the text always gets more marks but misquotes can backfire. So, be careful.*

3.   *For the Question "**Everybody during the last lesson is filled with regret. Comment".** you can use the value points from those given below:*

   a.   *Language of a country -part of identity of that nation- identity of people threatened when debarred- regrets for the time lost - could have been utilized.*

   b.   *Order from Berlin forbidding -teaching of French -schools of Alsace and Lorraine-all full of regrets -having ignored the language.*

   c.   *M. Hamel blames himself -given a holiday at the cost of a lesson- to go fishing himself- get his flowers watered -instead of making them attend their lessons.*

   d.   *Villagers regretted -paid less heed to learning the language – show their regret by sitting quietly - last rows of the class – for last lesson.*

   e.   *Franz -on the verge of tears -wished had attended the classes more often -paid more attention to the lessons - usually found uninteresting.*

   f.   *M Hamel ends the lesson - appeals to the people in the class - preserve 'French' - holding on to their language -keep them united -leaves the classroom after writing "Viva la France" on the board.*

12.   **(6 Marks)**

William Dane was a close friend of Silas Marner. He was a little older to Silas and their friendship was such that the

Lantern Yard brethren called them David and Jonathan. Silas considers himself fortunate to have a friend like William and a fiancée like Sarah. However, little did he know that his friend and fiancée would be his nemesis at Lantern Yard. In fact, one tends to derive a lot from William's "narrow slanting eyes and compressed lips" in contrast to Silas's "defenseless, dear-like gaze"that he is a scheming person. He became friends with Silas Marner primarily because they shared the same religious sect in Lantern Yard and he feels he will benefit from this association. However very early in the novel we get to see that each time that Silas wants his friend to rise to the occasion or some emergency, William fails him. In case of Silas's cataleptic fit which happened during one of the prayer-meetings, it is William's suggestion alone which jarred with the general sympathy of the rest of the people that the trance looked more like a visitation of Satan than a proof of divine favour. Despite this Silas trusts him only to be framed by William in a crime of a larger magnitude. Since Silas's knife is found at the scene of crime and the empty bag, which earlier had the money of the church was found in Silas's room, all are convinced of Silas's guilt. Even though in reality Silas's knife had been last used to cut a strap for William and then he had not put it back to its designated place, Silas does not reveal this fact to the others. However, far from owning to this truth, William does not hesitate in betraying Silas. He even manages to marry Silas's fiancée later.

OR

The burglary at the Vicarage occurs in the 'small hours of Whit Monday' at around 4 am. It is done by Griffin since all his money was exhausted and he needed cash to continue with his research and make the payment to Mrs Hall.

Griffin left the inn and entered the vicarage. Since he was invisible, he was not seen by the vicar and his wife even though they could hear the noise made by the opening and closing of the door. Once they approach the study, they can hear the ruffling sound of papers and a match being struck to light the candle. A violent sneeze also confirmed the presence of someone. However, despite all this, Griffin after entering the study, opened the drawers, searched it and stole 'two pounds ten in half sovereigns'which were put in the drawer and left the vicarage without being identified since he was invisible. The sound of the slamming of the kitchen door confirmed that someone had left the Vicarage.

![Note]

Note

1. *Adhere to the word limit. Answer must reveal your deep knowledge of the text.*
2. *For e.g. the question **'Why and how did Griffin rob the Vicar's house'** divide your answer into WHY and HOW and then answer the question.*

a. *WHY – All of Griffin's money was exhausted - needed cash to continue with his research - make payment to Mrs Hall. Burglary occurs - 'small hours of Whit Monday' - 4 am.*

b. *HOW - Griffin left the inn - entered the vicarage - was invisible - so not seen by the vicar and his wife - could hear the noise - opening and closing of the door- ruffling sound of papers- match being struck – candle lighted- violent sneeze- despite all this, Griffin enters the study, opens drawers- steals 'two pounds ten in half sovereigns'- left the vicarage without being identified since was invisible*

13.   **(6 Marks)**

The portrayal of Dunstan Cass's character and whatever happens to him in the course of the novel is a perfect example of the proverb "Evil begets Evil". He is the Squire's youngest son and the younger brother of Godfrey. He is portrayed as a lazy, manipulative and greedy person who can say or do anything to get what he wants. He blackmails his brother Godfrey into selling of his favourite horse Wildfire in order to give the money to the Squire as the rent. His knowledge of the secret marriage of Godfrey with Molly and the awareness that the Squire will never approve of the same is his weapon to blackmail Godfrey. In his greed to strike a good bargain with Bryce, he gets the horse killed. He also has no qualms about stealing Silas's money and then vanishes. It is no surprise that his disappearance at the time of Silas's money being stolen is not questioned since he is known to vanish for long periods. His remains are discovered sixteen years later in a drystone pit wedged between two stones with all the money and Godfrey's golden whip. It is concluded that he might have drowned. His evil deeds ultimately lead to a lonely and undignified death.

OR

Mrs Hall was the owner of the inn 'Coach and Horses'. She was a typical business-woman who joyously took the god sent opportunity to have guests at her inn. Since it was winter, Griffin's visit was an opportunity for her to make some money since they hardly had any guests in such a harsh and rough weather.Therefore, in her excitement, she ignores the appearance of the guest. Instead, she makes all attempts to make him feel at home right from lighting the fire to preparing the meals herself and offering to take off his coat and hat for drying in the kitchen. Despite being rebuffed time and again throughout the novel, Mrs Hall does not stop being inquisitive. It is clear that she suspects Griffin's involvement in the burglary at the Vicarage when she tells him to always come through the door even though she is scared at that time. She is more decisive and vocal when compared to her husband. She is also quite practical and most of her decisions are guided by monetary considerations.

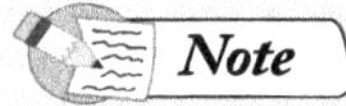

Note

1. This question tests understanding, appreciation, analysis and interpretation of the incident/character. So, thorough reading of the text is required.

2. Adhere to the word limit and answer the question.

3. Avoid giving details which you are not sure of.

4. For e.g. the question **"Attempt a character sketch of Mrs. Hall,"** use at least 4-5 value points from those given below:

    a. Mrs Hall - owner of the inn 'Coach and Horses.'

    b. Typical business-woman - joyously took the god sent opportunity to have guests at her inn- winter, Griffin's visit - an opportunity to make some money - hardly had any guests in harsh and rough weather- in her excitement-ignores the appearance of the guest.

    c. Makes attempts to make him feel at home - lighting the fire - preparing the meals herself - offering to take off his coat and hat - drying in the kitchen.

    d. Rebuffed time and again throughout the novel - does not stop being inquisitive-suspects Griffin's involvement in the burglary at the Vicarage - more decisive and vocal - compared to her husband - quite practical - most of her decisions guided by monetary considerations.

CBSE Board Solved Paper

Time Allowed : 3 Hours   *Maximum Marks : 100*

General Instructions:

(i) This paper is divided into three Sections : A, B and C. All the sections are compulsory.

(ii) Separate instructions are given with each section and question, wherever necessary. Read these instructions very carefully and follow them faithfully.

(iii) Do not exceed the prescribed word limit while answering the questions.

SECTION A: Reading

(30 Marks)

1. Read the passage given below carefully:

   1. For four days, I walked through the narrow lanes of the old city, enjoying the romance of being in a city where history still lives– in its cobblestone streets and in its people riding asses, carrying vine leaves and palm as they once did during the time of Christ.

   2. This is Jerusalem, home to the sacred sites of Christianity, Islam and Judaism. This is the place that houses the church of the Holy Sepulchre, the place where Jesus was finally laid to rest. This is also the site of Christ's crucifixion, burial and resurrection.

   3. Built by the Roman Emperor Constantine at the site of an earlier temple to Aphrodite, it is the most venerated Christian shrine in the world. And justifiably so. Here, within the church, are the last five stations of the cross, the 10th station where Jesus was stripped of his clothes, the 11th where he was nailed to the cross, the 12th where he died on the cross, the 13th where the body was removed from the cross, and the 14th, his tomb.

   4. For all this weighty tradition, the approach and entrance to the church is non-descript. You have to ask for directions. Even to the devout Christian pilgrims walking along the Via Dolorosa - the Way of Sorrows - first nine stations look clueless. Then a courtyard appears, hemmed in by other buildings and a doorway to one side. This leads to a vast area of huge stone architecture.

   5. Immediately inside the entrance is your first stop. It's the stone of anointing: this is the place, according to Greek tradition, where Christ was removed from the cross. The Roman Catholics, however, believe it to be the spot where Jesus body was prepared for burial by Joseph.

6. What happened next? Jesus was buried. He was taken to a place outside the city of Jerusalem where other graves existed and there, he was buried in a cave. However, all that is long gone, destroyed by continued attacks and rebuilding: what remains is the massive– and impressive– Rotunda (a round building with a dome) that Emperor Constantine built. Under this, and right in the centre of the Rotunda, is the structure that contains the Holy Sepulchre.

7. "How do you know that this is Jesus' tomb?" I asked one of the pilgrims standing next to me. He was clueless, more interested, like the rest of them, in the novelty of it all and in photographing it, than in its history or tradition.

8. At the start of the first century, the place was a disused quarry outside the city walls. According to the gospels, 'Jesus crucifixion occurred' at a place outside the city walls with graves nearby.......' Archaeologists have discovered tombs from that era, so the site is compatible with the biblical period.

9. The structure at the site is a marble tomb built over the original burial chamber. It has two rooms, and you enter four at a time into the first of these, the Chapel of the Angel. Here the angel is supposed to have sat on a stone to recount Christ's resurrection. A low door made of white marble, partly worn away by pilgrims' hands, leads to a smaller chamber inside. 'This is the room of the tomb', the place where Jesus was buried.

10. We entered in single file. On my right was a large marble slab that covered the original rock bench on which the body of Jesus was laid. A woman knelt and prayed. Her eyes were wet with tears. She pressed her face against the slab to hide them, but it only made it worse.

On the basis of your understanding of this passage answer the following questions with the help of given options:

(a) How does Jerusalem still retain the charm of ancient era?
- (i) There are narrow lanes,
- (ii) Roads are paved with cobblestones.
- (iii) People can be seen riding asses.
- (iv) All of the above

(b) Holy Sepulchre is sacred to ____
- (i) Christianity
- (ii) Islam
- (iii) Judaism
- (iv) Both (i) and (iii)

(c) Why does one have to constantly ask for directions to the church?
- (i) Its lanes are narrow.
- (ii) Entrance to the church is non-descript.
- (iii) People are not tourist-friendly.
- (iv) Everyone is lost in enjoying the romance of the place.

(d) Where was Jesus buried?
- (i) In a cave
- (ii) At a place outside the city
- (iii) In the Holy Sepulchre
- (iv) Both (i) and (ii)

Answer the following questions briefly :

(e) What is the Greek belief about the 'stone of anointing'?

(f) Why did Emperor Constantine build the Rotunda?

(g) What is the general attitude of the pilgrims?

(h) How is the site compatible with the biblical period?

(i) Why did the pilgrims enter the room of the tomb in a single file?

(j) Why did 'a woman' try to hide her tears?

(k) Find words from the passage which mean the same as:
- (i) A large grave (para 3)
- (ii) Having no interesting features/dull (para 4)

2. Read the passage given below:

1. We often make all things around us the way we want them. Even during our pilgrimages we have begun to look for whatever makes our heart happy, gives comfort to our body and peace to the mind. It is as if external solutions will fulfil our needs, and we do not want to make any special efforts even in our spiritual search. Our mind is resourceful - it works to find shortcuts in simple and easy ways.

2. Even pilgrimages have been converted into tourism opportunities. Instead, we must awake our conscience and souls and understand the truth. Let us not tamper with either our own nature or that of the Supreme.

3. All our cleverness is rendered ineffective when nature does a dance of destruction. Its fury can and will wash away all imperfections. Indian culture, based on Vedic treatises, assists in human evolution, but we are now using our entire energy in distorting these traditions according to our convenience instead of making efforts to make ourselves worthy of them.

4. The irony is that humans are not even aware of the complacent attitude they have allowed themselves to sink to. Nature is everyone's Amma and her fierce blows will sooner or later corner us and force us to understand this truth. Earlier, pilgrimages to places of spiritual significance were rituals that were undertaken when people became free from their worldly duties. Even now some seekers take up this pious religious journey as a path to peace and knowledge. Anyone travelling with this attitude feels and travels with only a few essential items that his body can carry. Pilgrims traditionally travelled light, on foot, eating light, dried chickpeas and fruits, or whatever was available. Pilgrims of olden days did not feel the need to stay in special AC bedrooms, or travel by luxury cars or indulge themselves with delicious food and savouries.

5. Pilgrims traditionally moved ahead, creating a feeling of belonging towards all, conveying a message of brotherhood among all they came across whether in small caves, ashrams or local settlements. They received the blessings and congregations of yogis and mahatmas in return while conducting the dharma of their pilgrimage. A pilgrimage is like penance or sadhana to stay near nature and to experience a feeling of oneness with it, to keep the body healthy and fulfilled with the amount of food, while seeking freedom from attachments and yet remaining happy while staying away from relatives and associates.

6. This is how a pilgrimage should be rather than making it like a picnic by taking a large group along and living in comfort, packing in entertainment, and tampering with environment. What is worse is giving a boost to the ego of having had a special darshan. Now alms are distributed, charity done while they brag about their spiritual experiences!

7. We must embark on our spiritual journey by first understanding the grace and significance of a pilgrimage and following it up with the prescribed rules and rituals - this is what translates into the ultimate and beautiful medium of spiritual evolution. There is no justification for tampering with nature.

8. A pilgrimage is symbolic of contemplation and meditation and acceptance, and is a metaphor for the constant growth or movement and love for nature that we should hold in our hearts.

9. This is the truth!

On the basis of your understanding of the above passage answer the questions that follow with the help of given options:

(a) How can a pilgrim keep his body healthy?
- (i) By travelling light
- (ii) By eating small amount of food

    (iii) By keeping free from attachments
    (iv) Both (i) and (ii)
 (b) How do we satisfy our ego?
    (i) By having a special darshan
    (ii) By distributing alms
    (iii) By treating it like a picnic
    (iv) Both (i) and (ii)

Answer the following as briefly as possible :

(c) What change has taken place in our attitude towards pilgrimages?

(d) What happens when pilgrimages are turned into picnics?

(e) Why are we complacent in our spiritual efforts?

(f) How does nature respond when we try to be clever with it?

(g) In olden days with what attitude did people go on a pilgrimage?

(h) What message does the passage convey to the pilgrims?

(i) Find words from the passage which mean the same as the following:
    (i) made / turned (para 3)
    (ii) very satisfied (para 4)

3. Read the passage given below:

It is surprising that sometimes we don't listen to what people say to us. We hear them, but we don't listen to them. I was curious to know how hearing is different from listening. I had thought both were synonyms, but gradually, I realised there is a big difference between the two words.

Hearing is a physical phenomenon. Whenever somebody speaks, the sound waves generated reach you, and you definitely hear whatever is said to you. However, even if you hear something, it doesn't always mean that you actually understand whatever is being said. Paying attention to whatever you hear means you are really listening. Consciously using your mind to understand whatever is being said is listening.

Diving deeper, I found that listening is not only hearing with attention, but is much more than that. Listening is hearing with full attention, and applying our mind. Most of the time, we listen to someone, but our minds are full of needless chatter and there doesn't seem to be enough space to accommodate what is being spoken.

We come with a lot of prejudices and preconceived notions about the speaker or the subject on which he is talking. We pretend to listen to the speaker, but deep inside, we sit in judgement and are dying to pronounce right or wrong, true or false, yes or no. Sometimes, we even come prepared with a negative mindset of proving the speaker wrong. Even if the speaker says nothing harmful, we are ready to pounce on him with our own version of things.

What we should ideally do is listen first with full awareness. Once, we have done that, we can decide whether we want to make a judgement or not. Once we do that. communication will be perfect and our interpersonal relationship will become so much better. Listening well doesn't mean one has to say the right thing at the right moment. In fact, sometimes if words are left unspoken, there is a feeling of tension and negativity. Therefore, it is better to speak out your mind, but do so with awareness after listening to the speaker with full concentration.

Let's look at this in another way. When you really listen, you imbibe not only what is being spoken, but you also understand what is not spoken as well. Most of the time we don't really listen even to people who really matter to us. That's how misunderstandings grow among families, husbands and wives, brothers and sisters.

(a) On the basis of your reading of the above passage make notes on it, using headings and sub-headings. Use recognizable abbreviations (wherever necessary - minimum four) and a format you consider suitable. Also supply an appropriate title to it.

(b) Write a summary of the passage in about **80** words.

(30 Marks)

4. Every year in the central park of the city a flower show is held in the month of February Your school has received a circular from the District Collector inviting your students to visit it. Write a notice in about **50** words informing the students about the show and advising them to go and enjoy it. You are Navtej/Navita, Head Boy/Head Girl Sunrise Public School, Surat.

OR

Sarvodaya Education Society, a charitable organisation is coming to your school to distribute books among the needy students. As Head Boy/Head Girl, Sunrise Public School, Surat, write a notice in about **50** words asking such students to drop the lists of books they need in the box kept outside the Principal's office. You are Navtej/Navita.

5. Recently you went to your native village to visit your grandparents. You saw that some of the children in the age group 5 - 14 (the age at which they should have been at school) remained at home, were working in the fields or simply loitering in the streets.

Write a letter in **120-150** words to the editor of a national daily analyzing the problem and offering solutions to it. You are Navtej/Navita, M-114 Mount Kailash, Kanpur.

OR

When cricket teams go abroad the members are allowed to take their wives, even friends along with them. Does this fact distract them or help them to focus on their game in a better way? If it is good, why don't we allow our athletes to enjoy the same privilege?

Write a letter to editor of a national daily in **120-150** words giving your views on the issue. You are Navtej/Navita. M-114 Mount Kailash, Kanpur.

6. Mobile phone of today is no longer a mere means of communication. Music lovers are so glued to it that they don't pay attention even to the traffic while crossing the

roads. This leads to accidents sometimes even fatal ones. Write a speech in **150-200** words to be delivered in the morning assembly advising the students to be careful in the use of this otherwise very useful gadget. Imagine you are Principal of your school.

OR

Power shortage has become a norm even in the metropolitan cities. One way to face this situation is by preventing the wastage of power.

Write a speech in **150-200** words on the importance of power in our daily life and how to save power at school and at home. Imagine that you are the Principal of your school.

7. In the year to come (if you have not already done this year) you are going to celebrate your 18th birthday. Write an article in **150-200** words on the joys and responsibilities of being eighteen. You are Navtej/Navita.

OR

Write an article in **150-200** words on how we can make India a carefree and enjoyable place for women when they can go wherever they like to without any fear of being stared at, molested or discriminated against. You are Navtej/Navita.

SECTION C: Textbooks and Long Reading Text

(40 Marks)

8. Read the extract given below and answer the questions that follow :

   I saw my mother,

   beside me,

   doze, open mouthed, her face

   ashen like that

   of a corpse and realized with

   pain

   that she was as old as she

   looked but soon

   put that thought away....

   (a) What worried the poet when she looked at her mother?

   (b) Why was there pain in her realization?

   (c) Why did she put that thought away?

   (d) Identify the figure of speech used in these lines.

   OR

   Far far from gusty waves these children's faces.

   Like rootless weeds, the hair torn round their pallor;

   The tall girl with her weighed-down head.

   (a) Who are these children?

   (b) What does the poet mean by 'gusty waves'?

   (c) What has possibly weighed-down the tall girl's head?

   (d) Identify the figure of speech used in these lines.

9. Answer any **four** of the following in **30 - 40** words each:

   (a) Who occupied the back benches in the class room on the day of the last lesson? Why?

   (b) Why did Douglas' mother recommend that he should learn swimming at the YMCA swimming pool?

   (c) What will counting upto twelve and keeping still help us achieve?

   (d) What does a thing of beauty do for us?

   (e) Which do you think is a better ending of Roger Skunk's story, Jo's or her father's? Why?

   (f) What could the Governor have done to securely bring Evans back to the prison from the 'Golden Lion'?

10. Answer the following in **120-150** words:

    Giving a bribe is an evil practice. How did the Tiger King bribe the British officer to save his kingdom? How do you view this act of his?

    OR

    Dr. Sadao was a patriotic Japanese as well as a dedicated surgeon. How could he honour both the values?

11. Answer the following in **120-150** words:

    Describe the difficulties the bangle makers of Firozabad have to face in their lives.

    OR

    The peddler declined the invitation of the ironmaster but accepted the one from Edla. Why?

12. Answer the following in **120-150** words:

    Describe the ironical situation in which Silas Marner had to leave Lantern Yard.

    OR

    Within a few days of his arrival in Iping, people became suspicious of Griffin. Why?

13. Answer the following in **120-150** words:

    Describe Dolly Winthrop as the most lovable character in George Eliot's 'Silas Marner'.

    OR

    Attempt a character sketch of Marvel.

Solutions

SECTION - A

1. (1 × 4 = 4 Marks)

(a) (iv) All of the above

(b) (i) Christianity

(c) (ii) Entrance to the church is non-descript

(d) (iv) Both (i) and (ii)

(1 × 6 = 6 Marks)

(e) The Greek belief about the 'stone of anointing' is that this is the place where Christ was removed from the cross.

(f) Emperor Constantine built the Rotunda to protect the Holy Sepulchre.

(g) The Pilgrims were mostly clueless about the traditions and history of the place. They were more interested in photographing it.

(h) The site is compatible with the biblical period as the archaeologists have found tombs from that era which says that Jesus' crucifixion occurred at a place outside the city walls with graves nearby.

(i) The pilgrims entered the 'room of the tomb' in a single file because there was a large marble slab that covered the original rock bench and it made the entrance very narrow.

(j) The woman tried to hide her tears because she didn't want anyone else to see her crying.

(k) (1 × 2 = 2 Marks)

(i) A large grave - Tomb

(ii) Having no interesting features/dull - Non-descript

 **Note**

Q.1. When answering the MCQs, choose the option which is the closest answer from amongst the options.

Passage 1:

1. *For Factual questions like e.g. **"Why did Emperor Constantine build the Rotunda"**, do not include information not given in the passage.*

2. *While answering the 'Why' question like **"Why did 'a woman' try to hide her tears"**, you may begin your answer with 'The woman tried to hide her tears because ....or a similar phrase.*

Passage 2:

1. *When answering MCQs choose the option which is the closest answer from amongst the options.*

2. *While answering the 'What' question like "What happens when pilgrimages are turned into picnics", you may begin your answer with ...When pilgrimages are turned into picnics, ...or a similar phrase.*

3. *While answering the vocabulary questions, check the part of speech, the tense of the word etc. Your answer should have the same part of speech, tense etc.*

4. *For e.g. Made/turned - rendered (NOT render or rendering).*

2. (2 × 1 = 2 Marks)

(a) (iv) Both (i) and (ii)

(b) (iv) Both (i) and (ii)

(1 × 6 = 6 Marks)

(c) The change that have taken place in our attitude towards pilgrimages is that we have begun to look for whatever makes our heart happy, gives comfort to our body and peace to the mind.

(d) When pilgrimages are turned into picnics, people take large groups along and live in comfort and tamper with the environment.

(e) We are complacent in our spiritual efforts because we make all the things around us the way we want and more comfortable. We also think that external solutions will fulfil our needs and therefore we do not make any special efforts even in our spiritual search.

(f) When we try to be clever with nature, all our cleverness is rendered ineffective and nature's fury can and will wash away all imperfection.

(g) In the olden days people went into pilgrimage with an attitude of belonging towards all and conveying a message of brotherhood among all.

(h) The message conveyed by the passage is that pilgrimage is symbolic of contemplation, meditation and acceptance.

(1 × 2 = 2 Marks)

(i) (i) Made/turned - rendered

(ii) Very satisfied - complacent

3. (a) **Note Making** (5 Marks)

Title – The art of listening

1. Hearing

   1.1   phy. phenomenon

   1.2   sound waves reach you

   1.3   hear what said

2. Listening
  2.1   hearing with full conc.
  2.2   applying mind
3. Barriers to listening
  3.1   prejudices / preconceived notion
  3.2   pretend to listen
  3.3   sit in jud.
  3.4   –ive mind-set
4. Importance of listening
  4.1   perfect comm.
  4.2   inter relationship gets better
  4.3   no tension/ negativity
  4.4   reduces misunderstanding

Key to Abbreviation

Abbreviation	Word
phy.	Physical
conc.	Concentration
jud.	Judgement
–ive	Negative
comm.	Communication
inter.	Interpersonal

(b) Summary   **(3 Marks)**

Listening and hearing are a lot different than we originally thought. Hearing refers to the sound waves we hear but do not fully understand and listening means hearing with full concentration. The barrier that comes between us and being good listeners are negative mindset, prejudices, misconceived notions etc. It is important to listen as it can improve communication, remove tension and interpersonal relationship gets better. If we really listen, we not only imbibe what is said but also understand the unspoken. Therefore, we should all try to be good listeners. (90 words)

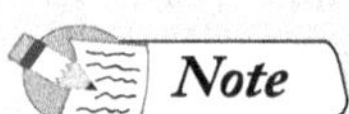 *Note*

1. *The passage is on the art of listening and the difference between hearing and listening. So, the title should have the key words 'Art', 'Science,' 'listening' or any synonym of the words.*
2. *It should always contain phrases. Avoid using complete sentences. For e.g.*
   1. Hearing
     1.1 phy. phenomenon
     1.2 sound waves reach you
     1.3 hear what said
   AND NOT Hearing is a physical phenomenon when ……..
3. *Include a minimum of 4-6 distinctly different recognizable short forms i.e. abbreviations of the words in the notes as done in the solution.*

4. Notice   **(4 Marks)**

NOTICE

SUNRISE PUBLIC SCHOOL, SURAT

15th February, 2019

CENTRAL PARK FLOWER SHOW

All the students are hereby informed that a flower show is being organized by the District administration in the Central park from 20th to 27th February. The timings are from 10 am- 4 pm. There is no entry fee for the students.

For more information, please contact the undersigned.

Navita
(Head Girl)

OR

NOTICE

SUNRISE PUBLIC SCHOOL, SURAT

15th November 2019

BOOKS FOR NEEDY STUDENTS

All the students are hereby informed that Sarvodaya Education Society will be visiting our school from 20th November to 27th November to distribute books among students. Interested students must drop the list of books they need in the box outside the Principal's Office latest by 2pm on 17th November, 2019.

Navita

(Head Girl)

---

5. Letter   **(6 Marks)**

M-114 Mount Kailash
Kanpur

15th March 2019

The Editor
Times of India
New Delhi

Subject: Lack of education among children in the villages

Sir/Madam,

Through the column of your esteemed newspaper, I would like to draw the attention of the concerned authorities regarding the illiteracy prevalent among children staying in the villages.

Recently I visited my grandparents in the village where I was aggrieved to see many children between the age group of 5-14 not attending school. They were either working in the fields or were simply loitering in the streets. None of these children had even visited the village government school, leave alone starting formal education there. Even the Parents seemed apathetic to the idea. I agree that parents need extra hands in the fields to work alongside them but I believe it should not be done at the cost of their children's education.

Therefore, through your newspaper, it is my humble request to the concerned authorities to act immediately and give free meals, books, uniform etc. so that the children feel motivated to go to school. After all these children are also the future of our country.

Yours Truly
Navita

OR

M-114, Mount Kailash
Kanpur

15th November 2019

The Editor
The Times of India
New Delhi

Subject: Discrimination towards athletes

Sir/Madam,

Through the columns of your esteemed newspaper, I would like to draw the attention of the concerned authorities towards the discrimination which our athletes have to face when compared to the cricketers. Cricket have been part of our culture since a very long time, and sometime due to the love that cricket gets, we forget about the athletes of other games.

We pamper our cricketers and give them the privileges which we don't offer to any other sport. The cricketers are allowed to take their wives and friends while playing abroad whereas other athletes are not allowed to do so. This in fact not only distracts the cricketers off their game, but also gives them a feeling of a vacation rather than a sporting event or a championship. The cricketers also break the discipline and the strict regimen which is essential to win games at the international level since they are with their families. Therefore, in my opinion these privileges should not be extended to any sport. This way parity will be maintained between all types of sports.

I hope this letter of mine will act as a wake-up call for the concerned authorities.

Yours Truly
Navita

6. Speech (10 Marks)

Good morning, my dear students and members of the staff!

Mobile phones have become an inseparable part of our lives. Something which started as a device used for just calling and messaging has now turned into a multi-functional gadget, which can perform almost any task a human mind can think of ranging from performing as a TV, radio, camera etc.

However, this device does not come with an instruction manual which tells you all how to use it safely as children. Our smart phones have many features which attracts all of you but none of you know whether it is acceptable to use these features at your age. Gaming is one such feature. Every day we read about incidents where children are busy playing games like PUBG ignoring their studies or listening to songs while crossing the roads etc. All this can lead to serious consequences. Furthermore, too much time devoted on mobiles can lead to exposure to radiation which can cause cancer and other complications.

Therefore, my dear children. My advice to you is, – use your mobiles but use it sparingly and judiciously, without risking your own self or others. Use your smart phones smartly and only after due permission and knowledge of your parents. I would also expect the staff to counsel our children on this.

Thank you and have a great day!

OR

Good morning my dear students and members of the staff.

We should consider ourselves blessed to be living in a world where we have uninterrupted electricity and power supply. However, like every other thing that we have, we abuse it a lot.

We abuse the power supply all the time, be it at our home or our school, due to our indifference and casual attitude. Leaving the classroom lights switched on while moving to the ground, leaving the monitors switched on while leaving the computer lab, the AC running in the staff room even if it is vacant: such are the daily examples in school. At home too lights of rooms are working even if there isn't anyone in the room, the TV keeps talking to the empty air in the living room, the charging point is switched on even if there isn't anything being charged - example like these are rampant. All this has led to power abuse and it is the right time to pledge that we will all refrain from repeating this in the future. I would expect all the class teachers to appoint Eco drive Champions in their classes so that they ensure proper switching off, of the various electrical points. We will shortly be sending an advisory to the Parents too so that they are aware of the measures taken at school and follow it themselves.

Thank you and god bless you all.

7. Article (10 Marks)

EIGHTEENTH BIRTHDAY

By *Navita*

We all have milestones in life. Milestones that we have achieved and milestones that we are yet to reach. There are milestones in age too such as sweet sixteen, turning 21, silver jubilee etc but for me turning 18 is the most special and wonderful milestone. Being 18 means being more responsible, mature, thoughtful and balanced. Some people say that age is just a number but not for me these platitudes.Turning 18 has led to a thousand new duties entrusted upon all of us who have reached that glorious age. In addition to initiation into adulthood, we have the right to vote in the elections, which personally is the best part as we get the chance to choose our democratic leader. We get our driving licence, and along with it, unlimited freedom.

However, with freedom comes responsibilities. Its the age when most of the teens go to college and it brings a lot of personality change since people look up to you as a responsible, mature young adult. There is greater accountability and childishness is discouraged. We get into an exploratory mode but with caution since now we have our careers to think of. We also start shouldering the family and household responsibilities. So being 18 comes with its own joys and travails.

OR

THE INDIAN WOMAN – HOW SAFE IS SHE

By *Navita*

Since time immemorial Women have been worshipped as the Shakti or the Mother. However, all this holds good for the past ages. With passage of time women were increasingly regarded as the weaker sex and were not given the equal rights or freedom. Even though in the modern scenario we claim that we have been successful in creating a well-balanced society where women are treated at par with men, the ground reality is extremely grim. The women are still stared at, stalked and even molested. There is exploitation at work-place, human trafficking, ill treatment of women in homes, violence against women in the rural areas but still we do nothing about it. The crime against women like rape also does not seem to abate despite stringent laws in place. Every other day

the newspaper headlines scream at us demanding justice for women. We therefore need to work not only towards effective implementation of laws protecting womens' rights but also changing the mind-set of the people. They need to understand that women are not commodities but an equal and necessary participant in all social, economic and national activity. Without women even Nature stands incomplete.

India is now developing at a fast pace. However, this development is meaningless if the female half of the society does not get its due. The sooner the members of the society wake up to this challenge and make amends, the better it will be for our society.

SECTION - C

8. (1 × 4 = 4 Marks)

(a) When the poet looked at her mother,she was worried about the fact that since her mother was getting old, this might be their last meeting. The old childhood fear of losing her mother came back to her.

(b) There was pain in her realization because the fact of the impending separation from her mother was unacceptable to her. She could not reconcile herself to the thought of losing her mother and the fact that very soon she would be left alone.

(c) She put that thought away since it was an unpleasant and painful one. She was also going away from her mother and therefore she wanted to leave happily and not carry that thought with her.

(d) The figure of speech used in these lines is a simile. "like that of a corpse".

OR

(a) These children are the children of an elementary school classroom in a slum. They are poor and deprived.

(b) The poet uses the phrase "gusty waves" to contrast the vitality and energy of the environment from which these children are far away to the actual environment in which they exist. The mainstream society in other words has better living conditions but these children are deprived of such conditions

(c) The tall girl's head has been possibly weighed down by the problems and responsibilities of her home. She is aware probably of the harsh realities of the world of the slums and unhappy due to the conditions surrounding their lives.

(d) The figure of speech used in these lines are simile- 'like rootless weeds', repetition-'far, far' and alliteration 'far, far, from' (Any One)

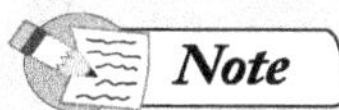

Reference to the Context:

1. *Be precise and to the point.*
2. *Look closely at the figures of speech and the special words.*
3. *E.g., **"Identify the figure of speech used in these lines"** (My Mother at Sixty Six)you may begin by ....The figure of speech used in these lines is a simile. "like that of a corpse".*

9.   **(3 × 4 = 12 Marks)**

(a) The people of the village like old Hauser, the former mayor, the former postmaster and several others occupied the back benches in the classroom on the day of the last lesson. They were sitting there to pay respect to the M Hamel for his faithful forty years of service and also as a show of respect and regret for not having learnt the French language all these years.

(b) Douglas's mother recommend that he should learn swimming at the YMCA swimming pool since it was only 2-3 feet deep at the shallow end and even though nine feet deep at the other end, the drop was gradual. In contrast to the Yakima river which was treacherous, the swimming pool was safe.

(c) Counting upto twelve and keeping still will help us find time to steer away from our mindless rush and give leisure for introspection and self-analysis. It will create an exotic moment of togetherness and we can once again strike a harmony with nature.

(d) A thing of beauty does many things for us. It removes the pall from our dark spirits and uplifts our mood. Since its loveliness keeps increasing, it becomes a source of eternal joy. It makes our life worth living in spite of despondence and gloomy days.

(e) The ending that Jo wanted is more appropriate since she wanted a happy ending for Roger Skunk in the story. From the perspective of the child, acceptance by the peers and their love is more important than an assertion of identity. She wanted the skunk to smell like roses so that he could play with the other animals and remain happy.

OR

The ending that Jack brings about is more appropriate since it underlines the acceptance of oneself as one is. In other words it is about identity and the way one needs to stick to it. He wanted the skunk to have its original smell and teach Jo that parents are the best judge. His ending is from the perspective of an adult and what Jo needs to learn.

(f) The governor could have travelled in the van himself with Evans to take him to the prison or at least checked the credentials of the officials escorting him to the prison.

Each 3-mark question must have at least two value points.

1. *So, for example – for the question "Who occupied the back benches in the class room on the day of the last lesson? Why," requires you to break the answer into two parts.*
2. *WHO- the people of the village - old Hauser-former mayor-former postmaster and several others - occupied the back benches in the classroom- day of the last lesson.*

WHY - Sitting there - pay respect to the M Hamel- faithful forty years of service -show of respect and regret- not having learnt the French language all these years

10.   **(6 Marks)**

The genesis of the problem which required the Tiger King to bribe the British officer can be traced to the king's birth where it was predicted by the astrologers that his death would be brought about by a tiger. In his desire to prove the astrologers wrong he vowed to kill one hundred tigers and ensure his longevity. So, hunting of tigers was prohibited in his kingdom. Even a high-ranking British officer who visited *Pratibandhapuram* was also not allowed to hunt or even get his photograph clicked with the carcass of the dead tiger. As a result of this the throne of the King was at stake. In order to make amends some fifty exquisite diamond rings was sent to the official's wife to choose from. However, the whole lot was accepted by the official's wife. The decision of the King cost him 3 lacs but it saved his crown.

It was no doubt an evil and foolish act of bribery but the King had no other option since what mattered more to him was the fulfilling of his vow.

OR

Dr Sadao was a patriotic Japanese as well as a dedicated surgeon. He loved his country and in spite of getting an education in America and finding a Japanese girl of his choice, he married her only after his father's permission as befitted his culture. He saved the life of the General by operating on him, fulfilled his duty as a Japanese citizen by informing the General about the American prisoner of War whom he had saved and also accepts the General's decision to send the assassins without any reluctance. He even keeps the door open for the assassins to enter.

In addition to this he even fulfils his duty as a surgeon. Notwithstanding the risk inherent in treating an enemy, and ignoring the fact that he does not like Americans, he takes the person home, operates him and provides post-operative treatment too. In course of time his faithful servants desert him failing to understand the humane side of Dr Sadao. Even his wife to a large extent does not favour his actions because she feels that he is not only risking himself but also putting the life of the family in jeopardy. Despite all these encumbrances on his way, he focusses on his primary duty as a surgeon and is able to balance both the values.

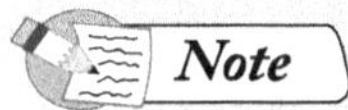 *Note*

1. *Each 6-mark question must have at least four value points.*

2. *Answer to the point including your own opinion in places where it is deemed necessary by the question.*

3. *Pick out specific examples from the text to support your answer.*

4. *Quote straight from the text wherever required but do so only when you are sure of the words.*

   *For e.g. the question **"Giving a bribe is an evil practice. How did the Tiger King bribe the British officer to save his kingdom? How do you view this act of his,"** divide your answer into: 1.Genesis of the problem 2. HOW did he bribe and 3. How do you view this act. Use the value points from those given below:*

   a. *Genesis of the problem - traced to the king's birth - predicted by the astrologers - his death would be brought about by a tiger - desire to prove the astrologers wrong- vowed to kill one hundred tigers - ensure longevity-hunting of tigers-prohibited.*

   b. *A high-ranking British officer - visited Pratibandhapuram - not allowed to hunt - get his photograph clicked with the carcass of the dead tiger - result - throne of the King - at stake*

   c. *In order to make amends - fifty exquisite diamond rings - sent to official's wife to choose from - the whole lot kept back. official's wife - cost him 3 lacs - saved the crown.*

   d. *No doubt an evil and foolish act of bribery - no other option - what mattered more to him- the fulfilling of the vow.*

11. (6 Marks)

The life of the bangle makers of Firozabad was quite difficult. They spend long hours in the glass furnaces with high temperatures, living in dingy cells without air and light and invite health problems. Working at night by the flickering and insufficient light of the oil lamps they weld pieces of coloured glass into circles of bangles. Their eyes are more used to the darkness inside their hutments rather than the light outside, often losing their eyesight before they are adults. They remain uneducated and live in houses which are like hovels with crumbling walls, wobbly doors and no windows. These hovels are crowded with families of human and animals co-existing

in a primeval state. They are unable to break away from the vicious cycle of exploitation by middlemen, money lenders, police and bureaucrats and lack a leader. They cannot even organise themselves into a cooperative as they fear that it might be treated as being illegal. In other words, burdened by the stigma of caste in which they are born with no initiative or daring left in their lives, the bangle makers continue with their 'god-given lineage'.

OR

The peddler declined the invitation of the ironmaster but accepted the one from Edla because of Eldas's persuasiveness. The Ironmaster had invited the peddler because he mistook him to be his former comrade Nils Olof. However when he realized that the peddler was not keen on going to his place, he did not insist much. He knew that Elda would be able to persuade him and therefore he send Elda to the Ramsjo Ironworks. Elda while talking to the peddler was firm yet polite. She even sympathized with the peddlar for the hard time he was facing. Noticing that the peddler seemed afraid, she even assured him that he would be free to leave whenever he desired. They just wanted to have company on Christmas Eve and after the Christmas celebration was over, he could leave. The friendly manner in which she said this won the confidence of the peddler and even though he still had the 30 kronors with him, the Peddler accompanies Elda to the manor house.

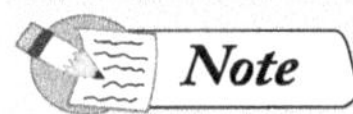 *Note*

1. *Adhere to the word limit given for the question.*

2. *Quoting from the text always gets more marks but misquotes can backfire. So, be careful.*

3. *For the Question **"The peddler declined the invitation of the ironmaster but accepted the one from Edla. Why?** divide your answer into WHY of both the actions on the part of the peddler. Use the value points from those given below:*

4. *The peddler declined invitation of the ironmaster -accepted the one from Edla because of Eldas's persuasiveness - Ironmaster invited the peddler - mistook him for his former comrade, Nils Olof- realized peddler not keen on going to his place - did not insist much*

   a. *Knew Elda would be able to persuade - sent Elda to Ramsjo Ironworks - Elda firm yet polite - sympathized with peddlar for the hard time he was facing - noticed peddler seemed afraid - assured him-free to leave whenever he desired-wanted to have company on christmas Eve- could leave after that-friendly manner won the confidence of the peddler.*

12.   **(6 Marks)**

Silas Marner, a weaver by profession was also a respected member of the church and known for his honesty, wisdom and exemplary life. He had a close friend William Dane who was a little older than Silas and their friendship was such that the Lantern Yard brethren called them David and Jonathan. Silas also had Sarah, his fiancée, whom he was set to marry in times to come. However, ironically, he is accused of theft based on flimsy evidence while he is taking care of the ailing deacon and performing a sacred duty for the church. He is framed by his friend, William Dane and since the empty bag, which had the church money is found in Silas's room and Silas's knife found at the scene of crime, his guilt is established. It is ironic that he is not even given a fair hearing and convicted through lots. This breaks Silas's faith in God since he knows that the Knife was last used to cut a strap for William.

A respected member of the Church thus departs from Lantern Yard convicted of a crime which he had not committed whereas ironically the actual guilty person goes scot free and even marries Silas's fiancée later.

OR

People become suspicious of Griffin within a few days of his arrival in Iping because of his appearance on the day of his arrival and his conduct thereafter. Griffin's arrives on a winter day walking from Bramblehurst railway station braving the biting wind and snow. He carried a little black portmanteau in his thickly gloved hand. He was also wrapped up from head to toe and the brim of his hat hid every inch of his face barring the shiny tip of his nose. He does not introduce himself and takes up a room in the Inn throwing a few sovereigns on the counter. It is very clear that he does not want to be social with anyone and rebuffs all advances of Mrs Hall to be friendly. As the story progresses, we see him keeping mostly to his room, talking to himself and looking strange with a muffled and bandaged head. He is rude with Teddy Henfrey and asks him to leave the room. Teddy also spreads rumours saying the stranger keeps himself wrapped to conceal his identity as he is wanted by the police. More incidents like these follow. All this arises the suspicion of the people of Iping.

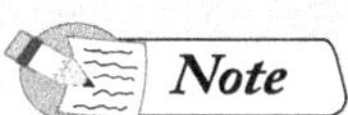
Note

1.   *Adhere to the word limit. Answer must reveal your deep knowledge of the text.*

2.   *For e.g. the question **"Within a few days of his arrival in Iping, people became suspicious of Griffin. Why"** requires a deep knowledge of the text. You can use the value points from those given below:*

   a.   *People become suspicious of Griffin - his appearance on day of arrival - conduct thereafter - worthy of suspicion*

   b.   *Arrives on a winter day walking from Bramblehurst - braving biting wind and snow - carried a little black portmanteau - thickly gloved hand - wrapped up from head to toe - brim of hat hiding every inch of face barring shiny tip of nose*

   c.   *Does not introduce himself - takes up a room in the Inn - throws a few sovereigns on the counter - did not want to be social - rebuffs all advances of Mrs Hall*

   d.   *Story progresses - keeping mostly to his room - talks to himself - looks strange with a muffled and bandaged head - rude with Teddy Henfrey- asks him to leave the room.*

   e.   *Teddy also spreads rumours - stranger keeps wrapped to conceal identity - wanted by the police - more incidents like these follow - arises the suspicion of the people of Iping.*

13.   **(6 Marks)**

Dolly Winthrop is the most lovable character in George Eliot's 'Silas Marner'. She is the wife of the wheelwright, Ben Winthrop and mother of Aaron who later marries Eppie. She is characterized as a "good wholesome woman," "a woman of scrupulous conscience", and someone who takes upon herself to help Silas. She visits Silas along with Aaron and a present of lard cakes and talks to Silas about going to church. Though initially she does not make any impact on Silas, she is the one who slowly bring him into the mainstream. She gets Eppie christened and that is the first time that Silas visits the Church . She later raises Eppie along with Silas and in due course of time becomes Eppie's godmother and mother-in-law. She herself believes in customs and traditions and persuades Silas to always trust in God and go to church. She is kind and patient, devoutly religious and open and friendly.

OR

Marvel was a poor, homeless tramp who did not have any job. He was a plump man with short limbs and wore shabby and old fashioned clothes along with equally shabby obsolete hat. He meets Griffin when he was sitting leisurely with his feet in the ditch by the roadside which was one and a half mile away from Iping. Marvel feels his imagination has gone wild when he hears a voice but does not see anyone. Griffin considers him foolish but since he requires someone to carry out his plan, he convinces Marvel to be with him. However the events later prove that he is far from being a foolish person. Marvel agrees as he feels he too will benefit by the power of Griffin's invisibility. He always portrays himself as fearful of Griffin and just as a puppet carrying out orders but he gives Griffin the slip and takes his notebooks and money to Port Burdock. He is smart enough to take protection in the cell and after Griffin's death, he benefits the most by getting all the money and the books. In the end he starts a little inn and names it 'The Invisible Man' through which he becomes quite rich.

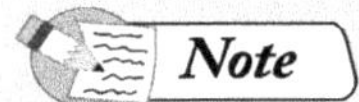 *Note*

1. *This question tests understanding, appreciation, analysis and interpretation of the incident/character. So, thorough reading of the text is required.*
2. *Adhere to the word limit and answer the question.*
3. *Avoid giving details which you are not sure of.*
4. *For e.g. the question "**Attempt a character sketch of Marvel,**" use at least 4-5 value points from those given below:*

    a. *Marvel a poor, homeless tramp - did not have any job - plump man with short limbs - wore shabby and old - fashioned clothes - shabby obsolete hat.*
    b. *Meets Griffin when sitting leisurely with his feet in the ditch by the roadside - one and a half mile away from Iping.*
    c. *Feels his imagination has gone wild - hears a voice - does not see anyone.*
    d. *Griffin considers him foolish - but requires someone to carry out plan- so convinces Marvel to be with him.*
    e. *Events later prove that he is far from a foolish person.*
    f. *Agrees as he too will benefit - power of Griffin's invisibility - portrays himself as fearful of Griffin - as a puppet carrying out orders - gives Griffin the slip - takes his notebooks and money to Port Burdock - smart enough to take protection in the cell.*
    g. *After Griffin's death - benefits the most - gets all the money - the books - starts a little inn - names it 'The Invisible Man' - becomes quite rich.*

CBSE Board Solved Paper

Time Allowed : 3 Hours   *Maximum Marks : 100*

General Instructions:

(i)   This paper is divided into three Sections : A, B and C. All the sections are compulsory.

(ii) Separate instructions are given with each section and question, wherever necessary. Read these instructions very carefully and follow them faithfully.

(iii) Do not exceed the prescribed word limit while answering the questions

SECTION A: Reading

(20 Marks)

1. Read the passage carefully and answer the questions that follow :

   1. Too many parents these days can't say no. As a result, they find themselves raising children who respond greedily to the advertisements aimed right at them. Even getting what they want doesn't satisfy some kids; they only want more. Now, a growing number of psychologists, educators and parents think it's time to stop the madness and start teaching kids about what's really important: values like hard work, contentment, honesty and compassion. The struggle to set limits has never been tougher — and the stakes have never been higher. One recent study of adults who were overindulged as children, paints a discouraging picture of their future: when given too much too soon, they grow up to be adults who have difficulty coping with life's disappointments. They also have a distorted sense of entitlement that gets in the way of success in the workplace and in relationships.

   2. Psychologists say that parents who overindulge their kids set them up to be more vulnerable to future anxiety and depression. Today's parents themselves raised on values of thrift and self-sacrifice, grew up in a culture where 'no' was a household word. Today's kids want much more, partly because there is so much more to want. The oldest members of this Generation Excess were born in the late 1980s, just as PCs and video games were making their assault on the family room. They think of MP3 players and flat-screen TVs as essential utilities, and they have developed strategies to get them. One survey of teenagers found that when they crave something new, most expect to ask nine times before their parents give in. By every measure, parents are shelling out record amounts. In the heat of this buying blitz, even parents who desperately need to say no find themselves reaching for their credit cards.

   3. Today's parents aren't equipped to deal with the problem. Many of them, raised in the 1960s and '70s, swore they'd act differently from their parents and have closer relationships with their own children. Many even wear the same designer clothes as their kids and listen to the same music. And they work more hours; at the end of a long week, it's tempting to buy peace with 'yes' and not mar precious family time with conflict. Anxiety about the future is another factor. How do well intentioned parents say no to all the sports gear and arts and language lessons they believe will help their kids thrive in an increasingly competitive world? Experts agree: too much love won't spoil a child. Too few limits will.

   4. What parents need to find, is a balance between the advantages of an affluent society and the critical life lessons that come from waiting, saving and working hard to achieve goals. That search for balance has to start early. Children need limits on their behaviour because they feel better and more secure when they live within a secured structure.

      Older children learn self-control by watching how others, especially their parents act. Learning how to overcome challenges is essential to becoming a successful adult. Few parents ask kids to do chores. They think their kids are already overburdened by social and academic pressures. Every individual can be of service to others, and life has meaning beyond one's own immediate happiness. That means parents eager to teach values have to take a long, hard look at their own.

   (a) Answer the following :
      (i) What values do parents and teachers want children to learn?

(ii) What are the results of giving the children too much too soon?

(iii) Why do today's children want more?

(iv) What is the balance which the parents need to have in today's world?

(v) What is the necessity to set limits for children?

(b) Pick out words from the passage that mean the same as the following :

(i) a feeling of satisfaction (para 1)

(ii) valuable (para 3)

(iii) important (para 4)

2. Read the passage carefully and answer the questions that follow :

1. I remember my childhood as being generally happy and can recall experiencing some of the most carefree times of my life. But I can also remember, even more vividly, moments of being deeply frightened. As a child, I was truly terrified of the dark and getting lost. These fears were very real and caused me some extremely uncomfortable moments.

2. May be it was the strange way things looked and sounded in my familiar room at night that scared me so much. There was never total darkness, but a street light or passing car lights made clothes hung over a chair take on the shape of an unknown beast. Out of the corner of my eye, I saw curtains move when there was no breeze. A tiny creak in the floor would sound a hundred times louder than in the daylight and my imagination would take over, creating burglars and monsters. Darkness always made me feel helpless. My heart would pound and I would lie very still so that 'the enemy' wouldn't discover me.

3. Another childhood fear of mine was that I would get lost, especially on the way home from school. Every morning, I got on the school bus right near my home — that was no problem. After school, though, when all the buses were lined up along the curve, I was terrified that I would get on the wrong one and be taken to some unfamiliar neighbourhood. I would scan the bus for the faces of my friends, make sure that the bus driver was the same one that had been there in the morning, and even then ask the others over and over again to be sure I was in the right bus. On school or family trips to an amusement park or a museum, I wouldn't let the leaders out of my sight. And of course, I was never very adventurous when it came to taking walks or hikes because I would go only where I was sure I would never get lost.

4. Perhaps, one of the worst fears I had as a child was that of not being liked or accepted by others. First of all, I was quite shy. Secondly, I worried constantly about my looks, thinking people wouldn't like me because I was too fat or wore braces. I tried to wear 'the right clothes' and had intense arguments with my mother over the importance of wearing flats instead of saddled shoes to school. Being popular was very important to me then and the fear of not being liked was a powerful one.

5. One of the processes of evolving from a child to an adult is being able to recognize and overcome our fears. I have learnt that darkness does not have to take on a life of its own, that others can help me when I am lost and that friendliness and sincerity will encourage people to like me. Understanding the things that scared us as children helps to cope with our lives as adults.

(a) On the basis of your reading of the above passage, make notes using headings and sub-headings. Use recognizable abbreviations, wherever necessary.

(b) Write a summary of the passage in not more than 80 words using the notes made and also suggest a suitable title.

SECTION B: Advanced Writing Skills

(35 Marks)

3. You were very upset about the reports on communal riots in various parts of the country. As a concerned social worker, design a poster in not more than 50 words, highlighting the importance of communal harmony. You are Vinay/Vineeta.

OR

The literary club of your school is putting up the play 'Waiting for Godot'. As secretary of the club, draft an invitation inviting the famous writer Sudeesh Gupta to be the guest of honour at the function. Write the invitation in not more than 50 words. You are Govind/Gauri.

4. Last week the newly built auditorium of your school was inaugurated. As Deepak/Deepti Saha, the head boy/girl of the school, write a factual description of the auditorium in 125 – 150 words.

OR

You had attended a workshop on personality development for students. Many eminent personalities had been present. Write a report in 125 – 150 words on how the workshop proved to be beneficial. You are Rajesh/Rajshree.

5. You are Anand/Arti of 14, Model Town, Delhi. You have seen an advertisement in *The Hindu* for the post of Chef in a 5-Star Hotel. Apply for the job with complete biodata. Write in 125 – 150 words.

OR

You are Prem/Parul of 16, TT Nagar, Bhopal. You would like to apply for the post of Marketing Manager in a reputed firm in Mumbai. Write a letter to the Public Relations Officer, Chantac Enterprises, Mumbai, applying for the job. Write the letter in 125 – 150 words giving your biodata.

6. Last week as you were coming back from school you happened to see a huge plastic bag full of leftovers of food being flung into the middle of the road from a speeding car. You wondered how people can be so devoid of civic sense. Write an article in 125 – 150 words on why we lack civic sense and how civic sense can be inculcated in children at a very young age. You are Shiva/Shamini.

OR

You saw a stray dog beaten to death by a group of boys. Their act infuriated you and you scolded them for their cruel act. You decided to write an article on cruelty to animals. Write the article in 125 – 150 words. You are Nikhil/Naina.

SECTION C: Textbooks and Long Reading Text

(45 Marks)

7. Read the following extract and answer the questions that follow :

Spite of despondence, of the inhuman dearth

Of noble natures, of the gloomy days,

Of all the unhealthy and o'er-darkened ways

Made for our searching: yes in spite of all,

Some shape of beauty moves away the pall

From our dark spirits.

(a) Name the poem and the poet.

(b) Why are we 'despondent'?

(c) What removes 'the pall from our dark spirits'?

OR

.... And yet, for these

Children, these windows, not this map, their world.

Where all their future's painted with a fog,

A narrow street sealed in with a lead sky

Far far from rivers, capes, and stars of words.

(a) Who are the 'children' referred to here?

(b) Which is their world?

(c) How is their life different from that of other children?

8. Answer any *two* of the following in about 30 – 40 words each :

(a) What was the poet's childhood fear?

(b) What is the sadness the poet refers to in the poem 'Keeping Quiet'?

(c) How are Aunt Jennifer's tigers different from her?

9. Answer any *six* of the following in about 30 – 40 words each :

(a) Why did Sophie long for her brother's affection?

(b) Why did Edla plead with her father not to send the vagabond away?

(c) What job did Saheb take up? Was he happy?

(d) Why were the elders of the village sitting in the classroom?

(e) Why did the Maharaja order the dewan to double the land tax?

(f) Why did Roger Skunk go to see the old owl?

(g) Why was Zitkala-Sa in tears on the first day in the land of apples?

10. Answer any *one* of the following in 100 – 125 words :
Why is the Champaran episode considered to be the beginning of the Indian struggle for Independence?

OR

What was the General's plan to get rid of the American prisoner? Was it executed? What traits of the General's character are highlighted in the lesson 'The Enemy'?

11. Both Derry and Lamb are physically impaired and lonely. It is the responsibility of society to understand and support people with infirmities so that they do not suffer from a sense of alienation. As a responsible citizen, write in about 100 words what you would do to bring about a change in the lives of such people.

12. Why did Dr. Mortimer need the service of the detective Sherlock Holmes? Answer in about 125 words.

13. Who is Laura Lyons? What confession did she make to Sherlock Holmes? Answer in about 125 words.

Solutions

1. **(a)**

(i) Teachers and parents want their children to learn the important lessons of life and to be hard working.

(2 Marks)

(ii) When kids are given too much too soon they grow up to be adults who have difficulty coping with life's disappointments. **(2 Marks)**

(iii) Today's children want more because there is so much more to want. **(1 Mark)**

(iv) The balance that parents need to have in today's world is a balance between the advantages of an affluent society and the critical life lessons that come from waiting, saving and working hard. **(2 Marks)**

(v) There is a necessity to set limits for the children because they feel better and more secure when they live within a secured structure. **(2 Marks)**

Note

1. Be brief and to the point.

2. For Factual questions like e.g. "What is the necessity to set limits for children", do not include information not given in the passage.

3. While answering the 'Why' question like "Why do today's children want more", you may begin your answer with 'Today's children want more because ....or a similar phrase.

4. While answering the vocabulary questions, check the part of speech, the tense of the word etc. Your answer should have the same part of speech, tense etc.

> *a. For e.g. Valuable- Precious*
>
> *b. Important- Critical/essential*

(b) **(1 × 3 = 3 Marks)**

(i) A feeling of satisfaction- Contentment

(ii) Valuable- Precious

(iii) Important- Critical/essential

2. **(a) TITLE: CHILDHOOD FEARS** **(5 Marks)**

1. childhood memories
   1.1 gener. happy
   1.2 carefree time
2. fear of darkness
   2.1 cur. moving
   2.2 heard loud noises
   2.3 felt helpless
   2.4 heart poun. heavily

3. fear of getting lost
   3.1 taking wrong bus
   3.2 scan. buses
   3.3 ask others
4. worst fear
   4.1 not being liked
   4.2 worried about the looks
   4.3 wore right clothes
5. evolving as an adult
   5.1 to recognize and overcome fear
   5.2 to realize that
      5.2.1. darkness doesn't take a life of its own
      5.2.2. others can help
      5.2.3. being friendly & sincere will help

Key to Abbreviation

Abbreviation		Word
1.	gener.	generally
2.	cur.	curtains
3.	poun,	pounded
4.	scan.	canned
5.	doesn't	does not
6.	&	and

(b) Summary **(3 Marks)**

Childhood mostly comprised of being happy or having free time but it also contained some moments of being deeply frightened. There were two great fears, first of darkness and second of getting lost. The former was caused due the movement of the curtains and some weird noise and the latter was because I feared getting lost. The most frightening part was that no one was going to like you.However when you grow up, you realize that these fears are without any foundation and if you do certain things, people will definitely like and help you.

Note

1. The passage is on the various kinds of fears that surround children. So, the title should have the key words ' Fear', 'children' or any synonym of the words.

2. It should always contain phrases. Avoid using complete sentences. For e.g.

> *1. childhood memories*
>
> *1.1 gener. happy*
>
> *1.2 carefree time*

3. Poster on Communal Harmony   **(5 Marks)**

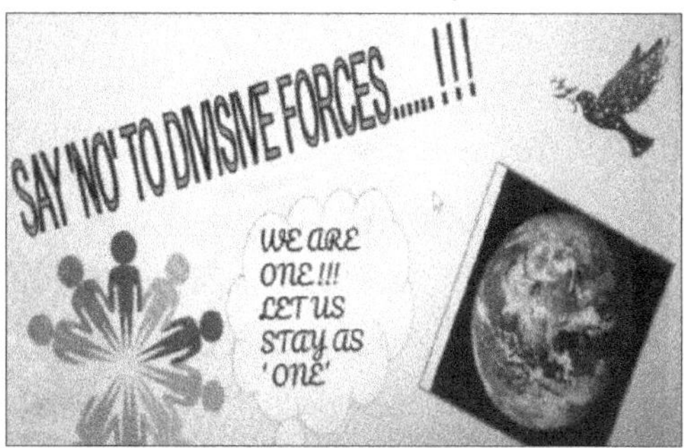

Issued in Public Interest by Vinay/Vineeta

OR

Formal Invitation

> Green Valley Iternational School
>
> Sector 24
>
> Lucknow
>
> 14th March 20XX
>
> Mr Sudeesh Gupta
>
> Sector 26
>
> Lucknow
>
> **Sub:** Invitation to be the Guest of Honour
>
> Respected Sir,
>
> It is with immense pride and pleasure that we inform you about the staging of Samuel Beckett's much acclaimed play " **Waiting for Godot**" by the budding artists of the Literary Club of the school in our school auditorium on the 25th of March 20XX from 4:00 pm-6:00. The event will be followed by high tea. We shall consider it a great honour if you could grace the occasion by consenting to be the Guest of Honour for the day. Your presence would go a long way in motivating our students.
>
> Soliciting a line of confirmation by e mail on sec.litclub.gvis@gmail.com.
>
> Yours faithfully
>
> Govind/Gauri
>
> Secretary
>
> Literary Club

4. Factual Description   **(10 Marks)**

Kamani Auditorium Inaugurated

By *Deepak Saha/Deepti Saha*

The long awaited inauguration of the Kamani auditorium was finally done on 12th March 20XX by the Chairman of the School Management Committee, Mr Aadarsh Dev Kumar. The Kamani auditorium is the last in the series of the auditoriums that have been built in all the schools of the Aadarsh Group. Inspired by the structure of the Globe Theatre, where Shakespeare is said to have acted and staged his plays, it has a seating capacity of a thousand people. It has three floors with the green rooms occupying most of the top floor. The stage is levelled in such a manner that irrespective of where you are sitting, you still can have a bird's eye view of all the action on the stage. The acoustics and the lighting are par excellence. It is said that the sound system has been done by the German company XXX, which is the best in the World. An estimated two crore has been spent on this auditorium.

OR

Report

Personality Development for Students

By *Rajesh/Rajeshree*

Lucknow, March 6: A week -long Personality Development workshop was organized at the Lucknow Skill Development Centre from 27th February 20XX to 5th March 20XX for the students of classes IX-XII. The main idea behind the workshop was to make the participants understand the changing contexts of the personality with reference to the twenty first century skills. The workshop was inaugurated by the noted academician Shri Bala Subramaniam and the opening session was conducted by the noted TV anchor, newsreader and personality development trainer Ms Usha Albequerque. In addition to the sessions with trainers from India and abroad, there were group discussions, movies and panel discussions. It taught the students on how to work with various professionals, people and groups, understand the challenges of life and work in the present context and maintain a fine balance between the two. The need to enhance communication and interpersonal skills so that one could function in professional and social settings effectively was also stressed upon. Time management skills along with effective planning tips were also shared during the week. Ashish, one of the participants said, "The best part about the workshop was the tips that were given on self- appraisal and the importance of introspection".

5. Letter   **(10 Marks)**

14, Model Town
Delhi

23 March, 20XX
Head HR
The Trident
New Delhi

Sub: Application for the post of Chief Chef

Respected Sir/ Madam,

This is with reference to the advertisement in 'The Hindu' on 20th March, 20XX for the post of the Chief Chef at

Trident. I wish to put forth my application for the same. I have a graduate degree in Culinary Arts from International Culinary Institute, Switzerland and have previously worked with the Taj and ITC Group.

I would request you to consider my application for the post.

Looking forward to a positive response

Yours Truly

Anand/Arti

RESUME

Name:	Ms Arti Sinha
Father's Name:	Mr Akash Sinha
Gender:	Female
Marital Status:	Unmarried
Address:	14, Model Town, Delhi
Email:	arti.sinha@gmail.com
Date of Birth:	05.07.20XX
Academic Qualifications:	
	Bachelor's Degree for Culinary Arts
Professional Qualifications:	
	Certification: American Culinary Federation
Work Experience:	Worked at ITC and Taj Group
Languages Known:	Hindi, English, Punjabi, French, Spanish & Mandarin
Hobbies:	Gardening, Listening to Music & travelling

Encl: Resume

OR

16, TT Nagar
Bhopal

23 March, 20XX

Public Relations Officer
Chantac Enterprises
Mumbai

Sub: Application for the post of Marketing Manager

Respected Sir/ Madam,

This is with reference to the opening for the position of Marketing Manager at Mumbai. I wish to put forth my candidature for the same. I have a degree in Marketing from Global Business School and Research Centre and have previously worked with the Reliance Group. I have excellent communication and inter -personal skills too.

I would request you to consider my application for the post.

Looking forward to a positive response

Yours Truly

Prem/Parul

RESUME

Name:	Ms Parul Singh
Father's Name:	Mr Vivek Singh
Gender:	Female
Marital Status:	Unmarried
Address:	16, TT Nagar, Bhopal
Email:	parul.sinha@gmail.com
Date of Birth:	05.07.20XX
Professional Qualification:	
	Bachelor's Degree In Marketing
Work Experience:	
	Worked at Reliance & Tata AIG
Languages Known:	Hindi, English, Punjabi, French, Spanish & Mandarin
Strengths:	Goal Oriented, Strong leadership skills, Excellent IT Skills
Hobbies:	Travelling, Meeting new people, Gardening, Reading

Encl: Resume

6. Article **(10 Marks)**
Civic Sense: A Forgotten Value

By *Siva/Shamini*

Since the time we became a civilized society, civic sense was considered an integral part of it. However, a recent escapade on the road when a speeding car threw a huge plastic bag full of leftover food from one of its widows set me thinking about how ingrained this virtue is into the bloodstream of our society! Talking about civic sense, it is an unspoken code of conduct or social norms for our society following which, living together become more amiable and pleasant. It is not just about keeping the roads, streets and public property clean but also abiding by the law, respecting others' point of view, etiquette, maintaining decorum in public places etc. However, the recent instances of vandalism, intolerance, road rage, rampant spit marks, random garbage, overflowing sewers at every nook and corner etc. reflect the poor state that our society is in. Roads are dirty not because nobody cleaned them, but because they are strewn with garbage which we threw in the first place.

The reasons behind all this is Us. Barring a few lessons in school or at home, not much attention is given to the civic behaviour of the children. We as a community therefore have to give a focused attention to transforming the life of our young ones by starting early. Civic sense comes from a 'sense of belonging' which creates pride and a sense of ownership. We need to develop a pro-active approach, build a sense of accountability and pride in our surroundings and personal behaviour. Civic education can be made mandatory and awareness through talks and documentaries can be spread. Incentives too can be given. Schools can run drives to encourage saving of food and avoiding wastage. In addition to these sone stringent laws against littering can be put in place and followed. If we practice the measures suggested above, the day is not far when we will transform into a civic society once again.

OR

Cruelty to Animals

By *Nikhil/Naina*

Cruelty towards animals has existed throughout the ages. People had harnessed muscle powerof animals and used their bodies for fuel, skin, food and countless other products. Animal muscle power was also needed in times of war. Horses carried soldiers and pulled chariots in battle and animals were sometimes used as weapons of war. Ancient Rome had often used them for entertainment in the Colosseum where they were kept below the arena floor and hoisted up for slaughter. They were also starved and goaded into attacking criminals in the Colosseum to amuse the crowds. However,one would think that times have changed and animals are nowadays treated with much more love and respect. A recent incident that I came across where a stray dog was killed by a group of boys set me thinking once again. One is forced to conclude that animal cruelty has existed in different guises at different points of time of history. However, since we are not living in the dark ages, we need to put a stop to such practices. In addition to the neglect and ill treatment of animals , we need to ensure that they are not used for commercial purposes. If only awareness is created through campaigns, drives and street plays, will things improve. Creating home shelters for the stray animals will also help in preventing the recurrence of such inhuman acts. We need to understand that they too are living things as much as we are.

SECTION - C

7.

(a) The poemis 'A Thing of Beauty' and the poet is John Keats. **(1 Mark)**

(b) We aredespondent because there is complete lack of noble people around us and we are surrounded by paths which are unhealthy and over darkened.

(2 Marks)

(c) Any shape of beauty or any manifestation of beauty removes 'the pall from our spirits'. **(1 Mark)**

OR

(a) The children referred to here are the children from the elementary school of the slum. **(1 Mark)**

(b) 'Their world' is the world of slum where there is deprivation and poverty. It is a world far away from rivers, capes and stars of words with a window which looks out into a narrow street which appears to be sealed in with a lead sky. **(1 Mark)**

(c) Their life is very different from that of the other children. Their future is bleak without any hope or progress and full of poverty and disease. Their education too seems unrealistic and without any practical use to them considering the situation in which they are living. **(2 Marks)**

1. *Be precise and to the point.*

2. *Remember the names of the poem and the poets with the correct spellings. For e.g. **"Name the poem and the poet"** (A Thing of Beauty) as asked this year.*

3. *Look closely at the figures of speech, the special words and the imagery used.*

4. *For e.g. the question **"Why are we 'despondent',"** you can write your answer in the following manner .....We are despondent because there is complete lack of noble people around us and we are surrounded by paths which are unhealthy and over darkened.*

8. **(2 × 2 = 4 Marks)**

(a) The poet's childhood fear was the fear of losing her mother due to her old age.

(b) The sadness that the poet refers to in 'Keeping Quiet' is the sadness of never understanding ourselves and nature since we never spend even a few seconds in keeping quiet and introspecting.

(c) Aunt Jennifer's tigers are exactly the opposite of Aunt Jennifer herself. The tigers are free, fearless, confident and proud whereas Aunt Jennifer is tied by the dominant nature of her husband. She cannot break free from the bondages that marriage has inflicted on her. She is meek, submissive and fearful even in her death. without any identity.

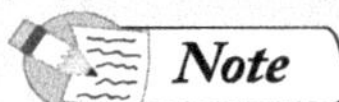

Note

1. *Each 2-mark question should have two value points.*

2. *So, for example – for the question **"How are Aunt Jennifer's tigers different from her"**, you can pick out the value points from those given below:*

   a. *Aunt Jennifer's tigers - exactly the opposite of Aunt Jennifer herself*

   b. *Tigers - free, fearless, confident and proud*

   c. *Aunt Jennifer- meek, submissive and fearful*

   d. *Aunt Jennifer - tied - dominant nature of her husband*

   e. *Cannot break free from the bondages- marriage has inflicted on her*

   f. *Fearful even in her death*

   g. *Without any identity*

3. *Do not make any spelling or grammatical errors as it may lead to deduction of marks.*

9. (6 × 2 = 12 Marks)

(a) Sophie longed for her brother's affection because to her he symbolized freedom and a part of the world that she aspired for. She trusted him more than any other member of the family and therefore he was the first with whom she shared her secrets. She hero worshipped him and longed for his approval since her father was critical and disapproving.

(b) Edla pleaded with her father not to send the vagabond away since it was Christmas eve and Edla wanted to keep the spirit of Christmas alive for the vagabond and in her house. She knew that he was lonely and therefore she wanted to provide him with a day of comfort and solace.

(c) Saheb took up a job in a tea stall. No, he was not happy.

(d) The elders of the village were sitting in the classroom to thank M Hamel, the French teacher, for his forty years of faithful service and to show their respect for the language and their country. Since they felt sorry for not having paid attention to the language all these years, this was their way to express regret for not having done so.

(e) The Maharaja ordered the Dewan to double the taxes in his frustration. He had already killed ninety-nine tigers but could not find the hundredth tiger to kill and fulfill his vow. He was therefore furious, and in his frustration,he ordered the Dewan to double the taxes.

(f) Roger Skunk went to see the old owl since he wanted a solution to his problem. He being a skunk had an awful smell because of which he was ignored by his friends and not involved in the play activities. He therefore wanted to seek advice from the owl for this problem of the awful smell.

(g) Zitkala-Sa was in tears on the first day in the land of apples because of the new environment that she was exposed to. The strict discipline of the place was something new for her. She also made mistakes like sitting down while all others were standing and then standing up while all others sat down. The fact that she felt exposed since her blanket had been stripped away added to her discomfort.

Note

1. *Each 2-mark question should have two value points.*

2. *So, for example – for the question **"Why did Sophie long for her brother's affection"**, you can pick out the value points from those given below:*

   a. *Longed for her brother's affection*

   b. *Symbolized freedom – was a part of the world that she aspired for*

   c. *Trusted him more than any other member of the family*

   d. *Was the first with whom she shared her secrets*

   e. *Hero worshipped him and longed for his approval*

   f. *Her father was critical and disapproving.*

3. *Do not make any spelling or grammatical errors as it may lead to deduction of marks*

10. (5 Marks)

The Champaran episode is considered to be the beginning of the Indian struggle for Independence since it was for the first time that the people gathered courage and spoke up for their rights. It was the first of the wins secured with the Gandhian style of fighting against the British- a style characterized by peaceful and patient agitation. The Champaran episode was also a turning point in the life of Gandhi ji since it grew out of an attempt tomake the sufferings of the poor peasants less severe. It did not begin as an act of defiance, but it was during this struggle that the farmers learnt courage as well as the fact that they had rights too. The Champaran episode was the beginning of the liberation from the fear of the British and a movement towards self-reliance and ultimately complete independence.

OR

The General's plan was to send two private assassins to Dr Sadao's house who would enter the bedroom of the injured American through the open outer partition of the room and kill him quietly. The assassins would also remove the dead body. The General just wanted Dr Sadao to keep the partition open on all the nights till the assassins arrived.

No. The plan was not executed.

The traits of the General's character which are highlighted in the lesson are that he cares for his own self before the country. Though he knows Sadao should be punished for treating an enemy, he avoids it as he knows Sadao is the only capable doctor who can save his life. He is self centred and lacks human consideration.

Note

1. Each 5-mark question must have at least four value points

2. Answer to the point including your own opinion in places where it is deemed necessary by the question.

3. Pick out specific examples from the text to support your answer

4. Quote straight from the text wherever required but do so only when you are sure of the words.

5. Sometimes you need to break the question into parts and then answer the same. For e.g. the question **"What was the General's plan to get rid of the American prisoner? Was it executed? What traits of the General's character are highlighted in the lesson "The Enemy"/**you need to first talk about the plan , then the result of that plan and finally the character traits of the General.

6. Pick out the value points from those given below :

    a. THE PLAN : to send two private assassins to Dr Sadao's house- enter the bedroom of American- through the open outer partition of the room- kill him quietly- assassins- remove the dead body- Dr Sadao to keep the partition open - all nights till - the assassins arrive

    b. RESULT : No - plan not executed

    c. TRAITS :

        i.   Cares for his own self before the country

        ii. knows Sadao should be punished- treating an enemy- avoids

        iii. Sadao the only capable doctor - save his life

        iv. Self centred and lacks human consideration

11.   **(5 Marks)**

Both Derry and Lamb from the lesson"On the Face of It" are physically impaired and lonely. As a responsible member of the society,we should understand and support people with infirmities so that they do not suffer from a sense of alienation. Being sympathetic does not really solve the problem. One has to be empathetic , like Mr Lamb and try to be as supportive as one can. They should be given equal opportunity. I am a supporter of inclusive education so that the other children can also understand the problems that are being faced by the differently abled and support them. Sensitization drives can also be conducted. Most importantly, they should be given a voice and heard with due respect. Lots of love, affection and smooth integration into the mainstream would really work wonders and empower them.

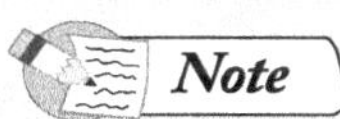
Note

1. Adhere to the word limit (100) given for the question.

2. Quoting from the text always gets more marks but misquotes can backfire. So, be careful.

3. Give your opinion wherever required

4. For the Question **"Both Derry and Lamb are physically impaired and lonely. It is the responsibility of society to understand and support people with infirmities so that they do not suffer from a sense of alienation. As a responsible citizen, write in about 100 words what you would do to bring about a change in the lives of such people".** you have to give your answer by taking examples from the story " On the Face Of It". Use the value points from those given below:

    a. Both Derry and Lamb the lessonare physically impaired and lonely

    b. Responsible member of the society- understand and support people with infirmities- do not suffer from a sense of alienation

    c. Being sympathetic does not really solve the problem

    d. Being empathetic more important , like Mr Lamb- as supportive as one can

    e. Should be given equal opportunity

    f. Personally - am a supporter of inclusive education - other children also understand the problems - being faced by the differently abled- support them

    g. Sensitization drives – conducted

    Should be given a voice and heard with due respect- Lots of love, affection - smooth integration into the mainstream- work wonders - empower

12.   **(8 Marks)**

Dr Mortimer needed the services of Sherlock Holmes since Sherlock Holmes was an expert in solving crimes. Having been a witness to the mysterious circumstances surrounding Sir Charles's death and in possession of the manuscript containing the reference to the story of Sir Hugo Baskerville and the ensuing curse on the generations of the Baskervilles , Dr Mortimer was apprehensive about the impending danger to Henry Baskerville. He had also apparently seen the footprints of a mighty hound at the death site. He, therefore, wanted to protect Henry by averting any future danger to his life. Therefore, he had gone to seek Sherlock's advice regarding the arrival of Henry Baskerville to the town.

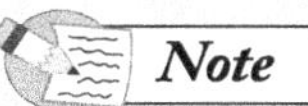
Note

1. Adhere to the word limit. Answer must reveal your deep knowledge of the text.

2. The 8 mark question must have 6-7 value points.

3. For e.g. the question **"Why did Dr Mortimer need the service of the detective Sherlock Holmes ? Answer in about 125 words"** requires not onlya knowledge of the text but also of the characters of the text. You can use the value points from those given below:

    a. Sherlock Holmes- an expert in solving crimes

    b. Dr Mortimer - apprehensive about impending danger to Henry Baskerville

c.   *Was a witness to the mysterious circumstances surrounding Sir Charles's death*

d.   *In possession of the manuscript - reference to the story of Sir Hugo Baskerville*

e.   *Aware of the ensuing curse on the generations of the Baskervilles*

f.   *Had also apparently seen the footprints- mighty hound at the death site*

g.   *Therefore, wanted to protect Henry - averting any future danger to his life*

h.   *Had gone to seek Sherlock's advice regarding the arrival of Henry Baskerville to the town*

13.   **(7 Makrs)**

Laura Lyons was the daughter of Mr Frankland. Since she had married against the wishes of her father, he had broken all relationship with her.

She tells Watson that in addition to Mr. Stapleton, Sir Charles had also been helping her to make the ends meet. She also says that she had written a letter to Sir Charles asking him to meet her on the day he died for some financial help. However, she did not go to meet her at the appointed hour. Later she confesses to Sherlock Holmes that Stapleton had forced Laura to write the letter to Sir Charles dictating to her even the wordings of the letter and then prevented her from meeting himby saying to Laura that it would hurt his self- respect if she went to some other person with such a request. He had also added that even though he was a poor man himself he would devote his last penny to removing the obstacles which divided Laura and him.

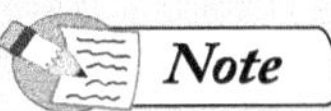

Note

1.   *This question tests understanding, appreciation, analysis and interpretation of the incident/character. So, a thorough reading of the text is required.*

2.   *Adhere to the word limit (**125 words only**) and answer the question.*

3.   *Avoid giving details which you are not sure of.*

4.   *For e.g. the question **"Who is Laura Lyons? What confession did she make to Sherlock Holmes? Answer in about 125 words**, break the question into two parts: a. Who is Laura b. The confession that she makes. Pick out the value points from those given below:*

a.   *WHO – i. Laura Lyons - daughter of Mr Frankland*

Delhi *2014*
CBSE Board Solved Paper

Time Allowed : 3 Hours   *Maximum Marks : 100*

General Instructions:
(i)   All the questions are compulsory.
(ii) Your answer should be to the point, try to stick to the word limit given.

(20 Marks)

1. Read the following passage and answer the questions that follow :

   1. Too many parents these days can't say no. As a result, they find themselves raising 'children' who respond greedily to the advertisements aimed right at them. Even getting what they want doesn't satisfy some kids; they only want more. Now, a growing number of psychologists, educators and parents think it's time to stop the madness and start teaching kids about what's really important : values like hard work, contentment, honesty and compassion. The struggle to set limits has never been tougher - and the stakes have never been higher. One recent study of adults who were overindulged as children, paints a discouraging picture of their future : when given too much too soon, they grow up to be adults who have difficulty coping with life's disappointments. They also have distorted sense of entitlement that gets in the way of success in the work place and in relationships.

   2. Psychologists say that parents who overindulge their kids, set them up to be more vulnerable to future anxiety and depression. Today's parents themselves raised on values of thrift and self-sacrifice, grew up in a culture where no was a household word. Today's kids want much more, partly because there is so much more to want. The oldest members of this generation were born in the late 1980s, just as PCs and video games were making their assault on the family room. They think of MP3 players and flat screen TV as essential utilities, and they have developed strategies to get them. One survey of teenagers found that when they crave for something new, most expect to ask nine times before their parents give in. By every measure, parents are shelling out record amounts.

   In the heat of this buying blitz, even parents who desperately need to say no find themselves reaching for their credit cards.

   3. Today's parents aren't equipped to deal with the problem. Many of them, raised in the 1960s and '70s, swore they'd act differently from their parents and have closer relationships with their own children. Many even wear the same designer clothes as their kids and listen to the same music. And they work more hours; at the end of a long week, it's tempting to buy peace with 'yes' and not mar precious family time with conflict. Anxiety about future is another factor. How do well intentioned parents say no to all the sports gear and arts and language lessons they believe will help their kids thrive in an increasingly competitive world? Experts agree : too much love won't spoil a child. Too few limits will.

   4. What parents need to find, is a balance between the advantages of an affluent society and the critical life lessons that come from waiting, saving and working hard to achieve goals. That search for balance has to start early. Children need limits on their behaviour because they feel better and more secure when they live within a secured structure.

   Older children learn self-control by watching how others, especially parents act. Learning how to overcome challenges is essential to becoming a successful adult. Few parents ask kids to do chores. They think their kids are already overburdened by social and academic pressures. Every individual can be of service to others, and life has meaning beyond one's own immediate happiness. That means parents eager to teach values have to take a long, hard look at their own.

   (a) Answer the following :
   (i) What values do parents and teachers want children to learn?
   (ii) What are the results of giving the children too much too soon?

(iii) Why do today's children want more?

(iv) What is the balance which the parents need to have in today's world?

(v) What is the necessity to set limits for children?

(b) Pick out words from the passage that mean the same as the following :

(i) a feeling of satisfaction (para 1)

(ii) valuable (para 3)

(iii) important (para 4)

2. Read the passage carefully.

1. I remember my childhood as being generally happy and can recall experiencing some of the most carefree times of my life. But I can also remember, even more vividly, moments of being deeply frightened. As a child, I was truly terrified of the dark and getting lost. These fears were very real and caused me some extremely uncomfortable moments.

2. Maybe it was the strange way things looked and sounded in my familiar room at night that scared me so much. There was never total darkness, but a street light or passing car lights made clothes hung over a chair take on the shape of an unknown beast. Out of the corner of my eye, I saw curtains move when there was no breeze. A tiny creak in the floor would sound a hundred times louder than in the daylight and my imagination would take over, creating burglars and monsters. Darkness always made me feel helpless. My heart would pound and I would lie very still so that 'the enemy' wouldn't discover me.

3. Another childhood fear of mine was that I would get lost, especially on the way home from school. Every morning, I got on the school bus right near my home - that was no problem. After school, though, when all the buses were lined up along the curve, I was terrified that I would get on the wrong one and be taken to some unfamiliar neighbourhood. I would scan the bus for the faces of my friends, make sure that the bus driver was the same one that had been there in the morning, and even then ask the others over and over again to be sure I was in the right bus. On school or family trips to an amusement park or a museum, I wouldn't let the leaders out of my sight. And of course, I was never very adventurous when it came to taking walks or hikes because I would go only where I was sure I would never get lost.

4. Perhaps, one of the worst fears I had as a child was that of not being liked or accepted by others. First of all, I was quite shy. Secondly, I worried constantly about my looks, thinking people wouldn't like me because I was too fat or wore braces. I tried to wear 'the right clothes' and had intense arguments with my mother over the importance of wearing flats instead of saddled shoes to school. Being popular was very important to me then and the fear of not being liked was a powerful one.

5. One of the processes of evolving from a child to an adult is being able to recognise and overcome our fears. I have learnt that darkness does not have to take on a life of its own, that others can help me when I am lost and that friendliness and sincerity will encourage people to like me. Understanding the things that scared us as children helps to cope with our lives as adults.

(a) On the basis of your reading of the above passage, make notes using headings and subheadings. Use recognizable abbreviations wherever necessary.

(b) Make a summary of the passage in not more than 80 words using the notes made and also suggest a suitable title.

SECTION B: Advanced Writing Skills

(35 Marks)

3. An interschool Kabaddi Competition is organized by your school. Write a notice, in not more than 50 words, requesting the students to be present at the venue to encourage the players. Invent all the necessary details. You are Arjun, the sports captain of your school.

OR

You possess an acre of land in the heart of the city. You want to dispose of this property since you have decided to buy a flat. Write an advertisement to be published in a national daily, giving all the necessary details. You are Krishan of Moti Nagar, Delhi.

4. Incessant rain has caused irrecoverable damage in your area. As an active participant in the flood relief programme, write a report in 125–150 words on the different flood relief measures carried out. You are Krishan/Krishna.

OR

You have visited a book exihibition in your neighbourhood. Write a report in 125–150 words on the exhibition. You are Rohan/Rohbini.

5. You are the librarian of Amla Public School. You had placed an order for text books with Dhanpati & Sons. Since the books did not arrive on time, you have decided to cancel the order. Write a letter to the Manager, Dhanpati & Sons, Chennai, cancelling the order.

OR

You are interested in doing a short-term course in computer graphics during your holidays. Write a letter to the Director, Easy Computers, enquiring about their short-term courses and asking for all the necessary details. You are Naresh/Nandini.

6. You are Rajendra Kumar, a social worker. You read an article in *The Hindu* on 'Health Care for Indian Workers'. Write a speech in 125 - 150 words on the importance of health care to be delivered at a public function to create awareness among the workers.

OR

Media has a strong hold on society. Write a speech in 125 - 150 words on how media influences public opinion to be delivered in the school assembly.

(45 Marks)

7. Read the following extract and answer the questions that follow :

   All lovely tales that we have heard or read;

   An endless fountain of immortal drink.

   Pouring unto us from the heaven's brink.

   (a) Name the poem and the poet.
   (b) What is the thing of beauty mentioned in these lines?
   (c) What image does the poet use in these lines?

   OR

   With ships and sun and love tempting them to steal ...

   For lives that slyly turn in their cramped holes

   From fog to endless night?

   (a) Who are 'them' referred to in the first line?
   (b) What tempts them?
   (c) What does the poet say about 'their' lives?

8. Answer any two of the following questions in about 30 - 40 words :

   (a) How does Kamala Das try to put away the thoughts of her ageing mother?

(b) Which is the exotic moment that the poet refers to in 'Keeping Quiet'?

(c) What are the difficulties that aunt Jennifer faced in her life?

9. Answer any six of the following questions in 30 - 40 words:

   (a) Why did Gandhiji feel that taking the Champaran case to the court was useless?
   (b) Why did the peddler derive pleasure from his idea of the world as a rattrap?
   (c) How is Mukesh different from the other bangle makers of Firozabad?
   (d) What tempted Franz to stay away from school?
   (e) Why did the maharaja ban tiger hunting in the state?
   (f) How was the skunk's story different from the other stories narrated by Jack?
   (g) Which words of her brother made a deep impression on Bama?

10. Answer the following in about 100–125 words.

    Has Sophie met Danny Casey? What details of her meeting with Danny Casey did she narrate to her brother?

    OR

    Describe the precautions taken by the prison officers to prevent Evans from escaping.

11. Read the following and answer the question that follows :

    The story "Deep Water" has made you realize that with determination and perseverance one can accomplish the impossible. Write a paragraph in about 100 words on how a positive attitude and courage will aid you to achieve success in life.

    Long Reading Text - The Hound of the Baskervilles

12. Write a character sketch of Mr. Barrymore in about 125 words.

13. Describe Miss Stapleton's first encounter with Sir Henry. (about 125 words)

Solutions

SECTION - A

1. **(a)**

(i) Teachers and parents want their children to learn the important lessons of life and to be hard working.

(2 Marks)

(ii) When kids are given too much too soon they grow up to be adults who have difficulty coping with life's disappointments. **(2 Marks)**

(iii) Today's children want more because there is so much more to want. **(1 Mark)**

(iv) The balance that parents need to have in today's world is a balance between the advantages of an affluent society and the critical life lessons that come from waiting, saving and working hard. **(2 Marks)**

(v) There is a necessity to set limits for the children because they feel better and more secure when they live within a secured structure. **(2 Marks)**

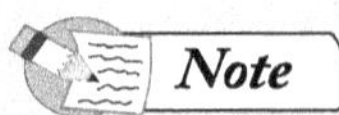 *Note*

1. *Be brief and to the point.*

2. *For Factual questions like e.g. **"What is the necessity to set limits for children"**, do not include information not given in the passage.*

3. *While answering the 'Why' question like **"Why do today's children want more"**, you may begin your answer with 'Today's children want more because ....or a similar phrase.*

4. *While answering the vocabulary questions, check the part of speech, the tense of the word etc. Your answer should have the same part of speech, tense etc.*

   a. *For e.g. Valuable- Precious*

   b. *Important- Critical/essential*

(b) **(1 × 3 = 3 Marks)**

(i) A feeling of satisfaction- Contentment

(ii) Valuable- Precious

(iii) Important- Critical/essential

2. **(a) TITLE: CHILDHOOD FEARS** **(5 Marks)**

1. childhood memories

   1.1 gener. happy

   1.2 carefree time

2. fear of darkness

   2.1 cur. moving

   2.2 heard loud noises

   2.3 felt helpless

   2.4 heart poun. heavily

3. fear of getting lost

   3.1 taking wrong bus

   3.2 scan. buses

   3.3 ask others

4. worst fear

   4.1 not being liked

   4.2 worried about the looks

   4.3 wore right clothes

5. evolving as an adult

   5.1 to recognize and overcome fear

   5.2 to realize that

      5.2.1. darkness doesn't take a life of its own

      5.2.2. others can help

      5.2.3. being friendly & sincere will help

Key to Abbreviation

Abbreviation		Word
1.	gener.	generally
2.	cur.	curtains
3.	poun,	pounded
4.	scan.	canned
5.	doesn't	does not
6.	&	and

(b) Summary **(3 Marks)**

Childhood mostly comprised of being happy or having free time but it also contained some moments of being deeply frightened. There were two great fears, first of darkness and second of getting lost. The former was caused due the movement of the curtains and some weird noise and the latter was because I feared getting lost. The most frightening part was that no one was going to like you.However when you grow up, you realize that these fears are without any foundation and if you do certain things, people will definitely like and help you.

Note

1. *The passage is on the various kinds of fears that surround children. So, the title should have the key words' Fear', 'children' or any synonym of the words.*

2. *It should always contain phrases. Avoid using complete sentences. For e.g.*

   1. *childhood memories*

      1.1 gener. happy

      1.2 carefree time

SECTION - B

3.   **(5 Marks)**

> ### NOTICE
> #### SUNRISE PUBLIC SCHOOL, NEW DELHI
> 15TH February, 2019
> #### INTER SCHOOL KABBADI TOURNAMENT
> All the students are hereby informed that an Inter School Kabbadi Tournament is being organized by the Sports Club of the School from 20th to 24th February 2019 in the school ground. The timings are from 10 – 4 pm. All the toprated schools will be participating in the competition. Therefore, all are requested to be present and boost the morale of the home team.
>
> For more information, please contact the undersigned.
>
> Arjun
> (Sports Captain)

> ### PROPERTY ON SALE
> An acre of land available for sale. Plot in the heart of the city near Apollo Hopital, easy accessibility to the railway station and the airport: location ideal for a play school/ company guest house etc. All documents in proper shape: Quick disposal. Price negotiable. Interested people may contact Mr Krishan at 9768745655.

4. Report   **(10 Marks)**

INCESSANT RAIN CAUSES HAVOC: RELIEF MEASURES IN PLACE

By *Krishan*

Agra, December 28: The Incessant rains in the past one and a half week has not only played havoc with the general routine of all the residents of the city of Agra but also led to a major loss of life and property. Most of the low-lying areas of the city have four feet of accumulated stagnant rainwater due to the continuous rainfall and the ill preparedness of the Municipal authorities. In some of the areas people have been forced to vacate their ground floor residences and move to the first floor or the terrace.

Relief measures are also in full swing. My school along with a handful of volunteers including me moved from place to place with the NDRF teams to rescue people who were stranded alone or without food supplies. Food supplies and other essential commodities were also distributed amongst the flood victims.

The Government has also announced a significant amount from the Prime Minister's Relief Fund. One only hopes that people from all over the country come forward in large numbers to support the cause and lend a helping hand in form of cash or the other essential commodities.

OR

BOOK EXHIBITION REKINDLES INTEREST IN PRINT

By *Rohini*

Delhi, February 22: The Delhi Golf Club in association with Times of India organized a weeklong Book Exhibition in Ramlila Ground from 15th February 20XX to 21st February 20XX. The exhibition which was inaugurated by Education Minister along with the acclaimed writer Ruskin Bond on 15th of February had publishers from both India and abroad as participants. The first day itself recorded a footfall of 75,000 visitors and it only increased in the days that followed. Visiting the exhibition on the very first day I could notice the variety of choices that book lovers would have in case they were interested in buying some books.

The books displayed were both academic and non-academic in nature with subjects ranging from adventure, sports, science-fiction, self-help, cookery etc. Another noteworthy feature was the special browsing sessions that was organized exclusively for the schools. It was also a pleasant sight to see schools reciprocating and taking an initiative to get the children to the Exhibition to not only browse but buy the books too. The sale of books touched a record height on the first day itself.

This, in itself was a testimony to the fact that books have not lost their relevance in the world of Internet.

5. Letter   **(10 Marks)**

Amla Public School
New Delhi
March 6, 20XX
The Manager
Dhanpati & Sons
Chennai

Subject: Cancellation of Order Number 2XX3056

Sir,

This is with reference to Order No - 2XX3056 dated 15th February placed with your company for the delivery of Science reference books for classes IX and X in the school library.

In this respect, I would like to inform you that despite repeated reminders the books have not been delivered at the school so far. The examination is just round the corner and since the books have not been delivered, the students are going to suffer. Therefore, I regret to inform you that the order stands cancelled from our side. You are also required to return the 50% advance payment that was made towards the billing of the books within a week of the receipt of this communication.

Failure to comply would lead to a strict action from our side.

Yours Truly

XYZ

(Librarian)

OR

28, Nehru Nagar

New Delhi

March 6, 20XX

The Director

Easy Computers

New Delhi

Subject: Request to furbish information about the short-term courses

Sir,

This is to inform you that I am a student of Std XII and am pursuing Commerce stream.

I had recently come across an advertisement of your institute wherein the names of some short-term courses were mentioned. I am interested in pursuing Computer Programming/ Computers graphics after I appear for my board examinations to utilize my free time. I would therefore request you to provide me some additional information like the admission criteria, the exact duration, the fee structure, the course material that would be provided etc. I would also like to know if there is any provision of student concession / scholarship.

I would appreciate if you could mail the details along with the prospectus on my email ID naresh.kumar@ yahoo.com.

Thanking you in anticipation

Your truly

Naresh Kumar

6. **Speech** (10 Marks)
Health Care for Indian Workers

Good Morning to the august gathering present here!

As I stand here today to talk about the importance of providing health care for the Indian workers, I am reminded of an article which I had recently read where, in addition to focusing on the present scenario, the article talked about increasing the insurance cover and other benefits to the workforce. In the present scenario the condition of the health and hygiene of workers is dismal with inadequate proper health care facilities for workers leading to poor general health, increased susceptibility to diseases, lack of post-operative and post-hospitalization care sometimes leads to untimely death. The reasons behind this are many ranging from lack of awareness of the programs floated by the government, lack of

adequate finances, unnecessary legal and governmental complications in completing the paperwork etc.

We therefore need to unplug the bottlenecks in the whole system. Awareness programs focusing on the need and the importance of health care should be organized with increased vigor. The government can take the help of the NGOs too. The workers should also be provided easy access to good hospitals and clinics. Some free camps can be organized for the workers residing in remote areas. The importance of health insurance and cashless treatment can be publicized too.

The role of govt. agencies, NGO's including individual volunteers and social workers is of paramount importance in such a scenario.

OR

Media: How it influences public opinion

Good Morning to all present here. Respected Principal Mam, teachers and my dear friends. Today I, XXX of class XII stand before you to deliver a speech on"How Media influences public opinion."

There is an old saying in the media circles that Media can't tell you what to think but it can tell you what to think about. However, in the current age of the onslaught of communication and easy flow of information the role of Media has gone for a sea change.

The primary role of Media was to create awareness and provide unbiased information to the general public so that they could be well-informed and be able to form an opinion about various national and International issues and affairs. With the advent of electronic media, the entertainment component too was well catered to. In other words, print and electronic media were the answer to all queries.

However, with passage of time Media has assumed gargantuan proportions and thanks to the Internet Age, people of all ages are exposed to multifarious information, some of which can play a debilitating role on the psyche of the children. Not only this, the elders too get influenced by the ongoing multiple debates creating a cacophony of sounds for some but appealing to the senses of some others. The scale at which media can influence public opinion can be gauged from the debates on TV before the elections and how opinions change after the debates are viewed. Not only this, in some cases, we pronounce people guilty of certain misdemeanors even before they are found guilty by the courts- all thanks to the media.

Therefore, we need to understand and take everything reported in the media with a pinch of salt lest we get swayed by the reports.

Thank you for your patient hearing

SECTION - C

7.   **(4 Marks)**

(a) The poem from which the above extract has been taken is 'A thing of Beauty' and the poet is John Keats. **(1 Mark)**

(b) The thing of beauty mentioned in these lines are the lovely tales of the mighty men that we have heard or read. **(1 Mark)**

(c) In this poem the poet uses the image of a fountain with the endless flow of the immortal drink from the heaven. The poet uses the image of the fountain to underline the perennial nature of beauty and how it can be a source of motivation to all human beings. **(2 Marks)**

OR

(a) The 'them' referred to in the first line are the children of the Elementary classroom in a slum. **(1 Mark)**

(b) The image of the outside world that is portrayed in their books which has 'ships and sun and love' tempts them since it is diametrically opposed to the world in which they live. Their world has darkness as opposed to the world of the books with all its radiance. **(1 Mark)**

(c) The poet says that these children spend their entire life in a miserable condition, living in 'cramped holes' which is actually their homes. Their days as well as nights are surrounded with endless darkness and there is no chance of any deliverance from such a situation. **(2 Marks)**

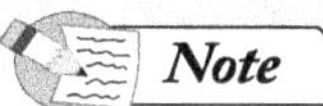 *Note*

1. *Be precise and to the point.*

2. *Remember the names of the poem and the poets with the correct spellings. For e.g.* **"Name the poem and the poet"** *(A Thing of Beauty) as asked this year.*

3. *Look closely at the figures of speech, the special words and the imagery used.*

4. *For e.g.* **"What image does the poet use in these lines"** *(A Thing of Beauty) you may begin by ………The poet uses the image of a fountain with the endless flow of the immortal drink from the heaven- to underline the perennial nature of beauty - how it can be a source of motivation to all human beings.*

8.   **(2 × 2 = 4 Marks)**

(a) Kamla Das tries to put away the thoughts of her aging mother by looking outside the window of her car at the trees which seemed to be moving at a fast pace and at the happy children who were running out of their homes.

(b) The exotic moment that the poet talks about in 'Keeping Quiet' is that moment in which all will keep still, count upto twelve and continue to be silent. It would be a moment without any movement, any rush or any thought. It would give everyone some moments to introspect and indulge in some self-analysis.

(c) The difficulties that Aunt Jennifer faced in her life were the difficulties that a woman faces in a difficult marriage. Throughout her life she had been dominated by her authoritarian husband so much so that she is not free of the fears even in her death. Even though the panel that she sews has fearless tigers on it, her life is exactly the opposite.

 *Note*

1. *Each 2-mark question should have two value points.*

2. *So, for example – for the question "How does Kamala Das try to put away the thought of her ageing mother", you can pick out the value points from those given below:*

   a. *Looking outside the window of her car - trees which seemed to be moving at a fast pace*

   b. *Looking at the happy children who were running out of their homes*

   c. *By not looking at her mother's old ashen face*

   d. *Distracting herself*

3. *Do not make any spelling or grammatical errors as it may lead to deduction of marks.*

9.   **(2 × 6 = 12 Marks)**

(a) Gandhi Ji felt that taking the Champaran case to court was useless because taking such cases to court does more harm than good. In his opinion the peasants were already fear stricken and crushed. Therefore, what was more important was to make them free from fear. In any case there was little hope for justice since the case was against British landlords.

(b) The peddler derived pleasure from his idea of the world as a rat trap because the world had never been kind to him. Therefore, he viewed this world as a rat trap and all men and women either trapped by it or else circling round the bait waiting to be trapped. However, he himself till date was untouched by the rat trap.

(c) Mukesh is different from the other bangle makers of Ferozabad because he still has not lost his ability to dream. He dreams of being a motor mechanic which is in a sharp contrast to the others who have surrendered themselves to the family tradition of bangle making. However, he wants to be his own master.

(d) There were lot of things that tempted Franz to stay away from school that day. He had not learnt his lesson of participles and therefore he feared

M Hamel's scolding. The warm and pleasant weather outside along with the chirping of the birds and the marching of the Prussian soldiers were the other attractions.

(e) The Maharaja banned tiger hunting in his state because he wanted to prove the astrologers' prediction of him getting killed by a tiger wrong. Since there was a limited population of tigers in his state, he wanted to hunt them all himself and ensure that he had killed all the tigers.

(f) Usually the other stories told by Jack had a happy ending. Therefore, Jo had always taken his stories well. However, the story of the Skunk had a twist where the smell of the skunk is changed back to his original smell and this is not acceptable to Jo since that meant Roger Skunk not being accepted by his friends. Jack wanted to prove that parents always know what is right but Jo wanted this ending to be changed the next day.

(g) The elder brother of Bama, while explaining why the elder of their community was carrying the food packet in such a manner explained that they were born in a community of untouchables and food touched by them was considered to be polluted. They were never given any honour or respect. If only they studied and stayed ahead of others, the people would come to them of their own accord. Only then would they be able to throw away those indignities.

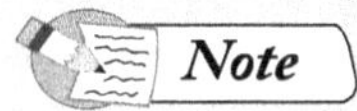 *Note*

1. *Each 2-mark question should have two value points.*

2. *So, for example – for the question "What tempted Franz to stay away from school ", you can pick out the value points from those given below:*

    a. *Lot of things that tempted Franz to stay away from school that day*

    b. *Had not learnt his lesson of participles - feared M Hamel's scolding*

    c. *The warm and pleasant weather outside along-chirping of the birds*

    d. *Marching of the Prussian soldiers- other attractions*

3. *Do not make any spelling or grammatical errors as it may lead to deduction of marks*

10.   **(5 Marks)**

No. Sophie has not met Danny Casey in reality.

In order to make her brother Geoff believe in the authenticity of her cooked up meeting with Danny, she gives the minutest details. She tells Geoff that she had met Danny Casey in the arcade while she was looking at the clothes in Royce's window. She spotted him standing there. Since Geoff is not willing to believe her, she describes Casey's Irish accent. She even adds that she wanted his autograph for little Derek, but since neither of them had a paper or a pen, she was unable to take the autograph. They chatted a little about the clothes in Royce's window and then he departed asking her to meet him the following week, if she wanted to. It was then that he would give her an autograph for little Derek.

OR

During Evans's O-level examination multiple precautions were taken by the prison authorities to prevent Evans' escape. Mr. Jackson, the senior prison officer on D wing and Stephens who was newly recruited to the forcevisited Evans' cell to check it thoroughly before the exam. Special seating arrangements with two square tables set opposite each other and two hard chairs were made in the cell. His razor, nail file and nail scissors were also removed from the cell to ensure that he did not have any device or instrument with him. A bugging device was installed in the cell so that the Governor could listen to any talk, if any, that was going on there. Stephens was also instructed to peep into his cell after every few minutes. Extra precautions were even taken at the gates. The doorsbetween Evans' cell and the yard with high walls were locked. All messages and phone calls were to go via the governor and a parson from St Mary Mags was deputed as the invigilator.

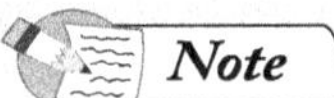 *Note*

1. *Each 5-mark question must have at least four value points*

2. *Answer to the point including your own opinion in places where it is deemed necessary by the question.*

3. *Pick out specific examples from the text to support your answer*

4. *Quote straight from the text wherever required but do so only when you are sure of the words.*

    *For e.g. the question **"Describe the precautions taken by the prison officers to prevent Evans from escaping"** pick out the value points from those given below :*

    a. *During Evans's O-level examination multiple precautions were taken- prevent Evans' escape*

    b. *Mr. Jackson- senior prison officer on D wing & Stephens- newly recruited visited Evans' cell-checked it thoroughly*

    c. *Special seating arrangements -two square tables opposite each other & two hard chairs- in the cell*

    d. *Razor, nail file & nail scissors removed from cell- ensure – no device or instrument*

    e. *A bugging device-installed in the cell -Governor could hear any talk*

f.   *Stephens- instructed to peep in cell after every few minutes*

g.   *Extra precautions at the gates*

h.   *Doors between Evans' cell & the yard with high walls – locked*

i.   *All messages & phone calls - via the governor*

Parson from St Mary Mags - deputed as the invigilator

11.   **(5 Marks)**

The story "Deep Water" makes us realize that one can accomplish the impossible with perseverance and determination. Douglas had a deep -seated fear of water because of his horrifying experience at YMCA swimming pool as a child and he finds the idea of enjoying swimming absolutely impossible. He is unable to learn it because of this fear and remains deprived of the joys of water sports too. However, with the help of his instructor and armed with the values of positive attitude, courage and determination, he is not only able to learn swimming but also able to overcome his fear of water. Similarly, other human beings too have their own fears. However, if one is determined to overcome his/hear fear, one will be able to do that in the same way as Douglas does.

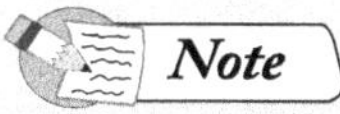
Note

1.   *Adhere to the word limit (100) given for the question.*

2.   *Quoting from the text always gets more marks but misquotes can backfire. So, be careful.*

3.   *Give your opinion wherever required*

4.   *For the Question "**The story "Deep Water" has made you realize that with determination and perseverance one can accomplish the impossible. Write a paragraph in about 100 words on how a positive attitude and courage will aid you to achieve success in life,** you have to give your answer by taking examples from the story "Deep water". Use the value points from those given below:*

a.   *"Deep Water" – underlying theme - the impossible achievable with perseverance and determination*

b.   *Douglas   deep seated fear of water- reason- horrifying experience at YMCA swimming pool as a child - finds swimming absolutely impossible*

c.   *Unable to learn it because of fear- deprived of the joys of water sports too*

d.   *Help of instructor - armed with the values of positive attitude, courage & determination- not only able to learn swimming - also able to overcome fear of water*

e.   *Like Douglas- other humans- have their fears- if one is determined – one can overcome fear- the same way as Douglas does.*

12.   **(8 Marks)**

Mr. John Barrymore was the trusted butler of the Baskervilles. He was tall and distinguished looking with a square black beard. He was also deaf and wished to leave Baskerville Hall due to the painful memories of Sir Charles and the new needs of Sir Henry as he would have more company. Mr Barrymore along with his wife are considered suspects, there being various reasons for the same. Mr Barrymore had the same black beard as the person following them in London. They also were aware of the will beforehand. In addition to this they would also get a permanent and comfortable home if the heir was scared away. His nightly wanderings added to the suspicion.

Mr Barrymore's relationship with his wife however was never under suspicion. He was devoted husband who even lied to conceal information about Selden, the convict and Mrs Barrymore's brother. He even provided Selden with food, shelter and clothes to make sure he survived. He went almost every night down the corridor where he would hold a candle to the window and signal to Selden.

Note

1.   *Adhere to the word limit. Answer must reveal your deep knowledge of the text.*

2.   *The 8 mark question must have 7-8 value points.*

3.   *For e.g. the question "**Write a character sketch of Mr Barrymore in about 125 words**" requires not only a knowledge of the text but also of the characters of the text. You can use the value points from those given below:*

a.   *Mr. John Barrymore - trusted butler of the Baskervilles*

b.   *Physical features – tall- distinguished looking - square black beard*

c.   *Deaf - wished to leave Baskerville Hall - painful memories of Sir Charles - new needs of Sir Henry as he would have more company*

d.   *Mr Barrymore & his wife - considered suspects – for various reasons*

e.   *Mr Barrymore - same black beard as the person following them in London- aware of the will beforehand*

f.   *Would get a permanent and comfortable home if the heir was scared away*

g.   *Nightly wanderings added to the suspicion*

h.   *Mr Barrymore's relationship with wife – good- devoted husband*

i.   *Even lied to conceal information about Selden, the convict - Mrs Barrymore's brother*

j.   *Provided Selden with food, shelter and clothes – ensured his survival*

Went almost every night down the corridor - hold a candle to the window - signal to Selden

13. **(7 Marks)**

Sir Henry made his acquaintance of Miss Stapleton at a luncheon organized at Merripit House. Sir Henry is strongly attracted to Miss Stapleton as soon as they come face to face with each other and it seems that the feeling is mutual. On the walk home, he keeps referring to her. Even later they continue meeting each other. On the moor she takes Watson for Sir Henry and tells him urgently to go back to London at once and never to return to the moor. However, she changes the subject as soon as Stapleton returns. She also appears anxious upon learning that she was talking to Watson and not Sir Henry.

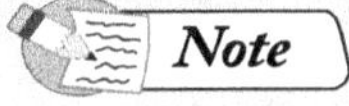
Note

1. *This question tests understanding, appreciation, analysis and interpretation of the incident/character. So, a thorough reading of the text is required.*

2. *Adhere to the word limit (125 words only) and answer the question.*

3. *Avoid giving details which you are not sure of.*

4. *For e.g. the question "Describe Ms. Stapleton's first encounter with Sir Henry in about 125 words, use the value points from those given below:*

a. *Sir Henry met Miss Stapleton at a luncheon - Merripit House*

b. *Strongly attracted to Miss Stapleton- face to face with each other - feeling mutual*

c. *On the walk homekeeps referring to her*

d. *Later continue meeting each other*

e. *On the moor takes Watson for Sir Henry - tells him urgently to go back to London at once - never to return to the moor*

f. *Changes the subject - as Stapleton returns*

g. *Also anxious upon learning - she was talking to Watson - not Sir Henry*

CBSE Board Solved Paper

Time Allowed : 3 Hours   *Maximum Marks : 100*

General Instructions:

(i)   This paper is divided into three Sections : A, B and C. All the sections are compulsory.

(ii)   Separate instructions are given with each section and question, wherever necessary. Read these instructions very carefully and follow them faithfully.

(iii) Do not exceed the prescribed word limit while answering the questions.

SECTION A: Reading

(20 Marks)

1. Read the passage given below and answer the questions that follow :

1. Air pollution is an issue which concerns us all alike. One can willingly choose or reject a food, a drink or a life comfort, but unfortunately there is little choice for the air we breathe. All, what is there in the air is inhaled by one and all living in those surroundings.

2. Air pollutant is defined as a substance which is present while normally it is not there or present in an amount exceeding the normal concentrations. It could either be gaseous or a particulate matter. The important and harmful polluting gases are carbon monoxide, carbon dioxide, ozone and oxides of sulphur and nitrogen. The common particulate pollutants are the dusts of various inorganic or organic origins. Although we often talk of the outdoor air pollution caused by industrial and vehicular exhausts, the indoor pollution may prove to be as or a more important cause of health problems.

3. Recognition of air pollution is relatively recent. It is not uncommon to experience a feeling of 'suffocation' in a closed environment. It is often ascribed to the lack of oxygen. Fortunately, however, the composition of air is remarkably constant all over the world. There is about 79 per cent nitrogen and 21 per cent oxygen in the air – the other gases forming a very small fraction. It is true that carbon dioxide exhaled out of lungs may accumulate in a closed and over-crowded place. But such an increase is usually small and temporary unless the room is really air-tight. Exposure to poisonous gases such as carbon monoxide may occur in a closed room, heated by burning coal inside. This may also prove to be fatal.

4. What is more common in a poorly ventilated home is a vague constellation of symptoms described as the sick-building syndrome. It is characterized by a general feeling of malaise, head-ache, dizziness and irritation of mucous membranes. It may also be accompanied by nausea, itching, aches, pains and depression. Sick building syndrome is getting commoner in big cities with the small houses, which are generally over-furnished. Some of the important pollutants whose indoor concentrations exceed those of the outdoors include gases such as carbon monoxide, carbon dioxide, oxides of nitrogen and organic substances like spores, formaldehydes, hydrocarbon aerosols and allergens. The sources are attributed to a variety of construction materials, insulations, furnishings, adhesives, cosmetics, house dusts, fungi and other indoor products.

5. By-products of fuel combustion are important in houses with indoor kitchens. It is not only the burning of dried dung and fuelwood which is responsible, but also kerosene and liquid petroleum gas. Oxides of both nitrogen and sulphur are released from their combustion.

6. Smoking of tobacco in the closed environment is an important source of indoor pollution. It may not be high quantitatively, but significantly hazardous for health. It is because of the fact that there are over 3000 chemical constituents in tobacco smoke, which have been identified. These are harmful for human health.

7. Micro-organisms and allergens are of special significance in the causation and spread of diseases. Most of the infective illnesses may involve more persons of a family living in common indoor environment. These include viral and bacterial diseases like tuberculosis.

8. Besides infections, allergic and hypersensitivity disorders are spreading fast. Although asthma is the

most common form of respiratory allergic disorders, pneumonias are not uncommon, but more persistent and serious. These are attributed to exposures to allergens from various fungi, molds, hay and other organic materials. Indoor air ventilation systems, coolers, air-conditioners, dampness, decay, pet animals, production or handling of the causative items are responsible for these hypersensitivity – diseases.

9. Obviously, the spectrum of pollution is very wide and our options are limited. Indoor pollution may be handled relatively easily by an individual. Moreover, the good work must start from one's own house.

(Extracted from *The Tribune*)

(a) (i) What is an air pollutant?

(ii) In what forms are the air pollutants present?

(iii) Why do we feel suffocated in a closed environment?

(iv) What is sick building syndrome? How is it increasing?

(v) How is indoor smoking very hazardous?

(vi) How can one overcome the dangers of indoor air pollution?

(b) Find the words from the above passage which mean the same as the following:

(i) giddiness (para 4)

(ii) constant (para 8)

(iii) humidity (para 8)

2. Read the passage given below and answer the questions that follow :

The term dietary fibres refers collectively to indigestible carbohydrates present in plant foods. The importance of these dietary fibres came into the picture when it was observed that the people having diet rich in these fibres, had low incidence of coronary heart disease, irritable bowel syndrome, dental caries and gall stones.

The foodstuffs rich in these dietary fibres are cereals and grains, legumes, fruits with seeds, citrus fruits, carrots, cabbage, green leafy vegetables, apples, melons, peaches, pears etc.

These dietary fibres are not digested by the enzymes of the stomach and the small intestine whereas most of other carbohydrates like starch and sugar are digested and absorbed. The dietary fibres have the property of holding water and because of it, these get swollen and behave like a sponge as these pass through the gastrointestinal tract. The fibres add bulk to the diet and increase transit time in the gut. Some of these fibres may undergo fermentation in the colon.

In recent years, it has been considered essential to have some amount of fibres in the diet. Their beneficial effects lie in preventing coronary heart disease, and decreasing cholesterol level. The fibres like gums and pectin are reported to decrease postprandial (after meals) glucose level in blood. These types of dietary fibres are

recommended for the management of certain types of diabetes. Recent studies have shown that the fenugreek (Methi) seeds, which contain 40 per cent gum, are effective in decreasing blood glucose and cholesterol levels as compared to other gum containing vegetables.

Some dietary fibres increase transit time and decrease the time of release of ingested food in colon. The diet having less fibres is associated with colon cancer and the dietary fibres may play a role in decreasing the risk of it.

The dietary fibres hold water so that stools are soft, bulky and readily eliminated. Therefore high fibre intake prevents or relieves constipation.

The fibres increase motility of the small intestine and the colon and by decreasing the transit time there is less time for exposure of the mucosa to harmful toxic substances. Therefore, there is a less desire to eat and the energy intake can be maintained within the range of requirement. This phenomenon helps in keeping a check on obesity. Another reason in helping to decrease obesity is that the high-fibre diets have somewhat lower coefficients of digestibility.

The dietary fibres may have some adverse effects on nutrition by binding some trace metals like calcium, magnesium, phosphorus, zinc and others and therefore preventing their proper absorption. This may pose a possibility of nutritional deficiency especially when diets contain marginal levels of mineral elements. This may become important constraints on increasing dietary fibres. It is suggested that an intake of 40 grams dietary fibres per day is desirable.

(Extracted from '*The Tribune*)

(a) On the basis of your reading of the above passage make notes on it in points only, using recognizable abbreviations wherever necessary. Also suggest a suitable title.

(b) Write a summary of the above in about 80 words.

SECTION B: Advanced Writing Skills

(35 Marks)

3. You are Smitha/Sunil, Secretary AVM Housing Society. You are going to organize a blood donation camp. Write a notice in not more than 50 words, urging the members of your society to come in large numbers for this noble cause. Invent all the necessary details.

OR

You are General Manager, Hotel Dosa, Gurgaon. You need a lady Front Office Assistant with sound knowledge of computers. She must be a graduate and good in communication skills with pleasing manners. Draft an advertisement in not more than 50 words to be published in Gurgaon Times.

4. Your school, Sun Public School, Poona, celebrated 'Environment Day' on 5th November. Write a report on the programme in 100-125 words for your school newsletter. You are Neeta/Naveen, Cultural Secretary of the school. Invent the necessary details.

OR

You are Deepak/Deepika, Secretary of Ahimsa Club, Parsva Public School, Delhi. On 2nd October your school observed 'International Day for Peace and Non-violence', organizing various activities such as visit to Raj Ghat, Charkha spinning, lectures by eminent Gandhians etc. Write a report on the same in 100 - 125 words.

5. As a regular commuter by bus from Noida to Delhi, you have been witnessing rash driving by the bus drivers daily without an exception. Write a letter to the Editor, 'The Times of India' drawing the attention of the General Manager, Delhi Transport Corporation to this problem. You are Priti/Prakash, 15, Udyog Vihar, Noida.

OR

Write a letter to Lightways Sports, Amrapalli, Thane, placing an order for sports articles (minimum 4) to be supplied to your school, ABC Matriculation School, Civil Lines, Poona. Sign as Ravi/Raveena, Sports Secretary.

6. Your family has recently shifted from Kota in Rajasthan to Ernakulam in Kerala, where your house is situated in the midst of beautiful flowering plants and fruit yielding trees. Every minute and every second, you are experiencing the joy of being in the lap of nature. Write an article in 150-200 words on the diversity of nature that you have experienced. You are Latha/Lalith of Class XII.

OR

Write an article in 150 - 200 words on the topic, 'Poverty is the cause of all evils', to be published in the Young World of 'The Hindu', Chennai.

SECTION C: Textbooks and Long Reading Text

(45 Marks)

7. Read the extract given below and answer the questions that follow :

Perhaps the Earth can teach us

as when everything seems dead

and later proves to be alive.

Now I'll count upto twelve

and you keep quiet and I will go.

(i) What does the Earth teach us?

(ii) What does the poet mean to achieve by counting upto twelve?

(iii) What is the significance of 'keeping quiet'?

OR

A flowery band to bind us to the Earth,

Spite of despondence, of the inhuman dearth

Of noble natures, of the gloomy days,

Of all the unhealthy and o'er-darkened ways

Made for our searching :

(i) What are we doing everyday?

(ii) Which evil things do we possess and suffer from?

(iii) What are the circumstances that contribute towards making humans unhappy and disillusioned with life?

8. Answer any three of the following in 30 - 40 words each :

(a) Why has the poet's mother been compared to the 'late winter's moon'?

(b) What message does Stephen Spender convey through the poem : 'An Elementary School Classroom in a Slum'?

(c) What was the plea of the folk who had put up the roadside stand?

(d) What will happen to Aunt Jennifer's tigers when she is dead?

9. Answer any three of the following questions in 30 - 40 words each :

(a) How did Franz react to the declaration that it was their last French lesson?

(b) What made the lawyer lose his job? What was funny about it? (Poets and Pancakes)

(c) How did the instructor turn Douglas into a swimmer?

(d) Why did Sophie like her brother, Geoff more than any other person?

10. Answer the following in 125 - 150 words :

What made the American publisher think that the novel, 'The Name of the Rose' won't sell well in America? What actually happened? What was the secret of its success?

OR

How did the peddler feel after robbing the crofter? What course did he adopt and how did he react to the new situation? What does his reaction reveal?

11. Answer the following in about 100 words :

Exploitation is a universal phenomenon. The poor indigo farmers were exploited by the British landlords to which Gandhiji objected. Even after our independence we find exploitation of unorganized labour. What values do we learn from Gandhiji's campaign to counter the present day problems of exploitation?

12. Answer the following in 125 - 150 words :

What is the bond that unites the two – the old Mr. Lamb and Derry, the small boy? How does the old man inspire the small boy?

OR

Do you think Dr. Sadao's final decision was the best possible one in the circumstances? Why / Why not? Explain with reference to the story, 'The Enemy'.

13. Answer the following in 30 - 40 words each :

(a) How does Charley, the narrator describe the third level at Grand Central Station?

(b) What unique opportunities does the Antarctic environment provide to the scientists?

(c) What sort of hunts did the Maharaja offer to organize for the high-ranking British officer? What trait of the officer does it reveal?

(d) What did Jo want the wizard to do when Mommy Skunk approached him?

Solutions

SECTION - A

1. (a)

(i) An air pollutant is any substance which is not normally found in the air, but sometimes it is present in the amount which is exceeding the normal concentrations and therefore harmful. **(1 Mark)**

(ii) Air pollutants are in various forms such as gaseous or particulate matter. Gases like carbon monoxide, carbon dioxide, ozone and oxides of Sulphur and nitrogen are some of the important gaseous air pollutants. The common particulate pollutants are dusts of various inorganic and organic matters. **(2 Marks)**

(iii) We feel suffocated in a closed environment due to lack of oxygen in the closed environment. **(1 Mark)**

(iv) Sick – building syndrome is a vague collection of symptoms such as headache, nausea, dizziness, irritation of mucous membrane, depression which a person experiences or complains of while living in a poorly ventilated home. It is increasing because a large part of the population lives in the big cities where people have small over furnished houses which lack proper ventilation. **(2 Marks)**

(v) Smoking indoors is hazardous because there are over 3000 chemical constituents in tobacco smoke which have been identified as harmful for human health. While one smokes indoors all these remain trapped in the closed environment of home impacting the residents in a harmful way. **(1 Mark)**

(vi) One can overcome the dangers of indoor pollution by the following means- **(2 Marks)**
 (a) We must ensure that our homes are properly ventilated
 (b) We must also ensure that our homes are free from tobacco smoke and dust
 (c) The indoor ventilation systems, ACs, Coolers are working fine and there is no dampness/decay within the home
 (d) The kitchen is well ventilated so that no harmful gases which are released during combustion remain trapped inside the house
 (Any Two)

(b) (i) dizziness **(1 × 3 = 3 Marks)**
 (ii) persistent
 (iii) dampness

Note

1. *Be brief and to the point.*

2. *For Factual questions like e.g.* **"What is an air pollutant ",** *do not include information not given in the passage.*

3. *While answering the* **'Why'** *question like* **"Why do we feel suffocated in a closed environment",** *you may begin your answer with 'We feel suffocated in a closed environment because ....or a similar phrase.*

4. *While answering the vocabulary questions, check the part of speech, the tense of the word etc. Your answer should have the same part of speech, tense etc.*

 a. *For e.g. giddiness- dizziness (NOT Dizzy)*

 b. *Constant –persistent (NOT persistence or persist)*

2. (a) **(5 Marks)**

Title – DIETARY FIBRES- THE WAY TO HEALTHY LIVING

1. Dietary Fibers and its Sources
 1.1 Indigestible carbs present in plant food
 1.2 Cereals, grains & legumes
 1.3 Fruits with seeds: all kinds of citrus fruits: apples, melons , peaches , pers etc
 1.4 Green leafy vegetablescabbage , carrots etc

2. Health Benefits of including Dietary Fibers in meals
 2.1 Low incidence of coronary heart disease
 2.2 ↓ incidence of irritable bowel syndrome
 2.3 Dental Caries are reduced
 2.4 Occurrence of Gall stones reduced
 2.5 PP blood sugar decreased-prevents diabetes
 2.6 ↓ incidence of Obesity through
 (a) Decreasing desire to eat
 (b) Low coefficient of digestibility
 2.7 Since hold water , stools are soft & bulky . ∴ No constipation
 2.8 ↓ time of ingested food in colon. ∴ decrease in incidence of colon Cancer

3. Mechanism of Digestion
 3.1 Remain undigested by enzymes of the stomach & the small intestine
 3.2 Hold water : ∴ swell up &behave like sponge
 3.3 Add bulk to the diet &increasethe transit time to the gut

4. Adverse effects
 4.1 Bind trace metals like Ca, Mg,P& Zn & prevent absorption by body

4.2   → nutritional deficiency

5.   Advised Intake

    5.1   40 gms/day

Key To Abbreviations

Abbreviation	Word
&	And
↓	Decreases
PP	Post prandial
∴	Therefore
Ca	Calcium
Mg	Magnesium
P	Phosphorus
Zn	Zinc
→	Leads to
gms	Grams
/	per

 *Note*

1. *The passage is on the dietary fibres and our eating habits which can give rise to a healthy living. So, the title should have the key words like 'Diet', 'habit,' 'healthy', etc or any synonym of the given words.*

2. *It should always contain phrases. Avoid using complete sentences. For e.g.*

    1. *Dietary Fibers and its Sources*

       1.1. *Indigestible carbs present in plant food*

       1.2. *Cereals, grains & legumes*

       1.3. *Fruits with seeds: all kinds of citrus fruits: apples, melons , peaches , pears etc*

       1.4. *Green leafy vegetables cabbage , carrots etc*

    AND NOT There are various sources of dietary fibres like the indigestible ………etc

3. *Include a minimum of 4-6 distinctly different recognizable short forms i.e. abbreviations of the words in the notes as done in the solution.*

2.   (b) Summary   **(3 Marks)**

Dietary fibers refer to the indigestible carbohydrates present in plant food. Cereals, grains, legumes, green leafy vegetables, citrus fruits etc are sources of dietary fibers. Their inclusion in our daily diet leads to significant health benefits viz preventing heart diseases, diabetes, obesity, colon cancer etc. However, its over consumption leads to nutritional deficiency as it binds important metals like calcium, zinc, phosphorus etc and prevent its absorption by the body. Therefore, a daily intake of 40 gm is recommended. (79 words)

3.   Notice   **(5 Marks)**

AVM Housing Society

NOTICE

Blood Donation Camp

March 23, 2013

All the members of the society are hereby informed that a blood donation camp will be organized as per the details given below. All are requested to come in large numbers and make the camp a great success. All are requested not to bring young children with them

    Date: March 29, 2013

    Time: 9 am to 5 pm

    Venue: The Community Hall

Please contact the undersigned for any other details

Sign

(Smitha)

Secretary

AVM Housing Society

OR

ADVERTISEMENT

SITUATION VACANT

Wanted a smart, efficient Lady Front Office Assistant for a leading hotel. The candidate must be a graduate with pleasing personality, good communication skills and sound knowledge of computers. Salary negotiable. Interested candidates should apply within 10 days with resume and photograph to GM , Hotel Dosa , Gurgaon- 12.

4.   Report   **(10 Marks)**

Environment Day Celebrated

By *Neeta*

Pune, November 5 : Recognizing the need to educate the students on the degradation in the environment and its bearings on the future, Environment Day was celebrated on 5th of November in the school campus. The day started with a special assembly where all the staff and students took the Green Pledge. Eco-rally, planting of saplings and an exhibition focusing on the need to protect the environment were also organized. The exhibition was inaugurated by the local environmentalist Shri A. K. Anthony. It displayed posters, models and scientific instruments highlighting the depletion in the ozone layer and suggested remedial measures. Parents of the senior children were also invited on the occasion. The younger children were also given green takeaways so that the message could reach their homes too.

OR

International Day for Peace and Non- Violence Celebrated

By *Deepika*

New Delhi, October 2: The International Day for Peace and Non-Violence was celebrated with great enthusiasm on 2nd of October within the school campus. The day started with a special assembly by the Ahimsa Club where the students were taken through a journey of the Gandhian Principals followed by two lectures by eminent Gandhians. The assembly ended with a pledge taken by all the staff and the students.

The Secondary wing of the school was taken to Raj Ghat and asked to pen down their feelings and present a PPT in the next assembly. Activities like a mock Dandi march, Charkha Spinning and the screening of the award winning film "Gandhi" were the other highlights of the day.

The students expressed their happiness over such an initiative by the school.

5. **Letter** (10 Marks)

15, Udyog Vihar

Noida

23 March, 2013

The Editor

Times of India

Respected Sir

Sub: Rash Driving by the Bus Drivers

Through the esteemed column of your newspaper, I would like to draw the attention of the General Manager, Delhi Transport Corporation to this problem of rash driving by the drivers of the DTC buses.

This is a daily practice which is threatening the safety of the daily commuters which include people of all ages. The drivers flout all directives of the desired speed limits often screeching to sudden halts at the bus stops. They do not even stop for all the passengers to deboard before moving further. Jumping of traffic lights is also a regular practice with them.

I believe that even a small warning or a fine would bring matters under control. I had earlier written to the concerned authorities but till date nothing has happened. I hope to draw the attention of the concerned authorities through this letter so that the live of the daily commuters is no further in jeopardy.

Yours truly

Priti

OR

Raveena

Sports Secretary

ABC Matriculation School

Civil Lines

Poona

23 March, 2013

Lightways Sports

Amrapalli

Thane

Sir,

Sub: Supply Order for Sports Good

Kindly arrange to supply at your earliest convenience the following sports items for our Sports Club at the discounted rates approved for the year 20XX-20XX.

S. No.	Particulars	Number of items/boxes
1	Crickets bats (JJ Jonex)	10 pieces
2	Cricket Balls (Dukes)	5 boxes
3	Table Tennis Racquet (Stag)	10 pieces
4	Table Tennis Balls (Pack of Six- Stag)	6 boxes

Please ensure that all the sports good are free from any defect. Payment will be released once the goods are received and found satisfactory by the Sports Committee.

Yours faithfully
Ravina

Sports Secretary

6. **Article Writing** (10 Marks)

India – A Natural Delight

By *Latha*

India, a land with a rich cultural heritage , is also a natural and visual delight and a fitting answer to a recuperating mind. From the snow- capped mountains of the Himalayas to the beautiful sand dunes of Rajasthan, the exotic beaches of Goa to the untouched wilds of the Sunderbans – it has an answer to every person's dreams.

I had the pleasure of experiencing this diversity when I shifted from Kota in Rajasthan to Eranakulum in Kerala. Moving from an extreme climate with scanty rainfall and little greenery of Kota to a land of unending lush green vegetation , I was transfixed by the beauty of Kerala.

A moderate humid tropical climate with a good amount of rainfall, due to its unique terrain and elevation, Kerala abounds in a rich variety of spices and medicinal oils. The landscape of Kerala has highland deciduous, evergreen forests which houses more than 1,000 species of trees. Not only this, some of the common flora in this region includes bamboo, palm, wild cardamom, black pepper and Vetiver Grass with amazing aroma.Kerala incidentally also happens to be a land of several architectural masterpieces, exemplified in the ancient temples and its natural beauty has inspired many a poets and artists.

OR

Poverty is the cause of all Evils

By *XYZ*

Even though we are in the 21st century and touted as a power to reckon with, India is still struggling when it comes to eradication of Poverty. It would not be an error to say that poverty is the root cause of all evils.

We find hordes of people around us who struggle daily for the basic amenities of life including one square meal a day. Clad in rags, they are either engaged in petty jobs which does not lead to a proper income or indulge in activities which are anti- social in nature. Criminal activities like robbery, thefts, murders, kidnapping etc are on the rise due to the abject conditions in which the unemployed youth of today are forced to live in. Added to this is the problem of malnutrition and over populationwhich again is a by-product of poverty.

No doubt, the Government has launched various poverty alleviation programs, but none of them has reached the grass root level due to official bottlenecks. Misappropriation of funds too has led to the weakening of the programs.

It is important therefore for the Government now to focus primarily on this problem so that poverty is eradicated completely, and one is free to live in a society free from all evils.

SECTION - C

(1 × 3 = 3 Marks)

7. (i) The Earth teaches us that there can be life under apparent stillness. Even though all seems dead and still, there is life beneath this dormant surface and it resurrects itself.

(ii) The poet wants us to pause for some time and introspect. Keeping still till the time he counts till 12, gives us time to put a stop to all that we are rushing with and give us the necessary respite for self- analysis and peace.

(iii) The significance of "Keeping quiet" is that it will give us time to introspect and help us understand what we are actually looking for. Unless we do that, we will be involved in the humdrums of life without any direction.

OR

(i) Everyday, we are weaving a flowery wreath which will bind us to the beauties of the Earth. In other words we are looking for something beautiful that

will give meaning to our existence and bring joy to us and our fellow beings.

(ii) The evil things that we possess and suffer from are utmost sadness, disappointment and despair. We also lack a noble nature.

(iii) The circumstances that contribute towards making humans unhappy and disillusioned with life can be enumerated as a the lack of hope and utter despair among human beings, a complete absence of noble qualities and the negative & dark ways that humans taker recourse to, to fulfill their aims and ambitions. This makes them unhappy.

Note

1. *Be precise and to the point.*

2. *Remember the names of the poem and the poets with the correct spellings.*

3. *Look closely at the figures of speech, the special words and the imagery used.*

4. *For questions pertaining directly to the poem , for e.g. the question "What does the Earth teach us'," you have to refer directly to the poem. You can write your answer in the following manner The Earth teaches us that there can be life under apparent stillness. Even though all seems dead and still, there is life beneath this dormant surface and it resurrects itself.*

8.   **(2 × 3 = 6)**

(a) The poet uses a simile to draw a comparison between her mother's age and the moon in the Winter season. The dull, weak & pale visage of her mother's is similar in look to the late winter's moon since it too lacks shine & brightness. Winter being the last season of the year is synonymous with lifelessness and dormancy. Similarly the poet's mother too is at the last stage of her life.

(b) The message that the poet conveys through the poem " An Elementary Classroom in a Slum" is that of social injustice and class inequalities and how this can be corrected. The poet presents two contrasting worlds- a world in the books through which the children are being provided the education and the actual world that the children experience in their day to day life. The poet also suggests ways by which the gap between the two worlds can be bridged.

(c) The plea of the folk who had put up the roadside stand was addressed to the city dwellers who would pass by their make shift shops.. The city dwellers were requested to stop by their stalls and buy something so that the poor folks also had some money and a participation in the flow of currency that sustained the commercial activities of the cities.

(d) Aunt's Jennifer's tigers will survive her even after she is dead as they have been immortalized by art.

Even though Aunt Jennifer will lie in death with hands which hand gone through terror and ordeals during her married life, the tigers will go on jumping – proud and unafraid.

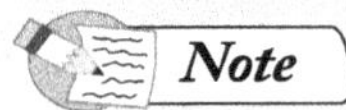

Note

1. *Each 2-mark question should have two value points.*

2. *So, for example – for the question **"What message does Stephen Spender convey through the poem: 'An Elementary Classroom In A Slum',** you can pick out the value points from those given below:*

a. *Message the poet conveys through the poem - social injustice and class inequalities- how this can be corrected*

b. *Poet presents two contrasting worlds- a world in the books- through which the children provided education - actual world that children experience everyday*

c. *Poet also suggests ways – bridge the gap between the two worlds*

3. *Do not make any spelling or grammatical errors as it may lead to deduction of marks.*

9. **(2 × 3 = 6 Marks)**

(a) Franz was extremely shocked to hear the unexpected announcement by M Hamel that it would be their last lesson that day. He now understood the reason behind the crowd at the notice board, the Sunday dress of M Hamel and the strange stillness in the room. He suddenly wanted to make full use of this day and realized with a heavy heart how much he loved the language.

(b) The lawyer lost his job because the Boss closed the Story Department and all the poets were asked to go home. The lawyer along with Subbu was a part of the said department and therefore he too lost his job. The funny part about this was that the lawyer lost his job because the poets were asked to go home.

(c) The instructor worked on Douglas' psychology first. Douglas has had a fear of water since his childhood due to certain unsavory incidents in his young days. He made Douglas practice with each part of his body separately. It was only after perfecting each part that Douglas was able to get rid of his fear of water. The trainer then integrated the whole and Douglas was able to gain complete confidence of his abilities.

(d) Sophie liked Geoff more than anyone else since he was someone whom she could talk to and share her secret fantasies with. Geoff listens to whatever Sophie has to say which is a sharp contrast to the domineering attitude of their father and the sarcastic comments of her younger brother. Geoff in fact is the first person to know about anything that happens to Sophie.

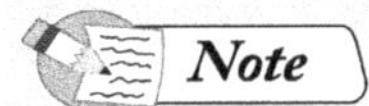

Note

Short Answers-Prose

1. *Each 2-mark question should have two value points.*

2. *So, for example – for the question **"How did Franz react to the declaration that it was their last French lesson",** you can pick out the value points from those given below:*

a. *Franz- extremely shocked to hear the unexpected announcement- M Hamel - last lesson that day*

b. *Now understood the reason behind the crowd at the notice board*

c. *The Sunday dress of M Hamel*

d. *Strange stillness in the room*

e. *Suddenly wanted to make full use of the day*

f. *Realized with a heavy heart- he loved the language*

3. *Do not make any spelling or grammatical errors as it may lead to deduction of marks*

10. **(10 Marks)**

The novel "The Name of the Rose" had the mention of things which were far away from the experiences of an average American.The American publisher opined that the book wouldn't sell for more than 3,000 copies since an average American might not have even seen a cathedral or studied Latin. In addition to this was the fact that lot of books had been written on the medieval past far before him and none of them were a huge success. However in reality, the novel sold for two or three million copies in the US.

As Umbert Eco mentions in his interview, that the success of the novel was a mystery to him too. However, there can be many reasons attributed to its success. Perhaps the time in history when it was written proved to be the reason for its success or as Mukund points out – the novel's setting in the medieval past might have contributed. In other words it is extremely difficult to point out any one reason for the novel's success.

OR

The peddler felt extremely delighted as soon as he was successful in robbing his generous host. Even though he had taken advantage of the faith and trust reposed in him, the peddler did not feel guilty initially. His primary motive was to keep himself and the stolen thirty kronor safe and it was for this reason that he decided to discontinue walking on the public highway and take to the woods.

The first few hours in the woods did not pose any difficulty to him but as time passed the forest started confusing him. The paths twisted back and forth and he kept on moving in circles. He realized slowly that he was coming back to the same position from where he had originally started.

The entire day had been wasted and he had not moved an inch further. It was at this point of time that he recalled his own thoughts about the world and the rat trap and discovered with an alarm that he too had been caught like a rat in the trap. The whole forest now seemed like an impenetrable prison from which he couldn't escape.

His reaction highlights the human predicament and how , if man wants, he can steer clear of this. Moreover, the reaction also reveals that he realized his folly.

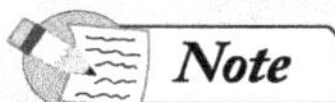
Note

1. *Each 10 -mark question must have at least 6-7 value points*

2. *Answer to the point including your own opinion in places where it is deemed necessary by the question.*

3. *Pick out specific examples from the text to support your answer*

4. *Quote straight from the text wherever required but do so only when you are sure of the words*

5. *Break the answer to the question "How did the peddler feel after robbing the crofter? What course did he adopt and how did he react to the situation? What does his reaction reveal?" First talk about the feeling of the peddler , then the course that he adopted, his reaction to the situation and finally what his reaction reveals.*

6. *Pick out the value points from those given below :*

   a. *FEELING OF THE PEDDLER*

      i. *Peddler felt extremely delighted- successful in robbing generous host*

      ii. *Even though - taken advantage of the faith and trust reposed -did not feel guilty initially*

      iii. *Primary motive- he and the thirty kronor should be safe*

   b. *COURSE THAT HE ADOPTED*

      i. *Decided to discontinue walking on the public highway*

      ii. *Took to the woods to ensure safety*

      iii. *First few hours -woods did not pose any difficulty*

      iv. *As time passed- forest started confusing him*

      v. *Paths twisted back and forth - kept moving in circles*

      vi. *Realized - coming back to the same position- from wherehad originally started*

      vii. *Panicked*

      viii. *Entire day wasted - not moved an inch further*

      ix. *Recalled his own thoughts -the world and the rat trap -discovered with an alarm that he too - caught like a rat in the trap*

      x. *Whole forest - an impenetrable prison from which he couldn't escape.*

   c. *REACTION AND REVELATION*

      i. *Highlights the human predicament*

      ii. *If man wants- can steer clear of the trap*

      iii. *Reaction also reveals that he realized his folly*

11.   **(5 Marks)**

Even though Exploitation is a universal phenomenon notwithstanding the boundaries of time and place, men have a right to protest against it. The exploitation of the poor indigo farmers of Champaran by the Britishers was rightly brought to the forefront by Gandhiji and the farmers were able to gain for themselves what they rightfully deserved. Gandhji's campaign for the Indigo farmers teaches us to counter the problems of exploitation in the present too. Firstly, the freedom from fear is an absolute must. The victims need to understand their own strengths and become self-reliant. They also need to work collectively since being united is the key to success.

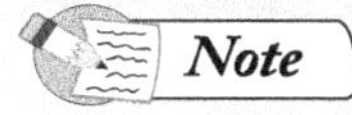
Note

1. *Adhere to the word limit (100) given for the question.*

2. *The 5-mark question must have at least 2 value points*

3. *Quoting from the text always gets more marks but misquotes can backfire. So, be careful.*

4. *Give your opinion wherever required*

12.   **(7 Marks)**

The bond that unites both Mr Lamb and Derry is that of physical impairment and loneliness. Half of Derry's face has been burnt by acid and Mr Lamb has a leg made of tin since his leg was blown off during the war. Both of them lack friends and have been mocked at by others. The similarities that they share becomes the common ground for their friendship.

Mr Lamb inspires Derry through his words of encouragement and positivity that makes Derry change his mind set and kindle a zest for living meaningfully. "Handsome is he as handsome does" is something which Derry understands by the end of the play and this helps him to move beyond his physical impairment and look at his other qualities.

OR

Yes, I think Dr Sadao's final decision was the best possible one in the given circumstances. Dr Sadao's primary duty as a doctor was to tend to the sick and the injured and make them whole. Therefore, despite the fact that time and again, he and his wife decide to turn the man in, they steer clear of the action. However, as a true patriot the burden of not only hiding but tending to an American soldier (an enemy) was a weighing heavily on his conscience. Therefore, he was torn between his primary humanitarian duty as a doctor and his duty as a citizen of a country at war.

He is able to prove his loyalty to the nation by telling the General about the American and even keeping the door open for the assassins to enter. He is also able to save his conscience by allowing the man to flee to safety.

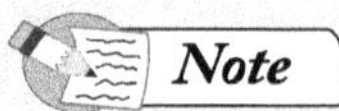 *Note*

1.   *Adhere to the word limit (120-150 words) . Answer must reveal your deep knowledge of the text.*

2.   *The 7mark question must have 4-5 value points.*

3.   *For e.g. the question **"Do you think Dr Sadao's final decision was the best possible one in the circumstances? Why/ Why not? Explain with reference to the story 'The Enemy'**, requires not only a knowledge of the text, the characters of the text but your own opinion too.*

4.   *You can use the value points from those given below:*

   a.   *YOUR VIEWPOINT*

      i.   *Yes, I think Dr Sadao's final decision was the best possible one in the given circumstances.*

   b.   *THE REASON*

      i.   *Primary duty as a doctor -tend to the sick and the injured - make them whole again*

      ii.   *Time and again, he and his wife decide - turn the man in – but- do not carry out the plan*

      iii.   *As a true patriot- burden of hiding & tending to an American soldier (an enemy) - weighing heavily – conscience*

      iv.   *Torn between primary humanitarian duty - a citizen of a country at war.*

      v.   *Able to prove his loyalty- tells the General – agrees to keep the door open - assassins to enter*

      vi.   *Able to save his conscience - allowing the man to flee to safety*

13.   **(2 × 4 = 8 Marks)**

   (a)   Charley says that there are three levels to the Grand Central railway Station in New York. The first two levels have the twentieth century trains and the suburban trains. However, contrary to what all believe there is a controversial third level too which Charley accidently stumbles upon and from where he tries to buy two tickets to Galesburg, Illinois. The people, their attire, the ambience, the platform, the lighting at the platform, the locomotives were all of the old style. Even the newspaper stand had "The World" on it, and that newspaper hadn't been published since years to the best of Charley's knowledge. When Charley went to buy the tickets he realized with a shock that even the currency being used at the third level was the kind that people used in 1894.

   (b)   The Antarctica provides the scientists various unique opportunities. They can study the Earth's past,

present and the future here and get an understanding of where we've come from and where we could possibly be heading too. Since the Antarctica holds within its ice-cores, half million years old carbon records, this can help the scientists study climate change and contribute to the raging debate on Global warming and possibly give the wakeup call to the humans.

   (c)   The Maharaja offered to organize any kind of hunt except tiger hunt. The British officer could go for a mouse, a boar or even a mosquito hunt but a tiger hunt was an absolute no. The episode reveals that the officer was a vain, image conscious man since he sends word to the Magaraja that he only needs to get his photograph alongside the dead body of the tiger and the Maharaja can himself kill the tiger.

   (d)   Jo was not too happy with the end of the story. Therefore she wanted the wizard to hit the Mommy Skunk right over the head with the magic wand when Mommy Skunk approached him.

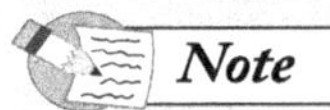 *Note*

1.   *Each 2-mark question should have two value points.*

2.   *These questions test understanding, appreciation, analysis and interpretation of the text etc*

3.   *Adhere to the word limit (330-40 words only) and answer the question.*

4.   *Avoid giving details which you are not sure of.*

5.   *For e.g. the question **"What sorts of hunts did the Maharaja offer to organize for the high- ranking British officer? What trait of the officer does it reveal**, break the question into two parts: a. The offered hunts for the official b. The trait of the officer*

6.   *Pick out the value points from those given below:*

   a.   *KINDS OF HUNT*

      i.   *Offered to organize any kind of hunt except tiger hunt*

      ii.   *The British officer could go for a mouse hunt - boar hunt - mosquito hunt- tiger hunt - an absolute no.*

   b.   *TRAIT OF THE OFFICER*

      i.   *The episode reveals – vanity of the officer*

      ii.   *image conscious man*

      iii.   *sending word to Maharaja - only needs to get his photograph alongside the dead body of the tiger*

      iv.   *Maharaja himself could kill the tiger- no issues in that*

www.ingramcontent.com/pod-product-compliance
Lightning Source LLC
LaVergne TN
LVHW080616200726
843509LV00007B/327